T0211058

Lecture Notes in Computer Science 10345

Commenced Publication in 1973
Founding and Former Series Editors:
Gerhard Goos, Juris Hartmanis, and Jan van Leeuwen

More information about this series at http://www.springer.com/series/7409

Feng Tian · Christos Gatzidis
Abdennour El Rhalibi · Wen Tang
Fred Charles (Eds.)

E-Learning and Games

11th International Conference, Edutainment 2017
Bournemouth, UK, June 26–28, 2017
Revised Selected Papers

Springer

Editors
Feng Tian
Bournemouth University
Bournemouth
UK

Wen Tang
Bournemouth University
Bournemouth
UK

Christos Gatzidis
Bournemouth University
Bournemouth
UK

Fred Charles
Bournemouth University
Bournemouth
UK

Abdennour El Rhalibi
Liverpool John Moores University
Liverpool
UK

ISSN 0302-9743   ISSN 1611-3349   (electronic)
Lecture Notes in Computer Science
ISBN 978-3-319-65848-3   ISBN 978-3-319-65849-0   (eBook)
https://doi.org/10.1007/978-3-319-65849-0

Library of Congress Control Number: 2017955728

LNCS Sublibrary: SL3 – Information Systems and Applications, incl. Internet/Web, and HCI

Printed on acid-free paper

This Springer imprint is published by Springer Nature
The registered company is Springer International Publishing AG
The registered company address is: Gewerbestrasse 11, 6330 Cham, Switzerland

Preface

Welcome to the proceedings of Edutainment 2017, the 11th International Conference on E-Learning and Games, which was held in June 26–28, 2017 in Bournemouth, UK.

Over the last decade, the E-Learning and Games conference has become an international forum for researchers and practitioners to present their latest research results in game-based learning and education, and share their experiences gained from this emerging area that combines education and entertainment. The scope of the conference is not limited to just the field of edutainment research, but also includes interdisciplinary subjects across virtual reality, augmented reality, and computer graphics technologies. Since the first conference held in Hangzhou, China, in 2006, the conference has taken place in many international cities including Hong Kong (China, 2007), Banff (Canada, 2009), Taiwan (2011), and now, in 2017, in the sunny southwest of England, in Bournemouth, UK.

Included in this volume of conference proceedings, we have contributions from academia and from industry, all of which aim to advance technology and address challenging issues in all fields related to education and entertainment, ranging from pedagogy, mobile applications, and computer graphics to multimedia, augmented and virtual reality, plus digital games. There were 47 submissions to Edutainment 2017, each of which was reviewed by at least two reviewers from our International Program Committee. 36 papers were accepted for presentation at the conference. The conference also hosted a satellite workshop: Next Generation Computer Animation Techniques.

We would like to thank all members of the International Program Committee for their devotion to the conference in the past years and their expert reviews of the papers, for which they provided valuable feedback to the authors. Many thanks also go to our three keynote speakers, Prof. Gabriel Brostow, Dr. Sylvester Arnab, and Prof. Paul Coulton for their inspirational plenary talks to the conference delegates. Last but not least, we would like to thank Bournemouth University for hosting and organizing the conference.

June 2017

Feng Tian
Christos Gatzidis
Abdennour El Rhalibi
Wen Tang
Fred Charles

Conference Organization

Honorary Chairs

Jianjun Zhang   Bournemouth University, UK
Joaquim Jorge   Instituto Superior Tecnico, Lisbon, Portugal

Conference General Chairs

Feng Tian   Bournemouth University, UK
Christos Gatzidis   Bournemouth University, UK
Zhigeng Pan   Hangzhou Normal University, China

Program Chairs

Wen Tang   Bournemouth University, UK
Abdennour El Rhalibi   Liverpool John Moores University, UK
Yongzhao Zhan   Jiangsu University, China
Koji Koyamada   Kyoto University, Japan

Publication Chairs

Minghui Sun   Jilin University, China
Maiga Chang   Athabasca University, Canada
Hongchuan Yu   Bournemouth University, UK

Local Chairs

Fred Charles   Bournemouth University, UK
Charlie Hargood   Bournemouth University, UK
Karsten Pedersen   Bournemouth University, UK

Technical Program Committee

Liarokapis Fotis   Masaryk University, Czech Republic
Theresa-Marie Rhyne   Consultant, North Carolina, USA
Leonel Morgado   INESC TEC/Universidade Aberta, Portugal
Andrés Navarro   Pontificia Universidad Javeriana, Cali, Columbia
Yam-San Chee   National Institute of Education, Singapore
Mingmin Zhang   Zhejiang University, China
Dhiya Al-Jumeily   Liverpool John Moores University, UK
Anthony Brooks   Aalborg University, Denmark
Panagiotis Petridis   Aston University, UK

William Hurst	Liverpool John Moores University, UK
Stephen Tang	Liverpool John Moores University, UK
Gabriel Brostow	University College London, UK
Paul Coulton	Lancaster University, UK
Sylvester Arnab	Coventry University, UK
Chang Jian	Bournemouth University, UK
Hongchuan Yu	Bournemouth University, UK
Carlo Harvey	Bournemouth University, UK
John Ferraris	Bournemouth University, UK
Alain Simons	Bournemouth University, UK
Karsten Pedersen	Bournemouth University, UK
Fred Charles	Bournemouth University, UK
Charlie Hargood	Bournemouth University, UK
Jon Cobb	Bournemouth University, UK
Jose Fonseca	Bournemouth University, UK
Simant Prakoonwit	Bournemouth University, UK
Xiaosong Yang	Bournemouth University, UK
Peter Allen	Bournemouth University, UK
Leigh McLoughlin	Bournemouth University, UK
Glyn Hadley	Bournemouth University, UK
David John	Bournemouth University, UK
Tom Davis	Bournemouth University, UK
Ambrose Seddon	Bournemouth University, UK
Andrew Watson	Bournemouth University, UK
Mohd Shahrizal	Sunar MagicX, Malaysia
Chen Wei	Zhejiang University, China
Dansong Chen	Harbin Institute of Technology, China
Zhongke Wu	Beijing Normal University, China
Ning Xie	University of Electronic Science & Technology, China
Dongwann Kang	Bournemouth University, UK
Hui Yu	University of Portsmouth, UK
Fengquan Zhang	Beihang University, China
António Coelho	University of Porto, Portugal
Koji Koyamada	Kyoto University, Japan
Feng Tian	Bournemouth University, UK
Abdennour El Rhalibi	Liverpool John Moores University, UK
Christos Gatzidis	Bournemouth University, UK
Wen Tang	Bournemouth University, UK
Wolfgang Mueller	University of Education Weingarten, Germany
Sud Sudirman	Liverpool John Moores University, UK
Yoshihiro Okada	Kyushu University, Japan
Matthias Rauterberg	Eindhoven University of Technology, The Netherlands
Xiaogang Jin	CAD & CG, Zhejiang University, China
Ruck Thawonmas	Ritsumeikan University, Japan
Gengdai Liu	OLM Digital Inc., China
Sarmad Abdulazeez	Liverpool John Moores University, UK

Marc Jaeger	CIRAD, France
Rajae El Ouazzani	Ecole Supérieure de Technologie, Morocco
Tianlu Mao	ICT, Chinese Academy of Sciences, China
Xiaopeng Zhang	Institute of Automation, Chinese Academy of Sciences, China
Minhua Ma	University of Huddersfield, UK
Minghui Sun	Jilin University, China
Suiping Zhou	Middlesex University, UK
Qingde Li	University of Hull, UK
Martin Goebel	Hochschule Bonn-Rhein-Sieg, Germany
Rafiq Swash	Brunel University, UK
Edmond Prakash	University of Westminster, UK
Yuanquan Wang	Hebei University of Technology, China
Zhigeng Pan	Hangzhou Normal University, UK
Claudio Palazzi	University of Padua, Italy
Dunwei Wen	Athabasca University, Canada
Xubo Yang	Shanghai Jiaotong University, China
Yuanyuan Shen	Liverpool John Moores University, UK
Xiamao Wu	Smartisense GmbH, Germany
Yueh-Min Huang	National Cheng Kung University, Taiwan
Thomas Connolly	University of the West of Scotland, UK
Mohd-Shahrizal Sunar	Universiti Teknologi Malaysia, Malaysia
Kashif Kifayat	Liverpool John Moores University, UK
Katerina Mania	Technical University of Crete, Greece
Daming Shi	Middlesex University, UK
Kok-Wai Wong	Murdoch University, Australia
Julien Gascon-Samson	University of British Columbia, Canada
Fuhua Lin	Athabasca University, Canada
Lihua You	Bournemouth University, UK
Kin-Chuen Hui	Chinese University, Hongkong, China

Contents

Graphics, Imaging and Applications

E-Learning and Game

Virtual Reality and Augmented Reality
in Edutainment

Representation of Intractable Objects and Action Sequences in VR Using Hand Gesture Recognition

Denis Savosin[1]([✉]), Simant Prakoonwit[1], Feng Tian[1], Jingui Liang[2], and Zhigeng Pan[3]

[1] Bournemouth University, Dorset, UK
{i7620684, sprakoonwit, ftian}@bournemouth.ac.uk
[2] Shihezi University, Xinjiang, China
[3] Hangzhou Normal University, Hangzhou, China

Abstract. We propose a novel approach on using static and dynamic gesture recognition in VR games to represent interactive objects in games, such as equipment system, weapons and handy-tools. We examine various applications of gesture recognition in games, learning, medicine and VR, including how developers currently use the bundles of HDM devices paired with hand tracking sensors. The proposed approach provides game developers with a control over recording gestures and binding them to in-game intractable objects and equipment.

Keywords: Games · Gesture recognition · Virtual reality

1 Introduction

In recent years, many innovative Human-Computer-Interaction (HIC) controllers have emerged into a process of creation the new gameplay experiences in video games [6, 13, 15]. Each of the 7th generation of game consoles – Xbox 360, PlayStation 3 and Wii has introduced their visions of the interaction with games. The most known example of those devices was a Kinect controller, which brought the gesture and human pose recognition into mass games products. Since that times, the gesture recognition field has been extensively studied, particularly the hand gesture recognition and facial recognition [6, 10]. The gesture recognition has been applied to solve various problems in human-computer interaction field, including 'serious games' and reha-bilitation applications, handwriting, numeral gesture recognition and Sign Language [12, 14, 16].

The 8th generation of gaming systems has not only brought the overall increase in graphics fidelity, the complexity of a gameplay and AI but also become a first ever generation to adapt a Virtual Reality Head Mounted Displays (HMD) to mass use and introduced the players to a new interactive entertainment experiences. The introduction of a new generation of HMD devices raised a question of adapting input controllers to act as complement (supplement) to VR devices to expose the potential of interaction with games [8, 13].

© Springer International Publishing AG 2017
F. Tian et al. (Eds.): Edutainment 2017, LNCS 10345, pp. 3–10, 2017.
https://doi.org/10.1007/978-3-319-65849-0_1

Several companies, such as Leap Motion Inc. and Oculus have made significant progress in combining the HMD devices and hand-recognition controllers [2–4].

Although the combination of the VR HMD device and a hand tracking controller allowed game developers start exploring the new opportunities to interact with the games, most of the existing games and prototypes use the simple 'mimic' of the hands in the virtual worlds [1]. Those games are mostly utilizing the hands as grasping and handling tools to interact with some interactive objects, like normally human do in the reality [1] or as a to give gesture commands to a game [13]. From the overview of a portfolio of VR games with gesture recognition we conclude that game developers have not been fully implementing games where the hands of the players should mimic weapons, gear and inventory items.

To address this limitation, we propose a novel approach for game developers, which will allow them to fully the expose the potential of the hand-tracking controllers in virtual-reality games, disregarding the genre of the game. Developers would have an API to create the custom database of hand gestures and bind each of the gesture to an interactive object or action sequence. In a genre, as first-person shooters played in a VR, the usage of a player's own hands as a weapon will act a natural way to interact with a game, completely immersing players into virtual reality. In Sect. 2 of the paper, we go through the explanation of the approach to implement this tool, including the justification of existing methodologies in this area. In Sect. 4 we present evaluation of the effectiveness of various gesture recognitions during a gameplay, followed by the conclusion in Sect. 6.

2 Methodology

We use a Leap Motion controller to capture the image of the hand, and extract the important data, such as fingertips positions, palm normal, and their directions and then passing that data to a Support Vector Machine classification learner [7] to train the system which must respond to a stream of data in real time and give the correct gesture recognition.

To train the recognition system, game developers must record all proposed gestures and build the database of the gestures. In our recognition system, we have proposed the "trigger-class" association approach. Game developers will have an option to create their class [7] and nominate it, for example: "shotgun". Then they can select that class response as active and start recording gestures. All data, extracted from a Leap controller will be marked accordingly to that class and feed into database table. Developers have an option of recording one gesture at a time, or record all gestures in one run, by switching active classes using keyboard or using timers.

Once the database is filled with data and class responders, the data are fed into a Multi-SVM [7] classifier to recognize the performed gestures. After the classifier has been trained, the database can be disposed optionally.

Developers then can assign each of the static gesture [5] variable to an item in a game and the dynamic gesture [9] variables to trigger action sequences, such as firing a gun or throwing an object. Here we introduce a concept of "gesture blending" – the smooth transition from a static object to an action sequence with that object.

The example is a "stone" object represented by player holding his hand in a fist and the sequence action "throw stone" where the player repeats a throwing move with his hand. This problem is discussed in the testing section.

3 Experiment Setup

To do tests and evaluate the viability of the proposed concept, the experimental setup has been implemented. The setup consists of the C++ console application, written using SDL2 library and Leap Motion SDK. The application is written and built using XCode 8 IDE under Mac OS X 10.12 operational system. The program kicks-out with adding Sample Listener – defines the list of call-back functions, who respond to events from a Controller instance (the interface for physical Leap controller). As the purpose of the program is to read data continuously from controller and write it to a file, alongside with response for keypresses, it implements basic events like controller connection and disconnection and the frame events – each frame is used to get a data from it.

The program reads the data outputs from a Leap Motion controller: the fingers positions, velocity and validity, alongside with a palm normal and velocity vectors. Values are written sequentially into a Comma Separated Values (.CVS) table (Figs. 1 and 2).

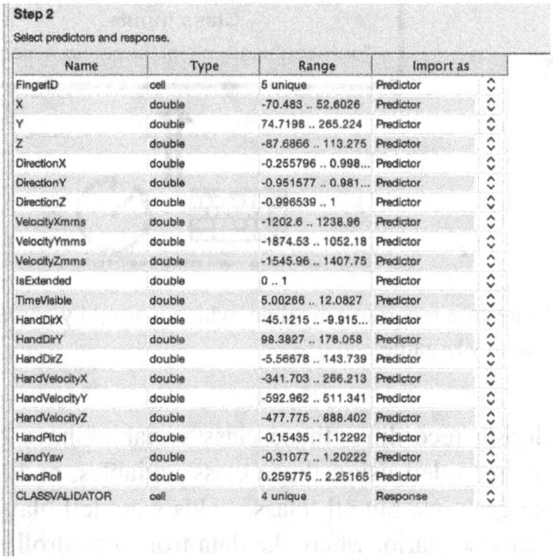

Name	Type	Range	Import as	
FingertD	cell	5 unique	Predictor	⟳
X	double	-70.483 .. 52.6026	Predictor	⟳
Y	double	74.7198 .. 265.224	Predictor	⟳
Z	double	-87.6866 .. 113.275	Predictor	⟳
DirectionX	double	-0.255796 .. 0.998...	Predictor	⟳
DirectionY	double	-0.951577 .. 0.981...	Predictor	⟳
DirectionZ	double	-0.996539 .. 1	Predictor	⟳
VelocityXmms	double	-1202.6 .. 1238.96	Predictor	⟳
VelocityYmms	double	-1874.53 .. 1052.18	Predictor	⟳
VelocityZmms	double	-1545.96 .. 1407.75	Predictor	⟳
IsExtended	double	0 .. 1	Predictor	⟳
TimeVisible	double	5.00266 .. 12.0827	Predictor	⟳
HandDirX	double	-45.1215 .. -9.915...	Predictor	⟳
HandDirY	double	98.3827 .. 176.058	Predictor	⟳
HandDirZ	double	-5.56678 .. 143.739	Predictor	⟳
HandVelocityX	double	-341.703 .. 266.213	Predictor	⟳
HandVelocityY	double	-592.962 .. 511.341	Predictor	⟳
HandVelocityZ	double	-477.775 .. 888.402	Predictor	⟳
HandPitch	double	-0.15435 .. 1.12292	Predictor	⟳
HandYaw	double	-0.31077 .. 1.20222	Predictor	⟳
HandRoll	double	0.259775 .. 2.25165	Predictor	⟳
CLASSVALIDATOR	cell	4 unique	Response	⟳

Step 2
Select predictors and response.

Fig. 1. Selecting the features from recorded database to be imported into MATLAB for testing. 4 unique CLASSVALIDATOR values are: 'unrecognized', 'pistol', 'fist', 'shooting action'

The last field in each table entry is an actual class variable – we use 4 class variables in our experimental setup: 'fist', 'pistol' – static gestures, 'pistol shot' – the dynamic gesture to define the shooting action sequence. The 'unrecognized' class is used to mark all fields, which are not intended to be classified as a gesture. By pressing

	A	B	C	D	E	F	G
1	Finger ID	X	Y	Z	DirectionX	DirectionY	DirectionZ
2	Thumb	-32.3269	220.184	37.7749	-0.005464	0.288962	-0.957325
3	Index	-30.416	202.135	-13.336	-0.319262	-0.001198	-0.947666
4	Middle	-42.6243	143.922	42.4189	-0.42981	-0.333249	0.839171
5	Ring	-40.7802	130.212	36.164	-0.842755	-0.528025	-0.104658
6	Pinky	-20.3064	130.04	39.7539	-0.890779	-0.387827	-0.236859
7	Index	-30.2807	202.095	-14.0295	-0.322641	0.002268	-0.946519
8	Thumb	-29.5654	219.252	37.4543	0.02227	0.262272	-0.964737
9	Middle	-42.3845	144.259	43.5251	-0.41175	-0.30869	0.857422
10	Ring	-41.0053	130.111	36.4187	-0.851775	-0.515393	-0.09407
11	Pinky	-20.5628	129.86	40.0201	-0.898501	-0.375358	-0.227602
12	Index	-30.1583	202.041	-14.6522	-0.325342	0.006577	-0.945573
13	Thumb	-27.7294	218.642	37.2126	0.036508	0.245267	-0.968768
14	Middle	-42.1514	144.583	44.5558	-0.396618	-0.288652	0.871421
15	Ring	-41.335	130.013	36.6707	-0.859883	-0.503498	-0.08421
16	Pinky	-20.9309	129.64	40.2562	-0.90545	-0.363473	-0.219196
17	Index	-30.0368	201.983	-15.2345	-0.326164	0.011228	-0.945247
18	Thumb	-26.5462	218.206	36.9911	0.044112	0.23443	-0.971132

	S	T	U	V	W
t	HandPitch	HandYaw	HandRoll	CLASS(VALIDATOR)	
	0.18102	0.218757	-0.776146	unrecognised	
	0.18102	0.218757	-0.776146	unrecognised	
	0.18102	0.218757	-0.776146	unrecognised	
	0.18102	0.218757	-0.776146	unrecognised	
	0.18102	0.218757	-0.776146	unrecognised	
	0.170692	0.214012	-0.791823	unrecognised	
	0.170692	0.214012	-0.791823	unrecognised	
	0.170692	0.214012	-0.791823	unrecognised	
	0.170692	0.214012	-0.791823	unrecognised	
	0.170692	0.214012	-0.791823	unrecognised	
	0.162209	0.209807	-0.806229	unrecognised	
	0.162209	0.209807	-0.806229	unrecognised	
	0.162209	0.209807	-0.806229	unrecognised	
	0.162209	0.209807	-0.806229	unrecognised	
	0.162209	0.209807	-0.806229	unrecognised	
	0.155922	0.206730	0.817051	unrecognised	

Fig. 2. Screenshots demonstrating the resulting. CSV table with data captured from a Leap Controller.

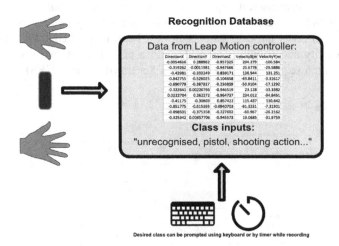

Fig. 3. Image shows the gesture recording pipeline, which is used by game developers to create and record gestures for their VR games.

corresponding keys during recording, those class variables have been recorded to a field. One data set was recorded using those class variables, and the second set was recorded with the same gestures, but all 'class' fields were left blank – this was due to simulation of the real case scenario, where the data from a controller is going to be fed into trained model in the real time (Fig. 3).

4 Testing and Evaluation

Resulting training set with recorded class variables has been uploaded to a MATLAB R2016b and used to train Multiple-SVMs classifiers. The first obtained performance and accuracy results allowed to make changes into process of the variable selection, as some variables have more effect on a prediction performance than others (Table 1).

Table 1. The table above shows performance and misclassification rates of Multiple-SVMs trained to recognize 'pistol' class.

Type of SVM model	True positive	True negative	Observations	Misc. rate
Medium Gaussian SVM	98%	2%	False: (33 + 3) True: (165 + 180) Total: 381	(33 + 3)/ 381 = 0.09
Fine Gaussian SVM	99%	1%	False: (12 + 2) True: (166 + 201) Total: 381	(12 + 2)/ 381 = 0.03
Cubic SVM	97%	3%	False: (15 + 5) True: (163 + 198) Total: 381	(15 + 5)/ 381 = 0.05
Linear SVM	72%	28%	False: (45 + 47) True: (121 + 168) Total: 381	(45 + 47)/ 381 = 0.24

After the classification algorithm has been trained, the second testing set with a class variables left blank has been used to evaluate resulting prediction model. The results of the prediction were satisfying enough, and we have obtained the correct predictions on all four trained classes, concluding, that a chosen concept is viable, and after more tweaking can be implemented as a full game engine plug-in.

Although the results of the experiments in a MATLAB were satisfying to continue exploring the concept in rather more sophisticated manner, further progress on the concept should be ideally supervised by the gameplay programmers, as problems discovered, such as solving the transition between static 'item' gestures and dynamic 'action' gestures in a runtime. Also, some genres of games are more dependent on the timings and a prediction speed rather than accuracy. The problem can be addressed on both sides: gameplay programmers and designers should adopt the gameplay logic, if an implementation, in other hand will be flexible to fit into games of various genres.

5   Future Work

As we are planning to continue working on the prototype and an approach, implementing the Unity and the Unreal Engine plug-in, which can be embedded into the editor. We prepared mock-ups to demonstrate concepts of how the final product might look like. Figures 4 and 5 show two plug-in windows on OS X system, where the first figure shows the 'Gesture Learner' window – setup and recording of gesture database. The second figure shows 'Linker' window – binding recorded gestures to an equipment or gearing system in game.

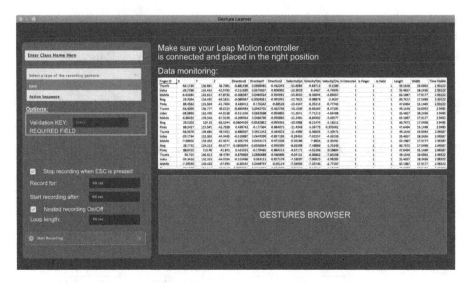

Fig. 4. Image shows a concept of the 'Gesture Learner' part and an editor window of the final product.

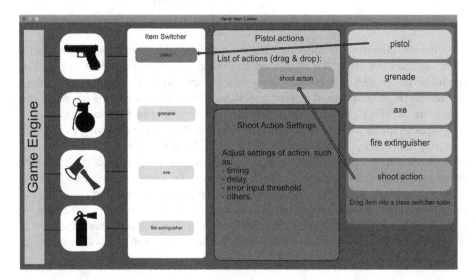

Fig. 5. Image shows a concept of the 'Linker' part and an editor window of the final product.

6   Conclusion

In this paper, we have proposed an approach for recording and predicting static gestures and actions, aiming to give game developers an opportunity to deeper explore the possible use cases for VR headsets bundled with tracking devices. Developers might also be able to adapt the gameplay experiences to immerse players into virtual reality.

By creating this prototype, we will investigate more about the opportunities for gesture recognition in Virtual Reality games. We also plan to further improve the design of the existing prototype and embed the tool into game engines, such as Unreal Engine and Unity as a plug-in. The concept presented here, and our discussion on how this concept can be adapted for VR games, certainly can further promote the research in this field and grab game developers' attention to this method, which can be used to create immersive VR experiences.

Acknowledgement. This paper is partially supported by the project – Virtual Visualization System for Culture Communications (2015BAK04B05) funded under the theme – National Science and Technology Supporting Project, China.

References

1. VR – Leap Motion Gallery: Gallery.leapmotion.com (2017). https://gallery.leapmotion.com/category/vr/. Accessed 6 Apr 2017
2. VR Setup: Leap Motion Developer (2017). https://developer.leapmotion.com/vr-setup/. Accessed 11 Apr 2017
3. Unreal: Leap Motion Developer (2017). https://developer.leapmotion.com/unreal#103. Accessed 11 Apr 2017
4. Unity: Leap Motion Developer (2017). https://developer.leapmotion.com/unity. Accessed 11 Apr 2017
5. Chen, Y., Ding, Z., Chen, Y., Wu, X.: Rapid recognition of dynamic hand gestures using leap motion. In: 2015 IEEE International Conference on Information and Automation (2015). doi:10.1109/icinfa.2015.7279509
6. Cheng, H., Yang, L., Liu, Z.: Survey on 3D hand gesture recognition. IEEE Trans. Circ. Syst. Video Technol. **26**, 1659–1673 (2016). doi:10.1109/tcsvt.2015.2469551
7. Cristianini, N., Shawe Taylor, J.: An Introduction to Support Vector Machines and Other Kernel-Based Learning Methods. Cambridge University Press, Cambridge (2000)
8. Ling, H., Rui, L.: VR glasses and leap motion trends in education. In: 2016 11th International Conference on Computer Science and Education (ICCSE) (2016). doi:10.1109/iccse.2016.7581705
9. Lu, W., Tong, Z., Chu, J.: Dynamic hand gesture recognition with leap motion controller. IEEE Sig. Process. Lett. **23**, 1188–1192 (2016). doi:10.1109/lsp.2016.2590470
10. Marin, G., Dominio, F., Zanuttigh, P.: Hand gesture recognition with leap motion and kinect devices. In: 2014 IEEE International Conference on Image Processing (ICIP) (2014). doi:10.1109/icip.2014.7025313
11. Mentzelopoulos, M., Tarpini, F., Emanuele, A., Protopsaltis, A.: Hardware interfaces for VR applications: evaluation on prototypes. In: 2015 IEEE International Conference on Computer and Information Technology; Ubiquitous Computing and Communications; Dependable, Autonomic and Secure Computing; Pervasive Intelligence and Computing (2015). doi:10.1109/cit/iucc/dasc/picom.2015.237
12. Naglot, D., Kulkarni, M.: Real time sign language recognition using the leap motion controller. In: 2016 International Conference on Inventive Computation Technologies (ICICT) (2016). doi:10.1109/inventive.2016.7830097
13. Rautaray, S., Agrawal, A.: Interaction with virtual game through hand gesture recognition. In: 2011 International Conference on Multimedia, Signal Processing and Communication Technologies (2011). doi:10.1109/mspct.2011.6150485

14. Sharma, J., Gupta, R., Pathak, V.: Numeral gesture recognition using leap motion sensor. In: 2015 International Conference on Computational Intelligence and Communication Networks (CICN) (2015). doi:10.1109/cicn.2015.86
15. Sonkusare, J., Chopade, N., Sor, R., Tade, S.: A review on hand gesture recognition system. In: 2015 International Conference on Computing Communication Control and Automation (2015). doi:10.1109/iccubea.2015.158
16. Spanogianopoulos, S., Sirlantzis, K., Mentzelopoulos, M., Protopsaltis, A.: Human computer interaction using gestures for mobile devices and serious games: a review. In: 2014 International Conference on Interactive Mobile Communication Technologies and Learning (IMCL 2014) (2014). doi:10.1109/imctl.2014.7011154

An Improved Augmented Reality Registration Method Based on Visual SLAM

Qing Hong Gao[1], Tao Ruan Wan[3], Wen Tang[2(✉)], Long Chen[2], and Kai Bing Zhang[1]

[1] College of Electronic and Information, Xian Polytechnic University, Xian, China
[2] Faculty of Science and Technology, Bournemouth University, Bournemouth, UK
wtang@bournemouth.ac.uk
[3] Faculty of Informatics, University of Bradford, Bradford, UK
t.wan@bradford.ac.uk

Abstract. Markerless Augmented Reality registration using standard Homography matrix is instable and has low registration accuracy. In this paper, we present a new method to improve the augmented reality registration method based on the Visual Simultaneous Localization and Mapping (VSLAM). We improved the method implemented in ORB-SLAM in order to increase stability and accuracy of AR registration. VSLAM algorithm generate 3D scene maps in dynamic camera tracking process. Hence, for AR based on VSLAM utilizes the 3D map of the scene reconstruction to compute the location for virtual object augmentation. In this paper, a Maximum Consistency with Minimum Distance and Robust Z-score (MCMD_Z) algorithm is used to perform the planar detection of 3D maps, then the Singular Value Decomposition (SVD) and Lie group are used to calculate the rotation matrix that helps to solve the problem of virtual object orientation. Finally, the method integrates camera poses on the virtual object registration. We show experimental results to demonstrate the robustness and registration accuracy of the method for augmented reality applications.

Keywords: Augmented Reality · SLAM algorithm · Virtual regristration and fusion · Point cloud

1 Introduction

Augmented Reality (AR) is the technology of mixing real scenes with virtual scenes, an emerging field of huge application potentials. The technology makes the use of computer-generated virtual information within the real world to enhance the human perception of the world. As defined by Azuma, it is an integration of virtual world and the real world with real-time interactions via three-dimensional registrations [2]. The recent rapid development of software as well as hardware technologies in virtual reality and computer vision, AR has a wider range of applications in medicine, military, entertainment and others [4,15]. Virtual registration, however, remains a challenge in AR research. Initially

© Springer International Publishing AG 2017
F. Tian et al. (Eds.): Edutainment 2017, LNCS 10345, pp. 11–19, 2017.
https://doi.org/10.1007/978-3-319-65849-0_2

Simultaneous Localization and Mapping (SLAM), as a probability algorithm, has been mainly used for positioning robots in unknown environments [3,14]. More recently, researchers have started to utilize the accuracy and real-time performance of SLAM for virtual registration in AR. Davison et al. [5,6] have used a monocular camera to achieve fast 3D modeling and positioning of cameras in unknown environments, which has presented many practical uses of the algorithm. Klein [9] applied a SLAM algorithm in the creation of three-dimensional point clouds, as well as Reitmayr [12] demonstrated the use of SLAM and sensor fusion techniques in an accurate virtual reality registration with markerless tracking.

The method of computing homography matrix in AR systems for the three-dimensional registration [7,11] is simple and efficient. This algorithm requires the detection of four point coordinates of a plane in order to determine the translation and rotation of the camera relative to the world coordinate system. In spite of its simplicity and efficiency, since it is based on the 2D plane registration, the four points of detection algorithm is prone to the error of misplacement of the virtual object registration, resulting in virtual objects being unstable with distracting visual effects (e.g. flashing visual artifacts). Previous approaches [9,12] have attempted to make the use of the three-dimensional map information generated by SLAM for this process. In this paper, we present a method of improvement to the registration and tracking process of virtual objects by using map information generated by VSLAM [12] technology. The three-dimensional information of a scene generated by VSLAM cannot be used directly, due to the interference points and the large error of point clouds. Therefore, a robust Maximum Consistency with Minimum Distance and Robust Zscore (MCMD_Z) [1] algorithm have been used to detect the 2D plane more accurately. Our improved MCMD_Z method computes plane point matrix by using the plane normal vector fund by Singular Value Decomposition (SVD). A method of lie group is then used to convert the normal vector into the rotation matrix to register the virtual object using the plane information. We use the precise positioning function of the VSLAM to change the camera poses to the rendering coordinate system under the camera perspective for the three-dimensional registration of the virtual object.

The main contribution of this paper is to develop a method that can effectively produce stable and high registration accuracy for virtual reality fusion.

2   AR System Overview

The AR system consists of two software modules: VSLAM module and registration module as shown in Fig. 1 for an overview of the system. Tracking in the VSLAM module is to locate the camera position through processing each image frame, and decide when to insert a new keyframe. Firstly, the feature matching is initialized with the previous frame and Bundle Adjustment BA [16] is used to optimize the camera poses. While the 3D map is initialized and the map is successfully created by the VSLAM module, the registration module is called.

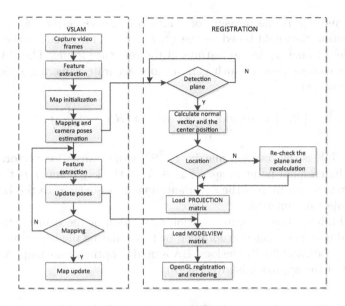

Fig. 1. System overview

Once the point cloud of the scene is generated, the computation for the plane detection is started, and the center and the normal vector of the plane are calculated. The center of the plane is used to determine the exact position of the virtual object and the normal vector is used to determine the orientation of the virtual object. Camera poses obtained by VSLAM are then transformed to the modelview matrix of OpenGL, which will be generated by the transformation of three-dimensional virtual objects to the center of the plane to achieve the virtual augmentation.

2.1   Tracking and 3D Map Building

Our system is based on a visual simultaneous mapping and tracking approach by extracting and matching the Oriented Features From Accelerated Segment Test (FAST) and Rotated Binary Robust Independent Elementary Features (BRIEF) (ORB) [13] feature points and compute two models: a homography matrix that is used to compute a planar scene and a fundamental matrix that is used to compute a non-planar scene. Each time two matrices are calculated, and a score ($M = H$ for the homography matrix, $M = F$ for the fundamental matrix) is also calculated as shown in Eq. 1. The score is used to determine which model is more suitable for the camera posture.

$$S_M = \sum_i \left(\rho_M \left(d_{cr,M}^2 \left(x_c^i, x_r^i \right) + \rho_M \left(d_{rc,M}^2 \left(x_c^i, x_r^i \right) \right) \right) \right) \qquad (1)$$

$$\rho_M \left(d^2 \right) = \begin{cases} \Gamma - d^2 \ if & d^2 < T_M \\ 0 & if \quad d^2 \geq T_M \end{cases}$$

where d_rc and d_cr is the measure of symmetric transfer errors [8], T_m is the outlier rejection threshold based on the χ^2, Γ is equal to, T_m, x_c is the features of the current frame, x_r is the features of the reference frame. The BA is used to optimize camera poses, which gets a more accurate camera position as in following equation.

$$\{R, r\} = \arg\min_{R,t} \sum_{i \in \chi} \rho \left(\left\| x^i - \pi \left(RX^i + t \right) \right\|_\Sigma^2 \right) \tag{2}$$

where $R \in \mathcal{SO}^3$ is the rotation matrix, $t \in \mathbb{R}^3$ is the translation vector, $\S^i \in \mathbb{R}^3$ is a three-dimensional point in space, $x^i \in \mathbb{R}^2$ is the key point, ρ is the Huber cost function, Sigma item is the covariance matrix associated to the key point, π is the projection function.

After obtaining the accurate position estimation of the camera, the three-dimensional map point cloud is obtained by triangulating the key frame through the camera poses, and finally the local BA is used to optimize the map. A detailed description of the approach is given in [10].

3   Plane Detection and Calculation of the Normal Vector

The map created in $\xi 2.1$ is composed of a sparse point cloud. Because of the error of the point cloud data with large number of abnormal values, MCMD_Z is used for plane detection. A MCMD_Z algorithm is used to fit the data according to a search model. The idea of this algorithm is to use Principal Component Analysis (PCA) for a reliable selection of the registration plane, using Robust Z-score to remove invalid points at once. This method not only effectively avoids the threshold setting, but also runs fast. The MCMD_Z algorithm detects the plane as follows:

Algorithm 1. The MCMD_Z algorithm

1: loop:
2: Randomly select any *3* points in the original point cloud, and calculate the corresponding initial plane and its *normal vector*;
3: Ranking the points according to the value of d_i that are the distance of the map point cloud to the initial plane;
4: Select the threshold $t = 2\sigma$. σ is the standard deviation of the point cloud to the initial plane model distance. When the $d_i > t$, the point is removed as an exception point, and vice versa as valid data retention, the number of valid data, P_num;
5: **if** The set of points reach the minimum Eigen values **then**
6:    Stop the loop.
7: Calculate Robust Z-score uses the Eq. 3. Zscore greater than 2 is considered an outlier and will be removed.

$$Rz_i = \frac{\left| od_i - \underset{j}{median}\,(od_i) \right|}{a \cdot \underset{i}{median}\left| od_i - \underset{j}{median}\,(od_i) \right|} \tag{3}$$

The detection of the plane determines the plane location, while providing a super-position of the location for a virtual object. Although the location of the virtual object is determined, virtual objects will not appear parallel to the plane but at a certain angle to the plane. In order to solve this problem, we need to calculate the normal vector of the plane and the rotation matrix.

The SVD of the matrix in the plane interior point is obtained, and the right singular vector corresponding to the minimum eigenvalue is the normal vector of the plane. Because there are two normal vectors in the plane, it is important that the normal vector direction is pointing outward. Specifically, the vector of the camera to the plane is found by the camera's posture. Through the vector and the relationship be-tween the plane vectors, we can then determine the direction of the normal vector. The rotation matrix is obtained from the known normal vector by Lie group using the following equation:

$$R_{3\times3} = exp\,(\hat{w}) = I + sin\,(\|w\|) \cdot \frac{\hat{w}}{\|w\|} + (1 - cos\,(\|w\|)) \cdot \frac{\hat{w}\hat{w}}{\|w\|^2} \tag{4}$$

$$w = \frac{n_y \times n_p}{\|n_y \times n_p\|} \cdot arctan\frac{\|n_y \times n_p\|}{n_y \times n_p}$$

Where n_y is $y - axis$ unit vector, n_p is normal vector of the plane, w is a column vector, $\hat{w}$ is the anti-symmetric matrix of the vector w. Finally, the transformation matrix of OpenGL is composed of a translation vector and a rotation matrix. The rotation matrix is obtained and the translation vector is found to be the center of the plane.

3.1   Virtual Registration

The virtual object is finally registered in the real world, which must go through the transformation of the coordinate systems (from the world coordinate system to the camera coordinate system to the crop coordinate system, and to the screen coordinate system). The transformation sequences can be described by Eq. 4 from left to right: the world coordinate system is transformed into the camera coordinate system by a rotation matrix $R_{(3\times3)}$ and a translation matrix $T_{(3\times1)}$. Those matrices are made up by the camera's position and the detected plane information. Then the camera coordinate system is then transformed into the screen coordinate system (u, v) by the focal length (f_x, f_y) and the principal point (d_x, d_y). These parameters are obtained by the camera calibration. Finally, the virtual object is registered in the screen to the real world.

$$\begin{bmatrix} u \\ v \\ 1 \end{bmatrix} = \begin{bmatrix} f_x & 0 & d_x & 0 \\ 0 & f_y & d_y & 0 \\ 0 & 0 & 1 & 0 \end{bmatrix} \begin{bmatrix} R_{3\times3} & T_{3\times1} \\ 0_{1\times3} & 1 \end{bmatrix} \begin{bmatrix} X \\ Y \\ Z \\ 1 \end{bmatrix} \tag{5}$$

4   Experiment and Evaluation

Our experiment is run under Ubuntu 14.04 system, CPU clocked at 2.3 GHz, 8 GB memory and graphics card for the NVIDIA GeForce GTX 960 MB. The camera resolution is 640 by 480 pixels at 30 Hz. The experimental scene is indoors and the length of the image collection is 1857 frames. Figure 2(a)–(b) show the indoor scene under the AR tracking and registration. We can see that the tracking and registration effect. Figure 2(c) shows the correct virtual object orientation.

(a)   (b)   (c)

Fig. 2. AR tracking and registration (left to right (a)–(c))

4.1   Plane Detection Analysis

Our method based on the CMCD_Z, which achieves better results than Random Sample Consensus (RANSAC). In contrast to these two algorithms, we use the Gaussian distribution to produce 1000 point with outlier percentages (10 and 20) using the same input parameters used previously. The inliers have means (15.0, 15.0, 10.0) and variances (10.0, 2.0, 0.5). The outliners have means (15.0, 15.0, 10.0) and variances (10.0, 2.0, 0.5). The program ran 1000 times. We compared Correct Identification Rate (CIR) and Swamping Rate (SR). The RANSAC sets iterations 50 times (Table 1).

4.2   Registration Error Analysis

A comparison method is used with fixed camera positions to evaluate the robustness of the method. The three-dimensional registration of the virtual object is carried out by using the described method and the standard homography matrix method. Six components of the three-dimensional registration results are analyzed. The difference between the transformation matrix of the current frame

Table 1. Correct Identification Rate (CIR), Swamping Rate (SR) and Time

Methods	Outlier percentage				Time (s)
	10		20		
	CIR	SR	CIR	SR	
RANSAC	100	24.3	100	8	0.307849
MCMD_Z	100	6	100	0.5	0.116869

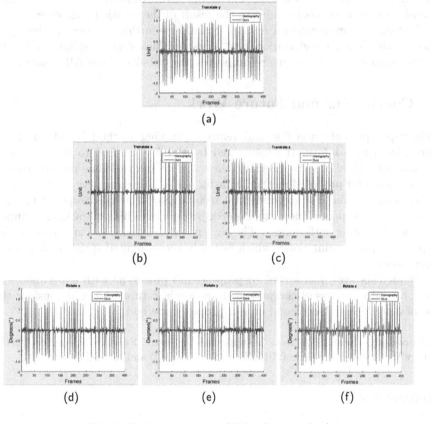

Fig. 3. Registration error (Color figure online)

and the corresponding component of the transformation matrix of the previous frame is used as the basis for comparison. The results are shown in Fig. 3, where Translate x, Translate y and Trans-late z are the errors of the translation components, respectively, and Rotate x, Rotate y, Rotate z are relative to the x, y, z axis of the rotation component error and where is obtained by subtracting the previous frame from the current frame. The result of the rotation component is obtained by dividing the respective components with the dot product of the corresponding coordinate axis, and the translation component is the result obtained by the normalization process.

In Fig. 3, the red curves in the figures are the results of using only the homography matrix. The blue curves are the results of the new registration method used in this paper. As can be seen from the Fig. 3, the use of the homography matrix method to register the virtual objects has produced large fluctuations of registration errors that are equivalent to virtual object registration instability. However, the new method tested on each rotation component has been kept the error in a small range below 0.5°. The errors with Translate x, Translate y and Translate z are also small similar to the result of the rotation components.

Through the experimental results, it can be seen that the new method produces stable virtual registration and solve the flickering phenomenon in the virtual reality registration, hence, improves the stability of the AR system.

5   Conclusions and Future Work

This paper presents a stable and realistic tracking method based on three-dimensional map information generated by VSLAM method to track the registration of virtual objects to ensure the stability and real-time performance of registration. Our proposed method is faster and is able to achieve more accurate registration results. The experimental results show that the proposed method can effectively suppress the virtual object jitter, have a higher tracking accuracy with good tracking performance. The current three-dimensional map used in this paper is a sparse point cloud, which can only access limited space configuration information.

While this work has served to propose and prototype with experiments to show the effectiveness of the proposed approach, future work will consider the use of dense point cloud based on our proposed method.

Acknowledgement. This work is supported by Shanxi Province Science and Technology Department: Projects (2016JZ026 2016KW-043) and (2016GY-047).

References

1. Azuma, R., Baillot, Y., Behringer, R., Feiner, S., Julier, S., MacIntyre, B.: Recent advances in augmented reality. IEEE Comput. Graphics Appl. **21**(6), 34–47 (2001)
2. Azuma, R.T.: A survey of augmented reality. Presence Teleoperators Virtual Environ. **6**(4), 355–385 (1997)
3. Bailey, T., Durrant-Whyte, H.: Simultaneous localization and mapping (SLAM): part II. IEEE Robot. Autom. Mag. **13**(3), 108–117 (2006)
4. Bimber, O., Raskar, R.: Spatial Augmented Reality Merging Real and Virtual Worlds. A K Peters Ltd., Natick (2005)
5. Davison, A.J., Mayol, W.W., Murray, D.W.: Real-time localization and mapping with wearable active vision. In: Proceedings of Second IEEE and ACM International Symposium Mixed and Augmented Reality, pp. 18–27, October 2003

6. Davison, A.J., Mayol, W.W., Murray, D.W.: Real-time workspace localisation and mapping for wearable robot. In: Proceedings of Second IEEE and ACM International Symposium Mixed and Augmented Reality, pp. 315–316, October 2003

7. Fiala, M.: Artag, a fiducial marker system using digital techniques. In: Proceedings of IEEE Computer Society Conference on Computer Vision and Pattern Recognition (CVPR 2005), vol. 2, pp. 590–596, June 2005

8. Hartley, R., Zisserman, A.: Multiple View Geometry in Computer Vision. Cambridge University Press, Cambridge (2000)

9. Klein, G., Murray, D.: Parallel tracking and mapping for small AR workspaces. In: Proceedings of the 6th IEEE and ACM International Symposium on Mixed and Augmented Reality, pp. 225–234, November 2007

10. Mur-Artal, R., Montiel, J.M.M., Tards, J.D.: Orb-SLAM: a versatile and accurate monocular SLAM system. IEEE Trans. Robot. **31**(5), 1147–1163 (2015)

11. Prince, S.J.D., Xu, K., Cheok, A.D.: Augmented reality camera tracking with homographies. IEEE Comput. Graphics Appl. **22**(6), 39–45 (2002)

12. Reitmayr, G., Eade, E., Drummond, T.W.: Semi-automatic annotations in unknown environments. In: Proceedings of the 6th IEEE and ACM International Symposium on Mixed and Augmented Reality, pp. 67–70, November 2007

13. Rublee, E., Rabaud, V., Konolige, K., Bradski, G.: Orb: an efficient alternative to sift or surf. In: Proceedings of International Conference on Computer Vision, pp. 2564–2571, November 2011

14. Strasdat, H., Montiel, J., Davison, A.J.: Visual SLAM: why filter? Image Vis. Comput. **30**(2), 65–77 (2012)

15. Szalaviri, Z., Gervautz, M.: The personal interaction panel - a two-handed interface for augmented reality. Comput. Graph. Forum **16**(3), C335–C346 (1997). http://onlinelibrary.wiley.com/doi/10.1111/1467-8659.00137/abstract

16. Triggs, B., McLauchlan, P.F., Hartley, R.I., Fitzgibbon, A.W.: Bundle adjustment—a modern synthesis. In: Triggs, B., Zisserman, A., Szeliski, R. (eds.) IWVA 1999. LNCS, vol. 1883, pp. 298–372. Springer, Heidelberg (2000). doi:10.1007/3-540-44480-7_21

Tenochtitlan - An Interactive Virtual Reality Environment that Encourages Museum Exhibit Engagement

Sebastian Garcia-Cardona[1,2(✉)], Feng Tian[1,2],
and Simant Prakoonwit[1,2]

[1] Faculty of Science and Technology,
Bournemouth University, Bournemouth BH12 5BB, UK
sebastian.garcia94@gmail.com
[2] Springer Heidelberg, Tiergartenstr. 17, 69121 Heidelberg, Germany

Abstract. With many cultural institutions experiencing declining visitor figures, a large number have begun introducing the use of engaging technologies to attract more visitors, the use of which seem especially appealing to the younger generations. Due to the steadily rising popularity of virtual reality, it is one of the more prominent technologies these institutions have incorporated. However, most uses of virtual reality result in small-scale exhibit recreations or immersive video with very little interaction. In this paper, we propose to create a large-scale virtual reality environment with an integrated interactive quiz system, which aims to offer an engagement level above that of traditional museum exhibits. Initial results of Tenochtitlan have been demonstrated positive. Participant interviews have shown that 87.5% experienced engagement levels in Tenochtitlan greater than that of a traditional museum exhibit, and 62.5% stated that their knowledge of the subject matter had increased.

Keywords: Museum virtual reality · Museum exhibit engagement · Interactive learning

1 Introduction

In recent years, many cultural institutions have seen their visitor figures stagnate or decline [1]. The heavy use of digital technology could be partly to blame, as it makes up a large percentage of how we choose to spend our leisure time [2], with younger generations even less likely to visit museums, galleries etc. One recent technology, in particular, seems to have captured the interest of these same young people: virtual reality [3].

Virtual reality technology has advanced massively in the last decade [4], to the point where consumer-level VR devices have become freely available to the public. Subsequently, virtual reality technology has seen a rise in popularity. Cultural institutions have tried to capitalise on this popularity by using virtual reality with their exhibits to attract visitors [5] in a time where figures have been falling.

Many current forms of virtual reality integration by museums currently exist, most of which result in a highly immersive experience. In 2015 the British Museum held the

© Springer International Publishing AG 2017
F. Tian et al. (Eds.): Edutainment 2017, LNCS 10345, pp. 20–28, 2017.
https://doi.org/10.1007/978-3-319-65849-0_3

'Virtual Reality Weekend' [6], an event where users could use a Samsung Gear VR to explore a Bronze Age roundhouse and view 3D-scanned exhibit artefacts. It proved extremely popular, attracting over 1,200 visitors during the two-day event. The National History Museum in London has employed VR technology in several ways [7, 8], the first example being a 360-degree VR video titled 'David Attenborough's Great Barrier Reef Dive'. They have also recently made many of their exhibits available to view remotely in VR using Google Cardboard, along with the option to see an ancient reptile swim around the user while they learn facts about it.

The methods in which the National History Museum have made use of virtual reality seem to be the most widespread amongst museums i.e. exhibit recreation in VR and 360 VR videos. However, these examples, as with many others, seem to overlook the capacity for interaction provided by the technology [9].

In this paper, we propose and develop an educational virtual reality environment, called Tenochtitlan. Tenochtitlan is intended to be used as a complementary tool to increase engagement levels with existing museum exhibits. The environment is explored in first person and integrates an interactive quiz system, designed to maximise information delivery and retention over that provided by traditional museum methods.

Participants who were asked to take part in Tenochtitlan's virtual reality quiz, and were subsequently interviewed, have produced positive initial results which will be discussed further in Sect. 4.

2   Suitability of Virtual Reality

Many museums already make use of multimedia technologies to complement existing exhibits as a means of making them more dynamic and engaging [10]. Virtual reality technology expands on this with the ability to wholly immerse the viewer in a realistic environment and gives them the opportunity to view artefacts in greater detail, resulting in a more engrossing experience.

In recent years, the benefits of virtual reality (and gamification) use in educational environments have been researched extensively, with many studies noting the positive outcomes in both education delivery and engagement levels [5, 6, 11].

Despite its benefits, virtual reality does have certain limitations not found in the traditional methods of information delivery currently found in museums [5]. Firstly, the employment of VR technology has been proved costly to museums [12]; and secondly, the creation of a VR application requires much more resources, in both time and people, than text-and-image based information delivery [13].

There also exists the need for a careful balance when creating virtual reality applications which include educational elements as one of their intended outcomes. The application must be designed in a way that avoids the appeal of the technology itself overshadowing the element intended to be presented to the user.

However, when executed well the resulting applications can prove highly effective. This has been shown in a study conducted by [14] testing the exhibit engagement levels in a children's science museum. These positive findings were echoed in a separate study by [15], which found that 70% of visitors agreed that the use of virtual reality "... enhanced the visitor experience".

Furthermore, a preliminary survey conducted across 50 individuals found a positive attitude towards virtual reality in museums, the results of which can be seen in Figs. 1 and 2.

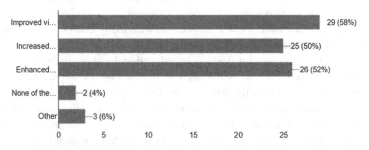

Fig. 1. 52% of respondents believe the inclusion of interactive VR would enhance visitor-exhibit engagement.

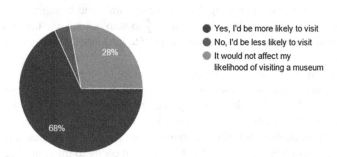

Fig. 2. 68% of those surveyed commented that the inclusion of a VR-integrated exhibit would increase their likelihood of visiting a museum.

3   Application Design

Our application Tenochtitlan has been tailored towards young adults aged 18–30, as this is the age group that museums seem to be struggling to attract the most [16]. As this element of the design mainly entailed regulating the language used and the questions within the quiz, Tenochtitlan could be modified to suit other target age groups relatively easily. Another consideration made during the design stage was that of the user's technological competence, which was assumed to be basic for the sake of this project. This allowed Tenochtitlan to remain accessible to as wide an audience as possible, without alienating individuals who lack experience with game technology.

3.1 The Application

Tenochtitlan is an interactive virtual reality environment which offers users the opportunity to explore a portion of an ancient Aztec city. Its purpose is to increase the user's engagement with, and knowledge of, the subject matter through the use of virtual reality technology. To achieve this Tenochtitlan incorporates two core design dynamics: exploration and educational delivery by means of a quiz system.

When the user starts up Tenochtitlan, they are greeted with a notice board with instructions on what their objectives are, and how they will interact with the environment. These introduction/instructions were kept short and make use of simple language to ensure that possible user confusion is kept to a minimum.

As the user explores the environment they will encounter several pop-ups along the way. Half of these are informational and display facts about the Aztecs to the user. This assists in the educational aspect of Tenochtitlan, which in an exhibit would normally be achieved through regular image/text information delivery methods [9].

The other half of these pop-ups contain questions, which form Tenochtitlan's main mechanic: the quiz system. The questions in these are tied directly to corresponding factual pop-ups. To answer these questions the player aims at their selection using the VR reticule and presses a button on the controller. Separate pop-ups, along with audio cues, inform the player if they have answered correctly or not. If they have answered correctly, then their level score will be updated to reflect this. The inclusion of a score mechanic as a positive feedback loop is one that aims to provide an incentive for the users to further explore the environment [17].

The quiz is completed when the user has found all the facts and answered all the quiz pop-ups. They are then free to explore further or exit the application.

3.2 Freedom to Explore, Freedom to Learn

One of the major aspects of Tenochtitlan is the freedom the user is given within the environment; this makes use of the 'Exploration' game mechanic as described by [18] to encourage users to explore and discover.

A study by [19] also demonstrated that the use of game design principles, such as the score system, lead to greater learning outcomes. This has been integrated to provide feedback to the user, but has been designed in a way that allows the user to learn at their own pace, gives them plenty of time to explore and immerse themselves in the environment.

3.3 VR Guidance and UI

Research into VR-specific development provided important considerations for the application.

To avoid breaking the user's immersion in the environment several precautions were taken. UI elements were kept minimal and unobtrusive (UI reticule, score's basic aesthetic) [20]; and audio cues were used to guide the player toward points of interest without the need of non-diegetic maps/arrows [21].

The large temples in the environment serve as permanent visual reference points in the player's line of sight, an aspect which helps to avoid user disorientation [21]. User visual comfort is further aided by making key elements in the environment provide subtle interactive visual feedback e.g. points of interest being highlighted [20].

4 Evaluation

Initial testing of Tenochtitlan has been conducted to gauge its effectiveness in its aim to increase user engagement. The initial sample size of 8 included participants aged 18–30, with varying degrees of technological knowledge i.e. first time VR users, experienced VR users, gamers and non-gamers. This helped to emulate a real-world museum situation in which the application would have to be suitable for a large variety of users.

4.1 Methodology

Participants were asked to complete a survey on museums and virtual reality before taking part in the interactive quiz. This survey allowed for an initial analysis of the attitudes and perceptions towards virtual reality use in museums. They were then briefed on the controls and their objectives within the environment before taking part in individual supervised play sessions. During these sessions, observations were made regarding each user's completion time, number of correct answers, perceived ease of controls and how they reacted/responded to the environment. Finally, participants were briefly interviewed after their session to determine how they rated their engagement levels, knowledge of the subject and how they would compare the application with a traditional exhibit.

4.2 Post-completion Interview Responses

An initial overview of the responses provided by the interviews show that 75% of participants rated their engagement levels in Tenochtitlan as "high" or "very high", with 87.5% rating their engagement with the subject matter higher than that of traditional text/image exhibit information delivery (Fig. 3), 62.5% also felt that they had learnt interesting new facts through the VR environment (Fig. 4). When asked whether they found the experience entertaining 87.5% answered "yes", with 62.5% going on to state that the application made them want to learn more about the Aztecs.

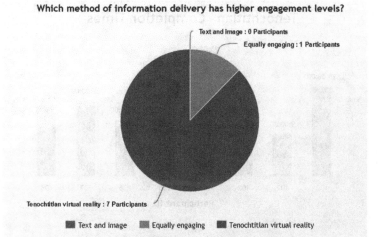

Fig. 3. Tenochtitlan participants' engagement level comparison

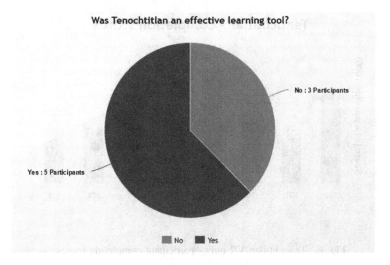

Fig. 4. Participants' opinions on Tenochtitlan's effectiveness as a learning tool

4.3 Data Analysis

Tenochtitlan was estimated to take between 12–15 min to complete. The longest play time lasted 25 min, the shortest was 9 min, and the average was 16 min (Fig. 5).

Users could score a maximum of 1000 points (100 per question). Only one participant managed a perfect score, the lowest was 400, and the average score was 675 (Fig. 6).

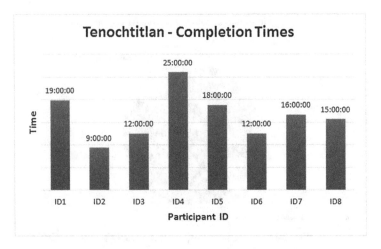

Fig. 5. Tenochtitlan VR quiz - participant completion times.

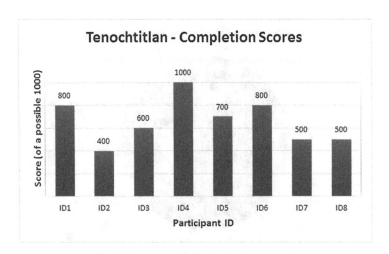

Fig. 6. Tenochtitlan VR quiz - participant completion scores.

Players moved much quicker between the set of ten questions than the set of 10 preceding facts. This may be due to players becoming familiar with movement in virtual reality.

5   Conclusion

In this paper, we have proposed and developed a VR application for young adults, Tenochtitlan, designed to increase user engagement with a museum exhibit, and enhance subject knowledge through interactive learning.

The initial evaluation results have shown that users found Tenochtitlan engaging and entertaining, more so than traditional exhibit information delivery methods, and improved their knowledge on the subject matter through the interactive quiz.

The mechanics within Tenochtitlan has been proved suitable for participants who were familiar with videogame controls and those who were not, an element that would be essential in a real museum setting.

This study was unable to test the application in a real museum environment, so direct comparisons with user engagement with a specific exhibit were unavailable.

Future work in this area would primarily look at creating a new application as a complementary tool for an existing museum exhibit, while studying and comparing the effectiveness of the VR application, in both engagement and education, against the physical museum environment.

References

1. Department for Culture, Media & Sport. https://www.gov.uk/government/uploads/system/uploads/attachment_data/file/562676/Focus_on_museums_and_galleries_final.pdf.   Last accessed 02 Apr 2017
2. Poser, S.: Leisure time and technology. In: European History Online (EGO), Institute of European History (IEG), Mainz, Germany (2011)
3. Statista. Virtual reality interest in the U.S. by age group 2015. https://www.statista.com/statistics/456812/virtual-reality-interest-in-the-united-states-by-age-group/. Last accessed 09 Apr 2017
4. Mujber, T., Szecsi, T., Hashmi, M.: Virtual reality applications in manufacturing process simulation. J. Mater. Process. Technol. **155–156**, 1834–1838 (2004). Elsevier, Amsterdam, Netherlands
5. Lepouras, G., Vassilakis, C.: Virtual museums for all: employing game technology for edutainment. Virtual Reality **8**(2), 96–106 (2004). Springer, London, UK
6. Rae, J., Edwards, L.: Virtual reality at the British Museum: what is the value of virtual reality environments for learning by children and young people, schools, and families? In: MW 2016: Museums and the Web 2016, Los Angeles, USA (2016)
7. National History Museum. Trailer for David Attenborough's Great Barrier Reef Dive. http://www.nhm.ac.uk/discover/david-attenborough-great-barrier-reef-dive-trailer.html. Last accessed 06 Apr 2017
8. TechRadar. VR takes you to London's Natural History Museum from anywhere in the world. http://www.techradar.com/news/wearables/vr-experience-helps-you-learn-from-london-s-natural-history-museum-anywhere-in-the-world-1328499. Last accessed 06 Apr 2017
9. Pujol Tost, L., Economou, M.: Exploring the suitability of Virtual Reality interactivity for exhibitions through an integrated evaluation: the case of the Ename Museum. In: Museology, vol. 4. Department of Cultural Technology and Communication, Greece (2007)
10. Bay, H., Fasel, B., van Gool, L.: Interactive museum guide: fast and robust recognition of museum objects. In: International Workshop on Mobile Vision, pp. 1–4. ACM Press, New York (2006)
11. Zoubola, N., Fokides, E., Tsolakdis, C., Vratsalis, C.: Virtual reality and museum: an educational application for museum education. Int. J. Emerg. Technol. Learn. (iJET) **3**, 89–95 (2008). International Association of Online Engineering

12. Roussou, M.: Immersive interactive virtual reality in the museum. In: Proceedings of Trends, Technology, Theming & Design in Leisure & Entertainment Conference, (2). Foundation of the Hellenic World, Greece (2002)

13. Döpker, A., Brockmann, T., Stieglitz, S.: Use cases for gamification in virtual museums. In: Jahrestagung der Gesellschaft für Informatik, pp. 2308–2321. Gesellschaft für Informatik, Koblenz, Germany (2013)

14. Podgorny, J.: Studying Visitor Engagement in Virtual Reality Based Children's Science Museum Exhibits (Doctoral dissertation, M.A. University of Chicago) (2004)

15. Carrozzino, M., Bergamasco, M.: Beyond virtual museums: experiencing immersive virtual reality in real museums. J. Cult. Herit. **11**(4), 452–458 (2010)

16. Brasseur, L.: Engaging with young people to create the museum of the future (Doctoral dissertation, University of Leicester) (2017)

17. Adams, E., Dormans, J.: Game mechanics: Advanced Game Design, 1st edn. New Riders, California (2012)

18. Perry, D., DeMaria, R.: David Perry on Game Design, 1st edn. Course Technology, Boston (2009)

19. Gauthier, A., Corrin, M., Jenkinson, J.: Exploring the influence of game design on learning and voluntary use in an online vascular anatomy study aid. Comput. Educ. **87**, 24–34 (2015). Elsevier, Amsterdam, Netherlands

20. Sherman, W.R., Craig, A.B.: Understanding Virtual Reality: Interface, Application, and Design. Morgan Kaufmann Publishers, San Francisco (2002)

21. Jerald, J.: The VR Book: Human-Centered Design for Virtual Reality. Morgan & Claypool Publishers, California (2015)

A Collaborative Aesthetic-Driven Virtual Fitness Game

Lizhen Han[1,2], Mingmin Zhang[1], Feng Tian[3], and Zhigeng Pan[4(✉)]

[1] Zhejiang University, Hangzhou, China
hlz-1@126.com, zhangmm95@zju.edu.cn
[2] Shandong University of Arts, Jinan, China
[3] Bournemouth University, Bournemouth, BH, UK
ftian@bournemouth.ac.uk
[4] Hangzhou Normal University, Hangzhou, China
zgpan@hznu.edu.cn

Abstract. By introducing a collaborative aesthetic-driven virtual fitness game, we give a possible solution to guide and encourage people who have sedentary lifestyle to do regular physical activity with enough intensity, duration and frequency. This method bridges physical interaction with a stationary bicycle and visual changes in a virtual environment, and combines it with a multiplayer game. During the test of game playing, individual participant's effort to meet their own target heart rate zone contributes to a team effort of aesthetic immersion overall.

Keywords: Aesthetic-driven interaction · Multiplayer collaboration · Aesthetic immersion · Real-time bio-feedback · Virtual fitness game

1 Introduction

Doing regular physical activity with enough amounts of intensity, duration and frequency is a healthy lifestyle. Helping people to form such a healthy lifestyle is a hot and challenging area in the fields of computer aided exergame design.

Aesthetic pleasure is a kind of powerful affective experience. It can enhance immersion and engagement of virtual reality environment. Based on this, we present a collaborative aesthetic-driven virtual fitness game as a low cost while pervasive solution to encourage effective fitness training. In this game, the aesthetic visual effects of a virtual world are tightly associated with the player's real-time heart rate level, while the heart rate level reflects the subject's physiological and psychological state accordingly. By physically acting on the control of the representation of one component part of the virtual world, players will be engaged to cooperate on the creation of aesthetically pleasing virtual surroundings, meanwhile, to immerse themselves into target fitness training zones. A pilot in-lab user study was conducted to evaluate the effectiveness and enjoyment of the game. We find that this kind of persuasive technology is helpful on encouraging effective exercise training.

© Springer International Publishing AG 2017
F. Tian et al. (Eds.): Edutainment 2017, LNCS 10345, pp. 29–35, 2017.
https://doi.org/10.1007/978-3-319-65849-0_4

The main contribution of this work lies in: 1. put forward a new idea for exergame design - the multiplayer game with the aesthetic experience act as the cooperation strategy and goal; 2. complete a prototype system to demonstrate this aesthetic cooperation method.

The rest of the paper is organized as follows. In Sect. 2, we give a general review of related works. Then, we describe our method of aesthetic cooperation and illustrate the game design in detail in Sect. 3. Finally, in Sect. 4, general conclusions are drawn.

2   Related Works

Our previous studies [1–3] have found that combine people's instinctive pursuit of beauty with their real-time bio-feedback and immersive somatosensory interaction into one well designed system, can help people to be happy to carry out regular and effective exercise. In such a system, individual players tend to perform better to stay in a relatively beautiful virtual world, rather than in a relatively ugly world. So, how will players behave in collaborative multiplayer mode? This is what this study will explore.

2.1   Exergame for Fitness Training

It is one of the hotspots of current research to encourage users to exercise regularly as well as promote health through fitness games. Many studies have proved the effectiveness of fitness games [4–7]. To encourage players to do more physical activity, some exergames aim to capture the player's action, emotion or the physiological data such as heart rate to control the gameplay [8, 9] or to auto-adapt the game level for fair game play experiences [10–12]. Some try to constrain the player for more quantity and intensity by setting higher objectives or goals [13, 14]. Others use competitions or award strategies to lure player spending more time [15].

Most of the approaches above adopt compulsive incentive strategies with constraints to attract and retain players. However, fitness training is not simply the faster the better. Exerciser may need to maintain their heart rate at a target level. Sinclair et al. [16] advocate that exergame should take the guidelines of American College of Sports Medicine as a scientific guarantee of true health, but few exergame abided it strictly.

2.2   Aesthetical Immersion in Virtual Reality

Immersion is vital for virtual reality system. It provides realistic experience, even though the virtual world may not simulate an actual real-world location. Using aesthetical immersion as incentive strategy for game play has not been explored in virtual reality application before.

Growing awareness has noticed that aesthetic design is a key component of usability [17], and a decisive aspect for marketplace success [18]. More and more researchers are exploring the potential usability of aesthetics on designing interactive systems. These researches can be divided into two directions. One takes beauty as an ornament for giving system more visual and emotional attraction [19]. Aesthetic aspects are most like an added bonus of the system and relatively independent from the system itself. Another one is the pragmatist approach, which looks aesthetics attributes from its practical and functional aspect. The representative work is the concept of aesthetic interaction [20].

Although the two directions of form and function are definite, researchers still struggling on come up with a methodological approach to the subjective concept of aesthetics, having typically concerned itself with more scientific methods [21].

3   Method

Aiming to be available for the public as much as possible, we choose the economy and pervasive technology to get basic immersion of virtual game scene. Figure 1 illustrate our method in the system implementation level. The use of advanced virtual reality devices than the use of this basic one can provide more exciting experience.

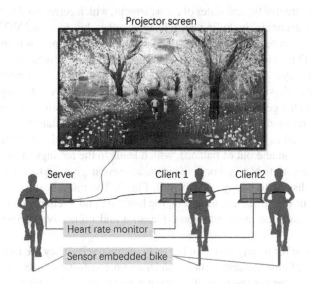

Fig. 1. Illustration of our system implementation.

In the multiplayer model, there are one server and multiple clients working together. Each player put on a wireless heart rate monitor and cycling on a sensor embedded bicycle. Her/his heart rate level, i.e. one's exercise intensity, is visualized as an element of a virtual scene. This element is selected from a library at the beginning of the gameplay by the player. The speed and direction of the player's bike are used to control the movement of their virtual avatar. By this way, during cycling, a virtual landscape which is composed of multiplayer's heart rate visualizations will be generated timely (Fig. 2). The strength of this game entry is the hands-on, physical interaction which feeds into a virtual experience.

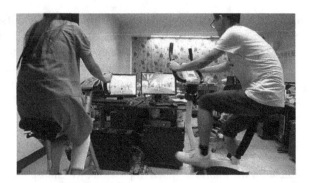

Fig. 2. Two players are playing our game with two sets of equipment. Wireless heart-rate monitors are worn on their chest.

Totally there are five typical states of each element, which correspond to five exercise training zones reasonably, including aerobic zone, anaerobic zone and VO2 Max zone. The virtual scene can be composed of several elements. Each element is being controlled by one player. Thus, variety of combination effects will be presented under the collaboration of each player's performance. Adding the extra dimension of multiple players contributing their physical effort together adds an interesting layer of complexity.

According to the gestalt theory of visual perception [22], aesthetic pleasure is often results from the harmony of the parts of the whole, and from the balance of the underlying driven force as well as the tension reducing. On the contrary, ugly often means disharmony, full of tension and out of balance, which leads to the feelings of uncomfortable. Accordingly, the variety of collaborative virtual scenes can give rise to different aesthetic emotion, from disgust to happy, as shown in Fig. 3. The more beautiful and vigorous the appearance of the virtual environment, the healthier and livelier each player's body status becomes and, the more emotional pleasure and immersive feeling the groups experiences.

Human pursue for beauty and avoid of ugly instinctively. They are more tolerant to stay in a beautiful environment rather than in an un-comfortable one. So, will all the players work together for the goal of creating a beautiful world which can be roamed and shared? Furthermore, do they really get the benefits of effective exercise by keeping their physical activity at the target exercise training zone? The results of a pilot in-lab user study (8 male and 4 females, graduate students, two or three persons one group, 15 min per ride, three times per person, random grouping each time) gave a positive response. The heart rate record data showed that the total effective rate of participants remaining in the target heart rate zone reached 82%. The questionnaire scores indicated that participants' willingness to collaborate was much higher than the willingness to act alone.

a) Harmony but different in aesthetic degree. Harmony means the players are in the same heart rate level at the same time. Different aesthetic degree means different body state and exercise intensity.

b) Disharmony, less beautiful. These picture indicate that the game players are not uniform in the exercise intensity. Disharmony leads to uncomfortable feelings of ugly.

Fig. 3. Illustration of some typical collaborative scenes in a two-player case. The two players could see each other nearby means they have the similar speed at the same place.

4 Conclusion

We address an interesting position on improving the interaction of a virtual world through aesthetic cooperation. Physiological measures which are coupled to the visual aspects of the game give guarantee to the effectiveness and individuality.

Whether it is in the public display space, or in the personal home environment, our virtual fitness game could be attractive. The reason lies in the followings: (1) Innovation. The use of biometrics to adjust the aesthetic sense of harmony in the scene is unique; (2) Collaboration. The concept of cooperation on create beauty as well as to maintain health is interesting. It will also push the boundaries of artistic creativity; (3) Interaction. The control of the game is natural, free and real-time; (4) Immersion. Somatosensory interaction and aesthetic pleasure will enhance the immersion of virtual reality; (5) Personality. The collaborative generated virtual world is unique and full of player's personal information of their inner body state. This is amazing.

We hope our work of aesthetically cooperation, can bring some inspiration to designers on how to develop exertion game or training system. In the future, in-depth user study is needed to evaluate the game design, a quantitative and qualitative analyses of its results is necessary for drawing a most precise conclusion. We also plan to enrich the elements library to give more creative freedom for the players. The quality of virtual scene's appearance will also be strengthened.

References

1. Han, L., Zhang, M., Tian, F., Wang, X.: Heart-creates-worlds: an aesthetic driven fitness training system. In: Zhang, Y.-J. (ed.) ICIG 2015. LNCS, vol. 9219, pp. 599–608. Springer, Cham (2015). doi:10.1007/978-3-319-21969-1_54
2. Han, L., Zhang, M., Pan, Z., Meng, Q., Tian, F.: Aesthetic-driven interaction: a pleasurable persuasive technology for health behavior change. In: SIGGRAPH ASIA Posters 2014, No. 15. ACM (2014)
3. Zhang, M., Xu, M., Han, L., Liu, Y., Lv, P., He, G.: Virtual network marathon with immersion, scientificalness, competitiveness, adaptability and learning. Comput. Graph. **36**(3), 185–192 (2012)
4. Sinclair, J., Hingston, P., Masek, M.: Considerations for the design of exergames. In: Proceedings of the 5th International Conference on Computer Graphics and Interactive Techniques in Australia and Southeast Asia, pp. 289–295. ACM (2007)
5. Baranowski, T., Buday, R., Thompson, D.I., Baranowski, J.: Playing for real: video games and stories for health-related behavior change. Am. J. Prev. Med. **34**(1), 74–82 (2008)
6. Berkovsky, S., Coombe, M., Freyne, J., Bhandari, D., Baghaei, N.: Physical activity motivating games: virtual rewards for real activity. In: Proceedings of the SIGCHI Conference on Human Factors in Computing Systems, pp. 243–252. ACM (2010)
7. Yim, J., Nicholas Graham, T.C.: Using games to increase exercise motivation. In: Proceedings of the 2007 Conference on Future Play (2007)
8. Hamilton, I., Imperatore, G., Dunlop, M.D., Rowe, D., Hewitt, A.: Walk2Build: a GPS game for mobile exergaming with city visualization. In: Proceedings of the 14th International Conference on Human-Computer Interaction with Mobile Devices and Services Companion, pp. 17–22. ACM (2012)

9. Lane, N.D., Lin, M., Mohammod, M., et al.: BeWell: sensing sleep, physical activities and social interactions to promote wellbeing. Mob. Netw. Appl. **19**(3), 345–359 (2014)
10. Park, T., Hwang, I., Lee, U., et al.: ExerLink: enabling pervasive social exergames with heterogeneous exercise devices. In: 10th International Conference on Mobile Systems, Applications, and Services (2012)
11. Buttussi, F., Chittaro, L., Ranon, R., Verona, A.: Adaptation of graphics and gameplay in fitness games by exploiting motion and physiological sensors. In: Butz, A., Fisher, B., Krüger, A., Olivier, P., Owada, S. (eds.) SG 2007. LNCS, vol. 4569, pp. 85–96. Springer, Heidelberg (2007). doi:10.1007/978-3-540-73214-3_8
12. Lamoth, C.J., Alingh, R., Caljouw, S.R.: Exergaming for elderly: effects of different types of game feedback on performance of a balance task. Stud. Health Technol. Inform. **181**, 103–107 (2012)
13. Masuko, S., Hoshino, J.: A fitness game reflecting heart rate. In: Proceedings of the 2006 ACM SIGCHI International Conference on Advances in Computer Entertainment Technology, p. 53. ACM (2006)
14. Doyle, J., Kelly, D., Patterson, M., Caulfield, B.: The effects of visual feedback in therapeutic exergaming on motor task accuracy. In: 2011 International Conference on Virtual Rehabilitation (ICVR), pp. 1–5. IEEE (2011)
15. Diakopoulos, N., Kivran-Swaine, F., Naaman, M.: Playable data: characterizing the design space of game-y infographics. In: Proceedings of the SIGCHI Conference on Human Factors in Computing Systems, pp. 1717–1726. ACM (2011)
16. Sinclair, J., Hingston, P., Masek, M., Nosaka, K.K.: Using a virtual body to aid in exergaming system development. IEEE Comput. Graph. Appl. **2**, 39–48 (2009)
17. Norman, D.A.: Emotional Design: Why We Love (or Hate) Everyday Things. Basic books, New York (2007)
18. Bloch, P.H.: Seeking the ideal form: product design and consumer response. J. Mark. **59**, 16–29 (1995)
19. Fogarty, J., Forlizzi, J., Hudson, S.E.: Aesthetic information collages: generating decorative displays that contain information, pp. 141–150 (2001)
20. Tractinsky, N.: Toward the study of aesthetics in information technology. In: International Conference on Information Systems, pp. 771–780 (2004)
21. Jung, H., Alteri, Y.L., Bardzell, J.: SKIN: designing aesthetic interactive surfaces. In: TEI 2010 Proceedings of the Fourth International Conference on Tangible, Embedded, and Embodied Interaction, pp. 85–92 (2010)
22. Arnheim, R.: Visual Thinking. University of California Press, Berkeley (1969)

A Virtual-Real Interaction Game Design Based on Motion Capture

Fengquan Zhang$^{(\boxtimes)}$, Yujie Zhao$^{(\boxtimes)}$, and Jiaojiao Guo$^{(\boxtimes)}$

North China University of Technology, Beijing, China
fqzhang@ncut.edu.cn, hyujiezhao@163.com,
jjiaoguo@163.com

Abstract. In this paper, we present a virtual-real game framework for human body interaction using passive optical motion capture device. In order to reduce the noise produced from motion capture, a noise reducing approach is firstly designed based on Kalman filter algorithm, which can estimate the position of marker and improve the accuracy of data. For the interaction of game, then a bounding box is created according to geometry of object for detecting collisions between virtual objects and real objects, preventing penetration during interaction. Finally, the game system is designed and implemented based on the capture device. The experimental results show that our system can preferably implement virtual-real interaction with diverse scenes such as human and rigid body, between virtual objects, human and real body objects.

Keywords: Motion capture device · Virtual-real interaction · Collision detection · Kalman filter

1 Introduction

Virtual-real interaction is a kind of technology which can combine computer-generated virtual scene with real scene [1]. It can provide a natural interaction and realistic simulation, which is a new human-computer interaction for user. In recent years, the virtual-real interaction based on motion capture has become a hot research field. Optical motion capture has a wider application than tradition devices, because it has a lager range of capture, and frees from cables and cumbersome hardware. However, occlusions of markers lead to produce of noise data; the problem limits the application range of it.

In this work, we use OptiTrack to obtain the motion data, and implement a virtual-real interaction game system [2]. In this system, users interact with virtual objects in real-time; the objects can be grabbed, moved and dropped. We focus on a noise reducing approach based on Kalman filter algorithm and improve effect of tracking. We also create bounding boxes to prevent penetration, and make the interaction of game more natural.

© Springer International Publishing AG 2017
F. Tian et al. (Eds.): Edutainment 2017, LNCS 10345, pp. 36–43, 2017.
https://doi.org/10.1007/978-3-319-65849-0_5

2 Data Processing Algorithm

Kalman filter includes two main processes: prediction and correction. Prediction establishes the prior estimation of the current state by time renewal equation, and calculates the variable of current state and the estimated value of error covariance timely, in order to establish the prior estimation of the next time state. Correction responsible for feedback, it establishes the improved posterior estimation of the current state by measuring renewal equation based on the prior estimation of prediction and the measurement variables of current [3]. Markers are often occluded, that lead to produce noise data during movement. Therefore, we apply Kalman filter algorithm to estimate the marker position of next frame, which can generate data more smoothly.

2.1 Kalman Filter Theory

Kalman filter algorithm predicts the motion state data of objects. We use the revised data as input for obtaining the data of next frame [4]. It is based on a state equation and an observation equation, which uses recursive method to predict the movement of objects. In this paper, Kalman filter algorithm estimates the position of marker and improves the accuracy of data. First, it predicts the current state k by the system process model, such as Eq. (1).

$$X(k|k-1) = FX(k-1|k-1) + BU(k) \tag{1}$$

where $X(k|k-1)$ is prediction result of last state, $U(k)$ is control variable of current state and sees it as 0. The covariance P of $X(k|k-1)$ is the Eq. (2). F' is the transpose of F, $P(k-1|k-1)$ is the covariance of $X(k|k-1)$, Eqs. (1) and (2) predict the system in time of k.

$$P(k|k-1) = FP(k-1|k-1)F' + Q \tag{2}$$

We calculate optimal estimation the current state value $X(k|k)$ by measured value and predictive the value of current state, as shown in Eq. (3).

$$X(k|k) = X(k|k-1) + Kg(k)(Z(k) - HX(K|k-1)) \tag{3}$$

where Kg is Kalman Gain, as shown in Eq. (4).

$$Kg(k) = P(k|k-1)H'/(HP(k|k-1)H' + R) \tag{4}$$

Then we calculate optimal estimation the current state value $X(k|k)$, covariance $P(k|k)$ updates in the Eq. (5). In this way, the Kalman filter runs end.

$$P(k|k) = (I - Kg(k)H)P(k|k-1) \tag{5}$$

where I is a matrix of 1.

2.2　Noise Reduction Processing

Kalman filter algorithm bases on last frame information to estimate the position of the present markers [5], we suppose the ith marker state vector at time k is $X(k)$.

$$X_i(k) = (x, y, z, x', y', z') \tag{6}$$

where x', y', z' is the rate of the marker along with x, y and z axis respectively. We have known the position of ith marker at time k, then we can estimate the state at the time of $k + 1$, as shown in the following.

$$X_i(k+1) = FX_i(k) + W(k) \tag{7}$$

where F is state transition matrix, $W(k)$ has a normal distribution $N(0, Q)$. When the next frame data was got, the model can be updated as follows. H is measurement matrix, $V(k)$ has a normal distribution $N(0, Q)$.

$$Y_i(k) = HX_i(k) + V(k) \tag{8}$$

The human body may cover markers, which lead to distortion in movement. During movement, we acquire human motion data, and then process the data by Kalman filter algorithm; finally the data is assigned to human avatar. Figure 1 is the left hand joint rotation data of X axis, the red indicates unprocessed data, whereas the blue indicates processed data. Obviously, the curve of processed data is smoother, so the algorithm can make the tracking of markers more accurately.

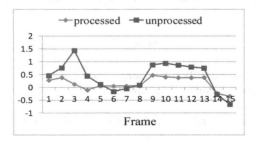

Fig. 1. The processes of left hand data image

3　Virtual-Real Interaction

Collision detection is an essential part of virtual-real interaction [6]. It can make virtual human to interact with objects in virtual reality interaction system, which realizes simulation of real environment. If there is not collision detection, penetration will happen during interaction. This phenomenon is no logical in reality. In terms of the game system, collision detection is mainly processing of interaction between virtual human and objects, such as human, birdcage and flowerpot.

In this paper, we adopt the collision detection algorithm based on Oriented Bounding Box (OBB) [7]. It defines right bounding box according to geometry and boundary conditions of objects. During collision detection, first, we determine if there is an intersection with bounding box, it is easier to intersect with the bounding box than objects, so we can quickly eliminate disjoint objects. If intersected, we just need a further step intersection test of the overlap bounding box. In this way, calculation of collision detection can be improved. However, how to find a best direction of axis is the key to the OBB collision detection algorithm [8]. We calculate the average vector μ of all vertex coordinates about bounding box, and take it as the center. Then we calculate covariance C. Finally, we obtain three axis vector of the OBB bounding box through the eigenvector of C.

We assume that p^i, q^i, r^i are the vertices of the ith triangle on basic geometric elements, then we calculate the average vector μ and the covariance C as the follow Eqs. (9) and (10).

$$\mu = \frac{1}{3n}\sum_{i=1}^{n}(p^i + q^i + r^i) \tag{9}$$

$$C_{jk} = \frac{1}{3n}\sum_{i=0}^{n}\left(\overrightarrow{p^i_j}\overrightarrow{p^i_k} + \overrightarrow{q^i_j}\overrightarrow{q^i_k} + \overrightarrow{r^i_j}\overrightarrow{r^i_k}\right)0 \leq j,k \leq 3 \tag{10}$$

where n is the number of triangles, $\overrightarrow{p^i} = p^i - \mu$, $\overrightarrow{q^i} = q^i - \mu$, $\overrightarrow{r^i} = r^i - \mu$ are three 3×1 vectors, for example $\overrightarrow{p^i} = (\overrightarrow{p^i_1}, \overrightarrow{p^i_2}, \overrightarrow{p^i_3})^T$. In order to determine the partial three axial of the OBB bounding box, we need get the eigenvector of C. In addition, we calculate the maximum and the minimum of all vertexes on three axes to determine the size of OBB bounding box.

We create the OBB bounding box for flowerpot, birdcage and human hand as shown Fig. 2. OBB collision detection algorithm can be offered through the Unity3D engine, and mesh of objects to get right box collider or capsule collider [9]. We mainly introduce the collision between human and birdcage. In interaction game, collier component is used to cover the surface of objects so as to prevent penetration. We analyze the effect of whether having bounding box or not on models. Figure 3 is game interaction with birdcage. Figure 3(a) and (b) have no bounding box, the virtual hand penetrates birdcage and cannot move birdcage. Figure 3(c) and (d) add bounding box, the hand can move birdcage and has no penetration.

Fig. 2. Bounding boxes of flowerpot, birdcage and human hand

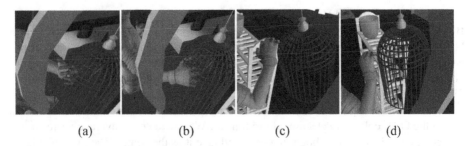

(a)   (b)   (c)   (d)

Fig. 3. Virtual-real interaction between hand and birdcage system design and implementation

3.1 Environment Construction

In our experiment, the hardware environment includes Intel Core i5-3317U 1.7 GHz CPU 4 GB, GeForce740 NVIDIA graphics card, and motion capture device is Opti-Track. The software environment includes Unity3D, Motive and OptiHub. Figure 4 shows the interaction game layout.

Fig. 4. The environment of interaction.

The system includes the environment construction, data processing, virtual-real interaction; the later parts have been stated in this paper. The environment construction mainly includes camera calibration and data acquisition.

During the calibration, we wave the T dynamic calibration stick and tries to cover all captured areas. Meanwhile, Motive records the movement track of markers on the stick. The next step is to calculate the Camera's parameters by markers' motion data, etc. On static calibration stick, long right angle side is z axis, short is x axis, using right-handed world coordinates. While Unity3D follows left-handed world coordinates, so data in Motive need to be multiplied by a transformation matrix, making them enjoy the same coordinates [10].

The data acquisition consists of human and rigid body. We get real-time motion data from objects with markers by OptiTrack, and transfer data to virtual-real inter-action system by data transmission interface, then controls virtual models. After Motive starts up, and interaction system is served as client, Motive as server, and client request data to server. Motive analyses collecting data from OptiTrack and saves their names and ID. Then system can get the position and rotation of markers in real time, and control the behavior of models.

3.2   Experiment

In our experiment, the objects divided into two types, which have markers, and others have no markers. The objects have markers such as human, flowerpot and watering can; those with no markers like birdcage. We design the objects with markers interacted each other, and virtual objects interaction with objects with markers. There is only one participant, and virtual human is rigid body. Therefore, we come up three types of interaction:

(1) Human-Rigid body interaction: Users operate rigid body with markers in real scene; corresponding models also have the same action in virtual scene. Users operate objects in real scene, as shown in Fig. 5. Virtual models are rendered as shown in Fig. 6.
(2) Rigid-Rigid body interaction: Rigid-rigid body with markers can also be interactive. The paper defines that watering can will pour water when it is titled to a certain angle. When the water particles collide with the flowerpot, a flower will grow out it, as shown in Fig. 7.
(3) Human-Virtual interaction: Virtual objects will respond accordingly when the collision between virtual human and virtual object is detected. As shown in Fig. 8, in the virtual scene, there is a birdcage; meantime a ray is created from the hand. The ray detects whether there is collision with the cage. The cage is forced to shake and butterfly flies out, when user collides with it.

Fig. 5. The interaction between human and rigid body (watering can, flowerpot, chair) in real scene.

Fig. 6. The interaction between human and rigid body (watering can, flowerpot, chair) in virtual scene.

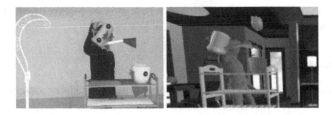

Fig. 7. The interaction between watering can and flowerpot.

Fig. 8. The interaction between human and pure virtual object (birdcage).

4   Conclusion

In the paper, we design and implement a virtual-real interaction game system. In the game system, virtual objects can be grabbed, moved and dropped by participants; the objects have the corresponding effect when specific events are triggered. This paper focuses on Kalman filter algorithm and collision detection. We design a denoised approach based on Kalman algorithm to process real-time motion data and reduce distortion. We create bounding box for virtual objects to prevent penetration. There are many interesting directions for future research, we should achieve hand interaction with complex objects, and raise immersion feeling in interaction.

Acknowledgment. This paper is supported by National Natural Science Foundation of China (61402016), Social Science of Ministry of Education (14YJCZH200), XN018001, Research Plan of Beijing (KM201610009008) and Youth Talent project of Beijing (2016000026833ZK09).

References

1. Han, Y.C.F.: Virtual pottery: a virtual 3D audiovisual interface using natural hand motions. Multimed. Tools Appl. **73**(2), 917–933 (2014)
2. OptiTrack Homepage: http://www.optitrack.com/. Accessed 8 Apr 2017
3. Welch, G., Bishop, S.: An introduction to the kalman filter. Univ. N. C Chap. Hill **8**(7), 127–312 (2006)
4. Sinopoli, B., Schenato, L., Franceschetti, M.: Kalman filtering with intermittent observations. IEEE Trans. Autom. Control **49**(9), 1453–1464 (2004)
5. Mo, Y.F., Sinopoli, B.S.: Kalman filtering with intermittent observations critical value for second order system. IFAC Proc. **44**(1), 6592–6597 (2011)

6. Martínez-Salvador, B., Pérez-Francisco, M., Del Pobil, A.P.: Collision detection between robot arms and people. J. Intell. Robot. Syst. **38**(1), 105–119 (2003)
7. Gottschalk, S., Lin, M.C., Manocha, D.T.: OBB tree: a hierarchical structure for rapid interference detection. In: Confrence on Computer Graphics and Interactive Techniques, pp. 171–180. ACM, USA (1997)
8. Fang, Z.F., Jiang, J.S., Xu, J.T.: Efficient collision detection using bounding volume hierarchies of OBB-AABBs and its application. In: International Conference on Computer Design and Applications, pp. 242–246. IEEE, China (2010)
9. LangYang, F.: Research of collision detection algorithm in Unity3D. Softw. Guide **13**(7), 24–25 (2014)
10. OptiTrack Documentation Wiki Homepage: http://wiki.optitrack.com/. Accessed 20 Mar 2017

Interactive Multimedia System for Chinese Traditional Costumes

Yan Jiang[✉], Rui-liang Guo, and Fen-fen Ma

Beijing Institute of Fashion Technology, Beijing 100029, People's Republic of China
jsjjy@bift.edu.cn

Abstract. The special natural and historical environment created representative Chinese clothing culture. The paper presents an interactive multimedia system based on Chinese traditional costumes. It can facilitate the clothing majors to have the self-study and understanding of the cutting and sewing features and also provide the learning platform to the people who has interests in clothing engineering. This System can fully demonstrate the characteristics of structures of the classic Chinese cheongsam. Three-dimensional virtual display technology is used to make and present the ancient garment, using two-dimensional garment CAD software to produce Chinese cheongsam pattern firstly, then using image processing software to process fabric images, and finally using CLO 3D system to produce three-dimensional model of clothing. In contrast with the traditional approaches of learning, the interactive system based on virtual reality technology shows the better intuitional and cognitive visual effect. Virtual reality technology is used as a tool to create the virtual clothing also as a part of the research work.

Keywords: Interactive multimedia system · Chinese traditional costumes · Virtual reality

1 Introduction

Clothing engineering learners need a capability to find new design inspirations by analyzing the structural features of the previous outstanding costumes and apply them to their own designs [1, 2]. With the continuous maturity and promotion of Virtual Reality Technology, a new teaching model comes forth in the current clothing engineering education, which is highly reputed as "Virtual Reality Interactive Teaching". Based on computer technology and combined with the relevant science and technology, VR can generate a range of real-world environment in vision, hearing, touch and other aspects of the digital environment with the necessary equipment and the digital environment objects [3]. Over the last decade a great deal of researches have been dedicated to implement cloth simulation. Some of them aim to reproduce the physical behavior of cloth [4]. Even more accurate ones [5], and others are able to context of interactive applications or games [6, 7]. Recently, some outstanding productions have been published, and used successfully in Europe textile and garment enterprises [8].

Nowadays, digital, internet and mobile communication technologies become the representatives of the new media with information widely spread out in various forms.

F. Tian et al. (Eds.): Edutainment 2017, LNCS 10345, pp. 44–51, 2017.
https://doi.org/10.1007/978-3-319-65849-0_6

Due to the changes in mass and communication media, the propagation of traditional clothing culture using the old way of exhibitions, such as physical static exhibition in museums and reports from paper, becomes unpopular. With virtual reality technology, the three-dimensional virtual presentation of "from reality to virtual reality and then back to reality" [9] and a new way of clothing culture propagation of "traditional clothing enters mobile client" become popular.

The research work presented in this paper follows on from that previous educational work. The interactive system described in this paper has the vital realistic significance as it can facilitate the clothing majors to have the overall study and understanding of the structural features of the classic models of some Chinese traditional costumes.

2   System Design

(1) System functions and development process design

As shown in Fig. 1, the Cheongsam interactive multimedia system structure includes three layers. There are five secondary menus under the main interface: overview of cheongsam, style change of cheongsam, beauty of cheongsam, production process, 3D interactive display. Each column contains the specific contents which are presented by text, illustration, picture, video, 3D models etc.

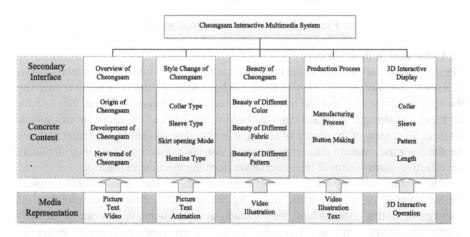

Fig. 1. Schematic diagram of system structure

In the process of system implementation, CLO 3D, 3ds Max, Flash and Unity 3D are selected as the tools to realize the interactive system. Firstly, CLO 3D should be used to build the original clothing model. CLO 3D design tool used in animated films and video game development for 3D character design, 3D art and 3D Models, especially for the garments with complex structure which are difficult to directly build three-dimensional model [10]. In the state of motion, CLO 3D has a good simulation of fabric texture, so we choose it as the main software for model making. While the special edge effects and metal buttons of the garment will be simulated by 3ds Max. In addition, if some traditional clothing is serious damaged, and photo collection of fabric patterns cannot be used, we have to recreate the fabric pattern in accordance with the original pattern ratio by Photoshop. Finally, we recreate a new texture for the garment model, and make it look like a new one.

Based on the virtual reality technology, this paper integrates the modern technology of computer graphics technology and sensor technology, combining with the related knowledge of traditional cultural protection, human-computer interaction, graphics and visualization to carry on the research about digital development of Chinese traditional cheongsam. The system implementation flow chart is shown in Fig. 2.

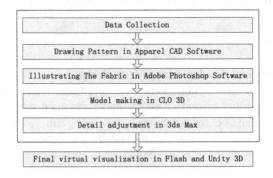

Fig. 2. System implementation flow chart

(2) Color design in the system

The significance of the color in the display system design should not be underestimated as it serves not only as a specific visual symbol but also an approach for better organizing the system information and the formation of the excellent system format. Not just for all these, the strongly designed color can additionally attract the users, arousing their interest. So in view of the choice of colors, it is important to identify the target and task for the color use, namely the communication assistance function of colors to facilitate the effective transmission of the information from the machine to the task.

This system is mainly intended to better promote the Chinese traditional cheongsam for the purpose of the systematic study, inheritance, protection and development of cheongsam, so this system adopts the popularly-accepted warm yellow hue as the basis supplemented with Purple and Tan to highlight the deep visual perception of its dignity and simplicity. The video information background inserted in the system is mainly involved with the traditional Chinese ink-and-wash paintings in clear and elegant hue.

(3) Interface design in the system

The interface design consists of four major Areas, respectively Title Area, Content Display Area, Interactive Control Area and Navigation Area, all of which are the Button Design for the purpose of simplicity, beauty and the clearly definitive target. Interactive function is designed in the form of cheongsam teaching contents and display models. The interface design for Content Display Area adopts the left-right sliding type to pave the way for the pending mobile platform APK support in later development. Navigation

Area is composed of five separate parts, respectively cheongsam Overview, cheongsam Changes, Beauty of cheongsam, Birth of cheongsam and 3D interaction, so each column has the second-level menu. Some of system interfaces are shown in Fig. 3.

Fig. 3. System interface

(4) Virtual figure design in the system
This system is the one to display the traditional Chinese cheongsam, so the leading virtual figure thus identified is the female image of the typical oriental features. The body proportion should be complied with the standards of the oriental females in the external appearance so as to bring into full play the features and styles of the traditional cheongsam and bring the personality and the entire color of the system into the total unity with the system.

3   Key Technologies for Realization of Virtual Clothing

(1) Data acquisition
The Ethnic Group Costume Museum in Beijing Institute of Fashion Technology has more than 10,000 precious traditional costumes of various ethnic groups, including not only Chinese traditional cheongsam collections but also some accessories for them. The collection covers a wide range of time, regional span, more complete types. By information collecting, mapping and recovering the structure of apparel samples, it formed the valuable first-hand information which provides important physical samples and data support for the establishment of the clothing 3D model. Each collection is carried on by the data information collection of its fabric, the lining, the edging and patterns. The holographic data information collection, recording, structure recovery and analysis for the structure pattern, structure pattern placement, pattern, fabric and craft of every part of the clothing specimens, which provides sufficient information to the later digital processing and protection. This paper explains the realization of virtual clothing process with the case of classic ladies long cheongsam in 1930's.

The size of cheongsam can be measured by tiling measurement. In this case, the classic ladies long cheongsam has medium sleeves. The specific measurements of this garment are shown in Table 1. The image of the garment is shown in Fig. 4.

Table 1. Measurements of cheongsam (unit: cm)

Length	Sleeve length	Chest girth	Hem girth	Cuff girth	Collar girth	Depth of front collar	Depth of back collar
136.0	30.4	86.0	84.5	33.8	40.9	5.9	3.3

Fig. 4. Cheongsam samples

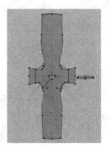

Fig. 5. 2D structure pattern

(2) Structure pattern drawing

According to the measurements of Data acquisition, the basic lines of cheongsam are drawn in apparel CAD software. Then, draw the details of the pattern, such as the sleeves and the neckline. Finally, the cheongsam of the two-dimensional paper pattern is shown in Fig. 5.

(3) Fabric pattern drawing

In order to make a clear garment pattern and facilitate the fabric mapping in CLO 3D system, the pattern with actual size was imported image processing software. In this paper, the DXF format patterns were imported into Adobe Illustrator software, filled with the fabric image. After filling operation was completed, the pattern was saved as a JPEG file as a fabric, as shown in Fig. 6.

Fig. 6. Fabrics adjustment

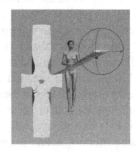

Fig. 7. 3D virtual sewing

(4) Virtual sewing

Because of the amount of geometrical details and the total number of polygons should be used to render the geometrical complexity of a give model, we ought to consider the available hardware limitations of the hosting platforms and the inherent constraints of any real time application. A careful preparation and optimization of the modeled 3D meshes is necessary in order to ensure real time simulation and interaction. Consequently, it is of prime importance to find a suitable compromise in the trade-off that exists between precision, performances and visual impact of the simulations, in order to guarantee an optimum balance in all the elements that participate in the virtual resti-tutions. In this section we will illustrate such concerns through the presentation of the modeling and mapping that have been applied to our case study.

For the realization of virtual clothing, sewing process is very important to understand the clothing structure, and this form of display also makes learning very intuitive, easy to accept. In this paper, we use CLO 3D and 3ds Max software to build the Cheongsam model. In the state of motion, CLO 3D has a good simulation of fabric texture, so we choose it as the main software for model making. While the special edge effects and metal buttons of the Cheongsam produced by the software 3ds Max. The process of virtual sewing is shown in Fig. 7.

(5) Interactive design

The interaction with the virtual models helps student to better understand the diversity of the garment design activity. At the meanwhile students may benefit of the possibility of interacting with the virtual model and, in this way, they stays more motivated [11]. In this system, there are different collar type, sleeve, length and pattern options. Learners are free to make adjustments according to their own preferences of the cheongsam's structure, and view their own design results in the real time. System interactive options and results are shown in Fig. 8. We have realized the digitization and interactive design for Qing Dynasty robe and Tibetan clothing by the same method.

Fig. 8. System interactive options and results

4   Extended Application

On the basis of the original function of the our system, we combined the somatosensory and augmented reality technology, and realized the somatosensory 3D Clothing Culture Display System. the system also describes the different costumes corresponding cultural background, knowledge of popular culture clothing of different costumes by means of text, images and other forms. Somatosensory 3D clothing culture display platform enhances cultural heritage innovation capacity of the school, especially provides a strong technical support to the exhibition of new clothing line technical.

In the past, the museum exhibits precious clothing collections protected by the restrictions, it can only be watched through the windows of the exhibits, allow visitors to make a simple understanding of the learning process but lack interactive entertainment. So the dress culture propagation is not ideal [7]. Figure 9 is traditional way to show the garments. The somatosensory 3D clothing culture display platform, with its good interactivity and realism, to make up for the limitations of traditional display mode.

Fig. 9. Traditional display mode   **Fig. 10.** Somatosensory 3D clothing culture showcase display effect

In September 2014, this system was meet with the general public at "National Science Day". The audience responded enthusiastically. Thousands of visitors to experience the 48 sets of clothing of system, Fig. 10 is the virtual fitting effect by the audiences.

5   Conclusion

Clothing is difficult to preserve because it is easily oxidized. Digital method can be used to protect and inherit other types of traditional clothing. This paper designs and implements an interactive multimedia system for Chinese traditional costumes by comprehensively applying clothing engineering, Virtual Reality technology, 3D visualization technology, digital media technology. So that more clothing engineering students and other learners who love the traditional costumes will be able to understand the abundant traditional costume culture. At the same time, the Virtual Reality Technology adopted in the system implementation process can be applied in other similar disciplines, thus enjoying the extensive development space.

Acknowledgement. This paper is sponsored by the science and technology project of Beijing Municipal Education Commission (SQKM201610012008), and research project of China Scholarship Council (NO. 201609970003).

References

1. Martin, K., Mauriello, D.: Motion and embodiment 3D simulations for historic fashion. Digit. Herit. Int. Congress (Digital Heritage) **2**, 329–332 (2013)
2. Martin, K., Ko, H.S.: Imagining historic fashion: digital tools for the examination of historic dress. In: 2011 Second International Conference on Culture and Computing, vol. 10, pp. 51–56 (2011)
3. Zhao, Q.P.: Virtual reality review. SCIENTIA SINICA Inf. **39**(1), 2–46 (2009)
4. Volino, P., Magnenat-Thalmann, N.: Comparing efficiency of integration methods for cloth animation. In: Proceedings of Computer Graphics International 2001, Hong-Kong, pp. 265–274 (2001)
5. Au, C.K., Ma, Y.S.: Garment pattern definition, development and application with associative feature approach. Comput. Indus. **16**, 524–531 (2010)
6. Ma, F.F., Jiang, Y.: Assistance of new media technology on the protection and inheritance of traditional costume culture. In: 9th Textile Bioengineering and Informatics Symposium, Melbourne, pp. 570–573 (2016)
7. Jiang, Y., Ma, W.X., Chen, J.H.: Kinect-based 3D costume culture display system. China Text. Lead. **03**, 74–76 (2015)
8. Meng, Y.W., Mok, P.Y., Jin, X.G.: Computer aided clothing pattern design with 3D editing and pattern alteration. Comput. Aided Des. **44**(8), 721–734 (2012)
9. Martin, K., Mauriello, D.: 3D simulation: a new embodiment for historic fashion. Int. Conf. Culture Comput. **2013**, 62–67 (2013)
10. Guo, R., Jiang, Y.: A 3D virtual visualization method for visualing chinese ancient clothing. In: 18th Annual International Foundation of Fashion Technology Institutes Conference, pp. 19–23 (2016)
11. Savage, N., Birch, R., Noussi, E.: Motivation of engineering students in higher education. J. High. Educ. Acad. Eng. Subj. Cent. Spec. Issue: Stud. Engagem. Eng. Educ. **6**(2), 39–46 (2012)

Towards Using an Augmented Reality Mobile Assistant for Improving Driving Skills

Gheorghe Daniel Voinea[✉], Cristian Postelnicu, and Mihai Duguleana

Transilvania University of Brasov, Brasov, Romania
{daniel.voinea,cristian.postelnicu,mihai.duguleana}@unitbv.ro

Abstract. Increasing road safety through the use of new technologies is of general interest. In this paper we present a mobile assistant that uses augmented reality. This assistant was tested in real driving conditions. The participants assessed the comprehensibility and usability through a questionnaire. Results show that novice drivers could improve their driving skills by using new technologies such as Augmented Reality.

Keywords: Mobile assistant · Real driving · Usability

1 Introduction

The process of advancing from a novice to an experienced driver takes hours of practice, although vehicle handling skills can be attained in short time. The driving task is determined by factors such as the road state, traffic rules and the presence of other drivers. The style of each driver depends on the speed, the following distance and the positioning on the road. Considering these choices, inexperienced drivers should aim at large safety margins in order to avoid dangerous situations. There are two main factors that can influence the safety of novice drivers: improvements in the instruction process and using technologies that monitor the traffic and the driving behavior [1].

Augmented Reality (AR) represents an emerging form of experience that enables participants to interact with digital information that is overlaid on top of the real world [2]. The authors in [3] found that the use of AR cues has improved participant's ability to maintain a safe headway distance when approaching pedestrian targets.

The use of on-board advanced driver assistive applications (ADASs) may lead to improvements regarding the perception and reaction to roadway hazards for drivers with visual impairments [4]. Several studies have shown the potential of increasing road safety by guiding the driver's attention in the case of hazardous situations through the use of collision avoidance systems [5].

The number of smartphone users is expected to reach around 2.87 billion until 2020, making smartphones a gateway to a new type of interaction between people and objects. Although the use of smartphones is not allowed while driving, around 70% of people have reportedly used them for texting, emailing, conversations or games [6].

While mobile driver assistant systems are proven to have a positive impact on road users [7], there is still a low adoption of such technologies in daily traffic activities [8].

© Springer International Publishing AG 2017
F. Tian et al. (Eds.): Edutainment 2017, LNCS 10345, pp. 52–55, 2017.
https://doi.org/10.1007/978-3-319-65849-0_7

Latest generation of cars come with built-in safety equipment that have a big impact on road safety, however a small percentage of drivers can afford them. Mobile assistants are susceptible to noise and weather conditions, thus making them less reliable, but they are accessible, easy to use and are becoming more intelligent as technology advances. The aim of this paper is to present an AR mobile assistant and to assess its usability and comprehensibility.

2   Application Architecture Overview

The architecture of the mobile assistant application is presented in Fig. 1. The first step is to obtain raw data from the back camera, as well as the built-in sensors (accelerometer, magnetometer, gyroscope, GPS). The processing module takes in the data and transforms it into meaningful parameters such as speed, traffic signs, headway, Time-To-Collision (TTC) and lane position. The last step consists of generating specific audio and visual alerts based on predetermined thresholds.

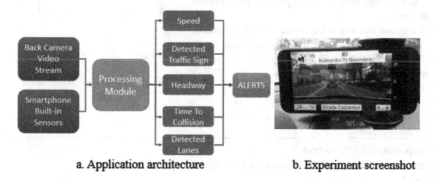

a. Application architecture   b. Experiment screenshot

Fig. 1. Mobile assistant architecture and experiment screenshot

The application uses AR to highlight detected traffic signs and lanes (see Fig. 1b), as well as TTC and headway. Audio warnings are generated only in situations classified as "dangerous" in order to avoid becoming annoying.

3   Method

A number of six participants aged between 19 and 34 years participated in the study. All participants possessed a valid Romanian driver's license for l at least two years and did not suffer of any neurological disease or other visual impairments.

The route for the driving test was the same for all participants and took around 30 min to complete, but different starting points have been chosen. Participants received a short briefing before the test about the features of the mobile assistant application and were asked to drive normally following a preprogrammed route.

At the end of the driving test, participants were asked to evaluate the application. We used a 20 item questionnaire to assess the usability and comprehensibility of the application. The statements for usability are from the System Usability Scale (SUS) [9] and the questions for comprehensibility are from a study that evaluates handheld augmented reality (HAR) systems [10]. Participants could rate how much they agree or disagree with the statements by using a seven-point Likert scale (1 is "strongly disagree" and 7 stands for "strongly agree").

4   Results and Discussion

Box plots were chosen to graphically represent the results. The statements used for the questionnaire and the resulting box plots are presented in Fig. 2.

Usability Measures:
1. I would like to use this system frequently.
2. I found the system unnecessarily complex.*
3. The system was easy to use.
4. I need the support of a technical person to be able to use this system. *
5. The various functions in this system were well integrated.
6. There was too much inconsistency in this system. *
7. I would imagine that most people would learn to use this system very quickly.
8. I found the system very cumbersome to use. *
9. I felt very confident using the system.
10. I needed to learn a lot of things before I could get going with this system. *

a. Usability box plots

Comprehensibility Measures:
1. Interacting with this application requires a lot of mental effort. *
2. The amount of information displayed on screen was appropriate.
3. The information displayed on screen was difficult to read. *
4. The information display was responding fast enough.
5. The information displayed on screen was confusing. *
6. The words and symbols on screen were easy to read.
7. The display was flickering too much. *
8. The information displayed on screen was consistent.

* These statements are negative and are supposed to receive a small score.

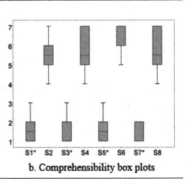

b. Comprehensibility box plots

Fig. 2. Questionnaire statements and corresponding box plots

Supplementary the authors added two statements to evaluate the acceptance of the presented mobile assistant. These are the following: "I felt that the warnings were annoying" and "I felt that using a mobile assistant could help me improve my driving skills". The participants gave an average score of 1.8 (mostly disagree) for the first statement and 5.5 (mostly agree) for the second statement.

There were 15 speed infractions and 10 lane departures that were augmented visually. Dangerous situations with a TTC smaller than 2 s were rare and only happened two times at one participant. The average speed was 34 km/h of all drivers, with a top speed of 67 km/h. Partial results regarding the driver's tendency to reduce speed in times of warnings are in accordance with conclusions from other studies [8].

5   Conclusions

This study was done in real driving conditions with a small number of participants. The results from the questionnaire conclude that using a smartphone mobile assistant can help improve a novice driver's skills. Participants rated warnings as having a low influence and expressed their intention of using the developed assistant in the future.

Acknowledgements.   This paper is supported by the Romanian Government, specifically MEN – UEFISCDI authority under the program PNII "Partnerships in priority areas", under the project number 240/2014 - NAVIEYES, supporting the collaboration between the company Route 66 and University Transilvania of Braşov.

References

1. European Commission Mobility and Transport, Road Safety: Novice drivers statement. https://ec.europa.eu/transport/road_safety/specialist/knowledge/young_en. Accessed 12 Feb 2017
2. Kearney, J.K., Rizzo, M., Severson, J.: Virtual reality and neuroergonomics. In: Parasuraman, R., Rizzo, M. (eds.) Neuroergonomics: The brain at work, pp. 253–274. Oxford University Press, New York (2009)
3. Schall Jr., M., et al.: Attraction without distraction: effects of augmented reality cues on driver hazard perception. J. Vis. **10**(7), 236 (2010)
4. Scott, J.J., Gray, R.: A comparison of tactile, visual, and auditory warnings for rear-end collision prevention in simulated driving. Hum. Factors **50**(2), 264–275 (2008)
5. Kramer, A.F., et al.: Influence of age and proximity warning devices on collision avoidance in simulated driving. Hum. Factors **49**(5), 935–949 (2007)
6. AT&T Newsroom: Smartphone Use Behind the Wheel Survey. http://about.att.com/story/smartphone_use_while_driving_grows_beyond_texting.html. Accessed 10 Feb 2017
7. Maag, C., Muhlbacher, D., Mark, C., Kruger, H.P.: Studying effects of advanced driver assistance systems (ADAS) on individual and group level using multi-driver simulation. IEEE Intell. Transp. Syst. **4**, 45–54 (2012)
8. Botzer, A., Musicant, O., Perry, A.: Driver behavior with a smartphone collision warning application – a field study. Saf. Sci. **91**, 361–372 (2017). ISSN:0925-7535
9. Usability Scale: System Usability Scale (SUS). https://www.usability.gov/how-to-and-tools/methods/system-usability-scale.html. Accessed 02 May 2017
10. Santos, M.E.C., Polvi, J., Taketomi, T., Yamamoto, G., Sandor, C., Kato, H.: Towards standard usability questionnaires for handheld augmented reality. IEEE Comput. Graph. Appl. **35**(5), 50–59 (2015)

Gamification for Serious Game and Training

Key Lightweighting Technologies of Web3D for Virtual Training of Metro Station Fire Evacuation

Fengting Yan[1], Yonghao Hu[1], Qinghua Guo[2], Kai Tang[3],
Jinyuan Jia[1(✉)], and Hehua Zhu[2]

[1] School of Software Engineering, Tongji University, Shanghai 201804, China
yanfengting2008@163.com, jyjia@tongji.edu.cn
[2] College of Civil Engineering, Tongji University, Shanghai 200092, China
[3] Hong Kong University of Science and Technology, Hongkong 999077, China

Abstract. It would be a horrible scene when a fire breaks out in any underground metro station, which could result in high human casualties. Therefore, the training of fire evacuation is highly necessary for the public. Among various current training methods, online fire evacuation training is a very popular one, owing to its low-cost and convenience. However, due to the huge size of data of both the representation of the metro station and the fire scenario, the limited bandwidth of network, and the weak rendering ability of web browser, the online fire evacuation training simulation usually runs extremely slow or is not able to run at all. This paper proposes a new virtual reality online training system for metro station fire evacuation. Firstly, a method based on semantic and voxelization component checking is introduced for light-weighting the large-scale metro station static scene, and the BIM (Building Information Modeling) data can be reduced by as much as 10 times. Next, we propose a smoke redundant-removing and normalization method, which is used for substantially light-weighting the dynamic FDS (Fire Dynamics Simulator) smoking data (as much as 200 times in our experiments). With the above methods, the metro station and smoke data can transmit through the internet quickly, and real-time rendering can be achieved on web pages by using a multi-thread mechanism. Finally, we present our *e*ACO (evacuation based on adaptive Ant Colony Optimization) algorithm which can be used for the planning of mass fire evacuation. A prototype system based on *e*ACO is implemented for VR (Virtual Realization) the fire evacuation training on Web, with which the user just needs to surf the internet (without loading and installing plug-ins) and take part in the fire evacuation training. The experimental results demonstrate that the proposed solution is feasible for online training in metro station fire evacuation. The technologies developed are also suitable for fire simulation and evacuation training in other urban infrastructures.

Keywords: Metro station fire evacuation · Web3D · IFC-based lightweight · Smoke lightweight · *e*ACO path planning

© Springer International Publishing AG 2017
F. Tian et al. (Eds.): Edutainment 2017, LNCS 10345, pp. 59–74, 2017.
https://doi.org/10.1007/978-3-319-65849-0_8

1 Introduction

It will be a horrible scene if a fire breaks out in any metro station. In the year of 2003, a fire broke out at the central subway station of Daegu city, South Korea, where at the time there were 600-odds passengers and among them 198 were dead, 146 injured, and 298 missing. In 2013, there was a metro station fire incident at the Russian central Moscow subway station; this time however, because many passengers had been partially trained in some evacuation training courses, of nearly 5000 passengers evacuated, only 11 people were injured, although the entire station was a mess after the fire. It can be seen that public fire evacuation training is necessary that all urban dwellers should take part in it. Obviously, there are many drawbacks and limitations for a real physical evacuation training course, which has huge potential safety risks, high costs, and can quickly get out of control. Computer simulated training then becomes a plausible alternative. As the matter of fact, nowadays fire evacuation training on Web3D is already a popular solution owing to its low-cost, convenience, and efficiency, especially considering that the public can participate in the fire evacuation training at anytime and anywhere via the Internet.

However, online fire evacuation training faces some major challenges, if such a training system is to provide a real-time interactive evacuation drill for the public: (1) the extremely slow transmission of massive data of the subway description and the fire scenario due to the limited bandwidth and speed of the network; (2) the limited rendering capabilities of the web browsers; and (3) the insufficient computing power of the web browsers. For example, for a subway station of 80 m in length and 50 m in width, the scene data would easily amount to around 1000 M, for which the data for 600 s smoke propagation exceeds 5 G in size. These challenges pose a variety of bottlenecks and difficulties for the online simulation of fire evacuation drill.

In this paper, a suite of solutions are proposed for lightweighting the online VR training system for subway station fire evacuation. First of all, a method based on semantic and voxelization component checking is proposed for lightweighting large-scale static BIM (Building Information Modeling) data [1, 2] of a metro station. As the result of this lightweighting, the data amount could be reduced by as much as 10 times. After that, a method of smoke redundant-removing and normalization for lightweighting the dynamic FDS (Fire Dynamics Simulator) smoke data [3] is proposed, which, based on our experiments, could lightweight the amount of smoke data by as much as 200 times. Both the lightweighted scene data and smoke data can now transit through the internet and be loaded onto the Web page in real-time, and a multi-thread mechanism is used to realize a lightweighted rendering of large-scale metro station fire scenario. At last, a multi-agent real-time evacuation algorithm (eACO) is presented, which is based on the adaptive ant colony path planning algorithm [4, 5]. Combining all of the above, a prototype system is then presented for the VR fire evacuation training on Web.

2 Related Works

As the memory and computing power of Web are always limited, currently it is almost impossible to achieve a real-time Web3D fire evacuation training platform. Notwithstanding a few studies on how people should evacuate from a fire scenario, the works on algorithms and technologies of computer simulated fire evacuation training system for masses are extremely scarce.

At present, there are already some pertinent industry software kits, such as the EXODUS emergency simulation system from the University of Greenwich, England [6], the legion series of software systems by the British Legion Company [7], the Myriad system by the Crowd Dynamics Company [8], and the Massive Software by the Massive Company of USA [9]. All these systems though are of offline type and PC-based. Some companies are now developing systems catering for the Internet. The vrEXODUS [6, 10] emergency simulation system software can be used to set up a 3D scene and then, based on the FDS smoke model, a simulation fire scenario can be simulated. However, at present there is no any online fire evacuation training system for a general public.

There are already some studies on crowd fire evacuation based on 3D spatial visualization techniques [11, 12]; additionally, research in crowd fire evacuation based on VR is also emerging [13, 14]. Meanwhile, the study on smoke poisoning and its visualization has been added to the research of crowd fire evacuation [14, 21]. In recent years, the training systems catering for Web3D techniques have gradually emerged, such as the Untiy3D tool [15] and WebGL engine [10, 17]. Sharakhow et al. [16] achieved a 3D scene loading and rendering on Mobile Web based on HTML5 [17]. Along with the more and more widespread applications of BIM building format in the construction industry, new Web3D fire crowd evacuation training techniques based on BIM format are emerging. For example, using Unity3D tools and BIM scene data, Chiu and Shiau [15] developed a fire scenario evacuation simulator. However, currently Unity3D is still not able to support massive online fire evacuation; this opens a wide foreground for the development of online fire evacuation training systems based on WebGL.

Heavy smoke must be considered in any fire scenario [19, 22], which takes up a huge amount of web memory resource and computing resource for an accurate evacuation path planning. At present, most of the existing solutions select the best path from some existing paths based on the rough smoke hazard statistic concept [13]. The fast marching match (FMM) method [18] sometimes is also used for fast path planning; but the method is not accurate enough for every agent in the crowd evacuation path planning. Regarding the large-scale crowd evacuation path planning considering individual agents' specific characters, AI (Artificial Intelligence) techniques have already been used [20]. For example, the ACO (Ant Colony Optimization) algorithm, as an effective, accurate, and efficient heuristic AI technique with pheromone reuse, has been used in crowd evacuation path planning [4, 5]. The ACO algorithm also has other capabilities, such as the positive feedback mechanism, and parallelism for path planning [5], which is very suitable for crowd evacuation path planning. Facing a sudden outbreak of fire, the crowd typically run away aimlessly, whose behavior is close to being random [23] and hence can be approximately modeled as a random process [24]. In particular, as reported in this paper, when combined with adaptive control by pheromone in case of dynamic smoke spread, the ACO algorithm can be used to accurately and efficiently plan an escape route for each of the agents in a multi-agent environment.

3   Architecture of the System

We adopt the B/S (Browser/Server) architecture to design our fire evacuation training system. At the Browser end, the JavaScript language and HTML5-oriented WebGL graphics engine tool are used for the Web page working, and this set of technology can cross the hardware platforms and run on most browsers (Google Chrome, Firefox, UC browser and so on) and facilitate the users participating in the fire evacuation training without plug-ins. At the Server end, the Java2EE language is used, and the static BIM scene data and dynamic smoke spreading data are preprocessed for the path planning and the visualization on the Web page. The static obstacle mapping (from the BIM scene data) and the dynamic obstacle mapping (from the spreading smoke data) comprise a series of time-ordered obstacle maps of the metro station. Additionally, according to the demand of path planning, the obstacle map is scheduled to dynamically calculate the optimization paths for multi-agents. After the optimization, the path array will be presented to the front users (Fig. 1).

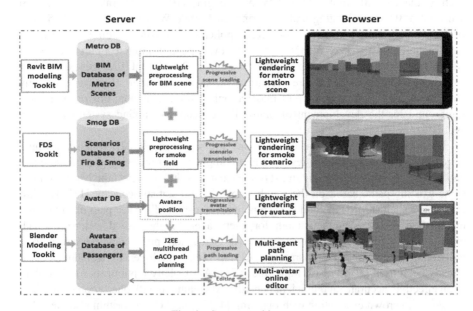

Fig. 1. System architecture.

The software deployed on the server is divided into the following modules according to the functions implemented: (1) the BIM scene lightweighting preprocessing module; (2) the smoke data lightweighting preprocessing module; and (3) the path planning module.

The fire evacuation training platform mainly caters to the traditional network transmission and P2P (Peer to Peer) transmission. The data on the server will be translated to the web clients; in case of the limited bandwidth or congestion, the P2P technique can be utilized to catch the required scenario data from the other devices which have the resources in demand. This kind of network transmission mechanism can suffice the web client's real-time visualization demand as well as real-time scenario interaction.

4 Key Technologies for Online Training of Metro Station Fire Evacuation

4.1 Lightweighting Preprocessing of Metro Station BIM Scenes

As metro stations and other types of public buildings are all large-scale scenes, public fire scenarios are very complex. We adopt the popular IFC (Industry Foundation Classes) of BIM [18, 25] as the format for scene data representation, which is advocated by the Chinese government and also used widely in the world, including the U.S. [2, 18]. After a careful analysis of the semantics of representative large-scale 3D BIM scenes, we propose a method for lightweighting BIM scene data and it is particularly suitable for Web3D. Firstly, as an initial lightweighting operation, through semantic analysis, we check for duplicate entities and, based on the consideration of geometric data reusing or stretching, remove the data redundancy and establish new data parameters accordingly. Then, catering to different characteristics of the visibility of indoor and outdoor of BIM structures, we proposes an algorithm for outdoor component separation based on the multi-view projection analysis and indoor spatial decomposition, so to granularly represent the BIM structural data. Thirdly, based on the results of indoor and outdoor processing, the TLHS (Three-Layered Hybrid Structure) data index is established; and the sparse voxel index of the outdoor scene is combined with the indoor spatial diagram, which enables the data granulation. Finally, by means of timely switching between the processing of indoor and outdoor, and adopting both the outdoor incremental interest area management (i.e., the incremental BIM Frustum of Interest, referred to as the iBIM-FOI) [2] and the indoor progressive spatial data loading, the obtained granular data can be effectively controlled and the system's resource utilization can be improved.

The above Web3D-based BIM data lightweighting solution has been experimentally proved by us to be able take full advantage of semantic information to significantly reduce the overall data in a BIM large data scene, forming a scene-indexing structure that supports instant network data loading. It can not only achieve efficient indoor and outdoor scenes' data redundancy removal, but also fully support incremental con pickup and space progressive loading, which is extremely desirable for reducing the rate of loading in online network transmission to BIM scenes. Ultimately, the huge three-dimensional BIM data can be effectively rendered in real-time on a web browser. Therefore, "Internet + BIM" is successfully achieved, and the average amount of lightweighted data is about 1/10 of the original data volume (Fig. 2).

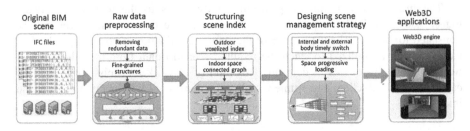

Fig. 2. Lightweighting preprocess of metro station BIM scenes.

4.2 Lightweighting Preprocessing of Spreading Smoke

For the representation of smoke, we adopt the dynamic smoke generation tool FDS to ensure the correctness of the dynamic smoke data. Based on the specific spatial geometric data of the real scene, the scene of the FDS is set up, and the fire source is placed in easy-to-occur fire spots to simulate the dynamic spreading smoke data at different times and with different durations.

The lightweighted smoke data obtained from the heavy smoke data can suffice the demand of Web3D-oriented visual rendering and the requirement of agent path planning. The specific lightweighting process is made of the following steps (as shown in Fig. 3):

(1) Obtain the heavyweight smoke data through FDS;
(2) Remove redundant content of the smoke data semantics;
(3) Use binary conversion to obtain the effective smoke data;
(4) Unify the smoke;
(5) Remove the geometrically repetitive smoke components; and finally
(6) Obtain lightweighted smoke data for Web Visualization.

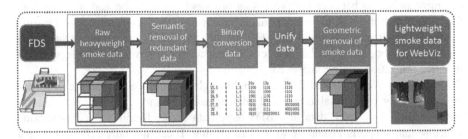

Fig. 3. Lightweighting process of heavy FDS smoke data.

All of the above tasks are carried out in the server.

After the above lightweighting work, the lightweighted smoke data volume has been tremendously reduced (e.g., in our experiments to only 1/30 of the original heavyweight data) and the preparation for visualization effects can be ensured. In addition, considering that smoke above the height of 1.6 m would not affect human beings, during the planning of the evacuation path we only consider the smoke below the 1.6 m height, which alone further lightweight the smoke data by 5–6 times. In all, the finally lightweighted smoke data could be reduced to as little as only 1/200 of the original heavyweight smoke.

The lightweighted smoke data can then be rendered as a volumetric opacity graph based on the smoke's volumetric density. We set $2^8 = 256$ levels of opacity, as illustrated below (Fig. 4):

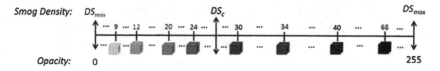

Fig. 4. Volumetric opacity graph based on the smoke's volumetric density.

where the opacity is calculated by the following equation:

$$Opacity = \frac{2^8(SD_c - SD_{min})}{SD_{max} - SD_{min}} \tag{1}$$

where SD_c is the point-wise density of the smoke, while SD_{min} and SD_{max} are respectively the minimum and maximum of SD_c in the entire volume of interest.

4.3 Parallel eACO Evacuation Path Planning Algorithm

We now describe our eACO algorithm, which takes the lightweighted metro station scene map and the also lightweighted smoke obstacle map as input and plans the dynamic evacuation route for every agent (person) at the scene. More specifically, based on the dynamic smoke data, the eACO algorithm plans the optimal escaping path every 3 s for each agent. As an evolution from the popular adaptive Ant Colony Optimization algorithm, eACO is a novel evacuation algorithm that utilizes the BIM static scene data and the FDS dynamic lightweighted scenario data and has the ability to plan a path with self-adaptive pheromone.

The core of the eACO algorithm is how to determine the next step for the ant movement. As illustrated in Fig. 5, the lightweighted volumetric smoke data not only is visualized via Eq. (1) but also is mapped into a floor map. In this paper, the smoke at the height of 1.6 m is chosen for constructing the 2D floor map. For any grid on this map, if the concentration of the smoke is more than 32 mg/m^3, it will be marked as an obstacle; otherwise, it is an accessible grid. E.g., the green points in Fig. 5 indicate accessible grids while the red ones are obstacles.

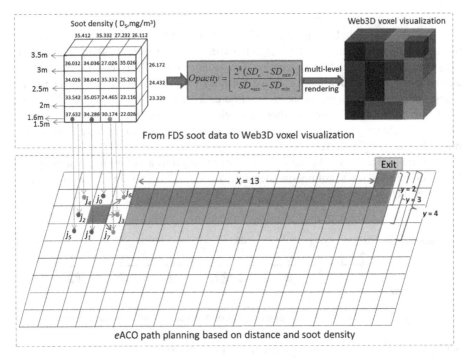

Fig. 5. Volumetric smoke visualization and the corresponding dynamic floor map of opacity (at height 1.6 m). (Color figure online)

To describe the path finding process, the following definitions are made for each ant k in the ant population.

Definition 1. Stagnation point: Each time ant k arrives at a new (grid) point, it is added to the current partial escaping route and this point is called a stagnation point.

Definition 2. Obstacle tabu list (OTL): This is the list of the static scene and dynamic smog obstacles on the floor map.

Definition 3. Tabu list of the passed points (PPTL): These are the points on the floor map that have already been passed by ant k in the current iteration.

Originally, the ant is at the current stagnation position and the eight neighboring grids $J = \{j_0, j_1, j_2, j_3, j_4, j_5, j_6, j_7\}$ (see Fig. 5) are the candidates for its next movement.

During the current search of the next point for the ant, any time when a neighboring point is visited, it will be removed from the candidate list J and added to the PPTL list. For example, referring in Fig. 5, suppose point j_0 has just been visited; it will then be removed from list J and added to list J_{PPTL}. As j_1, j_2 and j_5 are also in the obstacle list J_{OTL}, the candidate list now becomes $J = \{j_3, j_4, j_6, j_7\}$, and the probability for the selection is:

$$P_{ij} = \begin{cases} \dfrac{\tau_{ij}(t)\eta_{ij}(t)}{\sum_{s \in allowed_k} \tau_{ij}(t)\eta_{ij}(t)}, & j \in allowed_k \\ 0, & others \end{cases} \tag{2}$$

The distance from the exit to each candidate location $j \in J$ is pre-calculated (just one time), e.g., in Fig. 5, $d_{(j,Exit)} = x + y$. Then $\eta_{ij}(t)$ can be calculated:

$$\eta_{ij}(t) = 1/d_{(j,Exit)} \tag{3}$$

Here, $\tau_{ij}(t)$ is the pheromone concentration at location j. The value of the pheromone concentration comes from the past accumulated summation. After the current iteration, the pheromone concentration value will be updated as:

$$\tau_{ij}(t) = \rho * \tau_{ij}(t-1) + \Delta\tau_{ij} \tag{4}$$

The coefficient ρ is the pheromone evaporation factor, which is set to be 0.95 in our current implementation based on our empirical tests. Pheromone that is self-adaptive to dynamic objects is a very powerful tool for speeding up the path planning.

$$\Delta\tau_{ij} = \begin{cases} \sum_{k=1}^{m} \Delta\tau_{ij}^k, & \text{there is no smoke obstacle in the neighbor grids} \\ \sum_{k=1}^{m} \Delta\tau_{ij}^k/2, & \text{there is smoke obstacle in the neighbor grids} \end{cases} \tag{5}$$

After m ants completing their paths at location j, the cumulative pheromone at location j is calculated based on whether there is any smoke obstacle at its 8 neighbor grids. If there is no smoke obstacle around j, $\Delta\tau_{ij}$ is set to be $\sum_{k=1}^{m} \Delta\tau_{ij}^k$; otherwise, it is set to be $\sum_{k=1}^{m} \Delta\tau_{ij}^k/2$.

If the algorithm is trapped at a local optimum, the pheromone adaptive updating is performed through pheromone subtraction. The algorithm tries to intelligently avoid the spreading smoke so to expedite the path planning process. The subtraction coefficient of pheromone is 0.95. From time $t-1$ to t, if at $t-1$, $(0.95\rho(t-1)) \geq \rho_{min}$, then $\rho(t)$ is set to be $0.95\rho(t-1)$; otherwise, $\rho(t)$ is set to be ρ_{min}. The ρ is pheromone intensity in each section of every time.

$$\rho(t) = \begin{cases} 0.95\rho(t-1), & if(0.95\rho(t-1)) \geq \rho_{min} \\ \rho_{min}, & others \end{cases} \tag{6}$$

5 Experimental Results

The training system is based on B/S mode and the implementation of the complete set of the proposed solutions is based on the following server environment and Web terminal environment (Table 1).

Table 1. Condition of the experiments.

Server environment	(Mobile) Web terminal environment
• **CPU:** Inter(R) Xeon(R) CPU E5-2640 v3 @2.60 GHz 2.6. GHz (2 processor) • **Memory:** 128 G • **OS**: Windows Server 2012 R2 Standard • **System style**: 64 bit OS, x64 based processor	• **Mobile Phone Style:** Hongmi mobile phone (note2) • **Fuselage memory:** 32 GB ROM • **Runtime memory:** 2 GB RAM • **OS:** Android • **Browser:** Google Chrome, FireFox, UC

To measure the performance of our lightweighting methods for public evacuation on Web, four indices are evaluated before and after the lightweighting: (1) the scene data; (2) the smoke data; (3) the refreshing frequency when multi-agents are evacuating in a fire scenario; and last (4) the people evacuation success rate.

5.1 Lightweighting the BIM Scene

For this test, 10 IFC files with different data quantities (see Table 2) are lightweighted. The experiment results can be seen from Fig. 6. Sometimes, the original IFC data could not be uploaded due to the huge volume and the SIO and IFC-Compressor immediately collapsed during the operation. In comparison, with the proposed methods, our lightweighting process (i.e., Redundancy removal and Outer body extraction) has achieved about 60% reduction in data volume and it also shows good robustness.

Table 2. Experimental data.

Number	Name	Data quantity (M)
1	Duplex_A_20110505.ifc	2.311
2	301110FZK-Hans-EliteCAD.ifc	7.191
3	301110FJK-Project-Final.ifc	14.275
4	0912102010-03-01 Project.ifc	50.726
5	161210Med_Dent_Clinic_Combined.ifc	109.996
6	DN_Shnz_Project.ifc	226.186
7	SG-M13-CZ-WNL-ARC.ifc	270.093
8	Zg_mobileRoom-1.ifc	369.151
9	Ch-Subway-130215.ifc	384.438
10	Cgm-Project-12.ifc	429.433

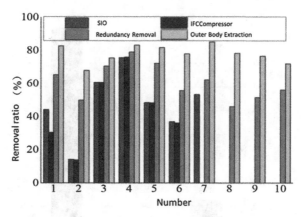

Fig. 6. Comparison with SIO and IFC-Compressor.

The item #9 with 384.438 M data quality in Table 2 is taken from a metro station; due to its huge volume it could not be loaded in Web by either SIO or IFC-Compressor. Whereas, by using the Redundancy removal or Outer body Extraction methods proposed in this paper, the data reduction ratios reach respectively 56% and 78%. The result shows that the BIM format large-scale metro station model is lightweighted, and the amount of total data can be reduced by about 10 times.

5.2 Lightweighting the Smoke

In this paper, the experiments are performed inside two metro stations respectively with a simple rectilinear structure and a curved structure. With the FDS tool, two sets of original data are obtained. And then, with the method proposed, the original data are lightweighted. After that, the smoke data of each step are measured. At last, the lightweighted smoke is used and examined for two purposes: (1) the visualization on Web3D; and (2) the path planning as obstacle data mapping in the path planning map. For a better description of the three key lightweighting results, two definitions are given here:

Definition 4. Visualization smoke data: The amount of lightweighted smoke data for visualization.

Definition 5. Path smoke data: The amount of lightweighted smoke data for path planning.

FDS is used to calculate the original heavyweight smoke data. The lightweighting results and their comparison are already shown in Fig. 7.

5.3 Lightweighting the Web3D Rendering of Smoke (FPS)

In a multi-agent fire evacuation scenario, 220 agents of different ages (i.e., children, youth, middle-aged, elder, women and men) in the metro station (of rectilinear structure) are rendered, whose movements are different from each other. In the smoking

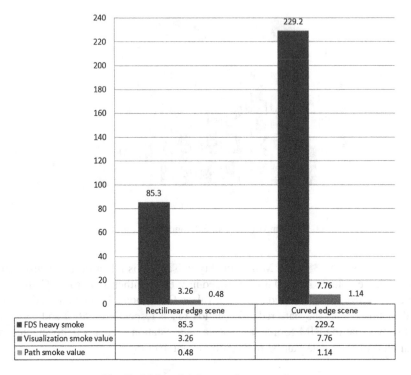

	Rectilinear edge scene	Curved edge scene
■ FDS heavy smoke	85.3	229.2
■ Visualization smoke value	3.26	7.76
■ Path smoke value	0.48	1.14

Fig. 7. Lightweighting results comparison.

metro station, smog is spreading from a supermarket in the metro station, and the 220 agents are evacuating following the dynamically optimally planned paths for them by the eACO algorithm. The entire-scene rendering rate recorded is in the range of 57–52 frame per second (FPS).

The training evacuation system uses the multi-thread technology to plan a path for each agent and renders all of them. During the path planning process, the multi-thread algorithm with pheromone is reused to accelerate the path planning performance. In the multi-agent rendering, the multi-thread algorithm with clone rendering accelerates the rendering performance.

At the onset of the fire, the page refreshing rate maintains at 57 FPS. Along with the increasing smoke data (as the fire is getting larger), the memory occupied for smoke rendering is increasing accordingly, and at last the page refreshing frequency becomes 52 FPS (Fig. 8).

5.4 Evacuation Success Rates

To evaluate the evacuation success rate (i.e., the ratio of the survivors over the original number of agents) achieved by the eACO algorithm, for comparison purpose, two benchmarking algorithms – the Random algorithm and the Greedy algorithm [24] – are

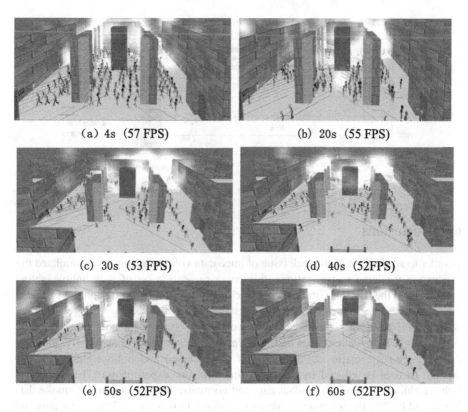

(a) 4s (57 FPS)   (b) 20s (55 FPS)

(c) 30s (53 FPS)   (d) 40s (52FPS)

(e) 50s (52FPS)   (f) 60s (52FPS)

Fig. 8. The visual evacuation process of 220 visual agents in a metro station under the *e*ACO algorithm.

also tested to compare with the performance of *e*ACO; the scene of the test is at the two metro station mentioned above.

The number of passengers in the test is 200. For each of the three algorithms, 5 experiments are conducted, and the experimental data are listed in Table 3 and shown in Fig. 9, which clearly show that the *e*ACO algorithm has the highest fire evacuation success rate whereas the Random algorithm the lowest.

Table 3. Crowd evacuation success rate.

Algorithms	Experiments					Mean values(%)
	1(%)	2(%)	3(%)	4(%)	5(%)	
*e*ACO algorithm	100	97	100	100	100	99.4
Greedy algorithm	99	94	100	100	73	93.2
Random algorithm	56	36	37	44	41	40.8

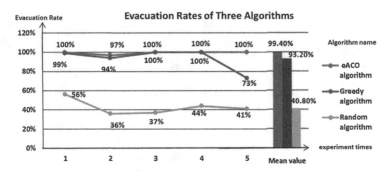

Fig. 9. Evacuation success rates by the three algorithms.

6 Conclusions

In order to address the bottleneck issue of huge data volume in computer simulated fire evacuation for large metro stations, this paper presents a set of data lightweighting solutions. On the basis of virtual Web3D technologies, a set of lightweighting solutions are proposed for online VR training systems of subway station fire evacuation. Specifically, we have presented the lightweighting solutions for both the large-scale metro station BIM static scenes and the dynamic FDS smoking data. Firstly, the BIM format large-scale metro station model is preprocessed and lightweighted, and the amount of data is reduced by about 10 times (in our experiments). Then, after the lightweighting of smoke-redundant data and normalization, the amount of smoke data is reduced by 200 times (again in our experiments). In this way, all the scene data and smoke data now become able to be transited through the internet and uploaded onto the Web page in real-time for rendering. And then, with the *e*ACO algorithm proposed in this paper and the multi-thread mechanism, the evacuation path planning can be finished within 3 s for a large-scale metro station. On the basis of the three above key technologies, a prototype system based on WebGL is developed for virtual fire evacuation training on web, and anyone can participate in virtual reality online fire evacuation training without downloading and installing the plug-ins. Our experiments confirm that the refresh rate on web by the *e*ACO algorithm is able to meet the public demands for virtual web training.

In the future, the following related research topics are planned. In order to assign an evaluation value for the best evacuation path, each trainee's evacuation path and the relative smoke data should be evaluated by the *e*ACO algorithm. The trainees can make comparison of the values and paths to improve the evacuation ability in fire evacuation. In that case, the training system can guide the public to increase the evacuation rate.

Acknowledgments. The authors appreciate the comments and suggestions of all the anonymous reviewers, whose comments help the authors significantly in their revising the paper. This work is supported by the Key Research Projects of Central University of Basic Scientific Research Funds for Cross Cooperation (201510-02), the Research Fund for the Doctoral Program of Higher Education of China (No. 2013007211-0035) and the Key project in scientific and technological of Jilin Province in China (No. 20140204088GX).

References

1. BIM WIKIPEDIA. https://en.wikipedia.org/wiki/Building_information_modeling. Last accessed 19 April 2017
2. Liu, X., Xie, N., Tang, K., Jia, J.: Lightweighting for Web3D visualization of large-scale BIM scenes in real-time. Graph. Models **88**, 40–56 (2016)
3. FDS Homepage, http://www.thunderheadeng.com/pyrosim/. Last accessed 19 April 2017
4. Gogna, A., Tayal, A.: Metaheuristics: review and application. J. Exp. Theor. Artif. Intell. **25**(4), 503–526 (2013)
5. Chiang, C., Huang, Y., Wang, W.: Ant colony optimization with parameter adaptation for multi-mode resource-constrained project scheduling. J. Intell. Fuzzy Syst. **19**(4, 5), 345–358 (2008)
6. Exodus Homepage. http://www.fseg.gre.ac.uk/index.html. Last accessed 19 April 2017
7. Legion Homepage. http://www.legion.com. Last accessed 19 April 2017
8. Myriad Homepage. http://www.crowddynamics.com/. Last accessed 19 April 2017
9. Massive Software Homepage. http://www.massiveoftware.com/. Last accessed 19 April 2017
10. Diez, H.V., Garcia, S., Mujika, A., Moreno, A., Oyarzun, D.: Virtual training of fire wardens through immersive 3D environments. In: ACM Web3D, pp. 43–50 (2016)
11. Benkoussas, B., Bouhdjar, A., Vauquelin, O.: Numerical security assessment in case of fire in underground transport spaces. Nat. Technol. **12**, 45–59 (2015)
12. Song, Y., Gong, J., Li, Y., Cui, T., Fang, L., Cao, W.: Crowd evacuation simulation for bioterrorism in micro-spatial environments based on virtual geographic environments. Saf. Sci. **53**, 105–113 (2013)
13. Cha, M., Han, S., Lee, J., Choi, B.: A virtual reality based fire training simulator integrated with fire dynamics data. Fire Saf. J. **50**, 12–24 (2012)
14. Xu, Z., Lu, X., Guan, H., Ren, A.: A virtual reality based fire training simulator with smoke hazard assessment capacity. Adv. Eng. Softw. **68**, 1–8 (2014)
15. Chiu, Y., Shiau, Y.: Study on the application of unity software in emergency evacuation simulation for elder. Artif. Life Robot. **21**(2), 232–238 (2016)
16. Sharakhov, N., Nicholas, P., Sforza, P.M.: SpeedSpy: a mobile Web3D platform for visualizing broadband data. In: ACM Web3D, pp. 208–208 (2013)
17. HTML5 Introduction. https://www.w3schools.com/html/html5_intro.asp. Last accessed 19 April 2017
18. Lin, Y., Liu, Y., Gao, G., Han, X., Lai, C., Gu, M.: The IFC-based path planning for 3D indoor spaces. Adv. Eng. Inform. **27**(2), 189–205 (2013)
19. Kinateder, M., Ronchi, E., Nilsson, D., Kobes, M.: Virtual reality for fire evacuation research. In: Proceeding of the 2014 Federated Conference on Computer Science and Information Systems, pp. 313–321. IEEE (2014)
20. Tian, Y., Zhou, T., Yao, Q., Zhang, M., Li, J.: Use of an agent-based simulation model to evaluate a mobile-based system for supporting emergency evacuation decision making. J. Med. Syst. **38**(12), 149 (2014)
21. Guest, J., Eaglin, T., Subramanian, K., Ribarsky, W.: Interactive analysis and visualization of situationally aware building evacuations. Inf. Vis. **14**(3), 204–222 (2015)
22. Benkoussas, B., Djedjig, R., Vauquelin, O.: Numerical assessment of conventional regulation effectiveness for smoke removal from a two level underground station. J. Fundam. Appl. Sci. **8**(2), 401–425 (2016)
23. Fang, X., Huang, P., An, H.: Progress in the research on crowd's emergency behaviors in large-scale events. Zhongguo Anquan Kexue Xuebao **21**(11), 22–28 (2011)

24. Duo, Q., Shen, H., Zhao, J., Gong, X.: Conformity behavior during a fire disaster. Soc. Behav. Pers. Int. J. **44**(2), 313–324 (2016)
25. IFC WIKIPEDIA. https://en.wikipedia.org/wiki/Industry_Foundation_Classes. Last accessed 19 April 2017

Game-Based Crisis Simulation and Generation Framework: Design and Implementation Structure

Pisit Praiwattana[✉] and Abdennour El Rhalibi

Department of Computer Science, Liverpool John Moores University, Byrom Street, Liverpool L3 3AF, UK
P.Praiwattana@2014.ljmu.ac.uk, a.elrhalibi@ljmu.ac.uk

Abstract. Crisis is an infrequent and unpredictable event. Training and preparation process requires tools for representation of crisis context. Particularly, Crisis Event consists of different situations which can occur at the same time combining into complex situation and becoming a challenge in collaboration of several crisis management departments. Studying of Resource distribution also improving an effectively in solving the ongoing crisis. By integrating modern game technology, development process of assistance and simulation system can become a cost-effective solution to allow observation and test practice procedures. Therefore, we aim to discuss and provide an implementation design choices of general framework tool for representing of coverage terrain, resources, different stakeholders and structure of crisis scenario using Unity3D game engine technology. The paper focuses on the procedural generation of complex 3D environment for crisis scenarios generation and disaster management, and introduces the framework, structure, functions and the visualization, and performance evaluation of the framework.

Keywords: Crisis simulation framework · Procedural computer generation · Agent-based system

1 Introduction

Currently, an occurrence of changing in world-environment states is commonly fast-paced and unpredictable. Such situation which may result in large scale of adversary impact on environment, population and resources can be considered as crisis situation. In preparation stage, the practices of distributing manpower, setting up tools, considering time expense are essentially required to derive an effective plan for complex situations. Fortunately, game-based application provides a cost-effective solution, as a game development technology such as Unreal Engine and Unity3D have been currently more accessible for researchers, and, thus, it becomes an affordable tool for integrating the visual representation and simulation process of emerging disaster to develop a practice application for crisis personal.

© Springer International Publishing AG 2017
F. Tian et al. (Eds.): Edutainment 2017, LNCS 10345, pp. 75–84, 2017.
https://doi.org/10.1007/978-3-319-65849-0_9

By representing and simulating ongoing crisis situation into description of scenario-based structure, it allows finding an answer to a question of what is the optimal responses in allocating, deploying, and prioritizing of available resource parameters and operation protocols. Regarding of the scope in crisis scenario representation, models can be designed using a level of information perception and possible interaction of participants. For instance, it can be designed with role-playing approach in first-person perspective on limited local perception of event, or it can have been further extended into real-time strategy observation approach in top-view with filtered information on resources and multiple events. Although both example models are aiming to reproduce a training experience in executing official procedures, the former design is suitable for training specific scope of crisis operational agents while the latter is often more appropriated for observing and testing large scale deployment plan on time-contesting situation. These design decisions strongly influence on how the final application will be deployed and evaluated.

In this paper, we provide a brief discussion on the existing scenario generation system then identify the core features of crisis simulation framework. Further, we discuss on general design decision and implementation of proposed framework in details. The remainder of this paper is organized as follows: In Sect. 2, we introduce backgrounds on automated content generation system and example of crisis simulation systems; In Sect. 3, we discuss implementation design of each component for our proposed framework; In Sect. 4, we discusses the result and evaluation of visualization stage; and, in Sect. 5, we conclude the paper.

2 Backgrounds

2.1 Automated Content Generation System

Modern serious games will required scenario and visual asset to provide content. There are also research which focus on procedural generation of such content.

Related researchers have tackled procedurally generated game environments with varying degrees of success. The most well known and most significant research has been carried out on the CityEngine [1], a system that is capable of producing realistic and detailed models. The generation algorithms are inspired by the modeling of natural phenomena in string grammars [2] and L-systems are used to construct road networks and buildings [1]. Procedural building generation has focused on the application of grammars to describe structure, like the Shape Grammars original proposed by [3]. These have been applied in various guises to the construction of building geometry [4].

In [5], the authors define a specific grammar to characterize building structure. This system defines rules to operate on shapes and can be used to design a range of detailed buildings in several architectural styles. Recently this approach has been extended to employ imaging techniques to aid in the acquisition of generation rules from existing building facades [6,7].

Other approaches include the application of intelligent agents [8], real-time frustum filling [9] and template based generation [10]. In [8,11] the authors propose to simulate the evolution of cities by modelling land use and evolving a city usage map over time that can be used later to create a cityscape. Real-time city generation has also been attempted.

In [9,11]the authors implemented a city generation system that is filling the view frustum rapidly with buildings of various shape combinations but their placement have been restricted to a road network consisting of a regular grid. In [10] the authors proposed an application of templates that encapsulate patterns such as raster radial to generate road networks.

Compared to these techniques, our approach introduces several novel aspects including: use of agent-based modeling for the game world generation, interoperability solution development using Unity 3D and allowing deployment across many platforms including web browsers, and multiple OS; instant in-game generation, rendering and recreation of 3D hexagonal cell-based and organic environments; agent AI Bots to interact with the environment after generation stage and according to other user-set constraints, and structural constraints induced by the game world and crisis scenario generation; and full control of the environment editing by the user.

2.2 Crisis Simulation Systems

There are several research of proposed crisis simulation system focusing on variety of implementation scopes which some have been built for specific platform and application. In general, the main objective of developing such a system is to provide practice experience on prepared protocols for related personals based on occurring crisis event. The deployment of simulation system may be integrated in complete game-based application, virtual equipment training, or combining real-system with content-simulation module. Furthermore, in simulating of real-world disasters on constrained situation of environments and stakeholders such as epidemic outbreak, wildfire and flood, deploying Agent-based model (ABS) architecture will provide ease of observance and flexibility to assign behaviors for appropriate entities [12,13].

For example, a multi-agent system WIPER [14] is using real GIS data for visualizing geographic terrain while each mobile phone user is having a movement activity tracked by tower cellular segments covering the area for a real-time response. The system allows observance of variety in movement and evacuation pattern with traffic situation. In SimGenis, it is proposed to design optimal, efficient, and appropriate rescue strategies, based on the initial state of victims, number of rescuers, and method of communication between rescuers. More precisely, the original aim of their research is determining how to response a dynamic large-scale emergency depends on the use of a centralized and decentralized collaborative rescue strategy with applying heuristic algorithm on each agent and component in simulator [15]. Robocup Rescue [16,17] which used the 1995 Kobe earthquake as the original test scenario. The system is aiming to represent the disaster situation sensory information then to incorporate the agent-simulation system to mitigate disaster and encourage large scale research collaboration based on optimization of the design and implementation of better action selection method. Moreover, PLAN-C [18,19] is also another ABS developed to predict the behavior of individual and collectively organized agents in large-scale emergency such as terrorist attack. Lastly, EpiSimS [20,21] is also another ABS developed to study the optimized parameters of resource and procedures in a SmallPox scenario model and influenza outbreak including the behavior of infected patients with deployment pattern of related officials. From our survey [22], crisis simulation systems shared similarities in: (1) abstracting the representation of real-world locations, participated stakeholders and environment entities; (2) reproducing crisis scenario based on knowledge and historical records; and, ultimately, (3) to train a crisis personal with appropriate response for any upcoming situations. The simulation stage also being benefit from having integrated automated content generation to tailor progression of crisis situations due to the nature of large scale disaster being very complex and restrained the time of crisis scenario designer.

In summary, these researches provided insight on possible core components of general crisis simulation framework which are representation and generation of terrain; process of distributing and storing key resource; procedures for facilities and specialized crisis agents in deployment, communication and collaboration; simulation of crisis event and integrating agent-based model to replicate responses of impacted stakeholders which can be individual citizens, responsible governing unit, specific department and personal using planning or rule-based approach; and finally integration of automated content generation on both terrain visualization and crisis scenario. We will propose and discuss the implemented of framework which aims to address the overall structure of these core components in the next section.

3   Crisis Scenario Simulation and Generation Framework

The crisis scenario simulation framework is separated into 2 focus groups of core components. The former is to consider representation structure of area, resources and stakeholder in the situation. Next, the latter is dealing with simulation of behaviors from these stakeholders respectively to their role and authority, while the crisis scenario generation will based on simulation framework to deliver a combination of these representations and tailoring sequence of event and situations logically or from the prescript of conditions. This section will only focus on initial setup of crisis simulation framework only. The uniqueness of application in proposed structure is that it adopts the variety of representation and simulation whether it is game-based model like SimCity or limited resource management situation on specific crisis context. Figure 1 shows the framework architecture with core components and Fig. 2 displays the implemented result in Unity3D.

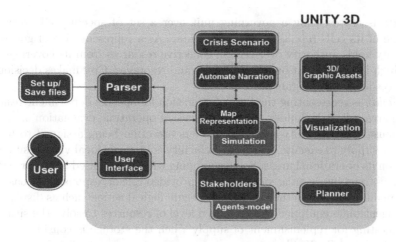

Fig. 1. Framework architecture with core components

Fig. 2. Framework architecture in Unity 3D

3.1 Map Representation

The map space for proposed framework is represented as abstract grid of hexagon cell (Hex Cell) which consists of 6 cell neighbors locating in cube coordinates on Cell(X, Y, Z). The distinct advantage from choosing hex cell over the traditional square cell lattice is that the distance between each direction to center of the cell would be symmetrical and, therefore, provide more realistic representation in traversing between coordinates. Each cell stored information of its terrain component type, elevation unit, resource supply being stocked, and other flags for determining the information of details such as road, river and etc. Necessary parameters for determining simulation event such as temperature or water mass can be added on specific cell individually.

3.2 Stakeholders

The stakeholders in crisis situation are being classified into three different representations accordingly; (1) City; (2) Facility; and (3) Personal Unit.

City is representing a governing unit over a set of specific cell areas and has one of its cells representing a city center. As a representative of governing unit, city holds authority over central collective resources from its coverage area with high-level information of crisis event and resources. City makes decision on resources and unit assignment.

Facility is representing the base of operation for specific department residing in one area cell. It includes a temporary base of operation, evacuation area, and storehouse. These facility-type stakeholders are often being assigned to hold a resource supply to execute action. Each facility is having a local view of situation based on its operational areas. Some equipping with agent-based behavior system will assess ongoing event associating with provided role of responsibility based on the remaining resources then decide to execute logical action such as dispatching crisis agent units equipped with required level of resources to solve the situation or requesting for replenishment of supply when the storage is considered to be not sufficient or depleted.

Personal Unit (or *Unit*) is, in general, a representation of quantity in mobile group of individual. There are two basic distinct roles of unit as a crisis personal squad and civilian. The former, squad is holding a responsibility role respectively such as Firemen, Medical doctors, Policemen and being assigned a quantity of resource supply from its facility owner for executing direct solving action on the crisis events.

The latter, civilians is representing represented in the situation such as injuries injured and escaping individuals from the impact area. These personal units have a low-level information perspective to only its specific role objective and, thus, will execute a fundamental action to reach the goal condition.

3.3   Crisis Scenario

To providing a basic structure, crisis scenario context will be described as a set of *Crisis Events*. For each event, it is also consisting of another set of *Disaster Situations* and starting time in the simulation clock called *Simulation Step* in which one step is including calculation of ongoing disaster flag such as fire and flood with evaluation of simulation parameters for state-changing.

Disaster Situation is considered as template for any anomaly of raise or decrease of simulation parameters similar to real-world problem. This allows us to describe the element of situation specifically in parameters and being reusable for similar context. For an example, the *"Heat surge"* situation would raise the temperature parameter of specific area with 30°–50° and, therefore, allowing *Fire Simulation Properties* to trigger a burning state if the condition is reaching the starting fire temperature threshold.

Crisis Event is considered to be an abstracted event combining different situations altogether. The event will consist of delay in simulation step which control the timing to be active state. Next, activated crisis event is to applying different disaster situations on designated cells. From the representation of crisis event, it allows us to represent a single event as a specific template which is reusable similar to disaster situations.

Lastly, *Crisis Scenario* is a high-level narrative of sequenced crisis events. With the collective representation of crisis events and disaster situations, the specific scenario can be reproduced with flexibility of alteration such as a random starting time of crisis event and range of disaster situation impact on parameter scale modifier.

3.4   Visualization

Fundamentally, Grid-based data structure allows us to represent the positioning of single strategic area space as cell and concept of residing resource, facilities, personals, and state of properties clearly. Therefore, visualization component is processing the map grid then, for each cell, calculates the vertices for terrain mesh triangulation from their coordinates and elevation. The quantity of resource supply is parsed into level of visual feature parameters for flexibility in 3D Assets preparation. Next, the placement of higher level abstraction will be *facilities* locating in the cell alongside with *personal unit* similar to visual representation of real-time strategy game. This similarity provides ease of perception using common game-metaphor and fast recognition to the user. As situation on each cell is varied based on its setup but, in general, it is to select a correct visual effect determining for specific situation. Optimization is preliminary done by using Built-in Unity3d Level-of-Detail object which switch preassigned different details of model or sprites based on camera distance.

3.5   Simulation of Environment

The simulation control will hold a local clock which is mentioned in Sect. 3.3 as simulation step. This step represents one loop to applying disaster situation parameters to associated components; evaluating the component's state; and simulating the impact of state such as transferring heat to nearby area, depleting fuel or flow the exceeding water mass respectively; applying damage value to residing personal units in the affected area. Lastly, adjust the visual effect or cell parameters as final result. The algorithm for example fire and flood disaster situation is initially designed by applying basic of a cellular automaton behavior considering the influence of nearby cells neighbors parameters to calculate and change internal state of each cell accordingly.

4   Result and Performance Evaluation

Crisis scenario simulation and generation framework has been implementing on Unity3d Game Engine for ease of visualization process. This section explains a result on process of terrain generation and visualization. The framework experiments was run in a Laptop with Core i7-5500U @2.40 GHz, 2 Cores with RAM 16 GB (10 GB Available), and Window 10 with GeForce 840m model. Figure 3 shows the overall visualized results from parsing terrain information on close-up detail and zoomed images on different size of terrain setups, (a) Small map with

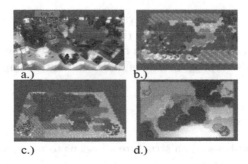

a.)   b.)

c.)   d.)

Fig. 3. Result for (a) Close-up; (b) Small map (c) Medium map (d) Large map

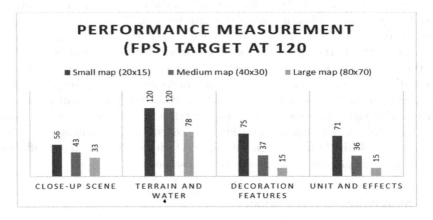

Fig. 4. Performance measurement in frame per seconds at target limit of 120 frames on (a) Close-up scene with all options on (b) Terrain and water only (c) Decoration features and 3D models (d) Placement of units and visual effects

grid size of 25 * 15 of total 300 cells; (b) Medium map with grid size of 40 * 30 of total 1200 cells; (c) Large map with grid size of 80 * 70 of total 5600 cells.

The overall visualization performance of proposed framework yielded general desirable for game application in small to medium map setup and drop to half framer-ate in large map setup. Terrain and water surface visualization were functioning on above average of 60 fps. Turning on the decoration map features resulted in linear decrease of framerate while units placement and visual effect rendering did not greatly slow down the system. In close-up scene view, size of the terrain map also represented linear decrease of framerate. Although small and medium map can still provide functional framerate during runtime, the large map size have suffered drop in framerate significantly to an average of 15 fps, when turning on visualization of scene features (Fig. 4).

5 Conclusion

This paper discusses the core components of proposed Crisis Scenario Simulation and Generation framework including its structure for representing terrain area, stakeholders, crisis scenario and visualization process.

The provided implementation result on representation of core component and testing in visualization stage from our framework shows that it is a flexible tool to support modeling, visualization and testing of general crisis scenario situation. Implemented on Unity3D game engine, the game-based application will be benefit from porting into different platform including web-based, providing accessibility to crisis scenario manager, designer, crisis personals and interested individuals. This work is preliminary, and whilst the planning system has been developed, the integration with visualization system and crisis generation scenario and simulation is on-going.

In the future work, our effort will focus on integration and evaluation of the agent-based model with planning capabilities to deliver a crisis plan with optimal actions.

References

1. Bekins, D., Aliaga, D.G.: Build-by-number: rearranging the real world to visualize novel architectural spaces. In: 2005 IEEE Visualization, VIS 2005, pp. 143–150. IEEE (2005)
2. Greuter, S., Parker, J., Stewart, N., Leach, G.: Real-time procedural generation of 'pseudo infinite' cities. In: Proceedings of the 1st International Conference on Computer Graphics and Interactive Techniques in Australasia and South East Asia, GRAPHITE 2003, pp. 87–ff. ACM, New York (2003). http://doi.acm.org/10.1145/604471.604490
3. Lechner, T., Watson, B., Wilensky, U., Felsen, M.: Procedural city modelling. Technical report, Northwestern University, November 2003
4. Lechner, T., Watson B, Ren, P., Wilensky, U., Tisue, S., Felsen, M.: Procedural modelling of land use in cities. Technical report, Northwestern University, August 2004
5. Müller, P., Wonka, P., Haegler, S., Ulmer, A., Van Gool, L.: Procedural modeling of buildings. In: ACM SIGGRAPH 2006 Papers, SIGGRAPH 2006, pp. 614–623. ACM, New York (2006). http://doi.acm.org/10.1145/1179352.1141931
6. Müller, P., Zeng, G., Wonka, P., Van Gool, L.: Image-based procedural modeling of facades. In: ACM SIGGRAPH 2007 Papers, SIGGRAPH 2007. ACM, New York (2007). http://doi.acm.org/10.1145/1275808.1276484
7. Parish, Y.I.H., Müller, P.: Procedural modeling of cities. In: Proceedings of the 28th Annual Conference on Computer Graphics and Interactive Techniques, SIG-GRAPH 2001, pp. 301–308. ACM, New York (2001). http://doi.acm.org/10.1145/383259.383292
8. Prusinkiewicz, P., Lindenmayer, A.: Modeling of cellular layers. In: Prusinkiewicz, P., Lindenmayer, A. (eds.) The Algorithmic Beauty of Plants, pp. 145–174. Springer, New York (1990). doi:10.1007/978-1-4613-8476-2_7
9. Stiny, G.: Introduction to shape and shape grammars. Environ. Plan. B Plan. Des. 7(3), 343–351 (1980). http://dx.doi.org/10.1068/b070343

10. Sun, J., Yu, X., Baciu, G., Green, M.: Template-based generation of road networks for virtual city modeling. In: Proceedings of the ACM Symposium on Virtual Reality Software and Technology, VRST 2002, pp. 33–40. ACM, New York (2002). http://doi.acm.org/10.1145/585740.585747

11. Wonka, P., Wimmer, M., Sillion, F., Ribarsky, W.: Instant architecture. ACM Trans. Graph. **22**(3), 669–677 (2003). http://doi.acm.org/10.1145/882262.882324

12. Wooldridge, M., Jennings, N.R.: Intelligent agents: theory and practice. Knowl. Eng. Rev. **10**(02), 115–152 (1995)

13. Challenger, R., Clegg, C., Robinson, M., Leigh, M.: Understanding crowd behaviours: simulation tools. UK Cabinet Office (2009)

14. Schoenharl, T., Madey, G.: Design and implementation of an agent-based simulation for emergency response and crisis management. J. Algorithms Computat. Technol. **5**(4), 601–622 (2011)

15. Saoud, N.B.B., Mena, T.B., Dugdale, J., Pavard, B., Ahmed, M.B.: Assessing large scale emergency rescue plans: an agent based approach. Int. J. Intell. Control Syst. **11**(4), 260–271 (2006)

16. Takeuchi, I.: A massively multi-agent simulation system for disaster mitigation. In: Ishida, T., Gasser, L., Nakashima, H. (eds.) MMAS 2004. LNCS, vol. 3446, pp. 269–282. Springer, Heidelberg (2005). doi:10.1007/11512073_20

17. Siddhartha, H., Sarika, R., Karlapalem, K.: Score vector: a new evaluation scheme for RoboCup rescue simuation competition 2009. Rescue Technical Committee (2009)

18. Mysore, V., Narzisi, G., Nelson, L., Rekow, D., Triola, M., Shapiro, A., Coleman, C., Gill, O., Daruwala, R.S., Mishra, B.: Agent modeling of a Sarin attack in Manhattan. In: Proceedings of the First International Workshop on Agent Technology for Disaster Management, ATDM, pp. 108–115 (2006)

19. Narzisi, G., Mysore, V., Mishra, B.: Multi-objective evolutionary optimization of agent-based models: An application to emergency response planning. Comput. Intell. **2006**, 224–230 (2006)

20. Barrett, C.L., Eubank, S.G., Smith, J.P.: If smallpox strikes portland. Sci. Am. **292**(3), 54–61 (2005)

21. Mniszewski, S.M., Del Valle, S.Y., Stroud, P.D., Riese, J.M., Sydoriak, S.J.: EpiSimS simulation of a multi-component strategy for pandemic influenza. In: Proceedings of the 2008 Spring Simulation Multiconference, pp. 556–563. Society for Computer Simulation International (2008)

22. Praiwattana, P., El Rhalibi, A.: Survey: development and analysis of a games-based crisis scenario generation system. In: El Rhalibi, A., Tian, F., Pan, Z., Liu, B. (eds.) Edutainment 2016. LNCS, vol. 9654, pp. 85–100. Springer, Cham (2016). doi:10.1007/978-3-319-40259-8_8

Snow White Is Missing: An Interactive Locative Story for Dementia Patients

Charlie Hargood[1]([✉]), Ben Hicks[2], Fred Charles[1], Samuel Lynch[1],
and Wen Tang[1]

[1] Creative Technology Department, SciTech, Bournemouth University, Poole, UK
chargood@bournemouth.ac.uk
[2] BUDI, SciTech, Bournemouth University, Poole, UK

Abstract. With the increasing prevalence of powerful mobile technology, interactive entertainment is also becoming increasingly mobile. This can also be said for a range of applications including those pertaining to mental and physical health which are also looking to take advantage of the increase in mobile technology to create digital interventions and other treatment based software for mobile devices that can benefit from the mobile deliver form. In this paper we propose a new form of serious game in this vein: therapeutic locative interactive fiction. These are interactive story experiences, read while on the move, that respond to the readers environment and location context, and have therapeutic value. The locative nature of these stories enables therapeutic activities connected with out door spaces, and allows for content to enrich users, the readers of locational context. We present a demonstration of this concept through our own therapeutic locative interactive narrative: Snow White is Missing, and detail both its design from an interactive narrative and therapeutic activity perspectives.

Keywords: Locative narrative · Interactive storytelling · Dementia

1 Introduction

Location Aware Narrative (LAN) promises an entertainment experience that contextually adapts to the users' environment [14]. This might mean asking them to travel to particular locations to view particular content, changing content to include the users surroundings, or a thematic pairing between the users' surroundings and the story. This can be used to enrich the users' experience of the surroundings through virtual tour guides, or fictional works unlocking local history, or enrich the content through games that involve physically travelling to relevant locations. As mobile technology with location sensors, particularly smartphones, becomes more prevalent this form of entertainment reaches a broader audience. A similar trend can be observed in digital Behaviour Change Interventions (dBCIs) [15]. These are programs of activities and supporting materials constructed by behaviour change scientists to elicit positive behaviour change

© Springer International Publishing AG 2017
F. Tian et al. (Eds.): Edutainment 2017, LNCS 10345, pp. 85–92, 2017.
https://doi.org/10.1007/978-3-319-65849-0_10

in participants such as losing weight or stopping smoking. While the move to a digital platform enables a great degree of personalisation [16], the move to mobile dBCIs enables context awareness and more timely interaction with the intervention [13].

In this paper we propose Therapeutic Locative Interactive Fiction (TLIF): a locative story which enhances its experience by taking the reader to particular locations while also providing the therapeutic advantages of a mobile dBCI. We present an example of this in 'Snow White is Missing' - a TLIF built using the StoryPlaces system [8] designed to be therapeutic for dementia patients. At present, over 46 million people live with dementia globally and this is predicted to rise to 131.5 million by 2050 [22]. Unsurprisingly this has resulted in a global focus on dementia, with the World Health Organisation identifying the condition as a priority area that needs to be addressed in the future health agenda. Our intervention is an interactive story that is designed to be read alongside a younger friend or family member, featuring a number of activities the readers can complete while physically moving to different locations set in Poole Park, Bournemouth, UK. This TLIF is a product of co-design between experts both in dementia from the department of psychology, and interactive fiction and game design from the department of creative technology, both from Bournemouth University.

The main contribution of this paper is the concept of TLIFs, including a completed example in 'Snow White is Missing', the co-designed structure and content of which we detail along with the therapeutic benefits of this approach in the context of contemporary literature in this area.

2   Background

2.1   Location Aware Narrative

Early examples of location-based narrative systems were often tour guides, for example the HIPS system [3] which connected location aware software to a knowledge base of information in order to generate personalised information pages based on current location. In more recent examples the focus has moved to the experience itself, often through the use of more evocative stories, such as location sensitive historical plays or tapestries of personal stories connected to space to build up a cultural picture [18]. Educational tools such as 'Gaius' Day in Egnathia' [1] push the interactive elements of this kind of storytelling by giving participants goals. In the case of 'Gaius' Day' this is in the form of exploration targets that they must identify by collecting location-based clues. The Chawton House project [23] also supports an educational experience, but in Chawton the activities themselves are non-digital, encouraging the participants to perform short creative exercises. A summary of this field should also include more entertainment focused and artist works such as location aware games and fiction. From the games sector works include 'Viking Ghost Hunt' [17] where players hunt down the ghosts of Dublin using an augmented reality system, or 'University of Death' [4] a hybrid reality system that requires its players to adopt specific roles and behaviours and utilise real world props and clues alongside digital information. In contrast, works of location aware fiction such as 'San Servolo, travel into the memory of an island' sometimes have more complex rules, based not just on location but other contextual factors such as weather and reader's history [21]. Location-based interactive fictions are comparable to 'Walking Sims', games where readers explore virtual spaces and interact with objects triggering narrative sequences, San Servolo even echoes the first popular example 'Dear Esther' which also takes place on an island [20].

2.2 Dementia Care and Intervention

'Dementia' is often used to describe a group of clinical syndromes [12]. These are associated with increasing age and are characterised by a progressive decline in cognition of sufficient severity to interfere with social and/or occupational functioning and may include other symptoms such as language and navigational difficulties, deterioration in the ability to perform activities of daily living and behaviour changes [10].

Although the global focus remains firmly on 'cure rather than care' [24], there is a growing recognition that without a silver bullet cure, more needs to be done to support people to live well with dementia. As such, a key aspect of the UKs current dementia policy directive has focused on promoting the social inclusion of people with dementia particularly those living in the community, where around two thirds of people diagnosed with the condition reside [7]. This involves using nonpharmacological or 'ecopsychosocial' initiatives to raise awareness of dementia and tackle the stigma and discrimination associated with the condition, as well as provide opportunities for people living with dementia to engage in activities that promote learning and personal growth and ensure they can continue to contribute economically, socially, culturally and politically [9].

Research has supported this policy agenda and demonstrated that enabling social inclusion through community activities, can promote physical, mental and social benefits, as well as address important psychological needs for people with dementia [19]. It provides them with opportunities to retain autonomy and identity, and experience pleasure, enjoyment, social connection, belonging and growth [5]. This is particularly the case for outdoor activities that enable connection with the natural environment [6]. Despite this focus, research has shown people with dementia still struggle to uphold their social inclusion. For instance, Innes et al. [11] found community-dwelling people with dementia faced difficulties when accessing leisure activities and spaces in Dorset, UK. This was attributed in part to the potential psychological stress people with dementia might incur if they became lost or encountered people who were misinformed or intolerant of their condition. This demonstrates the importance for further research that facilitates the social inclusion of community-dwelling people with dementia and offers them opportunities to engage in new activities that promote learning and personal growth as well as socially connect with their local environment and others who reside there.

3   Snow White Is Missing!

Snow White Is Missing is a TLIF designed to be therapeutic for those suffering dementia. It is designed to be experienced as a pair: a dementia sufferer and a young family member. The story has been written for a younger target audience, to engage the younger reader whilst providing an entertaining outdoors activity for the individual affected by dementia to enjoy for 1–2 h. The TLIF helps to both raise awareness and understanding of dementia, as well as providing a focus for someone affected by it to leave their home and spend time with others.

Our hypothesis is that such locative narrative technology may provide a means to support social inclusion by enabling people living with the dementia condition to overcome some of the challenges they encounter. Research in this rapidly developing field has challenged the assumption that people with dementia are disinterested or incapable of using modern technology, as well as demonstrated how it can support the social inclusion of this population [2]. TLIFs therefore have the potential to offer an innovative and interesting activity that can both facilitate social inclusion amongst community-dwelling people with dementia and promote mental, physical and social well-being.

In *Snow White Is Missing* TLIF, GPS technology is integrated to support safer walking for people with dementia by reducing their navigational difficulties and so decreasing their fear of getting lost, and so encourage people with dementia to re-engage with their local environment. The proposed technological device, therefore, has the potential to offer an interesting activity that can both facilitate social inclusion amongst community-dwelling people with dementia and promote mental, physical and social well-being. The interactive story can provide a fun method for people with dementia to socially connect with their younger relatives and care partners, while the process of engaging with the activity may offer important mental and physical stimulation as well as an opportunity to learn something new.

3.1   The Story

The story is designed with dementia patients and young children as intended readers, specifically, it needs to have simple and easy-to-follow narrative and understandable vocabulary. Given these pertinent pre-conditions for our story, *Snow White Is Missing* leverages an existing story which the users both older and younger generations can more easily identify with and relate to. Being locative aware narrative, the setting should be as relevant to the story as possible, while being easily accessible to people with dementia. This includes but is not limited to facilities such as places to rest, café/restaurant, ease of parking and lavatories. We highlighted various potential venues in Bournemouth and surrounding areas, and settled upon Poole Park as it met all criteria, and also included facilities for children such as play areas, while also being large enough to facilitate a reasonably-sized location aware narrative without difficulty to navigate. The next stage was to explore the location, retrieve photographs and their accompanying GPS co-ordinates for generating narrative nodes, whilst noting potential 'problem-spots' for those of limited mobility or navigation.

The story of Snow White featuring multiple dwarves led to the design of multiple narrative arcs (about each dwarf) that the reader could explore in any order. Given the scenario, each dwarf was designed to subtly refer to issues that people with dementia generally encounter after diagnosis: a dwarf that is intelligent but frequently forgetful; a dwarf that intends to help but is always too physically tired to do so; a dwarf who is angry for always being labelled as angry; and a pair of dwarves in which one means well, but ultimately causes the other to depend on him too much, to the point of losing independence. The story nodes can be read and reached in any order, affording the reader an indirect feeling of choice (albeit control). The nodes are positioned in such a way that present an easily recognisable optimal route on the map for participants to follow.

Structurally we can describe our story in terms of the CDP model [14] as a hybrid of the form Canyon-Plain-Canyon, this is due to its open exploration element sandwiched between two linear stretches as shown in Fig. 1. This is a common structure within interactive fiction where the author retains narrative control over the beginning and end but allows for immersive agency in-between in the manner of a foldback pattern [8].

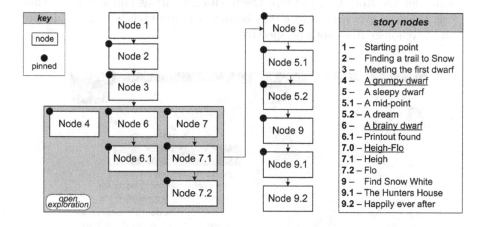

Fig. 1. Story nodes from *Snow White Is Missing*.

3.2   The Accompanying Activities

A key focus of the story was to raise awareness and understanding of dementia, and the problems they encounter. The intention was for readers with dementia to be accompanied by children; either their own or grandchildren. To retain attentiveness of the children, as well as to promote interaction between the readers, we included activities for them to complete as they explore the story. These activities were made explicit to the readers as part of the narrative, and designed alongside the story. The activities could be completed with or without the activity booklet, whilst promoted interaction between the person with dementia and the younger person. For instance, the activities were to list unique qualities about one another or taking a souvenir photograph.

3.3 Implementation and StoryPlaces

We have implemented *Snow White Is Missing* using the StoryPlaces system [8] as a general location aware narrative platform that is able to support the delivery of content paired to locations - all as a web application. The TLIF itself is constructed as a StoryPlaces story and then uploaded to the server where it is available to read on smartphones browsers as depicted in Fig. 2. Our co-design approach for this story between our experts from both game design and psychology underwent a four stage process:

1. **Concept**: initially experts from both game design and psychology met to share their own approach to content design for a TLIF, and a number of candidate locations and themes for the story were reviewed.
2. **Structure and Activity Design**: regular meetings were held to discuss both the location and story structure of the TLIF and its activities. Game design experts provided advice on engaging structures, while advice from a psychology expert was used for creating effective activities.
3. **Writing**: following the structure and activity design our writer prepared a script for the story that included the required locations and activities. This was reviewed over several meetings between experts from both game design and psychology from both perspectives.

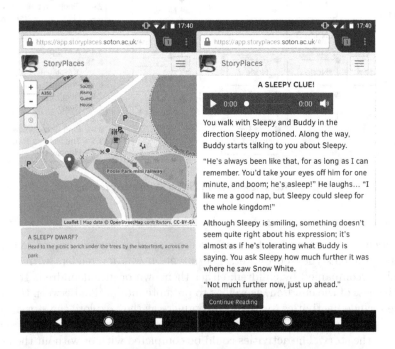

Fig. 2. Screenshots of Snow White Is Missing! as rendered by storyPlaces

4. **Implementation**: finally the agreed story was codified for StoryPlaces to deliver the TLIF, audio recordings were made for the text on every page, and photographs to illustrate the story were taken.

4 Conclusions and Future Work

In this paper we have proposed TLIF - Therapeutic Locative Interactive Fiction - as a serious application of interactive entertainment for health. We presented an example of this, *Snow White is Missing*, implemented within the StoryPlaces framework as an example of how the TLIF concept might be applied. The story makes use of a number of techniques to both take advantage of its delivery form and deliver effective intervention. Tailoring content to the users surroundings provides additional context to the intervention, both giving motivation to travel to these places and to use the setting to provide thematic backing to the story itself. The use of real world activities in this particular story also bring this in line with the work on mixed reality games, as part of the motivation for our work is to increase time spent together between the dementia patient and a friend/relative this mixed reality approach with real world interaction allows us to encourage this without the use of digital interaction which may be less effective as well as increasing development cost.

While this work has served to propose and prototype the TLIF concept future work points in two directions. First is an exploration of the efficacy of TLIFs as treatment, which would require user evaluation, possibly using a larger or greater variety of stories to explore the impact of this application. Secondly, if the efficacy of the approach is shown to be positive work would need to be done to explore design guidelines for TLIFs to better enable others to be created.

References

1. Ardito, C., Buono, P., Costabile, M., Lanzilotti, R., Pederson, T.: Mobile games to foster the learning of history at archaeological sites. In: Visual Languages and Human-Centric Computing (2007)
2. Bowes, A., Dawson, A., McCabe, L.: Remodem: Delivering support for people with dementia in remote areas. Dementia (2016). doi:10.1177/1471301216643848
3. Broadbent, J., Marti, P.: Location aware mobile interactive guides: usability issues. In: Proceedings of the Fourth International Conference on Hypermedia and Interactivity in Museums, pp. 162–172 (1997)
4. Bunting, B., Hughes, J., Hetland, T.: The player as author: Exploring the effects of mobile gaming and the location-aware interface on storytelling. Future Internet **4**(1), 142–160 (2012)
5. Fortune, D., Mckeown, J.: Sharing the journey: Exploring a social leisure program for persons with dementia and their spouses. Leisure Sci. **34**, 1–15 (2016)
6. Gilliard, J., Marshall, M.: Transforming the Quality of Life for People with Dementia Through Contact with the Natural World: Fresh Air on My Face. Jessica Kingsley, London (2012)

7. Green, G., Lakey, L.: Building Dementia-Friendly Communities: A Priority for Everyone. Alzheimers Society, London (2013)
8. Hargood, C., Hunt, V., Weal, M., Millard, D.E.: Patterns of sculptural hypertext in location based narratives. In: Proceedings of the 27th ACM Conference on Hypertext and Social Media. ACM, New York (2016)
9. Hicks, B.: Exploring the use of a commercial digital gaming Technological Initiative to enable social inclusion for community-dwelling older men with dementia in rural England. Ph.D. thesis, Bournemouth University (2016)
10. Innes, A., Manthorpe, J.: Developing theoretical understandings of dementia and their application to dementia care policy in the UK. Dementia **12**(6), 682–696 (2013)
11. Innes, A., Page, S.J., Cutler, C.: Barriers to leisure participation for people with dementia and their carers: An exploratory analysis of carer and people with dementia's experiences. Dementia **15**, 1643–1665 (2015)
12. Kitwood, T.: Dementia Reconsidered: The Person Comes First. Open University Press, Buckingham (1997)
13. Lathia, N., Pejovic, V., Rachuri, K., Mascolo, C., Musolesi, M., Rentfrow, P.J.: Smartphones for large-scale behaviour change intervention. IEEE Pervasive Comput. **12**(3), 66–73 (2013)
14. Millard, D.E., Hargood, C., Jewell, M.O., Weal, M.J.: Canyons, deltas and plains: towards a unified sculptural model of location-based hypertext. In: Proceedings of the 24th ACM Conference on Hypertext and Social Media (2013)
15. Morrison, L.G., Hargood, C., Pejovic, V., Geraghty, A.W., Lloyd, S., Goodman, N., Michaelides, D.T., Weston, A., Musolesi, M., Weal, M.J., et al.: The effect of timing and frequency of push notifications on usage of a smartphone-based stress management intervention: an exploratory trial. PLoS ONE **12**(1), e0169162 (2017)
16. Nahum-Shani, I., Smith, S.N., Tewari, A., Witkiewitz, K., Collins, L.M., Spring, B., Murphy, S.: Just in time adaptive interventions (jitais): An organizing framework for ongoing health behavior support. Methodology Center, Technical report (2014)
17. Naliuka, K., Carrigy, T., Paterson, N., Haahr, M.: A narrative architecture for story-driven location-based mobile games. In: Luo, X., Cao, Y., Yang, B., Liu, J., Ye, F. (eds.) ICWL 2010. LNCS, vol. 6537, pp. 11–20. Springer, Heidelberg (2011). doi:10.1007/978-3-642-20539-2_2
18. Nisi, V., Oakley, I., Haahr, M.: Location-Aware Multimedia Stories: Turning Spaces into Places. Universidade Cátolica, Portuguesa, pp. 72–93 (2008)
19. Nyman, S.R., Szymczynska, P.: Meaningful activities for improving the wellbeing of people with dementia: beyond mere pleasure to meeting fundamental psychological needs. Perspect. Public Health **136**(2), 99–107 (2016)
20. Pinchbeck, D.: Dear esther: an interactive ghost story built using the source engine. In: Joint International Conference on Interactive Digital Storytelling (2008)
21. Pittarello, F.: Designing a context-aware architecture for emotionally engaging mobile storytelling. In: IFIP Conference on Human-Computer Interaction (2011)
22. Prince, M.J.: World Alzheimer Report 2015: the global impact of dementia: an analysis of prevalence, incidence, cost and trends (2015)
23. Weal, M., Cruickshank, D., Michaelides, D., Millard, D., Roure, D., Howland, K., Fitzpatrick, G.: A card based metaphor for organising pervasive educational experiences. In: Pervasive Computing and Communications Workshops (2007)
24. Whitehouse, P.J.: The end of alzheimer's disease - from biochemical pharmacology to ecopsychosociology: a personal perspective. Biochem. Pharmacol. **88**, 677–681 (2014)

Affective Classification of Gaming Activities Coming from RPG Gaming Sessions

Fabrizio Balducci[(✉)] and Costantino Grana

Dipartimento di Ingegneria "Enzo Ferrari", Università degli Studi di Modena
e Reggio Emilia, Via Vivarelli 10, 41125 Modena, MO, Italy
{fabrizio.balducci,costantino.grana}@unimore.it

Abstract. Each human activity involves feelings and subjective emotions: different people will perform and sense the same task with different outcomes and experience; to understand this experience, concepts like Flow or Boredom must be investigated using objective data provided by methods like electroencephalography. This work carries on the analysis of EEG data coming from brain-computer interface and videogame "Neverwinter Nights 2": we propose an experimental methodology comparing results coming from different off-the-shelf machine learning techniques, employed on the gaming activities, to check if each affective state corresponds to the hypothesis fixed in their formal design guidelines.

Keywords: Classification · EEG · Brain-computer interfaces · Games

1 Introduction

The concepts of 'play' and 'learn' are strictly connected at various degrees: the best method to learn how to safely execute a task is to transform an assignment in a playing activity from which to gain experience for future goals [7]: this is the basis of the *gamification* and *serious gaming* theories which try to introduce playful aspects in all the daily interactive tasks. Lindley [4] defines a game as a goal-directed and competitive activity conducted with agreed rules: "to play" involves learning the internal rules and mechanics that characterize its dynamics and denote each game genre (the gameplay); it becomes crucial to consider player's feelings and preferences to personalize the player experience tailoring each gaming session to specific needs and desires.

Studies from Mandryk *et al.* [11] have successfully demonstrated how psychophysiological techniques (like EEG) evidence human emotions and cognitive activity. The terms "affect" and "emotion" are often used interchangeably and refer to a short-time emotional peak while a "mood" or "affective state" denotes a continuous lasting emotional trend which may involve more emotions and may influence the reactions [6]. Brainwaves allow to evaluate basic emotions and infer the affective states that a subject experiences. A useful scheme to evaluate basic emotions is the *Circumplex model of affect* by Russell *et al.* [14]. In the

© Springer International Publishing AG 2017
F. Tian et al. (Eds.): Edutainment 2017, LNCS 10345, pp. 93–100, 2017.
https://doi.org/10.1007/978-3-319-65849-0_11

field of computer science BCI has been used with various purposes like measure mnemonic and cognitive efforts [8], classify tasks [10] and improve usability [15]. In this paper we use different machine learning approaches to infer, from organized EEG data, the affective state (namely Boredom or Flow) experienced by the player: different classifiers are compared and tested on two game levels designed to induce specific sets of emotions. In this study we use a virtual world as research environments because it is cheap and easy to monitor and control, but it is easy to extend the proposed methodology to real-world (learning) tasks, for example by designing different time-limited versions of them and integrate the classic evaluation methodologies (interviews, think aloud, cognitive walkthrough) with objective evaluation coming from physiological data.

Section 2 summarizes the two proposed game levels and Sect. 3 briefly illustrates the technical system architecture, the experimental setup and the data format. Section 4 describes the proposed methodology for data analysis and Sect. 5 shows the classification results from three machine learning classifiers; finally, conclusions and suggestions for future work are drawn in Sect. 6.

2   Affective Design for Role-Playing Videogames

As shown in Lankoski [9] the RPG genre is based on statistics, object inventory and environmental exploration and its gameplay focuses on strong story plot, choices, skill progression, proactive and interactive allies, world exploration, people collaboration, interaction based on dialogues.

The works of Balducci et al. [1,2] takes inspiration from what Nacke et al. [12] has experienced with First-Person Shooter (FPS) genre: two sets of formal design guidelines, with one of their possible development, were proposed for a RPG game with the aim to induce the Boredom affective state and the Flow one.

Csíkszentmihályi [5] defines *Boredom* like a state in which player's skills are greater than required: the proposed game level features linearity and

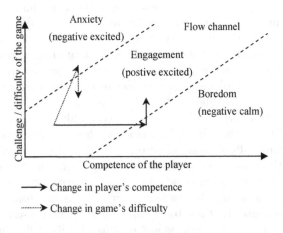

Fig. 1. The flow zone

Fig. 2. The same activity (dialogue) differently developed for the two game levels

repetitiveness with poor gratification, minimal plot-story, weak visual assets, plain dialogues (Fig. 2) and unnecessary allies.

The notion of *Flow* is characterized by constant balance between challenges and skills: hard challenges will produce *anxiety* while very high skills will increase the perceived boredom (Chanel *et al.* [3], Fig. 1). The proposed game level features complex dialogues and multiple goals, proactive and interactive allies which helps to accomplish profitable activities while the level structure and the visual assets encourage environmental exploration (Fig. 3).

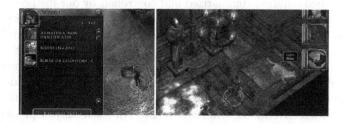

Fig. 3. Activities in the flow game level: "chest opened" and "group fight" with allies

3   Experimental Setup

The Emotiv EPOC headset is a wireless neuro-signal system with 14 wet sensors (+2 reference) capable of detecting brainwaves at 128 Hz sequential sampling rate; sensors are placed around the pre-frontal and frontal brain regions according to the international 10–20 standard system The headset exposes two type of data: the raw (from each sensor) and the pre-classified by internal algorithms (Engagement, Excitement, Frustration, Meditation, Long-Term Excitement); to characterize the gaming activities we will consider the second set.

Neverwinter Nights 2 has a visual level editor with a scripting language that allows to manage internal game variables and permits to customize the User Interface. We used the NWNX [16] tool to deploy a C++ plugin that permits the communication between the game and the headset allowing textual messages exchange in the server version of the game; in this way, a game script calls the extern plugin to iteratively manage the internal (game variables) and the external (EEG) data. The scheme of the system architecture is in Fig. 4.

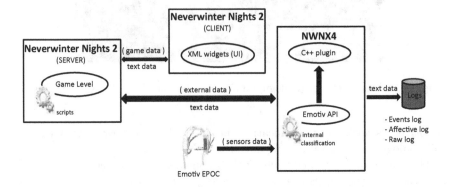

Fig. 4. The architecture for the data gathering tool

The experiment has a two-treatment (boredom/flow) within-subject design, with 'game level' as independent variable factor; the dependent variables are the five pre-classified emotion summarized and controlled by our method.

The subjects involved are 19 students (13 male, 6 female) which play both game levels in each session. The *Setup* step consists in headset and sensors placing with signal tuning and, after this, a brief explanation about the study is provided followed by a pre-questionnaire about subject's gaming preferences; next the *Tutorial* game level allows to familiarize with the commands and the user-interface (we also consider this steps a way to induce relaxation and a neutral initial affective mood, similarly to [13,17]). Each subject plays with the same game character with all RPG statistics set to average values and, at the end of a session, a post-questionnaire about the player experience is compiled.

After each experiment we have different data sources: a video capture of the gaming session, the pre- and post-questionnaires and three textual files featuring the synchronized game and EEG data.

The *events log* contains at each row the timestamp and the tag of the occurred event; an entry in *affective log* contains the same timestamp, the game area in which the player was (XY coordinates) and the punctual values of the five internal pre-classified emotions (values in range 0–1) while each row of the *raw log*, similar to the previous, collects the values of the 14 sensors.

4   Proposed Methodology

In order to interpret data which greatly change over time, analyzing a gaming session using all the log entries results impractical due to the time length; furthermore each game activity can have different duration and it is hard to identify a precise moment in which an affective stimulus appears.

Our approach is to split the log, identifying limited sequences for each activity faced during the gaming session: we remove the rows that don't belong to the tasks and events designed with the formal guidelines and, in this way, we can isolate those semantic units of time and make them more easily treatable.

The boredom game level has an average of 14 activities while the flow one offers the double having more activity types (which are *simple/dubbed/riddle dialogue, single/group fight, chest open, skills upgrade* and *stealing task*); notice that the second game level results longer since reaching a flow state requires more time to evolve the RPG gameplay in a natural way to the player's eyes.

We obtain our data by crossing the *events log* with the *affective log*: the first one provides the identifier and the initial time of each activity, while the second provides the affective values, synchronized by the same timestamp.

The fact that each game level has been designed and developed with formal guidelines permits to label as "Flow" or "Boredom" each of their activities depending on the membership: in this way we have a dataset implicitly annotated and so, using binary classification algorithms, it is possible to check if the affective data of an activity are characteristic enough to differentiate among the two levels; if this occurs for a substantial number of activities, then player's emotions have been well manipulated between the gaming sessions.

To describe the affective mood of an activity and use it in a machine-learning algorithm, we take the five pre-classified EEG emotions and, for each of them, we compute five numerical *features*:

- the *angular coefficient* β and the *intercept* α from a regression line, calculated considering the time T as a positive variable which constantly increases on the x-axis; it suggests the presence of an affective trend for the emotion E
- the *Pearson correlation coefficient* between time T and an emotion E: for a sample of n rows, if $r_e > \pm 0.7$ then there is evidence of strong local correlation, direct (positive sign) or inverse (negative sign).
- the *arithmetic mean* $\overline{E}$ and the *variance* σ_E^2 that give quantitative information on the affective values of emotion E.

This results in a 790×25 predictors matrix M: rows represent the labeled activities (277 boredom, 513 flow) and columns the features (five for each emotion); we balance this training dataset increasing the boredom cases by randomly sampling 236 examples from the original ones, finally giving a 1026×25 matrix.

5   Classification and Results

Three supervised classification techniques have been tested, trained with a "leave-one-out" setup: two employ Support Vector Machines (linear and Radial Basis Function kernel) and the third consists in binary Decision Trees. Results are provided in Tables 1, 2 and 3 respectively.

The *Decision Trees* method has the best performance: it is able to correctly separate 96% of the gaming activities, confirming the correctness of design and development phases by following the guidelines and, moreover, the validity of the proposed methodology.

Table 1. SVM-linear classification results

	Boredom	Flow	Tot.
Original events	513 (ext.)	513	1026
Classified events	610	416	1026
True positives	408	311	719
False negatives	105	202	307
Accuracy			0.73%

Table 2. SVM-RBF classification results

	Boredom	Flow	Tot.
Original events	513 (ext.)	513	1026
Classified events	542	484	1026
True positives	489	460	949
False negatives	24	53	77
Accuracy			0.92%

Table 3. Decision trees classification results

	Boredom	Flow	Tot.
Original events	513 (ext.)	513	1026
Classified events	507	519	1026
True positives	488	494	982
False negatives	25	19	44
Recall	0.95%	0.96%	
f1-score	0.96%	0.96%	
Accuracy			0.96%

5.1 Classification for Game Level Areas

Considering the areas by which each game level is composed, from Table 4 and 5 we can understand the best-designed parts: the 90% good classification for boredom areas suggests that they were constantly recognized as repetitive and tedious; it is also remarkable that while the first two areas have the same structure, the third reduces the perceived boredom introducing very small variations.

For the flow game level, the classification performance varies, but it is always above 95%: the correlation grows from 95.4% for the first area up to 98.3% for the fourth one; the second area contains the largest number of activities (163) so we observe a slight decrease with respect to the typical progressive involvement associated to the flow affective state (the fifth smallest area is not significant since it was reached by only 3 subjects).

5.2 Classification for Activity Types

Tables 6 and 7 show which activity types are the best classified: in the boredom game level *chest opened* is the best classified (96.7%) followed by *dialogue* (95.5%) while all classification ratings are over 93%.

In the flow game level, with the activities specifically developed for its gameplay, *stealing action*, *skills upgrade* and *dubbed dialogue* are 100% but the first two have a reduced extent; also here *chest opened* (98.8%) is the best of the activities followed by *group fight* (97%); all classification ratings are over 94%.

Table 4. Mood-congruent events by area: boredom game level

	Total (ext.)	Correct	Rate
area1	176	165	93.7%
area2	211	207	98.1%
area3	126	116	92.1%
Tot.	513	488	95.1%

Table 5. Mood-congruent events by area: flow game level

	Total	Correct	Rate
area1	130	124	95.4%
area2	163	159	97.5%
area3	157	150	95.5%
area4	60	59	98.3%
area5	3	2	66.7%
Tot.	513	494	96.3%

Table 6. Mood-congruent events by type: boredom game level

	Total (ext.)	Correct	Rate
Dialogue	224	214	95.5%
Single fight	136	127	93.4%
Chest opened	153	147	96.7%
Tot.	513	488	95.1%

Table 7. Mood-congruent events by type: flow game level

	Total	Correct	Rate
Dubbed dialogue	46	46	100%
Riddle dialogue	18	17	94.4%
Dialogue	159	152	95.6%
Single fight	153	144	94.1%
Fight vs. a group	37	36	97.3%
Chest opened	85	84	98.8%
Skills upgrade	11	11	100%
Stealing action	4	4	100%
Tot.	513	494	96.3%

6 Conclusions and Future Work

The positive results prove that well-designed formal guidelines can help to manipulate emotions and moods, that the proposed methodology effectively handles the time-duration issues and that good affective experimentations are possible even with cheap and easy-to-buy headsets. Finally it results that EEG data (although after the pre-classification of frequencies) can be effectively treated by the robust and reliable machine learning methods exploited here.

The next steps will expand this study to the gamification of real-world serious tasks (medical, teaching), even managing the raw data; furthermore, analyzing differences between male and female subjects can help product-placement and market segmentation.

References

1. Balducci, F., Grana, C., Cucchiara, R.: Classification of affective data to evaluate the level design in a role-playing videogame. In: 2015 7th International Conference on Games and Virtual Worlds for Serious Applications (VS-Games), Skovde, pp. 1–8 (2015)

2. Balducci, F., Grana, C., Cucchiara, R.: Affective level design for a role-playing videogame evaluated by a brain-computer interface and machine learning methods. Vis. Comput. **33**(4), 413–427 (2017). http://dx.doi.org/10.1007/s00371-016-1320-2

3. Chanel, G., Rebetez, C., Bétrancourt, M., Pun, T.: Boredom, engagement and anxiety as indicators for adaptation to difficulty in games. In: Proceedings of the 12th International Conference on Entertainment and Media in the Ubiquitous Era, pp. 13–17. MindTrek 2008. ACM, New York (2008)

4. Craigh, L.: Game taxonomies: a high level framework for game analysis and design. Gamasutra. www.gamasutra.com/features/20031003/lindley_01.shtml

5. Csikszentmihalyi, M.: Beyond boredom and anxiety. Jossey-Bass (2000)

6. Frasca, G.: Simulation versus narrative: introduction to ludology. In: The Video Game Theory Reader, pp. 221–236. Routledge, New York (2003)

7. Gee, J.P.: Learning and games. Ecol. Games Connecting Youth Games Learn. **3**, 21–40 (2008)

8. Grimes, D., Tan, D.S., Hudson, S.E., Shenoy, P., Rao, R.P.: Feasibility and pragmatics of classifying working memory load with an electroencephalograph. In: Proceedings of the SIGCHI Conference on Human Factors in Computing Systems, pp. 835–844. ACM (2008)

9. Lankoski, P.: Models for story consistency and interestingness in single-player RPGS. In: Proceedings of International Conference on Making Sense of Converging Media, AcademicMindTrek 2013, pp. 246:246–246:253. ACM, New York (2013)

10. Lee, J.C., Tan, D.S.: Using a low-cost electroencephalograph for task classification in HCI research. In: Proceedings of the 19th Annual ACM Symposium on User Interface Software and Technology, UIST 2006, New York, NY, USA, pp. 81–90 (2006)

11. Mandryk, R.L., Inkpen, K.M.: Physiological indicators for the evaluation of co-located collaborative play. In: Proceedings of the 2004 ACM Conference on Computer Supported Cooperative Work, pp. 102–111. ACM (2004)

12. Nacke, L., Stellmach, S., Lindley, C.: Electroencephalographic assessment of player experience: A pilot study in affective ludology. Simul. Gaming **42**(5), 632–655 (2011)

13. Obbink, M., Gürkök, H., Plass-Oude Bos, D., Hakvoort, G., Poel, M., Nijholt, A.: Social interaction in a cooperative brain-computer interface game. In: Camurri, A., Costa, C. (eds.) INTETAIN 2011. LNICSSITE, vol. 78, pp. 183–192. Springer, Heidelberg (2012). doi:10.1007/978-3-642-30214-5_20

14. Russell, J.A.: A circumplex model of affect. J. Pers. Soc. Psychol. **39**(6), 1161 (1980)

15. Smith, M.E., Gevins, A., Brown, H., Karnik, A., Du, R.: Monitoring task loading with multivariate eeg measures during complex forms of human-computer interaction. Hum. Factors J. Hum. Factors Ergon. Soc. **43**(3), 366–380 (2001)

16. Stieger, I.: Neverwinter nights extender v. 4. http://www.nwnx.org/, http://www.nwnx.org/

17. Vachiratamporn, V., Moriyama, K., Fukui, K., Numao, M.: An implementation of affective adaptation in survival horror games. In: 2014 IEEE Conference on Computational Intelligence and Games, CIG 2014, Dortmund, Germany, 26–29 August 2014, pp. 1–8 (2014)

Application of Virtual Simulation Technology in Maintenance Training

Qiang Song$^{(\boxtimes)}$, Jianda Zhang, Chunpeng Li, and Zhaoqi Wang

Institute of Computing Technology of the Chinese Academy of Sciences,
University of Chinese Academy of Sciences, Beijing 100190, China
songqiang@ict.ac.cn

Abstract. The rising complexity of large-scale machines means higher skill requirements for maintenance workers. Thence training more workers with practiced maintenance skills is significant to those manufacturers and service providers. This article proposes *a method to simulate virtual human's motion synthesis* in virtual maintenance through researching on the virtual simulation technology, and then *implements a virtual maintenance simulation analysis system* which can be used to instruct the training for maintenance workers.

Keywords: Virtual maintenance · Virtual human · Behavior planning · Human kinematics · Ergonomics analysis

1 Introduction

With the advance of science and technology, the complexity of large-scale equipment is rapidly rising and the equipment maintenance diculty is also greatly increased. Therefore, maintenance training for workers has become an important part of producing processes. Virtual maintenance is a technology based on virtual reality which simulates the maintenance processes through establishing maintenance operator models and creating virtual scenes so that it can help workers to master the maintenance skills without any entity machines.

Virtual maintenance technology was firstly used in the field of military and aerospace. In the 1900s, the NSNA trained their astronauts by using the virtual maintenance system and finally succeeded in completing the Hubble telescope maintenance tasks [1]; In order to guarantee the reliability of airplanes, Boeing Company established the Virtual Reality Lab to help designers to check the feasibility of maintenance tasks so that it can reduce the costs of design changes [2]. In research field, the Virtual Environment Center in University of Salford researched on the simulation of interactive assembly and maintenance evaluation to help the maintenance training. In recent years, Tang Zhi-bo and his teammates did their research on hand recognition in virtual maintenance training [3];

Fund Supported Num: CXJJ-15M022, KFZD-Sw-407.

F. Tian et al. (Eds.): Edutainment 2017, LNCS 10345, pp. 101–107, 2017.
https://doi.org/10.1007/978-3-319-65849-0_12

Zhao Chao came up with a control method of concurrent operation for collaborative virtual maintenance [4]; Yuan-Yuan researched on the application of gesture in virtual maintenance [5].

Note that virtual human is the main factor in maintenance processes, so the model and analysis of virtual human is the key to the whole simulation. This paper analyzes the human behavior in maintenance processes deeply and demonstrates a method to simulate the virtual human motion synthesis and then implements a virtual maintenance simulation system to help the trains for maintenance.

2   Key Technology of Maintenance Process Simulation

2.1   Maintenance Task Modeling

Virtual maintenance simulates the changes and the interactions among human, machine and environment. The whole maintenance process can be considered as a sequential combination of multiple maintenance operations on the timeline. The cost would be extremely high if trying to control the virtual human by controlling its every joint. Therefore, this paper proposes the maintenance process hierarchical controlling method to guarantee the simulation running efficiently. The maintenance process hierarchical controlling method divides the whole process into three logic layers: the task layer, the instruction layer and the therblig layer.

The task layer is the most advanced abstraction of virtual human behaviors which presents the whole progress of virtual human's motions from the beginning state to the target state. It usually contains movement, posture adjustment, handling, maintenance and other more actions. These actions can be considered as basic units of the whole task. They consist of the instruction layer and are called maintenance instructions. In the entire virtual maintenance simulation, each maintenance task is defined by different arrangement of these maintenance instructions. The therblig layer is composed by different maintenance therbligs. Maintenance therbligs, the indivisible and semantically distinct units of motions, are the bottom expressions of virtual human behaviors. A maintenance instruction can be seen as a combination and repetition of several maintenance therbligs.

2.2   Virtual Human Behavior Planning

Virtual human behavior planning is a significant issue in the research of interaction between human motions and virtual environment. In maintenance scenes, virtual human's behavior mainly contains its own behavior and the interaction behavior with the environment. The interaction behavior cannot only change the human's status but also the machine's and environment. To generate motion sequences (maintenance instructions) by combining different therbligs, this paper adopts the interactive task planning method based on interactive behavior graph [6] to synthesize different maintenance therbligs into maintenance instructions.

In this method, virtual human behavior planning are abstracted into a limited stage Markov Decision Process (MDP). Different maintenance therbligs are considered as different states and the rational behaviors in this state are seen as the actions so that we can get the transition state-action graph called Interactive Behavior Graph. Then we adopts Reinforcement Learning [7] method to get the optimal policy to synthesize complete maintenance instructions. The main steps of the algorithm are as follows:

(1) Abstract different maintenance independent therbligs as different states in data preprocessing stage and then construct the Interactive Behavior Graph according to the interactive feathers between therbligs and environments.

(2) In the learning stage, define the state and action sets and construct the reward function firstly. Under the instruction of Policy Iteration in the Q-Learning algorithm [7], update the state-value function in each iteration. Then we can get the optimal motion policy.

(3) Given the initial state and target state of the virtual human, we can synthesize the therbligs into a motion sequence according to the optimal motion policy above (Fig. 1).

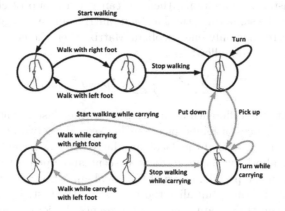

Fig. 1. This figure shows an interactive behavior graph. The vertices represent virtual human's current states and edges are the rational behaviour can be done in each state. The black edges are the basic behavior of the virtual human and the red are the interactive actions with the environment. (Color figure online)

2.3 Parametric Synthesis for Maintenance Therbligs

Virtual human is a complex model with high degrees of freedom. Thence creating a maintenance therbligs dataset can help reducing the complexity, improving simulation efficiency and making the behaviors more vivid. To obtain maintenance therbligs, we use the Vicon optical body movement capture device to collect human body three-dimensional motion data and collect multiple differentiated action data for each therblig to implement the parametric synthesis for

maintenance therbligs. For instance, when virtual human walks, different parameters can correspond to different strides. What's the human pose at this strides?
Actually, the essence of the parametric synthesis for maintenance therbligs is to
solve a problem that how to synthesize the target human pose through controlling limbs' positions. It belongs to the category of human inverse kinematics.

To solve the problem above, a method to analyze the pose space based on self-
organizing map (SOM) is adopted firstly. The SOM is a kind of neural network,
which can transform the input of arbitrary dimension into a low-dimensional
discrete grid subject to a neighborhood preserving constraint. We expand the
SOM model to unit quaternion space and then analyze the complex pose space
which contains multiple different motion types through divide and conquer strategy. This method combines the structure analysis and non-linear dimensionality
reduction properly and can not only construct rational pose spaces, but also can
deal with the complex pose spaces.

However, rational pose space is just a static presentation of human motion,
we also need to learn its change laws. Therefore, we use the method based on
Jacobian Matrix Learning [8] to solve the problem. It mainly contains two steps:

(1) In the learning stage, reduce the dimension of the pose space first and
    perform clustering operations, then we can get a group of cluster centers
    $\{W_k\}_{k=1}^n$, at the same time, the Jacobian Matrix can be also gotten. Assum-
    ing each cluster has only one Jacobian Matrix, then the error function can
    be formulated as the follow:

$$E = \frac{1}{2}\sum e^2 = \frac{1}{2}\sum ||\Delta p - J^+ \cdot \Delta g||^2$$

    Δp represents the difference from any pose to the cluster center, Δg repre-
    sents the differences of joints' positions between these two poses. J^+ repre-
    sents the pseudoinverse of the Jacobian Matrix. In this formulate. Optimize
    the formula above by using gradient descent and update the J^+ in each
    iteration, then the pseudoinverse of the Jacobian Matrix can be learned.
(2) In the synthesis stage, Initialize the pose $P_0 = W_c$ first, W_c is the nearest
    pose to the constraint target pose. g represents the joints' positions of the
    target pose. Compute the joints' positions of the current pose through human
    kinematics $g_i = f(P_i)$ and get the differences of the target and current poses
    $\Delta g_i = g - g_i$. Then according to the initial pose P_0 and the following iteration
    formula

$$P_{i+1} = P_i + \alpha \cdot J^+ \cdot \Delta g_i$$

    When Δg_i is tiny enough or not changed any more, the current P_i can be
    seen as the target pose. α is represents the learning rate– a number between
    0 and 1.

2.4   Ergonomics Analysis

The ergonomics analysis, combined with the interactions between virtual
human and environment, analyzes the physiological state, safety, comfort and

accessibility of virtual workers and then feedbacks all aspects of the information of virtual workers so that it can instruct the maintenance training.

In maintenance processes, the operations cannot go beyond the visibility and reachability of virtual human, otherwise the maintenance task could not be normally completed. The visibility of virtual human depends on its cone range and the head rotation range. The reachability of virtual human depends on the relative positon between virtual human and the target objects if there are rational solution spaces or not. Force analysis is to calculate the forces and moments on virtual humans each joint in maintenance processes. It can guarantee the force on each joint in a safe range to avoid workers being too tired or injured.

3   Virtual Maintenance Simulation System

3.1   The Design of the Maintenance Simulation System

The main target of virtual maintenance simulation system is to simulate the maintenance process and analyze the ergonomics. To complete the target above, the system is designed into two parts: maintenance simulation and simulation analysis. The maintenance simulation part is to build a virtual reality simulation environment based on existing Pro/E model [9], including establishing the 3D models of equipment and virtual, dividing maintenance tasks into maintenance instructions and executing these instruction in order. Simulation analysis refers to evaluating the feasibility of maintenance plans, and analyzing the ergonomics.

According to the design, we implement the whole system by dividing it into three layers: engine layer, simulation layer and analysis layer. The engine layer mainly includes the three-dimensional graphics engine, the physical simulation and the realistic drawing. The simulation layer consists of the simulation of the attitude of the equipment model, the maintenance attitude of the virtual man, the space environment and the virtual maintenance process. And the analysis layer contains the evaluation of the maintenance plan and real-time display of evaluation results.

3.2   System Implementation and Application Demonstration

To facilitate the realization of virtual maintenance simulation system, Neoaxis3D is adopted as the graphics engine and C# is used as the programing language. In this paper, we also offer a demostration in the mantenance of aircrafts to show how this system works in maintence training.

In this maintenance scene, we set the virtual machine in model editor and use scene editor to build the virtual environment. Then build a new maintenance task and set the parameters of each instructions. When compiling the maintenance task, the system will edit virtual human's behaviors according to the initial pose and the order of instructions by using the method of virtual human behavior plan referred in Sect. 1. Then the whole simulation process will be shown in the form of animation and the users can watch the maintenance process in any perspective by moving the observation point. At the same time, the system will analyze the ergonomics in real time and show the results on the screen. Through this process, workers can learn the whole process, grasp the key of maintenance and improve their maintenance skills (Fig. 2).

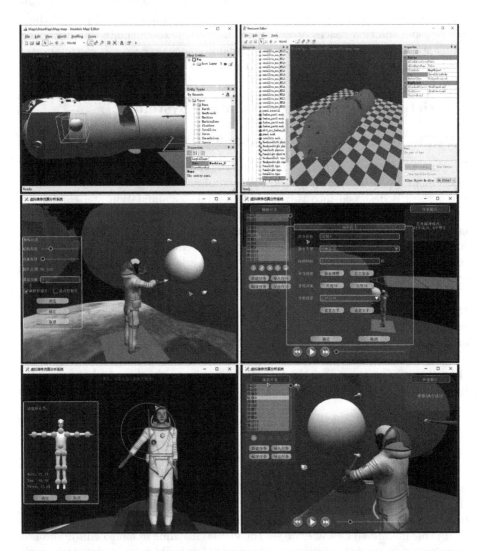

Fig. 2. These Screenshots show an application of virtual maintenance training which can instruct astronauts to repair the aircraft by using our system

4   Conclusion

By using virtual simulation technology, setting 3D models of machines and human and simulating the maintenance process, this paper designs and implements a virtual maintenance simulation system to instruct maintenance training. This system, adopting the methods of virtual human behavior plan and parametric synthesis for maintenance therbligs, simplifies the controlling and interactives between virtual human and machine and improves the simulation efficiency greatly. This paper provides some new ideas and shows a bright future of virtual simulation technology in maintenance training.

References

1. Hubble's Optics. http://hubblesite.org/
2. Boeing. http://www.boeing.com/
3. Zhi-Bo, T.: Hand recognition in virtual maintenance training. J. Comput. Eng. Des. **32**, 4278–4288 (2012)
4. Chao, Z., Xing-Xin, L.: Control method of concurrent operation for collaborative virtual maintenance. J. Comput. Syst. Appl. **23**, 198–201 (2012)
5. Yuan, Y.: Control research on the application of gesture in virtual maintenance. In: 2015 4th International Conference on Computer Science and Network Technology (ICCSNT), pp. 1375–1378 (2015)
6. Dan, Z.: Research on Behavior Planning based on Virtual Maintenance for Virtual Human. Degree Thesis of Chinese Academy of Sciences (2012)
7. Sutton, R.S., Barto, A.G.: Reinforcement Learning: An Introduction. The MIT Press, Cambridge (2012)
8. ChunPeng, L.: Research on Virtual Human Motion Synthesis Using Real Human Motion Characteristics. Degree Thesis of Chinese Academy of Sciences (2008)
9. Pro/ENGINEER. http://www.ptc.com/cad/pro-engineer/

The Gamification of Cybersecurity Training

Natalie Coull[1]([⊠]), Iain Donald[1], Ian Ferguson[1], Eamonn Keane[3], Thomas Mitchell[1], Oliver V. Smith[1], Erin Stevenson[1], and Paddy Tomkins[2]

[1] Abertay University, Bell Street, Dundee DD1 1HG, Scotland
n.coull@abertay.ac.uk
[2] Droman Crime Solutions Ltd., 4.9 Techcube, 1 Summerhall, Edinburgh EH9 1PL, Scotland
[3] Police Scotland, Scottish Crime Campus, Craignethan Drive, Gartcosh G69 8AE, Scotland

Abstract. Due to the rapidly and continued evolving nature of technology, there is a constant need to update police officers' training in cyber security to ensure that the UK continues to be a secure place to live and do business. Rather than deliver traditional classroom-based training, our project assesses the effectiveness of the delivery of cyber security through the use of games based learning to simulate cybercrimes and provide training in incident response. The aim of our research is to transform the delivery of first responder training in tackling cybercrime.

Through the use of a Game Jam and subsequent prototype development, we have trialed training materials that are based on serious games technology. The game poses a common incident reported to the police, for example the problem of a virtual person receiving offensive messages via Facebook and the training reflects the dialogue with that person and the technical steps to ensure that a copy of the evidence has been preserved for further investigation. Evaluation has been conducted with local police officers. Overall, this approach to the large-scale provision of training (potentially to a whole force) is shown to offer potential.

Keywords: Gamification · Serious games · Cybersecurity

1 Introduction

Many of the crimes frequently reported to the Police involve some aspect of digital technology. Cybercrime is no longer limited to describing criminal events where a computer or digital device is the target or tool, e.g. hacking or identity theft. Indeed, technology can play a key part in virtually any criminal investigation. For example, Police Officers responding to reports of a murder may need to investigate the mobile phone of a victim to establish which route they took to their destination, and the browsing history of the murderer could be used to establish intent. Consequently, crime scenes in the 21st century can contain a number of different digital devices, all of which may contain crucial evidence. First responders (those police officers who are the first ones on the scene when dealing with an incident) may be tasked with identifying and seizing those devices and due to the volatile nature of digital evidence, how they interact with those devices can impact the availability and integrity of evidence. Training police officers in the appropriate handling of digital devices is crucial to ensure that law

F. Tian et al. (Eds.): Edutainment 2017, LNCS 10345, pp. 108–111, 2017.
https://doi.org/10.1007/978-3-319-65849-0_13

enforcement can manage crime effectively. Although classroom-based training can be an effective mechanism for delivering cybercrime training, it is expensive and time consuming. There is a clear need to explore alternatives to traditional classroom based training.

2 Gamification of Cybersecurity Training

Computer games afford visually rich, interactive and immersive environments that allow exploration of complex problem spaces, both for entertainment purposes and in serious contexts. Existing research evidences that games can be engaging for a variety of different users [1] and are an effective mechanism for encouraging participation in activities. It is also shown that games enable users to interact with an environment that replicates the real world and have a positive impact on motivation, enjoyment, positive feelings and happiness [2], which consequently can encourage learning and retention of knowledge [3, 4].

2.1 Our Solution

Ensuring timely and cost-effective training of cybersecurity to police officers is a key priority for many law enforcement agencies. Serious games is one method that can deliver engaging and measurable training in a relatively cheap manner. A collaboration between academia, industry and law enforcement has led to the completion of a pilot project, described here. We have created a prototype using 3 crime scenarios and conducted an initial evaluation with local law enforcement personnel. Through this project, we have aimed to demonstrate that serious games can provide continually updated training in a way that is engaging for the user, which doesn't take officers off the streets for days at a time to sit in a classroom, and which can be delivered at a fraction of the cost of traditional training techniques. Our project, "First Responder's Guide" is a novel fusion of cybersecurity and computer games technology. The first stage in our research, described here, has led to the creation of a prototype that contains a virtual environment with 3 different crime scenarios. This stage consisted of 3 core activities: (1) Game jam, (2) Prototype development, (3) Initial evaluation.

Activity 1: The Game Jam

A game jam, typically popular in the gaming community, is an event where a mix of software developers, artists and game designers meet in a physical location to create one or more games over a short period of time (typically 1 to 2 days). These game jams provide an excellent opportunity to focus participants' efforts on developing games around a particular theme and challenge the participants to develop rapid prototypes which can be presented to peers and industry at the end of the game jam.

Our Game Jam was delivered over a 2 day period for the first stage of our prototype development. We used the Game Jam as a mechanism for identifying a broad range of game ideas and designs that could be utilized in a serious games environment to train Police Officers in responding to cybersecurity incidents. We invited students from across all our digital degree courses to participate in the Game Jam. At the beginning of the game jam, we provided students with a project brief, which outlined the challenges involved in the seizure, acquisition and analysis of digital devices. The students then formed teams to produce their 'asset', i.e. their proposed game to train police officers in cybersecurity. At the end of the 2-day period, each team presented their asset to a team of judges and were scored according to their proposed design, computer graphics, modularity and adaptability. The winning team were then invited to participate in the next stage of the project: Prototype Development.

Activity 2: Prototype Development
The next stage of the project involved developing the winning asset from the game jam into a prototype. The student team worked with representatives from Police Scotland to develop the scenarios which were incorporated into the prototype. The scenarios were developed to simulate the types of crimes involving a digital element that Police Scotland typically encounter. The scenarios can be classified as:

1. A pre-planned operation involving indecent images of children.
2. A reactive enquiry in which a complainant has received threatening messages via social media.
3. A spontaneous enquiry involving an attempted fraud of a business via spear-phishing.

Each scenario is built around a virtual environment, which the player can explore using either a 2nd or 3rd navigation mode. Within the environment are various different objects, depending on the particular scenario. Objects include laptops, mobile phones, credit cards, smart televisions etc. The user is able to inspect the objects and is presented with various different options for interacting with the objects, for example the user can chose to switch off a mobile phone, place it in a faraday cage or seize it for further investigation. For each level of game play, the user is presented with a description of the particular scenario, prior to entering the virtual property. After inspecting the virtual crime scene, the user can choose to leave the property and is then presented with their scores and feedback as to the appropriate course of action.

Activity 3: Evaluation
A short, qualitative evaluation was conducted with a small group of ten police officers to gather feedback on the appropriateness of the prototype. The purpose of the evaluation was to establish police officers current knowledge of cybercrime and incident response and their attitude towards using games for training. Each participating officer was interviewed using hypothetical scenarios, prior to playing the game. Scores for each participant were recorded during game play, before completing a questionnaire on game play and usability.

Results
Although all participants had received some form of training in cybersecurity prior to playing the game, there was some disparity between the interview answers and game play answers. Analysis of the questionnaire responses indicated that some participants found the wording of the questions vague. The navigation controls were also challenging

for some participants. This feedback will be invaluable for the next stage of the game development, which will focus on refining the scenarios and in-game text, and removing the joy-stick navigation option so that the controls are more typical of a normal smart 'phone application. Overall, participants were overwhelmingly positive about using games for training purposes.

3 Conclusion

Cyber security is a rapidly developing field with increasing impact on society and attracting the challenges of large and complex data sets on networked computing devices. This impact is reflected in patterns in crime: most of the crimes that Police Scotland investigate now involve computer technology to some extent and so training in this area is imperative. Typical classroom based training can be expensive and time consuming. Using serious game to train police officers in cybersecurity is a viable option. The prototype developed as part of our project is a novel fusion of cyber security and computer games technology to provide a new training tool that harnesses the interactivity of serious games. Importantly, this tool has demonstrated the potential for more effective training to be delivered at a significantly reduced cost, to more staff and without the need for lengthy and expensive classroom-based sessions. Improving the cybersecurity skills of law enforcement personnel will lead to improved response to cybercrime and better preservation of digital evidence.

References

1. Zelinski, E.M., Reyes, R.: Cognitive benefits of computer games for older adults. Gerontechnol. Int. J. Fundam. Aspects Technol. Serve Ageing Soc. **8**(4), 220–235 (2009)
2. Glover, I.: Play as you learn: gamification as a technique for motivating learners. In: Proceedings of World Conference on Educational Multimedia, Hypermedia and Telecommunications 2013. AACE, Chesapeake (2013)
3. Kumar, J.: Gamification at work: designing engaging business software. In: Marcus, A. (ed.) DUXU 2013. LNCS, vol. 8013, pp. 528–537. Springer, Heidelberg (2013). doi: 10.1007/978-3-642-39241-2_58
4. Mekler, E.D., Brühlmann, F., Opwis, K., Tuch, A.N.: Do points, levels and leaderboards harm intrinsic motivation? An empirical analysis of common gamification elements. In: Proceedings of the First International Conference on Gameful Design, Research, and Applications, pp. 66–73. ACM (2013)

Graphics, Imaging and Applications

3D Point Cloud Classification Based on Discrete Conditional Random Field

Xinying Liu[1,2], Hongjun Li[3(✉)], Weiliang Meng[1,2], Shiming Xiang[1,2],
and Xiaopeng Zhang[1,2(✉)]

[1] NLPR-LIAMA, Institute of Automation, CAS, Beijing, China
xiaopeng.zhang@ia.ac.cn
[2] University of Chinese Academy of Sciences, Beijing, China
[3] Beijing Forestry University, Beijing, China
lihongjun69@bjfu.edu.cn

Abstract. The advantage of the conditional random field (CRF) lies in the construction of the discriminant model and efficient parameter optimization. In the topic of the classification of three-dimensional point cloud, the parameters of the CRF are usually learnt through Gradient Descent and Belief Propagation, in order to optimize the objective energy function of the CRF. These optimization methods do not guarantee the highest global classification accuracy with a high classification accuracy on the smaller classes. In addition, differential features of the point cloud are not sufficiently utilized. In this paper, we use the local geometric shape features to construct the CRF, including the nearest neighbor tetrahedral volume, Gaussian curvature, the neighbourhood normal vector consistency and the neighbourhood minimum principal curvature direction consistency. We propose four discrete criteria for CRF parameter optimization to design the explicit functions, and present concrete solution procedures, in which Monte Carlo method and supervised learning method are employed to estimate the CRF parameters iteratively. Experimental results show that our method can be applied to the classification of the scene of 3D point cloud with plants, especially under the proposed second criterion that maximizing the accuracy with interclass weights. It can be used to improve significantly the classification accuracy of small scale point sets when different classes have great disparity in number.

Keywords: Point cloud classification · Feature extraction · Conditional Random Field · Parameter optimization criterion · Confusion matrix

1 Introduction

Point cloud refers to a set of multiple vertices with coordinate information, and the vertices position coordinates set sampled from the surface of 3D objects is a typical type of this data. Besides the position coordinate information, other auxiliary information can be attached to each vertex such as the color

© Springer International Publishing AG 2017
F. Tian et al. (Eds.): Edutainment 2017, LNCS 10345, pp. 115–137, 2017.
https://doi.org/10.1007/978-3-319-65849-0_14

information (RGB) or the intensity information. The point cloud data can be from scanning real scenes via terrestrial LiDAR [1] or the airborne 3D laser scanner [2], or reconstructing from the photos based on visual methods [3,4]. With the increasing performance of three-dimensional laser scanners, cameras and other hardware devices in recent years, the acquisition of point cloud data from the objects become easier than ever before, which in turn to promote point cloud analysis and process for widely applying in the industries of measurement, aviation, architecture, gardens, urban planning, digital city, monitoring and etc. Point cloud analysis and processing involves a variety of basic tasks, including point cloud denoising, feature calculation, segmentation, key points and lines recognition, object detection, surface reconstruction [5], registration and visualization, etc. The reconstruction based on the three-dimensional point cloud can generate more realistic three-dimensional models, and bring a stronger sense of immersion in the application of digital entertainment, education and so on.

The point cloud classification is a hot topic of the current research with the deepening needs of the applications. For example, through the analysis of the scene point cloud data, the roads, vegetation, buildings, bridges, vehicles, pedestrians and even windows can be identified. Compared with the image-based target recognition methods, the point cloud data realistically records the three-dimensional information of the objects in the scene, and we can get more accurate parsing results of the scene, which is conducive to the scene semantic analysis and reproduction.

As the basis for understanding the scene, point cloud classification is a difficult problem because of the huge data size, data noise, loss of partial information, and unknown geometric topology of data. Although a lot of related works have been done, the accuracy of point cloud classification is still to be further improved. On the one hand, the existing point cloud feature description methods don't fully introduce the local discriminant information; on the other hand, the existing point cloud classification methods don't combine the global geometric information with the discriminant classification methods effectively.

We adopt the discriminant information based on the both local neighborhood and global model, and improve the performance of point cloud classification by constructing new cloud point feature description methods and make a classification. Specifically, the idea of nearest neighbor classification is introduced into the local neighborhoods of each vertex in the cloud data, and the local geometric shape description method is constructed based on the nearest neighbor tetrahedron volume, the Gaussian curvature, and the pairwise potentials. Then the Conditional Random Field (CRF) model for point cloud data is built and the CRF parameter optimization criteria are designed to improve the classification performance. Experiments show that our discrete criteria for CRF parameter optimization have a better effect on improving the quality of the point cloud classification results, especially the proposed second criterion that based on the maximization accuracy with interclass weights.

2   Related Works

The related works mainly include three aspects: point cloud feature description, point cloud classification based on CRF, and point cloud classification based on pattern analysis.

2.1   Point Cloud Feature Description

The point cloud classification is mainly dependent on the local features of each vertex in the point cloud. The feature vector can be constructed by the 3D shape contexts and the harmonic shape contexts for point cloud shape recognition methods with high dimension eigenvectors [6]. In order to reduce the eigenvectors' dimension, the histogram of the local point cloud feature [7,8] and the surface feature histograms [9] can be used for analysis. The local features of the point cloud that used to build the histograms can be points scatterness, linearity and surfaceness [10]. In addition, normal vectors and the local flatness degree can also be taken as the features for point cloud classification [11]. Weinmann et al. [12] proposed a series of local shape features including the k-nearest neighbor's height difference, density, linearity, planarity, scattering, omni-variance, anisotropy, eigen-entropy, sum of eigenvalues, change of curvature and two-dimensional projection features. Yang et al. [13] proposed using local point cloud depth, density and deviation angles between normals to build local feature descriptor for point cloud recognition. Plaza-Leiva et al. [14] gave a general framework for supervised learning classifiers in which the support region features are defined by the voxels themselves.

2.2   Point Cloud Classification Based on CRF

The Conditional Random Field (CRF) is a probability graph model proposed by Lafferty et al. [15], which can be used to segment or classify sequence data and text. Then Kumar et al. [16] brought it in computer vision and constructed Discriminative Random Fields for region labeling and classification of natural images. Munoz et al. [17] proposed a 3D point cloud classification method based on Directional Associated Markov Network. Shapovalov et al. [2] extended this method to Non-Associated Markov Networks to distinguish vegetation points, and in turn a high-order Markov network is built by Najafi et al. [18]. Besides the position coordinates, echo amplitude, echo width and other property values associated with the vertex can also be used for point cloud classification. Rutzinger et al. [19] used these information to identify the higher plants (trees and shrubs) better. Niemeyer et al. [20] argued that the CRF is a generalization of the Markov random field, and using CRF is more suitable than the Markov random field. Husain et al. [21] classified the indoor point cloud by establishing a CRF. Wolf et al. [22] used the random forest classifier to initialize the unary potentials of the CRF and the parameters related to the pairwise potentials are deduced from the training set, in turn to accomplish indoor point cloud classification. Niemeyerar et al. [23] construct a 2-level CRF model for point cloud classification, where the second layer can correct the initial classification error. Lang et al. [24] proposed an adaptive CRF model to achieve the outdoor point cloud classification. Ni et al. [25] use reflectance-based features, descriptor-based features, and the geometric features for Random Forests in order to classify airborne laser scanning point clouds.

As a typical classification method based on graph discrimination, the graph structure of CRF makes connections between vertices in the point cloud data through local neighbors, which in turn to provide a global discriminant learning model for classification. The core of the CRF lies in the construction of the discriminant model and the efficient parameters optimization. Existing methods mainly use the idea of discriminant regression to construct the discriminant model, which cannot make the best of the distribution of point cloud data. In addition, they mainly use the descending method to solve the parameters, making the result very sensitive to the initial value, gradient updating rate and other factors, and the parameter optimization process is inefficient.

2.3   Point Cloud Classification Based on Pattern Analysis

Besides the CRF model, pattern analysis can also be used for point cloud classification. In recent years, most commonly used discriminant analysis methods in the field of pattern analysis and machine learning have been preliminarily transferred to apply in point cloud classification tasks. Specifically, Wang et al. [26] and Zhang et al. [27] used the Latent Dirichlet Allocation model for point cloud classification; Rodrguezcuenca et al. [28] used anomaly detection algorithm to identify column objects; Deep Convolutional Neural Networks (DCNN) [29] and spindle descriptors [30] were also proposed for point cloud classification method. Kang et al. [31] employed the geometric features from the point clouds with the spectral features from the optical images to train an optimal Bayesian network structure for classification. Maligo et al. [32] proposed a two-layer classification model, with the first layer that a GMM trained in an unsupervised manner and the second layer that corresponds to a grouping of the intermediary classes into final classes. Li et al. [33] showed that the local geometric features of the nearest neighbor tetrahedron volume, Gaussian curvature, point potential energy (neighbourhood normal vectors consistency and the neighbourhood minimum principal curvature directions consistency) had a good effect on point cloud classification. Based on the pattern analysis of these features, we construct our CRF to achieve point cloud classification and improves the classification accuracy.

3   Construction of CRF

In this paper, we use the position coordinate information of the point cloud to construct the CRF in order to determine the classification type of each vertex. Let (x_i, y_i, z_i) denote position of the i-th vertex P_i in the point cloud, and assume that the point cloud data can be divided into m class, denoted by $\mathcal{L} = \{l_1, l_2, \cdots, l_m\}$ respectively. First, we need to extract the local shape features of each vertex in the point cloud.

3.1   Local Shape Features Extraction

The local shape features of the vertex are the basis of the point cloud classification [33], and we mainly use the nearest neighbor tetrahedral volume, the
Gaussian curvature, and pairwise potentials as the local shape features for our
classification.

Nearest neighbor tetrahedral volume. The nearest neighbor tetrahedral
volume $\mathcal{V}_i$ of vertex P_i describes the density and position relation of the nearest
neighbors, which can be calculated as and the mixed product of the three vectors
constructed by three the nearest neighbor P_{1_i}, P_{2_i}, P_{3_i} of the vertex P_i as follows:

$$\mathcal{V}_i = \frac{1}{6}\|(\overrightarrow{P_iP_{1_i}} \times \overrightarrow{P_iP_{2_i}}) \cdot \overrightarrow{P_iP_{3_i}}\| \tag{1}$$

Gaussian curvature. The Gaussian curvature $\mathcal{K}_i$ reflects the bending degree of
the local surface where vertex P_i is located, and the value equals to the product
of two principal curvatures k_{1_i} and k_{2_i}, i.e., $\mathcal{K}_i = k_{1_i}k_{2_i}$. The calculation of the
principal curvature for the vertex P_i in the point cloud can be approximately
calculated as in [34] based on the position information of the k nearest neighbor
vertices of P_i.

Pairwise potentials. Pairwise potentials reflect the relationship between neighborhood pairs, including the neighbourhood normal vectors consistency σ_i and
the neighbourhood minimum principal curvature directions consistency δ_i. The
consistency of the normal vectors between an arbitrary vertex P_i and its k nearest
neighbor $\{P_{j_i}, j = 1, 2, \cdots, k\}$ can be used directly for point cloud classification.
The neighbourhood normals vector consistency σ_i can be denoted by the variance (θ_{j_i}) of the cosine of the angles between the normal vector of P_i and normal
vector of its k nearest neighbourhood P_{j_i} where $j = 1, 2, \cdots, k$).

$$\sigma_i = \frac{1}{k}\Sigma_{j=1}^k(\theta_{j_i} - \overline{\theta}_i)^2 \tag{2}$$

where $\theta_{j_i} = \overrightarrow{n}_i \cdot \overrightarrow{n}_{j_i}$ and $\overline{\theta}_i = (\Sigma_{j=1}^k\theta_{j_i})/k$. Here $\overrightarrow{d}_i$ is the normal vector of P_i,
and $\overrightarrow{n}_{j_i}$ is the normal vector of $P_{j_i}(j = 1, 2, \cdots, k)$.

Similarly, we define the neighbourhood minimum principal curvature directions consistency δ_i as

$$\delta_i = \frac{1}{k}\Sigma_{j=1}^k(\tau_{j_i} - \overline{\tau}_i)^2 \tag{3}$$

where $\tau_j = \overrightarrow{d}_i \cdot \overrightarrow{d}_{j_i}(j = 1, 2, ..., k)$ and $\overline{\tau}_i = (\Sigma_{j=1}^k\tau_{j_i})/k$. Here $\overrightarrow{d}_i$ is the
minimum principal curvature direction of P_i, and $\overrightarrow{d}_{j_i}$ is the minimum principal
curvature direction of $P_{j_i}(j = 1, 2, \cdots, k)$.

According to the above equations, we can get the local shape features of
an arbitrary vertex P_i, i.e., the nearest neighbor tetrahedron volume, Gaussian
curvature, and pairwise potentials, and our CRF can be constructed based on
these features.

3.2   CRF Objective Energy Function

Essentially, the CRF is an undirected graph, denoted as $G = <V, E>$, where V is the vertices set in which every vertex P_i in the point cloud Ω is taken as a vertex of the CRF, and E is the edge set. The user can specify an edge between two points within a certain distance [21]. In our case, considering that the distances between vertices in the point cloud may be non-uniform due to the occlusion, this edge definition may lead to an unconnected graph G, which makes the number of vertices in a subgraph is too small to determine its local shape, even with many isolated points. Therefore, we use the k nearest neighbors $\{P_{j_i}, j = 1, 2, \cdots, k\}$ of vertex P_i to define k edges correspondingly. Note that for vertex P_i and vertex P_j, P_j may be one of P_i's k nearest neighbors, while the reverse may be not true. For each vertex in the graph G, the corresponding degree is no less than k. The typical value of k is 20 in our tests.

As CRF G has the Markov property, i.e., the local shape at any vertex P_i is mainly determined by the P_i's nearest neighbor vertices P_{j_i}, we can construct the objective energy function $\mathcal{E}(\mathcal{L}, \Omega; w)$ based on our extracted features with the neighborhood volume $\mathcal{V}_i$, the Gaussian curvature $\mathcal{K}_i$, the point potential energy (including the neighbourhood normal vectors consistency σ_i and the neighbourhood minimum principal curvature directions consistency δ_i) as follows:

$$\mathcal{E}(\mathcal{L}, \Omega; w) = w_1^{(l)}\mathcal{V}_i + w_2^{(l)}\mathcal{K}_i + w_3^{(l)}\sigma_i + w_4^{(l)}\delta_i \tag{4}$$

Define $w = \{w_1^{(l)}, w_2^{(l)}, w_3^{(l)}, w_4^{(l)}\}$, and the optimal solution of w can be obtained by maximizing the following conditional probability $P(\mathcal{L}|\Omega, w)$ [21].

$$P(\mathcal{L}|\Omega, w) = \frac{e^{\mathcal{E}(\mathcal{L}, \Omega; w)}}{\Sigma_{l \in \mathcal{L}} e^{\mathcal{E}(\mathcal{L}, \Omega; w)}} \tag{5}$$

The optimization process of conditional fandom field (CRF) parameter w can be found in Sect. 3.4, and the final optimized CRF parameter value is denoted as w^*.

3.3   Point Cloud Classification

For the given point cloud Ω and the CRF parameter w^*, the vertex is classified according to the maximum value of the calculated posterior probability [21].

$$\mathcal{L}^* = \arg\max_{l \in \mathcal{L}} P(\mathcal{L}|\Omega, w^*) \tag{6}$$

If both the vertices number n and the classification number m are large, then the number of CRF parameters will be larger, and the computational complexity will be higher. In this case, belief propagation algorithm can be used for approximate calculation [35].

3.4   Parameter Learning

Parameter optimization is the core to the CRF. For a given training set Ω_0 and the identity labels of each vertex $\mathcal{L}_0$, the likelihood function can be constructed by regularized log likelihood probability [21, 36].

$$L(w) = \lambda \|w\|^2 - \Sigma_{l_i \in \mathcal{L}_0} \ln P(l_i | P_i; w) \tag{7}$$

And then we use the gradient method to get the optimal solution. The criterion for CRF parameter optimization in Eq. (7) is the maximum of the correct classification probability (the minimum of the likelihood function). However, the classification accuracy (i.e.,the number of correctly classified vertices) is usually taken as the main criteria for evaluating the classification methods, while minimizing the likelihood function does not necessarily lead to the maximum of classification accuracy. Therefore, we propose a new parameter optimization criterion to maximize the classification accuracy $\varepsilon(w)$, called the parameter optimization criterion I, i.e.

$$w^* = arg \quad \max \; \varepsilon(w) \tag{8}$$

The discrete calculation of this parameter optimization criterion is in the following form:

$$\varepsilon(w) = \frac{1}{n} N(w) = \frac{1}{n} \sum_{j=1}^{m} \sum_{i=1}^{n} \Psi \left(l_j = l^* \right) \tag{9}$$

where

$$l^* = arg \; \max \{ P(l_1 | P_i; w), \cdots, P(l_m | P_i; w) \} \tag{10}$$

and the explicit function Ψ is:

$$\Psi \left(l_i = l^* \right) = \begin{cases} 1, \; l_i = l^* \\ 0, \; l_i \neq l^* \end{cases} \tag{11}$$

Our criterion I in Eq. (8) is a discrete optimization problem that is not suitable to solve by the gradient method, while Monte Carlo (MC) Method [37] can be used for the parameter inference.

The problem of the parameter optimization criterion Eq. (7) that is commonly used in the literature, is that the classification accuracy is not guaranteed even when the sum of the probability of correct classification of the whole vertices is the maximum. Our parameter optimization criterion I is the discrete optimization criterion based on the optimal classification accuracy, and can obtain better classification result. However, this criteria I (Eq. (8)) may lead to relatively lower classification accuracy of the small scale vertices set for the case that the different classes with great disparity in number. In view of this defect, we propose another parameter optimization criterion that maximizes the accuracy with interclass weights, which is called the parameter optimization criterion II, i.e.,

$$w^* = arg \quad \max \; \varepsilon_2(w) \tag{12}$$

Here, $\varepsilon_2(w)$ is called interclass weighting accuracy, and denoted as

$$\varepsilon_2(w) = \frac{1}{m} \sum_{j=1}^{m} \frac{1}{n_j} \left(\sum_{i=1}^{n} \Psi\left(l_j = l^*\right) \right) \tag{13}$$

where n_j is the number of vertices of the l_j class for the training set, and l^* is calculated according to the Eq. (10). Compared with our criterion I (Eq. (8)), our criterion II (Eq. (12)) pay more attention to the accuracies of different classes to balance the overall classification accuracy.

3.5   Flowchart of Our Algorithm

Figure 1 shows the flowchart of our algorithm, which mainly include two stages: the training stage and the testing stage. The target of the training stage is to calculate the CRF parameters of objective energy function, in order to using in the testing stage to acquire the classification result. On the training stage, we construct CRF from the input training set of point cloud, extract the features, and use one of our criteria to calculate the CRF parameters of the objective energy function iteratively. Stopping iterations has two conditions: (1) The changing of objective energy function value is less than the user-specified threshold; (2) The number of iterations reaches a maximum value that the user sets, as we have tested that when the iteration times is large enough, the improvement of optimized result tends to be stable and has little effect after each iteration. When the iteration is stopped, the corresponding optimized parameters' values are recorded, and if not, we use Monte Carlo method to get a new group of parameters for the next iteration. On the testing stage, we still firstly extract the features, and then use those CRF parameters obtained from the training stage to classify the testing set directly to generate the final classification result.

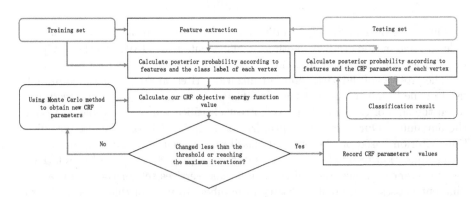

Fig. 1. Flowchart of our algorithm. The blue arrows guide the workflow of the training stage, while the red arrows guide the workflow of the testing stage. (Color figure online)

4   Experiments

All the experiments are done on a laptop computer, with an Intel Core i7-4710MQ CPU@2.50 GHz processor and 4.0 G memory. Our algorithm is implemented in C/C++ language with OpenGL to classify outdoor point cloud data. Usually outdoor point cloud data contain plants/vegetation information, so the main goal of our experiments is to distinguish the plants/vegetation area from the scene. We tested multiple point clouds sets with different sizes, different sources, and different complexities.

4.1   Classification of Terrestrial Lidar Scanning Point Cloud

Distinguishing the plants and the ground from the terrestrial LiDAR scanning point cloud is vital to environmental analysis and geographical investigation. A natural scene data opened by the French Nicolas Brodu point cloud classification work [38] is employed in our experiments, referred as *Canupo* point cloud data.

(a) The groundtruth of the classification.

(b) Classification result based on our criterion I.

(c) Classification result based on our criterion II.

Fig. 2. Ground and vegetation classification result of *Canupo* point cloud. The data is from http://nicolas.brodu.net/en/recherche/canupo/.

The *Canupo* data is made up of the ground data and plants data, as shown in Fig. 2(a), where the ground point cloud includes 40069 vertices and the plants point cloud is made up of 4608 vertices. The white part in the scene is the missing point cloud caused by occlusion. Figure 2(b) and (c) are the results of our methods, which can separate ground and plants in general. In the figures, the blue vertices denote the ground vertices that are wrongly classified as plants, while the red vertices denote the plants vertices that are wrongly classified as the ground.

The total classification accuracy based on our criterion I is 87.3%, and the corresponding confusion matrix is shown in Table 1; the total classification accuracy based on our criterion II is 84.58%, and the corresponding confusion matrix is shown in Table 2. Both the classification accuracies are close to each other.

Table 1. The confusion matrix of our classification of *Canupo* point cloud based on our criterion I.

	Ground	Plants	Total
Ground	34598(86.35%)	5471(13.65%)	40069
Plants	203(4.41%)	4405(95.59%)	4608

Table 2. The confusion matrix of our classification of Canupo point cloud based on our criterion II.

	Ground	Plants	Total
Ground	33293(83.09%)	6776(16.91%)	40069
Plants	114(02.47%)	4494(97.53%)	4608

4.2   Classification of Airborne LiDAR Scanning Point Cloud

Unlike terrestrial LiDAR scanner, the airborne LIDAR scanner has a larger scan range, and the captured point clouds are primarily on the top of the objects. In this section, an airborne scanning scene (abbreviated as GML_A point cloud data) which comes from the Graphics and Media Lab (GML) at Lomonosov Moscow State University in Russia is used for our classification tests. The laboratory used non-joint Markov network method [2] for point cloud classification, accompanied by an accurate result of the point cloud classification. The GML_A point cloud data contains $1,002,668$ vertices, where the plants point cloud includes 539799 vertices and the remaining vertices number is 462869, as shown in Fig. 3(a).

For GML_A point cloud data, the total classification accuracy based on our criterion I is 78.05% with the classification result in Fig. 3(b), and the corresponding confusion matrix is shown in Table 3; the total classification accuracy based on our criterion II is 78.58% with classification result in Fig. 3(c), and the corresponding confusion matrix is shown in Table 4. From our experiments, we can see that the classification accuracies based on our two criteria are almost same.

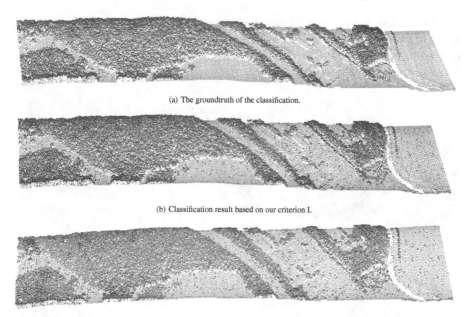

(a) The groundtruth of the classification.

(b) Classification result based on our criterion I.

(c) Classification result based on our criterion II.

Fig. 3. Ground and vegetation classification result of GML_A point cloud The data is from http://graphics.cs.msu.ru/en/node/922.

Table 3. The confusion matrix of our classification of GML_A point cloud based on our criterion I.

	Ground	Plants	Total
Ground	416068(89.89%)	46801(10.11%)	462869
Plants	173309(32.11%)	366490(67.89%)	539799

Table 4. The confusion matrix of our classification of GML_A point cloud based on our criterion II.

	Ground	Plants	Total
Ground	412396(89.10%)	50473(10.90%)	462869
Plants	164299(30.44%)	375500(69.56%)	539799

For the comparison on the testing set, we take another piece of point cloud data (abbreviated as GML_B point cloud data) from the Graphics and Media Lab (GML) at Lomonosov Moscow State University, and divide GML_B into GML_B training point cloud data and GML_B testing point cloud data. The GML_B training point cloud data includes 1544660 vertices, in which 1389385 vertices represent the ground, 155275 vertices are plants as shown in Fig. 4(a), and the GML_B testing point cloud data consists of 1160717 points, in which

1032766 vertices are the ground part accounting for 88.98%, and 127951 vertices are plants accounting for 11.02% as shown in Fig. 4(a). Please note that both the training point cloud data and the testing point cloud data include 3 blocks with 2 obvious blanks between them.

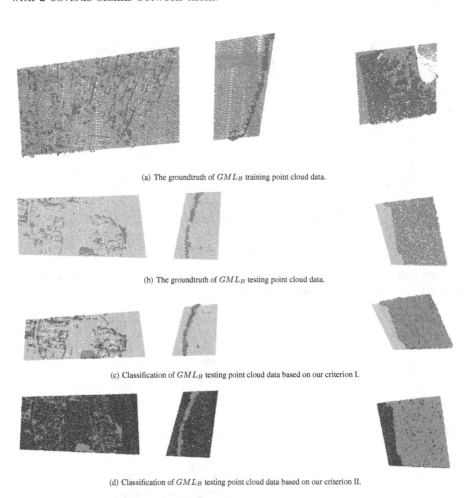

(a) The groundtruth of GML_B training point cloud data.

(b) The groundtruth of GML_B testing point cloud data.

(c) Classification of GML_B testing point cloud data based on our criterion I.

(d) Classification of GML_B testing point cloud data based on our criterion II.

Fig. 4. Classification result of ground and plants in GML_B point cloud data. The data is from http://graphics.cs.msu.ru/en/node/922.

According to our criterion I (Eq. (8)), the classification result of GML_B testing point cloud data after parameters optimization is shown in Fig. 4(c) with the classification accuracy of 94.16%. Although the classification accuracy is relatively high, the classification for plants point cloud is very bad seen from the corresponding confusion matrix (Table 5): many vertices belonging to the plants are wrongly classified as the ground, which are shown as the red dots in Fig. 4(c).

Table 5. The confusion matrix of our classification of GML_B testing point cloud data based on our criterion I.

	Ground	Plants	Total
Ground	1015321(98.31%)	17445(1.69%)	1032766
Plants	50398(39.39%)	77553(60.61%)	127951

By using our criterion II (Eq. (12)) to evaluate the parameters for the GML_B testing point cloud data, the result is shown in Fig. 4(d). The total classification accuracy is 78.1%, which is lower compared to the result based on our criterion I (Eq. (8)). However, the classification accuracy for plants is increased from 60.61% to 94.41%, with the classification accuracy for the ground preserving at an acceptable rate 76.09% as shown in Table 6.

Table 6. The confusion matrix of our classification of GML_B testing point cloud data based on our criterion II.

	Ground	Plants	Total
Ground	785858(76.09%)	246908(23.91%)	1032766
Plants	7152(5.59%)	120799(94.41%)	127951

4.3   Classification for Branches and Leaves of Tree Point Cloud

Another kind of experiments is to distinguish the branches and leaves from the tree point cloud collected by ourselves. The tree point cloud is scanned from a pine tree, denoted as $Pine1$ which consists of $487,555$ points with $27,763(5.7\%)$ branches vertices and $459,792(94.3\%)$ leaf vertices as shown in Fig. 5. We choose part vertices from the $Pine1$ for training to obtain CRF parameters.

The classification results are shown in Fig. 6. The top row is the classification result based on our criteria I (Eq. (8)) with the classification accuracy of 86.79%, and the bottom row is the classification result based on our criterion II (Eq. (12)) with the classification accuracy of 71.79%. By comparing the confusion matrix Tables 7 and 8 corresponding the classification results based on our two criteria respectively, we can see that the classification accuracy for the branches is much lower based on our criterion I. For the classification result based on our II, the classification accuracy for both branches and leaves are good with a slight loss on the overall classification accuracy compared to using our criterion I. This means the classification method based on the our criteria II can better balance classification the accuracy between the various classes and more stable to achieve a satisfied classification result.

Fig. 5. Point cloud *Pine*1.

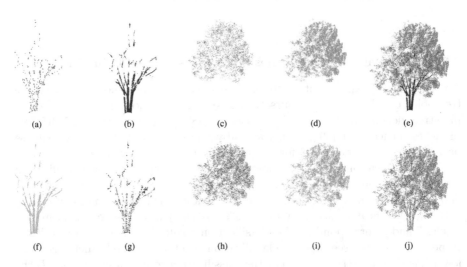

Fig. 6. The classification results of poind cloud *Pine*1. The top row (a–e) shows the classification results based on our criterion *I* (Eq. (8)), and the bottom row (f–j) shows the classification results based on our criterion *II* (Eq. (12)). From the left to right in each row, the subgraphs are correct branches point cloud, branches point cloud that wrongly classified as leaves, leaves point cloud that wrongly classified as branches, correct leaves point cloud, and the result combining the four previous subgraphs respectively.

Table 7. The confusion matrix of our classification for branches and leaves of $Pine1$ based on our criterion I (Eq. (8)).

	Branches	Leaves	Total
Branches	424(1.53%)	27339(98.47%)	27763
Leaves	37066(8.06%)	422726(91.94%)	459792

Table 8. The confusion matrix of our classification for branches and leaves of $Pine1$ based on our criterion II (Eq. (12)).

	Branches	Leaves	Total
Branches	25098(90.40%)	2665(9.60%)	27763
Leaves	134898(29.34%)	324894(70.66%)	459792

4.4 Performance Analysis

Computational complexity analysis. In order to quickly and accurately extract the features based on k nearest neighbors of each vertex, we use the Kd-tree [39] for data organization, and calculate the normal vectors and the main curvature directions by the method [34]. The complexity of constructing Kd-tree is $O(n)$, and the complexity of the k nearest neighbors query is $O(log(n))$, leading to the complexity of the normal vectors calculation and main curvature directions calculation are both $O(nlog(n))$. In the training stage, the iterations for parameter learning is related to the convergence rate of the Monte Carlo algorithm in the data classification, and each iteration is $O(1)$. In the testing stage, the complexity of the feature extraction is the same with the training stage, and the classification process is $O(1)$ level, making the whole algorithm is linear logarithm $O(nlog(n))$.

The relationship between the iteration and the accuracy. We uses the $Canupo$ and GML_A point clouds data to illustrate the relationship between the iteration and the accuracy. The size of these two poind clouds are quite different, but in the process of obtaining the optimal CRF parameters during the training stage, we find that both the numbers of iterations to achieve the best accuracy are close to each other. As shown in Fig. 7, when the number of iterations reaches 100, both the accuracies increasing rates become slow.

4.5 Comparison with Other Works

One of the recent works in point cloud classification is based on the probability mixture method [33]. We test this probability mixing method to classify the GML_B point cloud data, and the result is shown in Fig. 8 with he confusion matrix shown in Table 9. Comparing Fig. 8 to Fig. 4(c) and (d), we can see that all classification effects are very well. Calculated from Table 9, the total classification accuracy of [33] is 97.29%, which is slightly higher than both the

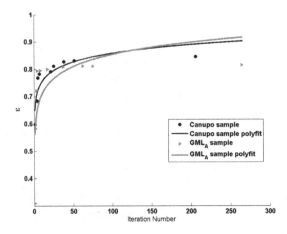

Fig. 7. The relationship between the iteration and the accuracy in the training stage.

Fig. 8. GML_B point cloud classification results based on [33].

classification accuracies based on our criterion I and criterion II (94.16% and 78.11% respectively). Compare Table 9) with Table 5, we can find that the classification accuracies for both the ground and plants based on probability mixture method [33] are slightly higher than the method based on our criterion I.

Table 9. The confusion matrix of GML_B point cloud classification results based on [33].

	Ground	Plants	Total
Ground	1032248(99.95%)	518(0.05%)	1032766
Plants	30957(24.19%)	96994(75.81%)	127951

However, comparing the confusion matrix Table 9 with Table 6, we can see that classification accuracy for plants on GML_B point cloud based on [33] is significantly inferior to the method based on our criterion II. The main reason is that the vertices number of plants is much smaller than the vertices number of the ground, and most of the methods such as [33] are based on the idea of maximizing the total accuracy, which makes them a priority to the classification accuracy of larger subclass and ignore the classification accuracy of smaller subclass. Based on our criterion II), we can classify small scale class better in the point cloud with great disparity in number between different classes.

5   Discussion of Criteria Design

Our criterion I and criterion II are designed according to the idea of maximizing the classification accuracy and maximizing accuracy with interclass weights. In fact, we can also design other criteria for classification. For example, in order to classify the data point cloud into two classes, we can design the criterion of maximizing the first class classification accuracy (denoted as parameter optimization criterion III) or the criterion of maximizing the second class classification accuracy (denoted as parameter optimization criterion IV) as follows.

Parameter optimization criterion III:

$$w^* = arg \quad \max \quad \frac{1}{n_1} \left(\sum_{i=1}^{n} \Psi \left(l^* = 1 \right) \right) \tag{14}$$

Parameter optimization criterion IV:

$$w^* = arg \quad \max \quad \frac{1}{n_2} \left(\sum_{i=1}^{n} \Psi \left(l^* = 2 \right) \right) \tag{15}$$

where the l^* is calculated as Eq. (10) both in criterion III and criterion IV.

We use two experiments to compare the classification effects of our four parameter optimization criteria. The first experiment uses another pine tree, denoted as $Pine2$ as shown in Fig. 9. The scanned point cloud $Pine2$ includes 269366 vertices, and the manual segmentation results are 20654 branches vertices and 248712 leaves vertices shown in Fig. 10. The corresponding classification accuracies for four criteria are shown in Table 10, where our first three criteria

Fig. 9. The manual classification result (groundtruth) of point cloud $Pine2$.

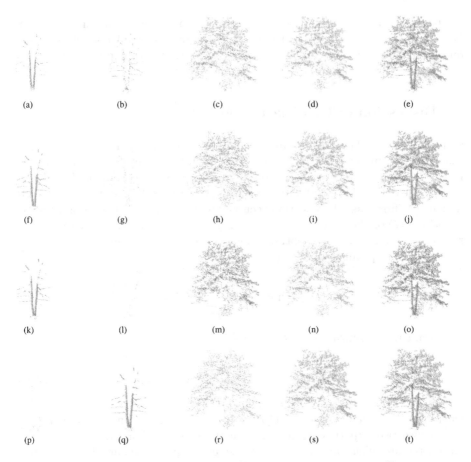

Fig. 10. The classification results of point cloud *Pine2* based on our four criteria, each row corresponding one criterion and from top to bottom are criterion *I, II, III,* and *IV* respectively. From the left to right in each row, the subgraphs are correct branches point cloud, branches point cloud that wrongly classified as leaves, leaves point cloud that wrongly classified as branches, correct leaves point cloud, and the result combining the four previous subgraphs in sequence.

can classify the branches better, and the criterion *IV* can classify leaves with best accuracy (79.61%).

Another experiment is on the multiple pines point cloud, denoted as *Forest* with the scan data shown in Fig. 11. *Forest* consists of 556, 308 vertices with manual segmentation of 151473 tree branches vertices and 414835 leaves vertices. The classification results based on our four criteria are shown in Fig. 12, and the corresponding classification accuracies are shown in Table 11, where the results are similar to the experiment on *Pine2*, that is, the first three criteria can extract the branches is better, and the criterion *IV* can classify the leaves with best accuracy (86.63%).

Table 10. The comparison of four confusion matrices corresponding the classification results of *Pine2* based on our four criteria.

Pine2	Classify branches as branches	Classify branches as leaves	Classify leaves as branches	Classify leaves as leaves
Criterion *I*	66.77%	33.23%	33.23%	66.77%
Criterion *II*	93.20%	6.80%	34.37%	65.63%
Criterion *III*	98.55%	1.45%	51.16%	48.84%
Criterion *IV*	2.19%	97.81%	20.39%	79.61%

Table 11. The comparison of four confusion matrices corresponding the classification results of *Forest* based on our four criteria.

Forest	Classify branches as branches	Classify branches as leaves	Classify leaves as branches	Classify leaves as leaves
Criterion *I*	76.35%	23.65%	33.72%	66.28%
Criterion *II*	84.12%	15.88%	38.44%	61.56%
Criterion *III*	93.45%	6.55%	56.95%	43.05%
Criterion *IV*	4.07%	95.93%	13.37%	86.63%

Fig. 11. The manual classification result(groundtruth) of point cloud *Forest*.

From these two experiments, we can see that our criterion *I* and criterion *II* are comparable in the overall classification effect, while criterion *II* can balance the classification accuracies between different classes. Criterion *uppercaseiv* has the best effect on the separation of the leaves, but the classification of the branches is not very well; on the contrary, our criterion *III* can distinguish the branches better, but the classification of the leaves is less than

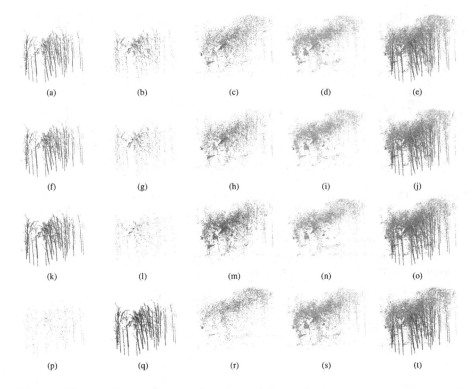

Fig. 12. The classification results of point cloud *Forest* based on our four criteria, each row corresponding one criterion and from top to bottom are criterion I, II, III, and IV respectively. From the left to right in each row, the subgraphs are correct branches point cloud, branches point cloud that wrongly classified as leaves, leaves point cloud that wrongly classified as branches, correct leaves point cloud, and the result combining the four previous subgraphs in sequence.

our criterion I and criterion II. When focusing on the extraction of a special class, criterion III and criterion IV can be taken as supplement control methods, and in common case, our criterion I and criterion II can satisfy our needs better.

6   Conclusion

In this paper, we have proposed new parameter optimization criteria in order to overcome the problem of current methods that maximizing the correct classification probability cannot guarantee the high classification accuracy. For the point cloud data, when the vertices numbers belong two classes of the point cloud data are not very different, our criterion I and criterion II can achieve better classification effects than previous methods; when different classes sets have great disparity in number, our criterion II can balance the accuracies between classes, and make the recognition of the class with small vertices number achieve better classification accuracy. Our criterion III and criterion IV can be used as supplement control methods for better classification on some special classes. Since all the parameter optimization criteria are discrete, the Monte Carlo method can be used for the parameter optimization process. Our algorithm is simple with the convergence of the algorithm a little slow. The efficient solution of our discrete parameter optimization problem could be an important direction in the follow-up studies.

Acknowledgements. This work is partly supported by National Natural Science Foundation of China with Nos. 61331018, 61372190, 61501464, 61571439, and 61561003, partly supported by the National High Technology Research and Development Program (863 Program) of China with No. 2015AA016402 and Project 6140001010207.

References

1. Zhang, X., Li, H., Dai, M., Ma, W.: Data-driven synthetic modeling of trees. IEEE Trans. Vis. Comput. Graph. **20**(9), 1214–1226 (2014)
2. Shapovalov, R., Velizhev, A., Barinova, O.: Non-associative markov networks for 3D point cloud classification. In: Photogrammetric Computer Vision and Image Analysis (2010)
3. Faugeras, O.: Three-Dimensional Computer Vision: A Geometric Viewpoint. MIT Press, Cambridge (1993)
4. Jin, H., Wang, X., Zhong, Z., Hua, J.: Robust 3D face modeling and reconstruction from frontal and side images. Comput. Aided Geom. Des. **50**, 1–13 (2017)
5. Berger, M., Tagliasacchi, A., Seversky, L.M., Alliez, P., Guennebaud, G., Levine, J.A., Sharf, A., Silva, C.T.: A survey of surface reconstruction from point clouds. Comput. Graph. Forum, n/a–n/a (2016)
6. Frome, A., Huber, D., Kolluri, R., Bülow, T., Malik, J.: Recognizing objects in range data using regional point descriptors. In: Pajdla, T., Matas, J. (eds.) ECCV 2004. LNCS, vol. 3023, pp. 224–237. Springer, Heidelberg (2004). doi:10.1007/978-3-540-24672-5_18
7. Himmelsbach, M., Luettel, T., Wuensche, H.-J.: Real-time object classification in 3D point clouds using point feature histograms. In: Proceedings of the 2009 IEEE/RSJ International Conference on Intelligent Robots and Systems, IROS 2009, pp. 994–1000. IEEE Press, Piscataway (2009)
8. Rusu, R.B., Blodow, N., Beetz, M.: Fast point feature histograms (fpfh) for 3D registration. In: IEEE International Conference on Robotics and Automation, pp. 3212–3217 (2009)
9. Paulus, S., Dupuis, J., Mahlein, A.K., Kuhlmann, H.: Surface feature based classification of plant organs from 3D laserscanned point clouds for plant phenotyping. BMC Bioinform. **14**(1), 1–12 (2013)
10. Lalonde, J.F., Vandapel, N., Huber, D.F., Hebert, M.: Natural terrain classification using three-dimensional ladar data for ground robot mobility. J. Field Robot. **23**(10), 839–861 (2006)
11. Vosselman, G.: Point cloud segmentation for urban scene classification. ISPRS - Int. Arch. Photogramm. Remote Sens. Spat. Inf. Sci. **XL–7/W2**(7), 257–262 (2013)

12. Weinmann, M., Jutzi, B., Hinz, S., Mallet, C.: Semantic point cloud interpretation based on optimal neighborhoods, relevant features and efficient classifiers. ISPRS J. Photogramm. Remote Sens. **105**, 286–304 (2015)
13. Yang, J., Cao, Z., Zhang, Q.: A fast and robust local descriptor for 3D point cloud registration. Inf. Sci. **346–347**, 163–179 (2016)
14. Plaza-Leiva, V., Gomez-Ruiz, J.A., Mandow, A., Garc-Cerezo, A.: Voxel-based neighborhood for spatial shape pattern classification of Lidar point clouds with supervised learning. Sensors **17**(3), 594 (2017)
15. Lafferty, J.D., McCallum, A., Pereira, F.C.N.: Conditional random fields: probabilistic models for segmenting and labeling sequence data. In: Proceedings of the Eighteenth International Conference on Machine Learning, ICML 2001, pp. 282–289. Morgan Kaufmann Publishers Inc., San Francisco (2001)
16. Kumar, S., Hebert, M.: Discriminative random fields. Int. J. Comput. Vision **68**(2), 179–201 (2006)
17. Munoz, D., Vandapel, N., Hebert, M.: Directional associative Markov network for 3-d point cloud classification. In: International Symposium on 3-D Data Processing, Visualization, and Transmission (2008)
18. Najafi, M., Taghavi Namin, S., Salzmann, M., Petersson, L.: Non-associative higher-order Markov networks for point cloud classification. In: Fleet, D., Pajdla, T., Schiele, B., Tuytelaars, T. (eds.) ECCV 2014. LNCS, vol. 8693, pp. 500–515. Springer, Cham (2014). doi:10.1007/978-3-319-10602-1_33
19. Rutzinger, M., Höfle, B., Hollaus, M., Pfeifer, N.: Object-based point cloud analysis of full-waveform airborne laser scanning data for urban vegetation classification. Sensors **8**(8), 4505–4528 (2008)
20. Niemeyer, J., Rottensteiner, F., Soergel, U.: Conditional random fields for lidar point cloud classification in complex urban areas. ISPRS Ann. Photogramm. Remote Sens. Spat. Inf. Sci. **I–3**(I–3), 263–268 (2012)
21. Husain, F., Dellen, L., Torras, C.: Recognizing point clouds using conditional random fields. In: 2014 22nd International Conference on Pattern Recognition, pp. 4257–4262, August 2014
22. Wolf, D., Prankl, J., Vincze, M.: Fast semantic segmentation of 3D point clouds using a dense CRF with learned parameters. In: IEEE International Conference on Robotics and Automation, pp. 4867–4873 (2015)
23. Niemeyer, J., Rottensteiner, F., Soergel, U., Heipke, C.: Hierarchical higher order CRF for the classification of airborne lidar point clouds in urban areas. ISPRS - Int. Arch. Photogramm. Remote Sens. Spat. Inf. Sci. **XLI–B3**, 655–662 (2016)
24. Lang, D., Friedmann, S., Paulus, D.: Adaptivity of conditional random field based outdoor point cloud classification. Pattern Recogn. Image Anal. **26**(2), 309–315 (2016)
25. Ni, H., Lin, X., Zhang, J.: Classification of ALS point cloud with improved point cloud segmentation and random forests. Remote Sens. **9**(3), 288 (2017)
26. Wang, Z., Zhang, L., Fang, T., Mathiopoulos, P.T.: A multiscale and hierarchical feature extraction method for terrestrial laser scanning point cloud classification. IEEE Trans. Geosci. Remote Sens. **53**(5), 2409–2425 (2015)
27. Zhang, Z., Zhang, L., Tong, X., Takis Mathiopoulos, P.: A multilevel point-cluster-based discriminative feature for ALS point cloud classification. IEEE Trans. Geosci. Remote Sens. **54**(6), 3309–3321 (2016)
28. Rodrguezcuenca, B., Garcacorts, S., Ordóñez, C., Alonso, M.: Automatic detection and classification of pole-like objects in urban point cloud data using an anomaly detection algorithm. Remote Sens. **7**(10), 12680–12703 (2015)

29. Hu, X., Yuan, Y.: Deep-learning-based classification for DTM extraction from ALS point cloud. Remote Sens. **8**(9), 730 (2016)
30. Chen, J., Fang, Y., Yong, K.C., Kim, C.: Principal axes descriptor for automated construction-equipment classification from point clouds. J. Comput. Civil Eng. **31**(2), 1–36 (2017)
31. Kang, Z., Yang, J., Zhong, R.: A bayesian-network-based classification method integrating airborne lidar data with optical images. IEEE J. Sel. Top. Appl. Earth Observ. Remote Sens. **10**(4), 1601–1609 (2017)
32. Maligo, A., Lacroix, S.: Classification of outdoor 3D lidar data based on unsupervised gaussian mixture models. IEEE Trans. Autom. Sci. Eng. **14**(1), 5–16 (2017)
33. Li, H., Liu, X., Zhang, X., Yan, D.: A semi-automatic 3D point cloud classification method based on probability mixture of local shape features. J. Zhejiang Univ. (Sci. Edn.) **44**(1), 1–8 (2017)
34. Zhang, X., Li, H., Cheng, Z., Zhang, Y.: Robust curvature estimation and geometry analysis of 3D point cloud surfaces. J. Inf. Computat. Sci. **6**(5), 1983–1990 (2009)
35. Xiang, S., Nie, F., Zhang, C., Zhang, C.: Interactive visual object extraction based on belief propagation. In: Cham, T.-J., Cai, J., Dorai, C., Rajan, D., Chua, T.-S., Chia, L.-T. (eds.) MMM 2007. LNCS, vol. 4351, pp. 24–33. Springer, Heidelberg (2006). doi:10.1007/978-3-540-69423-6_3
36. Sutton, C., McCallum, A.: An introduction to conditional random fields. Found. Trends Mach. Learn. **4**(4), 267–373 (2012)
37. Chen, Y., Raudenbush, S.W.: Maximum likelihood estimation in generalized linear: large mixed models using monte carlo methods: application to small-area estimation of breast cancer mortality. Chin. J. Appl. Probab. Stat. **22**(1), 69–80 (2006)
38. Brodu, N., Lague, D.: 3D terrestrial lidar data classification of complex natural scenes using a multi-scale dimensionality criterion: applications in geomorphology. ISPRS J. Photogramm. Remote Sens. **68**(1), 121–134 (2012)
39. Mount, D.M.: Ann programming manual (2006). http://www.cs.umd.edu/mount/ANN/Files/1.1. Accessed 6 Apr 2012

Lightweight Web3D Visualization Framework Using Dijkstra-Based Mesh Segmentation

Wen Zhou[✉] and Jinyuan Jia

School of Software Engineering, Tongji University, Shanghai 201804, China
zhouwen606@126.com, jyjia@tongji.edu.cn

Abstract. With the advent of the era of "Internet plus", there are great achieve-ment in Web3D technology areas, furthermore, more and more focuses have put on how to more effectively show dense models on browser. The paper proposes a framework to lightweight process the 3D shape based on Web Browser. This framework is based on Mesh Segmentation. Therefore, a new Dijkstra-based mesh segmentation approach is presented. The framework splits models and creates corresponding components, moreover, some repetitive components can be detected by our proposed framework. Firstly, a model barycenter is computed as a start point, besides, global distance is presented as the shortest path basis. Then, mesh triangles begin to diffuse until the conditions are not met. Secondly, according to the triangles diffuse, the original model will be re-indexed in order to acquire the segmentation files. Last but not least, repetition detection algorithm has been proposed, the components will be detected to confirm whether or not there exists the repetitive relationship of each other. In addition, experimental results on the Stanford and SHREC 2007 datasets show that our approach is accurate and feasible.

Keywords: Web3d · Lightweight · Mesh segmentation · Global distance · Repetition

1 Introduction

With the constant increase in availability of 3D model, more and more interest has been induced in 3D shape analysis algorithm, for which 3D mesh segmentation is considered as one of the most challenging problems. Besides, 3D mesh segmentation has been applied into many areas, such as Component-based Shape Synthesis [1], which makes use of segmentation and labeling to produce new models by transferring corresponding segments from one model to others, 3D scene analysis, part-based recognition, 3D video compression and 3D object retrieval [2, 3].

What's more, with the internet plus era coming, VR technology has been quickly developing, more and more emphasizes have been put on web browsers. Surely, the 3D model isn't exception. Furthermore, Contradiction between the limited load capacity and huger and huger data demand is more and more obvious. Therefore, the mesh segmentation is one of the most effective solution of the bottleneck of Web3D visuali-zation.

© Springer International Publishing AG 2017
F. Tian et al. (Eds.): Edutainment 2017, LNCS 10345, pp. 138–151, 2017.
https://doi.org/10.1007/978-3-319-65849-0_15

In this paper, we propose a new framework based on mesh segmentation oriental to repetition detection. Moreover, we illustrate our proposed Dijkstra-based segmentation algorithm, which is an import part of our proposed framework. Besides, we propose re-indexing-based mesh split algorithm in order to segment an individual mesh into parts. Last but not least, voxelization-based component repetition detection methods are proposed, which is the last part of our framework.

The remainder of this article is organized as follows: Sect. 2 reviews the relevant literature. Section 3 introduce our proposed framework and related approach. Section 4 present the proposed related approach and algorithm in detail. Section 5 is the part of experiment and validate the correctness of our proposed method. Section 6 concludes the article.

2 Related Works

3D segmentation isn't an easy job. Several methodological frameworks have been developed to present this underlying challenge. Golovinskiy et al. [4] introduced graph clustering method to balance the intra-mesh and inter-mesh segmentations. This method builds the connection by matching points between meshes aligned rigidly. However, it handles only limited model types for the requirement of global rigid alignment. Xu et al. [5] classify the meshes according to their styles and then establish part correspondences in each style group. But the group generation process is computationally expensive. Kraevoy et al. [6] create a consistent segmentation by matching the parts generated from an initial segmentation. Huang et al. [7] jointly consider the segmentation of individual meshes by a linear programming. Nevertheless, the segmentations, generated by these two methods, can't guarantee the consistency across the whole set even if they are mutually consistent. Sidi et al. [8] analyze the descriptor space via spectral clustering to segment a set of shapes with large variability. Meng et al. [9] cluster the primitive patches to generate initial guess and improve the co-segmentation results by the multi-label optimization. Hu et al. [10] generate the segmentation by grouping the primitive patches of the meshes directly and obtain their correspondences simultaneously. This method achieves some success benefiting from the observation that patches belonging to the same part are likely to be in one common subspace in the feature space. Liu et al. [11] introduce the low-rank representation into semantic mesh segmentation and labeling. Nonetheless, this method still exists several limitations, such as model style etc.

Besides, many mesh segmentation methods exist in the graphics literature that aim to decompose a mesh into functional parts. Shamir et al. [16] and Agathos et al. [17] proposed a survey to summary different methods. Attene et al. [18] made a comparison between several algorithms. These approach aim to create segments that are well-formed according to some pre-defined low-level criteria, that is, the segments are convex, boundaries lie along concavities etc. K-means [19], graph cuts [20], hierarchical clustering [21, 22], random walks [23], core extraction [24], tubular primitive extraction [25], spectral clustering [26], and critical point analysis [27] are used. Theologou et al. [28] present a comprehensive survey on 3D mesh segmentation, it show the current trends in 3D mesh segmentation.

On the other side, many 3D models are man-made, consisting of a wide range of components, which means these models are easily segmented according to the connectivity. It's worth nothing that similar components with different rigid geometry transformations usually exist in these 3D models. Shikhare et al. [12] and Cai et al. [13] proposed the repetition detection approach to find similar components in 3D models. Nevertheless, their matching methods are not accurate due to the limitations of their strategies. Wen et al. [14] presented a similarity-aware 3D model reduction method, called Lightweight Progressive Meshes, which can search similar component and reuse them through the construction of a Lightweight Scene Graph. However, this method depended on manual segmentation.

3   Proposed Framework

In this section, we will present our proposed framework (see Fig. 1), it's not hard to find that our framework consists of four parts. That is mesh segmentation, mesh split, component repetition detection, assemble. In order to solve the problem of how correctly assemble the removed part models to the whole 3D shape, the pose normalization approach is adopted in the assemble part in our proposed framework. We will introduce these four parts in detail in Sect. 4.

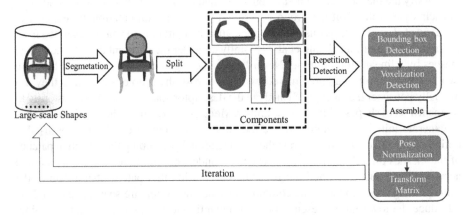

Fig. 1. The overview of proposed framework

4   Description

4.1   Dijkstra-Based Mesh Segmentation

The process of Mesh Segmentation is relevant in several CAD/CAM areas such mesh compression, parameterization, shape feature identification etc. we proposed a new algorithm based on Dijkstra shortest path approach. Dijkstra is an algorithm for finding the shortest paths between nodes in a graph, which may represent. We will consider a triangle as a node. Then, a model will be converted into a road networks, which network will be separated into several regions based on the triangle diffuse. Then, realize the segmentation (Fig. 2).

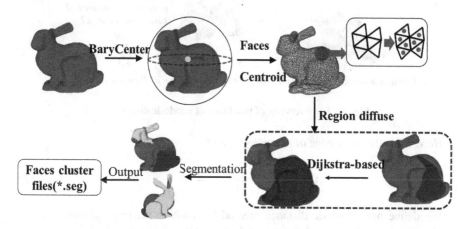

Fig. 2. The overview of our proposed segmentation algorithm

The process of mesh segmentation will be described as following:

1. We calculate the position of barycenter of the model, then acquire the nearest triangle (T_0) with the barycenter, which is the diffusion source position, S_0.
2. The centroids of all triangles will be calculated as the node of networks, $C = \{C_1, C_2, C_3, ..., C_n\}$, n is the quantity of triangles in model.
3. T_0 is the center of region. We will get the neighbor triangles of T_0 **Neigh$_0$**.
4. We calculate the global distance between region center triangle and its neighbor triangles, we build the topological networks. Dijkstra algorithm can acquire the shortest paths, **PATH$_0$** from S_0, If C_K belong to **PATH$_0$**, and then C_K belong to the region, which S_0 is the center position.
5. Update the region center, we re-calculate the region center of position, that is update the coordinate of S_0.
6. We iterate step 4, 5 until the number of steps exceeds the number of max iterations or the shortest paths have not existed. Then, we build new diffusion source, S_i.
7. Repeat Sects. 4 and 5. Then, we will acquire the cluster index of each triangle. Last but not least, we will output this into files (*.seg).

Due to Dijkstra algorithm depending on distance, we present two kinds of different geodesic distance, one is centroid distance (*CD*) and the other is angular distance (*AD*) (See Fig. 3).

$$CD_{i,j} = Distance\,(C_i, SE) + Distance\,(C_j, SE) \tag{1}$$

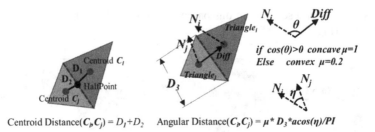

Centroid Distance$(C_i, C_j) = D_1 + D_2$ Angular Distance$(C_i, C_j) = \mu * D_3 * acos(\eta) / PI$

Fig. 3. The overview of two kinds of geodesic distance

Here, SE is the share edge of triangle C_i, and C_j.

$$AD_j^i = \frac{\mu * D_3 * acos(\eta)}{PI} \tag{2}$$

We define new geodesic distance method to combine the centroid distance and angular distance, called global distance, *GD*. D_3 denotes the length of *SE*.

$$GD = \frac{CD + \varphi * AD}{BBDiagonal} \tag{3}$$

Then, φ is empirical value, which determines the ratio of angular distance to global distance, though experiment, $\varphi \in [0, 500]$. The larger the value is, the greater the ratio of the angular distance in the global distance formula, the stronger the streamline of the model. In this paper, we set the value of φ to 300. Besides, *BBDiagonal* denotes the diagonal length of the bounding box.

In Fig. 4, the process of region diffuse has been shown.

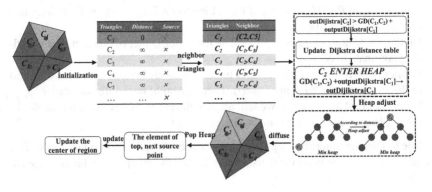

Fig. 4. The process of region diffuse

4.2 Re-indexing Based Mesh Split

In the previous section, we have get the cluster file. In this file, each triangle belongs to the region that has been recorded. In this section, we will present how to split the mesh according to the files. Due to a lot of share edges and vertices existing, therefore, many edges and points belong to many different regions. Then, we must re-index the vertices and triangles in order to split the mesh. Surely, the triangles that belong to which region are easily represented. However, vertices are not easily represented. In this paper, we use the half-edge data structure [15] to denote the vertex-triangle relationship. In order to re-index the vertices, we must visit its vertices from a triangle index. The process of re-indexing based mesh split will be seen in Fig. 5.

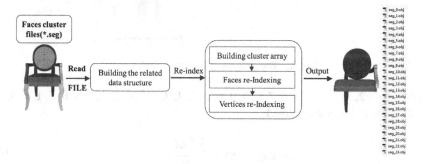

Fig. 5. The overview of mesh split process

4.3 Voxelization-Based Repetition Detection

According to the previous section, we will acquire many segmentation files. In this section, we mainly present how to detect the repetitive component. Repetition detection can reduce the size of model. Moreover, many man-made models exist a lot of repetition component. Our proposed approach mainly is divided into three steps. We will detail these as following.

1. To each component, we calculate the sum of its every triangles area.
2. Acquire a larger component, that is, the total number of triangles exceed 2% of the total number of triangles in the original model. Therefore, we will ignore small components.
3. Compare the area relationship of the component, if the area difference is small, then put into the list of repetition tables.
4. We can choose the same voxel size, and then compare the similarity relation of the voxels in the component repetition table, in order to finally confirm the repetition components.

The process will be seen in Fig. 6. In this paper, we set the voxel size is 0.01 * 0.01 * 0.01, which voxel precision is 0.001. In order to compare the voxel box of different components, we index each voxel. As known to all, each voxel is consisted of 12 triangles. Therefore, we denote each voxel as following.

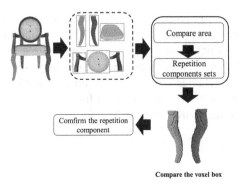

Fig. 6. The process of repetition detection

{0, 1, 2, 0, 2, 3, 3, 2, 6, 3, 6, 7, 0, 7, 4, 0, 3, 7, 4, 7, 5, 7, 6, 5, 0, 4, 5, 0, 5, 1, 1, 5, 6, 1, 6, 2} is the index of each voxel.

$$Similarity\,(A, B) = \frac{\sum_{i}^{N} \Delta(i)}{N} \tag{4}$$

$$\Delta(i) = \begin{cases} 1 \;\; if \;\left| Vol(A_i) - Vol(B_i) \right| \le precision \\ 0 \;\; otherwise \end{cases} \tag{5}$$

$$Vol\bigl(\varPsi_i\bigr) = \prod_{j}^{j\in\{1,5,14\}} vox(j+i) - vox(i) \tag{6}$$

According to the above formula, we can calculate the similarity relation between two components. **Vol** ($\varPsi_i$) denotes the volume of the ith voxel box. In this paper, we set the number of voxel is 4096, that is, $N = 4096$. In other words, any component has been represented by 4096 voxels. Hence, it will be better to compare the similarity of components. The specific process is shown in Fig. 7

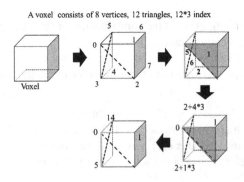

Fig. 7. The process of calculating volume.

4.4   Pose Normalization

Pose Normalization method was proposed by Wen et al. [14]. We adopt and implement this method in this paper. This main process of this method is as following. The objective of the pose normalization is to make the components of a model in the canonical coordinate system so that we can assemble the removed part models to the whole 3D models. It includes translation-invariant, rotation-invariant, and scaling-invariant transformation. Every component would individually conduct these transformations. In this process, the transform matrix associated to each component of the model has to be recorded for restoration later. By optimizing the process, in particular, by adding a symmetry-invariant transformation after the rotation-invariant transformation using PCA, the alignment of similar components will be overlapped with each other.

5   Experiment and Results

In this section, we will validate and test our methods by some experiments. We need test our proposed segmentation approach, repetition detection methods. Our experiment does in Stanford Shape Net, which is one of most famous 3D model datasets. In order to evaluate our segmentation algorithm, we compare our method with the other state-of-the art approach in Watertight Track of SHREC 2007 datasets. Many segmentation algorithms conduct related experiment in this datasets.

The method presents in this paper has been implemented using C++ program language and is executed on PC under Windows 7 OS, Intel core I5-M580 processor, 4G memory size.

5.1   Mesh Segmentation

In general, our algorithm can work in the two methods, one is automatic selecting number of segmentation, and the others is according to user input. In the Fig. 8, it's automatic selecting number of segmentation. Moreover, in the Fig. 9, it's showed the result of segmentation according to user input. In Fig. 10, we do a comparison experiment between the different methods. With the size of model having become bigger, we find that the time consumption become bigger and bigger in the method 1. Therefore, the method 1 better fits the small size model.

Besides, we compare our proposed method with the other state-of-the-art approach in Watertight Track of SHREC 2007 dataset. Watertight Track of SHREC 2007 dataset consist of 380 mesh models, which belong to 19 categories. The compared other state-of-the art approach include as following, K-means [19], graph cuts [20], random walks [23], core extraction [24]. The result show our method is not only robust but also efficient. In Table 1, we compare ours with others methods in user input requirements. Our proposed method obviously has stronger robustness and lower input requirements. Therefore, our proposed method can adapt and segment 3D shape in different conditions. In Table 2, the comparison result in compute time faces will been showed, the time consumption of our algorithm is less.

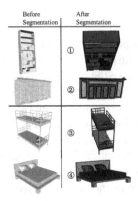

Fig. 8. The result of segmentation according to automatic selection

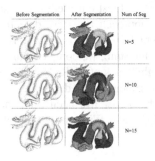

Fig. 9. The result of segmentation according to user input

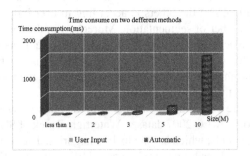

Fig. 10. The comparison figure on time consumption

Table 1. The comparison results between ours and other methods

Methods	Number of segments as input	
	Need take?	Need not take?
K-means	YES	NO
Graph cuts	YES	NO
Random walks	YES	NO
Core extraction	NO	YES
Ours	YES	YES

Table 2. The comparison result in compute time (measured on a 2.4 GHz PC).

Segmentation algorithms	Average Compute time(s)
K-means	1.6
Graph cuts	43.2
Random walks	0.9
Core extraction	18.3
Ours	1.8

Furthermore, a benchmark for 3D mesh segmentation was proposed by Chen et al. [29], which describe a benchmark for evaluation of 3D mesh segmentation algorithms. The benchmark comprises a data set with 4300 manually generated segmentation for 380 surface meshes of 19 different object categories. Four different indicator have been proposed by CHEN [29], that are cut discrepancy (*CD*), Hamming Distance (*HD*), Rand Index (*RI*), Consistency Error (*CE*).

$$CD(S_1, S_2) = \frac{mean\{d_G(p_1, C_2), \forall p_1 \in C_2\} + mean\{d_G(p_2, C_1), \forall p_1 \in C_1\}}{avgRadius} \quad (7)$$

Here, *avgRadius* denote the average Euclidean distance from a point on the surface to centroid of the mesh. C_1, C_2 denote sets of all points on the segment boundaries of segmentations S_1 and S_2, respectively. Then $d_G(\cdot, \cdot)$ measures the geodesic distance between two points on a mesh.

$$HD(S_1, S_2) = \frac{1}{2 * \| s \|} \left(\sum_i \| s_2^i \backslash s_1^i \| + \sum_j \| s_1^j \backslash s_2^j \| \right) \quad (8)$$

Where $\| s \|$ is the total surface area of the polygonal model, "\" is the set difference operator.

$$RI(S_1, S_2) = \binom{2}{n}^{-1} \sum_{i,j,i<j} [C_{ij}P_{ij} + (1 - C_{ij})(1 - P_{ij})] \quad (9)$$

Here, $C_{ij} = 1$ iff $s_i^1 = s_j^1$ and $P_{ij} = 1$ iff. $s_i^2 = s_j^2$. Then, $(1 - C_{ij})(1 - P_{ij}) = 1$ indicates that face i and j have different IDs in both S_1 and S_2.

CE indicator consists of Global Consistency Error (*GCE*) and Local Consistency Error (*LCE*).

$$GCE\left(S_1,S_2\right) = \frac{1}{n}\min\left\{\sum_i \frac{\left\|R(S_1,f_i)\backslash R(S_2,f_i)\right\|}{\left\|R(S_1,f_i)\right\|}, \sum_i \frac{\left\|R(S_2,f_i)\backslash R(S_1,f_i)\right\|}{\left\|R(S_3,f_i)\right\|}\right\} \qquad (10)$$

Here, $R\left(S_1,f_i\right)$ denotes a segment set which is in segmentation S_1 that contains face f_i.

$$LCE\left(S_1,S_2\right) = \frac{1}{n}\sum_i \min\left\{\frac{\left\|R(S_1,f_i)\backslash R(S_2,f_i)\right\|}{\left\|R(S_1,f_i)\right\|}, \frac{\left\|R(S_2,f_i)\backslash R(S_1,f_i)\right\|}{\left\|R(S_2,f_i)\right\|}\right\} \qquad (11)$$

The comparison result in the above indicators will be shown in Fig. 11. It is not hard to find that our proposed method is more approaching the benchmark than others methods.

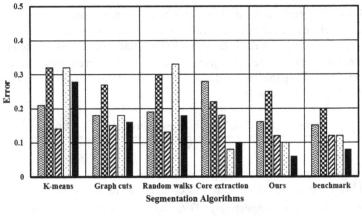

Fig. 11. The comparison result in five different indicators

5.2 Repetition Detection

In this section, we will test our repetition detection method. By this approach, we will verify the rightness and robustness of proposed approach.

In Fig. 12, we test our segmentation component. It is not hard to find that our result met the human judgment. In this paper, if the similarity value is greater than 0.85, we will judge that the two components are similar.

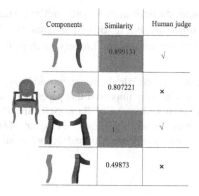

Components	Similarity	Human judge
	0.899131	√
	0.807221	×
	1	√
	0.49873	×

Fig. 12. The repetition detection test

5.3 Results

According to the above experiment result, we can split an individual mesh into many different components, then, by repetition detection, we will reduce the size of model (Fig. 13).

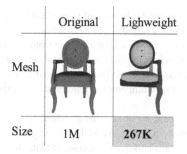

	Original	Lighweight
Mesh		
Size	1M	267K

Fig. 13. The comparison test of our framework

In Fig. 12, it's not hard to find the result is very obvious, after our proposed framework processing. Our framework can obviously reduce the size of model, furthermore, it will improve the efficiency of model transmission on web browser. Furthermore, Pose Normalization [14] method was used in order to correctly assemble the whole 3D shapes.

6 Conclusions

In this paper, we propose a new lightweight framework to process the model in order to better visualize in web browser. Moreover, Dijkstra-based mesh segmentation is presented, it can quickly split individual mesh into many components. Besides, voxelization-based repetition detection approach is proposed, the related experiments show our method is totally feasible.

However, there are some shortcomings in our method, such as the segmentation dependence on geometric topology, but ignoring the semantic. Therefore, our methods can get better result in symmetric man-made models, such as furniture models etc.

Acknowledgments. The authors appreciate the comments and suggestions of all anonymous reviewers, whose comments significantly improved this paper. This work is supported by The Key Research Projects of Central University of Basic Scientific Research Funds for Cross Cooperation (201510-02), Research Fund for the Doctoral Program of Higher Education of China (No. 2013007211-0035) and Key project in scientific and technological of Jilin Province in China (No. 20140204088GX).

References

1. Kalogerakis, E., Chaudhuri, S., Koller, D., et al.: A probabilistic model for component-based shape synthesis. ACM Trans. Graph. **31**(31), 1–11 (2012)
2. Theologou, P., Pratikakis, I., Theoharis, T.: A review on 3D object retrieval methodologies using a part-based representation. Comput. Aided Des. Appl. **11**(6), 670–684 (2014)
3. Savelonas, M.A., Pratikakis, I., Sfikas, K.: An overview of partial 3D object retrieval methodologies. Multimedia Tools Appl. **74**(24), 11783–11808 (2015)
4. Aleksey, G., Funkhouser, T.: Consistent segmentation of 3D models. Comput. Graph. **33**(3), 262–269 (2009)
5. Xu, K., Li, H., Zhang, H., et al.: Style-content separation by anisotropic part scales. ACM Trans. Graph. (TOG) **29**(1), 184 (2010)
6. Kreavoy, V., Dan, J., Sheffer, A.: Model composition from interchangeable components. In: Pacific Conference on Computer Graphics and Applications, pp. 129–138 (2007)
7. Huang, Q., Koltun, V., Guibas, L.J., et al.: Joint shape segmentation with linear programming. In: International Conference on Computer Graphics and Interactive Techniques, vol. 30, No. 6 (2011)
8. Sidi, O., Kaick, O.V., Kleiman, Y., et al.: Unsupervised co-segmentation of a set of shapes via descriptor-space spectral clustering. ACM Trans. Graph. **30**(6), 126:1–126:10 (2011)
9. Meng, M., Xia, J., Luo, J., et al.: Unsupervised co-segmentation for 3D shapes using iterative multi-label optimization. Comput. Aided Des. **45**(2), 312–320 (2013)
10. Hu, R., Fan, L., Liu, L.: Co-segmentation of 3D shapes via subspace clustering. In: Computer Graphics Forum, pp. 1703–1713. Blackwell Publishing Ltd. (2012)
11. Liu, X., et al.: Low-rank 3D mesh segmentation and labeling with structure guiding. Comput. Graph. **46**, 99–109 (2015)
12. Shikhare, D., Bhakar, S., Mudur, S.P.: Compression of large 3D engineering models using automatic discovery of repeating geometric features. In: Vision Modeling and Visualization Conference. Aka GmbH, pp. 233–240 (2001)
13. Cai, K., Wang, W., Chen, Z., et al.: Exploiting repeated patterns for efficient compression of massive models. In: International Conference on Virtual Reality Continuum and ITS Applications in Industry. ACM, pp. 145–150 (2009)
14. Wen, L., Jia, J., Liang, S., et al.: LPM: lightweight progressive meshes towards smooth transmission of Web3D media over internet. In: Virtual Reality Continuum and its Applications in Industry, pp. 95–103 (2014)
15. Kettner, L.: Using generic programming for "Designing a Data Structure for Polyhedral Surfaces". Comput. Geom. **13**(1), 65–90 (1999)

16. Shamir, A.: Segmentation and shape extraction of 3D boundary meshes. In: State of the Art Report Eurographics (2006)
17. Agathos, A., Pratikakis, I., Perantonis, S., et al.: 3D mesh segmentation methodologies for CAD applications. Comput. Aided Des. Appl. **4**(6), 827–841 (2007)
18. Attene, M., Katz, S., Mortara, M., et al.: Mesh segmentation - a comparative study. In: IEEE International Conference on Shape Modeling and Applications, p. 7. DBLP (2006)
19. Shlafman, S., et al.: Metamorphosis of polyhedral surfaces using decomposition. Comput. Graph. Forum **21**(3), 219–228 (2002)
20. Katz, S., Tal, A.: Hierarchical mesh decomposition using fuzzy clustering and cuts. ACM Trans. Graph. **22**(3), 954–961 (2003)
21. Garland, M., Willmott, A., Heckbert, P.S.: Hierarchical face clustering on polygonal surfaces. In: Symposium on Interactive 3D Graphics, Si3d 2001, Chapel Hill, NY, USA, March, pp. 49–58. DBLP (2001)
22. Inoue, K., Itoh, T., Yamada, A., et al.: Face clustering of a large-scale CAD model for surface mesh generation. Comput. Aided Des. **33**(3), 251–261 (2001)
23. Lai, Y., Hu, S., Martin, R.R., et al.: Rapid and effective segmentation of 3D models using random walks. Comput. Aided Geom. Des. **26**(6), 665–679 (2009)
24. Katz, S., Leifman, G., Tal, A., et al.: Mesh segmentation using feature point and core extraction. Vis. Comput. **21**(8), 649–658 (2005)
25. Mortara, M., Patane, G., Spagnuolo, M., et al.: Plumber: a method for a multi-scale decomposition of 3D shapes into tubular primitives and bodies. Stat. Methods Appl. 339–344 (2004)
26. Liu, R., Zhang, H.: Segmentation of 3D meshes through spectral clustering. In: Pacific Conference on Computer Graphics and Applications, pp. 298–305 (2004)
27. Lin, H.S., Liao, H.M., Lin, J., et al.: Visual salience-guided mesh decomposition. IEEE Trans. Multimedia **9**(1), 46–57 (2007)
28. Theologou, P., Pratikakis, I., Theoharis, T., et al.: A comprehensive overview of methodologies and performance evaluation frameworks in 3D mesh Segmentation. Comput. Vis. Image Underst. **135**, 49–82 (2015)
29. Chen, X., Golovinskiy, A., Funkhouser, T.: A benchmark for 3D mesh segmentation. ACM Trans. Graph. **28**(3), 1–12 (2009)

Dynamic Gesture Recognition Based on Edge Feature Enhancement Using Sobel Operator

Mingmin Zhang[1], Bing Wang[2], Shengle Zhou[1], and Zhigeng Pan[3(✉)]

[1] Zhejiang University, Hangzhou, China
zhangmm95@zju.edu.cn, 787306873@qq.com
[2] Jiangnan University, Wuxi, China
wangbing100@foxmail.com
[3] Hangzhou Normal University, Hangzhou, China
443922077@qq.com

Abstract. Aimed at the present situation that dynamic hand gestures recognition rate is low and the effect is not ideal, this paper uses Sobel operator to detect the edges in gesture image sequences, enhancing the edge features in dynamic gesture image. In order to prevent the information loss of gesture image after edge detection, the paper will fuse the HOG, HOG^2 feature of gesture image sequences after edge detection with that of the original gesture image sequences to enhance edge features without losing other information. In the experiments, Nearest Neighbor Interpolation (NNI) is used to normalize the image sequences to the same length with all gesture video from CVRR-HANDS 3D database, then Sobel operator is used to detect the edges in all gesture image sequences (including RGB data and the Depth data) for subsequent processing, we called edge detection image sequences for Sobel CVRR-HANDS 3D database, the original data for NonSobel CVRR-HANDS 3D database. Next we extract the HOG and HOG^2 features from NonSobel CVRR-HANDS 3D database and Sobel CVRR-HANDS 3D database, and incorporating these features. Finally, we respectively use Support Vector Machine (SVM) of the linear Kernel (LIN) and Histogram intersection Kernel (HIK) to recognize dynamic hand gestures. The experimental results show that the recognition rate from our method improves more than two percentage points compared with the traditional method on LIN and HIK kernel of SVM.

Keywords: Sobel operator · Edge detection · SVM · HOG features · HOG^2 features

1 Introduction

Gestures play an important role in our daily life, and they can help people convey information and express their feelings. In particular, interfaces incorporating hand gestures have gained popularity in many applications. Dynamic gestures recognition is the main research field and gets much attention of scholars. However dynamic gestures recognition also has many difficulties for accurate recognition [1]. These difficulties coupled with poor lighting conditions, camera's inability to capture dynamic gesture in focus, occlusion due to finger movement, color variations due to lighting conditions have introduced myriad of obstacles in realizing a true HCI.

© Springer International Publishing AG 2017
F. Tian et al. (Eds.): Edutainment 2017, LNCS 10345, pp. 152–163, 2017.
https://doi.org/10.1007/978-3-319-65849-0_16

Gesture recognition research is mainly divided into two kinds, one kind needs external devices, such as gloves and sensors. In 2015, Cheng studied Chinese Sign Language Recognition [6] using Accelerometer and Surface Electromyography Sensors. Dekate et al. Recognize gestures using Magic Glove [7]; the other kind which based on the video camera to capture data and identify gestures is more difficult. The gestures are identified according to features of the video image sequences. This paper belongs to this kind. At present the study of dynamic hand gestures recognition adopts a series of space-time descriptor [8–10], which can be used to extract features from depth image or color image. For every feature, SVM can be used to identify dynamic hand gestures.

Edges are the basic outline of an object, and the edge will change during the object moving and deforming. Thus the changing of object edges generally represents the object's actual situation. Due to most of the information from the dynamic gesture are hidden by the hand edge changing, the edge detection for each frame in dynamic gesture image sequences can strengthen the feature of dynamic gesture image.

As the improvement of resolution ratio with depth camera and ordinary camera, the research of gesture recognition around color and depth map gets more and more attention of scholars. At present the dynamic gesture recognition mainly around two big modules: the one mainly around the dynamic gesture feature extraction. Cheng uses HOG feature in gesture recognition [11]. Ohn-Bar first uses HOG^2 features in behavior recognition [8], then he introduces HOG^2 features to recognize gesture and achieves good results [12]. Klaser presents a three dimensional gradient HOG3D [9], then Ohn-Bar takes HOG3D into the dynamic gesture recognition and achieves good result [13]. Pathak proposes a novel algorithm for extracting of key frames to recognize dynamic hand gesture [2], he extracted hand shape, hand motion and hand orientation features and use Multiclass Support Vector Machine as classifier, but it doesn't work well with complex hand gesture. Ren uses Finger-Earth Mover's Distance to recognize gesture [17]. Wang captured hand 3D trajectory by leap motion, then quantified and coded the orientation characteristics as the feature to recognize dynamic hand gestures (numbers 0–9) [2]. Pang extracted divergence features, vorticity features, and hand motion direction vector as the feature and use traditional HMM to verify these features [4]. In [5], take the hand shape and motion orientation as the feature [5]. Premaratne used centroid tracking of hand gestures that captures and retains the time sequence information for feature extraction [18]. Although this method can identify 16 kinds of dynamic hand gestures, dynamic hand gestures should be very specific and simple. The other module is mainly around the classifier, at this time the feature of the dynamic hand gestures are also different. Doliotis uses the DTW (dynamic time warping) algorithm as a classifier to recognize dynamic hand gestures [15]. Although the DTW algorithm has an effect on dynamic gesture recognition, but dynamic hand gestures is more complex, and the image sequences length of each gesture movement varies a lot. Those issues bring very great difficulty to the DTW. The HMM model is also used in dynamic hand gestures recognition [16, 22, 24], which is good at identifying the simple dynamic hand gestures, and poor to more complex gestures. Heung-Il Suk propose a new method for recognizing hand gestures in a continuous video stream using a dynamic Bayesian network [21], he achieved a good result with 10 kinds of gestures. Muhammad R. Abid used support vector machine (SVM) and bag-of-feature (BOF) for dynamic hand gestures classification [23]. Stern considered the recognition of dynamic gestures based on representative sub-segments of a gesture, then using a modified longest common subsequence (LCS) measure, it gets good result, but it can only use a gesture that representative sub-segments [3].

2   Feature Extraction

In this paper, we use HOG + HOG^2 feature, which is validated by [13] as the best feature combination for recognition to validate the performance of our algorithm.

HOG: From a dynamic hand gesture video whose length is T, we extract the HOG features of every frame image, and then make a complete HOG feature, as shown in formula (1).

$$\phi(I_1, \ldots I_T) = [h_1, h_2, \ldots, h_T] \tag{1}$$

h_t is the HOG feature from frame t. $\phi(I_1, \ldots I_T)$ is the cascaded HOG feature of a whole video. In all of our experiments, we set the cell size 4 * 4 and set the orientation bins 9.

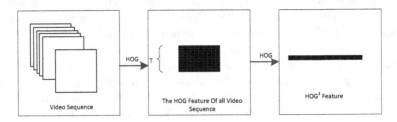

Fig. 1. Calculating HOG2 feature

HOG^2: From a dynamic hand gesture video whose length is T, we extract the HOG features of every frame image, and then the features form a two-dimensional array. HOG^2 feature is extracted through this two-dimensional array as shown in the formula (2). Figure 1 is the calculation process of HOG^2 feature.

$$\varphi(I_1, \ldots I_T) = HOG\left(\begin{bmatrix} h_1 \\ \ldots \\ h_T \end{bmatrix}\right) \tag{2}$$

3   The Proposed Gesture Recognition

During dynamic hand gestures recognition, the hand movement which composes dynamic gesture can be detected according to the edge changing of hand image sequences. Therefore we use Sobel operator to detect the edge of RGB and Depth image sequences in CVRR-HANDS 3D database. We called edge detection image sequences as Sobel CVRR-HANDS 3D database and the original data as NonSobel CVRR-HANDS 3D database. After edge detection, we calculate HOG, HOG^2 features of RGB and Depth data from Sobel CVRR-HANDS 3D database and NonSobel CVRR-HANDS 3D database respectively. Finally the dynamic gesture is identified through SVM training. In order to verify the performance of our algorithm, we incorporate the following two kinds of kernel function in SVM:

Given two data points, $x_i, x_j \in R^N$, the linear kernel is given as

$$K(x_i, x_j) = x_i^T x_j$$

The histogram intersection kernel (HIK) is given as

$$K(x_i, x_j) = \sum_{k=1:N} \min(x_{ik}, x_{jk})$$

Our algorithm includes the following six steps:

Step 1: As the number of images in each gesture videos from CVRR-HANDS 3D database are inconsistent, all dynamic gesture video frames should be normalized to T frames firstly by Nearest Neighbor Interpolation (NNI) algorithm. NNI pseudo code is shown as follows:

$$NNI(imgSequence, T)$$
$$imgLen = length(imgSequence)$$
$$rate = imgLen/T$$
$$for\ i \leftarrow 1\ to\ T$$
$$I_i^N = imgSequence(round(i^*rate))$$

imgSequence is an original dynamic gesture image sequences before NNI, T is the normalized length of the image sequences of a hand gesture video, I_i^N is the image sequences after NNI. In our experiment, $T = 32$.

Step 2: Dynamic gesture image sequence from CVRR-HANDS 3D database uses Sobel edge detection algorithm to get edge detection image sequences which corresponds to each dynamic gesture image sequence. The result data set is called as Sobel CVRR-HANDS 3D database. The original data set is called NonSobel CVRR-HANDS 3D database.as shown in formula (3) below.

$$I^S = Sobel(I^N)$$

I^S is the gesture image sequences after Sobel edge detection, $I^S = [I_1^S, \ldots, I_T^S]$; I^N is calculated at Step 1, $I^N = [I_1^N, \ldots, I_T^N]$.

Part of the gesture image after the edge detection is shown Fig. 2.

(a) Gray-scale image after edge detection   (b) Depth image after edge detection

Fig. 2. Images after edge detection

Step 3: Calculate HOG features and HOG^2 features for NonSobel CVRR-HANDS 3D database, constitute a new feature HOG + HOG^2 through the combination of the two kinds of features, as shown in formula (3) below.

$$F_{Nonsobel} = [\phi_{Nonsobel}(I_1^N, \ldots I_T^N), \varphi_{Nonsobel}(I_1^N, \ldots I_T^N)] \tag{3}$$

Where $\phi_{Nonsobel}(I_1^N, \ldots I_T^N)$ represents the HOG feature of the dynamic gesture image sequences, $\varphi_{Nonsobel}(I_1^N, \ldots I_T^N)$ represents HOG2 feature and $F_{Nonsobel}$ represents HOG + HOG2 feature from NonSobel CVRR-HANDS 3D database.

Step 4: Calculate HOG features and HOG^2 features for Sobel CVRR-HANDS 3D database. Constitute feature HOG + HOG^2 through the combination of the two kinds of features, as shown in formula (4) below.

$$F_{Sobel} = [\phi_{Sobel}(I_1^S, \ldots I_T^S), \varphi_{Sobel}(I_1^S, \ldots I_T^S)] \tag{4}$$

Where $\phi_{Sobel}(I_1^S, \ldots I_T^S)$ represents the HOG feature of the dynamic gesture image sequences, $\varphi_{Sobel}(I_1^S, \ldots I_T^S)$ represents HOG^2 feature and F_{Sobel} represents HOG + HOG^2 feature from Sobel CVRR-HANDS 3D database.

Step 5: Fusing the features from the Step 3 and Step 4, we will generate a new feature for each gesture sequences, as shown in formula (5) below

$$F_{Nonsobel + Sobel} = [F_{Nonsobel}, F_{Sobel}] \tag{5}$$

Where $F_{Nonsobel + Sobel}$ represents the feature after fusion.

Step 6: According to step 5 to extract the feature of each dynamic hand gestures, using leave-one-subject-out cross validation method and SVM classifier [14] to identifying and testing dynamic gesture. Step 6 pseudo code is shown as follows:

For i=1 to subjectNum do

    a. select Train Feature ($F_{Nonsobel+Sobel}$) about all subject except i

    b. using *feature* from a to train SVM

    c. *select Test Feature* ($F_{Nonsobel+Sobel}$) about subject i

    d.using SVM and *feature* from c to test accuracy,get accuracyList[i]

end

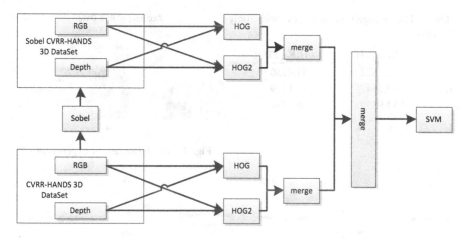

Fig. 3. Strengthen dynamic gesture recognition based on edge feature

Where subjectNum is the number of subjects in CVRR-HANDS 3D database. In our experiment, the subjectNum = 8, the final Accuracy is our dynamic hand gestures recognition result.

Figure 3 shows the design framework of our algorithm. From this framework, we can see the proposed algorithm differed from the traditional algorithms that only use original data feature, we apply both features calculated by original data and new data after edge detection by Sobel algorithm. These two kinds of information are fused together and finally classified by SVM.

4   Experimental Result and Discussion

The database of our experiment is CVRR - HANDS 3D [13], which including 19 kinds of gestures, 885 dynamic gestures video. Each gesture has both RGB data and Depth data. In our experiment, we use leave-one-subject-out to cross validation. In our method, HOG features and HOG^2 features are fused to be used as a characteristic of dynamic hand gestures. Three experiments are used to illustrate and verify the performance of our algorithm.

Experiment One: Experiment One only use RGB data to calculate the accuracy of hand gestures recognition, it has three parts: (a) Calculate the accuracy of hand gestures recognition with Original RGB data; (b) Calculate the accuracy of hand gestures recognition with RGB data after sobel edge detection; (c) Calculate the accuracy of hand gestures recognition with RGB data after sobel edge detection and original RGB data. Figure 4 show the structure of algorithms. Table 1 and Fig. 3 give the result of hand gestures recognition, for only RGB data, the recognition accuracy in part (c) is the best compare to part (a), part (c) Increased by 2 percentage points. So we can get a conclusion that sobel edge detection data have positive effect on hand gestures recognition. In addition, compare part (b) with part (a) in HIK, we can get this conclusion that though edge detection can enhance the edge region feature, edge detection

Table 1. The recognition accuracy with only RGB data

	LIN [13]	HIK [13]
(a)	50.1822	54.4136
(b)	50.7947	52.1129
(c)	54.9339	56.4178

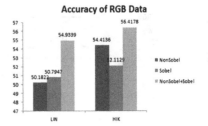

Fig. 4. The histogram of experiment one results

(a) The structure of hand recognition using Original RGB data

(b) The structure of hand recognition using RGB data after sobel edge detection

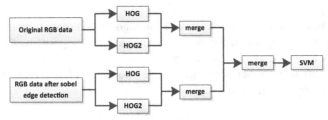

(c)The structure of hand recognition using RGB data after sobel edge detection and original RGB data

Fig. 5. Compare the accuracy of hand recognition between sobel edge detection data with original data using RGB (Color figure online)

also result in other region feature loss. So in HIK, the result of part (b) is less than part (a). In Fig. 6, the red line is the hog features of hand region in original RGB image (As shown in the red box in Fig. 5(a)), the blue line is the hog features of hand region in edge detection RGB image (As shown in the red box in Fig. 5(b)), we can see edge detection in RGB image enhanced the hog features of some regions, but it also weaken some regions, But the average hog value of edge detection hand region in RGB image is larger than the original hand region, show in Fig. 7.

Experiment Two: Experiment Two use Depth data to calculate the accuracy of hand gestures recognition. It also has three parts: (a) Calculate the accuracy of hand gestures recognition with Original Depth data; (b) Calculate the accuracy of hand gestures recognition with Depth data after sobel edge detection; (c) Calculate the accuracy of hand gestures recognition with Depth data after sobel edge detection and original Depth data. The structure of algorithms in Experiment Two is same as Experiment One, just

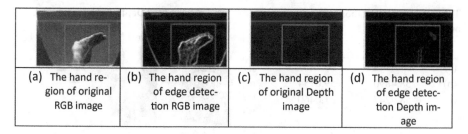

(a) The hand re-gion of original RGB image	(b) The hand region of edge detec-tion RGB image	(c) The hand region of original Depth image	(d) The hand region of edge detec-tion Depth im-age

Fig. 6 The hand region of images (Color figure online)

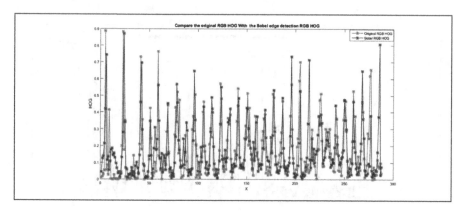

Fig. 7. The HOG features of the original RGB hand region and the edge detection RGB region

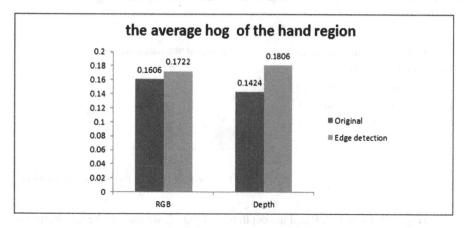

Fig. 8. The average hog of the hand region

the input data difference. Table 2 and Fig. 8 give the result of Experiment Two, we can get the similar conclusion as Experiment One. Figure 9 give us the hand region hog feature difference between original depth image (Fig. 5c) and edge detection depth

Table 2. The recognition accuracy with only depth data

	LIN [13]	HIK [13]
(a)	57.4818	60.7437
(b)	58.4890	59.0154
(c)	58.9247	61.0460

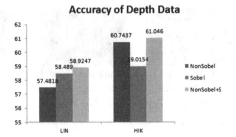

Fig. 9. The histogram of Experiment Two Results

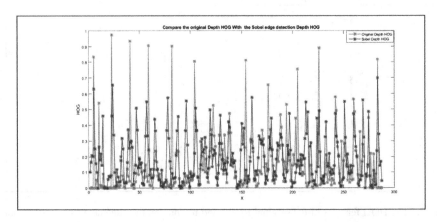

Fig. 10. The HOG features of the original depth hand region and the edge detection depth region

Table 3. The recognition accuracy with RGB data and depth data

	LIN [13]	HIK [13]
(a)	61.3195	64.6917
(b)	63.5800	66.7576

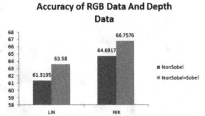

Fig. 11. the histogram of Experiment Three results

image (Fig. 5d). From Fig. 9 and the depth part of Fig. 7, we can get the hog feature in depth is same as Experiment One (Figs. 10) and 12.

Experiment Three: Experiment Three use RGB data and Depth data to calculate the accuracy of hand gestures recognition. It also has two parts: (a) Calculate the accuracy of hand gestures recognition with original RGB data and original Depth data; (b) Calculate the accuracy of hand gestures recognition with RGB data, RGB data after

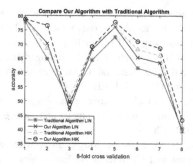

Fig. 12. The comparison about our algorithm with traditional algorithm in 8-fold cross validation

sobel edge detection, Depth data and Depth data after sobel edge detection. Through Experiment One and Experiment Two we know that edge detection have positive effect on hand gestures recognition, So we want to know what's going to happen when the feature of original RGB data and depth data combine with the feature of RGB data and Depth data after sobel edge detection. Figure 2 show the structure of (b). Table 3 and Fig. 11 give the result of hand gestures recognition. Compare to traditional method that using original data, we find our method achieve a good result. Our method accuracy increased by 2.2605% and 2.2605% under the two types of SVM kernel respectively. Figure 11 give us the results of 8-fold cross validation, in the majority of cross validation, out method is better than traditional method.

5 Conclusion

In this paper, dynamic gesture recognition after Sobel operator to strengthen the edge feature takes good effect compared with the traditional algorithm. The dynamic gesture recognition accuracy will be improved by 2% to verify our idea that strengthening the edge feature is a worthy research for dynamic hand gesture. But our algorithm has higher feature dimensions which increases the training time and test time, traditional algorithm test rate is 32 fps in i5 processor, but our algorithm test rate is 16 fps, higher feature dimensions increased test time. In the future work, we will focus on how to reduce the feature dimension under the guarantee of recognition accuracy.

References

1. Premaratne, P.: Human Computer Interaction using Hand Gestures. Springer International Publisher, Singapore (2014)
2. Wang, Q., Xu, Y.R., Bai, X., et al.: Dynamic gesture recognition using 3D trajectory. In: 2014 4th IEEE International Conference on Information Science and Technology (ICIST), pp. 598–601. IEEE (2014)
3. Stern, H., Shmueli, M., Berman, S.: Most discriminating segment–longest common subsequence (MDSLCS) algorithm for dynamic hand gesture classification. Pattern Recognit. Lett. **34**(15), 1980–1989 (2013)

4. Pang, H., Ding, Y.: Dynamic hand gesture recognition using kinematic features based on hidden markov model. In: Yang, Y., Ma, M. (eds.) (GCN 2012): Volume 5. LNEE, vol. 227, pp. 255–262. Springer, Heidelberg (2013). doi:10.1007/978-3-642-35398-7_32

5. Duc-Hoang, V., Huynh, H.H., Nguyen, T.N.: Modeling dynamic hand gesture based on geometric features. In: 2014 International Conference on Advanced Technologies for Communications (ATC), pp. 471–476. IEEE (2014)

6. Cheng, J., Chen, X., Liu, A., et al.: A novel phonology-and radical-coded chinese sign language recognition framework using accelerometer and surface electromyography sensors. Sensors 15(9), 23303–23324 (2015)

7. Dekate, A., Kamal, A., Surekha, K.S.: Magic glove-wireless hand gesture hardware controller. In: 2014 International Conference on Electronics and Communication Systems (ICECS), pp. 1–4. IEEE (2014)

8. Ohn-Bar, E., Trivedi, M.: Joint angles similarities and HOG2 for action recognition. In: Proceedings of the IEEE Conference on Computer Vision and Pattern Recognition Workshops, pp. 465–470 (2013)

9. Klaser, A., Marszałek, M., Schmid, C.: A spatio-temporal descriptor based on 3D-gradients. In: BMVC 2008–19th British Machine Vision Conference, vol. 275, pp. 1–10. British Machine Vision Association (2008)

10. Wang, H., Kläser, A., Schmid, C., et al.: Dense trajectories and motion boundary descriptors for action recognition. Int. J. Comput. Vis. 103(1), 60–79 (2013)

11. Cheng, S.Y., Trivedi, M.M.: Vision-based infotainment user determination by hand recognition for driver assistance. IEEE Trans. Intell. Transp. Syst. 11(3), 759–764 (2010)

12. Ohn-Bar, E., Tran, C., Trivedi, M.: Hand gesture-based visual user interface for infotainment. In: Proceedings of the 4th International Conference on Automotive User Interfaces and Interactive Vehicular Applications, pp. 111–115. ACM (2012)

13. Ohn-Bar, E., Trivedi, M.M.: Hand gesture recognition in real time for automotive interfaces: a multimodal vision-based approach and evaluations. IEEE Trans. Intell. Transp. Syst. 15(6), 2368–2377 (2014)

14. Chang, C.C., Lin, C.J.: LIBSVM: a library for support vector machines. ACM Trans. Intell. Syst. Technol. (TIST) 2(3), 27 (2011)

15. Doliotis, P., Stefan, A., McMurrough, C., et al.: Comparing gesture recognition accuracy using color and depth information. In: Proceedings of the 4th International Conference on PErvasive Technologies Related to Assistive Environments, p. 20. ACM (2011)

16. Keskin, C., Cemgil, A.T., Akarun, L.: DTW based clustering to improve hand gesture recognition. In: Salah, A.A., Lepri, B. (eds.) HBU 2011. LNCS, vol. 7065, pp. 72–81. Springer, Heidelberg (2011). doi:10.1007/978-3-642-25446-8_8

17. Ren, Z., Meng, J., Yuan, J.: Depth camera based hand gesture recognition and its applications in human-computer-interaction. In: 2011 8th International Conference on Information, Communications and Signal Processing (ICICS), pp. 1–5. IEEE (2011)

18. Premaratne, P., Yang, S., Vial, P., Ifthikar, Z.: Dynamic hand gesture recognition using centroid tracking. In: Huang, D.-S., Bevilacqua, V., Prashan, P. (eds.) ICIC 2015. LNCS, vol. 9225, pp. 623–629. Springer, Cham (2015). doi:10.1007/978-3-319-22180-9_62

19. Kanopoulos, N., Vasanthavada, N., Baker, R.L.: Design of an image edge detection filter using the Sobel operator. IEEE J. Solid-state Circ. 23(2), 358–367 (1988)

20. Pathak, B., Jalal, A.S., Agrawal. S.C., et al.: A framework for dynamic hand gesture recognition using key frames extraction. In: 2015 Fifth National Conference on Computer Vision, Pattern Recognition, Image Processing and Graphics (NCVPRIPG), pp. 1–4. IEEE (2015)

21. Suk, H.I., Sin, B.K., Lee, S.W.: Hand gesture recognition based on dynamic Bayesian network framework. Pattern Recognit. 43(9), 3059–3072 (2010)

22. Morguet, P., Lang, M.: Spotting dynamic hand gestures in video image sequences using hidden Markov models. In: 1998 International Conference on Image Processing, ICIP 1998 Proceedings, pp. 193–197. IEEE (1998)
23. Abid, M.R., Meszaros, P.E., d Silva, R.F., et al.: Dynamic hand gesture recognition for human-robot and inter-robot communication. In: 2014 IEEE International Conference on Computational Intelligence and Virtual Environments for Measurement Systems and Applications (CIVEMSA), pp. 12–17. IEEE (2014)
24. Wang, X., Xia, M., Cai, H., et al.: Hidden-markov-models-based dynamic hand gesture recognition. Math. Probl. Eng. **2012** (2012)

How Can 3D Game Engines Create Photo-Realistic Interactive Architectural Visualizations?

Joseph Ratcliffe[✉] and Alain Simons

Bournemouth University, Fern Barrow UK, Bournemouth BH12 5BB, UK
{i7218183,asimons}@bournemouth.ac.uk

Abstract. Architectural Visualizations are the evolution from a once used technique of Architectural Rendering. Through the proliferation of modern technology, the industry has progressed by using more contemporary applications to produce three dimensional (3D) renders for the output of images and videos. Using such applications allows for "photo-realistic" visuals that have an uncanny representation to a real-life environment, for clients to visualize proposed buildings, which can offer both interior and exterior environments. However, such applications lack a key component that could extend the platform that the visualization industry currently uses. Through recent technological developments pertaining to game engines, virtual game environments can render high fidelity visuals in real-time whilst providing interactive elements for deployment to various devices. This paper aims to create and implement an alternative method to the conventional three-dimensional pre-rendered visualizations, using a 3D game engine that can provide an interactive based solution, distributed to a computer device, for both the industry and the end user to experience.

Keywords: Photo-realistic · Visualization · Architectural · Interactive · Real time · Game engine

1 Introduction

Over the past decade, the need for 3D computer generated graphics has become ubiquitous in a variety of entertainment and industrial industries. They provide a certain kind of visual communication that allows for users or clients to understand the ideas being conveyed to them. In the architectural industry, being able to communicate such ideas has previously been dominated with the use of two dimensional (2D) renders. Although the traditional techniques are still being used in the industry today, by using 3D representations of a proposed office space, flat, etc. allows for visualization companies to create highly detailed environments that can aid in the promotion of their client's business by enticing potential buyers of properties [1].

Predominantly, within the industry, 3D rendering software is used. Applications, such as Chaos Theory's "V-Ray", allow for creators to render visualizations as frames to produce a video representation instead of having to run the environment in real-time. A benefit of such methods allows for greater visuals as the scene can have additional

© Springer International Publishing AG 2017
F. Tian et al. (Eds.): Edutainment 2017, LNCS 10345, pp. 164–172, 2017.
https://doi.org/10.1007/978-3-319-65849-0_17

lighting, higher density models and high quality textures. On the other hand, such methods can cause the issue of slow render times.

Another area that needs to be considered for the visualization is the product. Commonly a short film will be produced from the 3D renders. Providing the client with a visual representation of how their prospective building will look, which can be used for construction and advertising purposes. Although this is useful to the client, they aren't interacting with the visualization. Having such interaction would allow for the client to be more engaged with the product and get a sense of how the user would act as if they were in the real-life scenario.

To achieve additional interaction an architectural visualization company could adopt the use of a 3D video game engine. Game engines are like that of a 3D rendering application however, the environments that are produced all run in real time and allow the user to walk through the environment as if they were there. Although there are slight visual discrepancies between the two, the benefit of a video game engine may outweigh the benefits of the 3D rendering application.

2 Previous Research

Architectural Visualizations are derived from a 2D technique called Architectural Rendering. However, as technology has progressed consumers/customers are wanting more interaction with architectural environments. Rosmani et al. (2014) [2] addresses this view by proposing that many architectural visualization developers want to give viewers a more realistic environment based on 2D photos by creating a three-dimensional adaptation.

Conventionally, within industry, computer-aided design (CAD) software is used. Per Szczepaniak (2016) [3], CAD software has become a required tool for companies that build complex machines and systems. An application such as Autodesk's "AutoCAD" functions as one of those tools. A report by "Research and Markets" (2016) [4] has forecasted that architectural rendering software such as Vray, Lumion and KeyShot as a market sector should grow by 29.37% during the period 2016–2020, illustrating that there shows little sign of moving away from the traditional techniques.

As mentioned previously, within both rendered and real time solutions of a visualization or environment, lighting is an influential area in creating a realistic expectation of an environment. In a book by Mark Karlen et al. (2012) [5], they discuss various elements on the basics of lighting design. Many of the principles that are mentioned within this source suggest that effective lighting should achieve "desired moods", "provide the proper amount of light" and "produce good colour". Many of these points directly coincide with how a visualization artist carries out their lighting systems within rendering engines and real time game engines.

Commonly architectural visualizations portray exterior designs or interior designs in 3D. In regards to interior design the use of colour can illustrate a certain life-style. Guangming Chen et al. (2016) [6] relays this point by suggesting a colour scheme can "convey particular design philosophy and design a specific household style". This can be influenced by the colour of a room and furniture. For many visualization designers, they will choose a colour palette for the entirety of the project. For a modernistic approach, they may go for a "cool" colour palette or to have a classic effect go with a "warm" colour palette.

In industry, the previous conventional method of producing textures was through the means of artistic software packages such as Adobe Photoshop, within many institutions and disciplines, texturing has been produced using such digital software packages as Carol Faber (2007) [7] discusses in her paper. However, as technology has progressed, the process of texturing has also advanced. As the industry, has moved away from the previous conventional methods, a new texturing technique called "Procedural Texturing" has been introduced. This still incorporates the use of artistic software packages. Fundamentally, the procedural technique involves "code segments or algorithm that specify some characteristic of a computer-generated model or effect" David Ebert et al. (2003). Ebert [8] this allows for artists to create textures within an efficient time frame.

Coinciding with the development of procedural texturing, a new method of material creation has been implemented called Physical Based Rendering (PBR). In a guide by Wes McDermott (2014) [9] expresses that "Light-Rays" are important to understand due to the way in which the light reacts with the surface of an object, that surface is governed by how the texture and material is made. In Volume 2 of the PBR guide by McDermott (2015) [10] PBR "is a method of shading and rendering that provides a more accurate representation of how light interacts with surfaces."

Currently game engines are being used to create a variety of solutions for different industries. As they contain powerful feature sets they become increasingly useful in creating highly detailed environments. Neal Bürger [11] considered the use of Unreal 3.5 and how it can be used to create a real time architectural visualization. In his paper, he summaries that the engine could output a solution that was "positively received".

A recent development in game engine technology has even provided the film industry with the means of creating high quality rendered characters and scenes with the use of real time game engines. The first company to use a game engine for this specific purpose was Industrial Light & Magic (ILM) in the recent film "Star Wars: Rogue One". This information was gathered from a keynote by Tim Sweeney, CEO of Epic Games during GDC [12] about how some scenes within the film involving droid "K-2SO" were shot and rendered in real time within Unreal 4. Illustrating that the film industry has been looking to new methods to produce photo-realistic content without the use of the traditional rendering engines, companies such as Disney's Pixar have also been collaborating with Epic Games on the use of real-time game engines.

3   Our Research

Based upon research discovered within the literature review, refinement of software tools to implement a solution was determined. Three areas require bespoke software to create an implementation that relates to a traditional based visualization. These areas are: Modelling, Texturing and Game Engine. A modern approach to the production pipeline would be preferred as it's more efficient whilst still attaining detail. Each piece of software chosen is used within both video game and visualization industries as there is some overlap, however, the pipeline used will be more akin to the video game industry. Various elements have been influenced directly by research into the production process to architectural visualizations within game engines. Many of the theories covered within the literature review have been considered during the implementation. Colour theory, lighting theory are a selection of theories that have been adapted to create an architectural visualization fitting a specific life-style theme.

Interactive elements for the research have been produced using a node based scripting system within Unreal 4 called "Blueprints" that is a visual representation of code using C ++. These blueprints have been applied to door and lighting assets. Each asset contains their own bespoke blueprint scripts as they both function differently. Specifically, the scripting method that Epic Games has produced for their engine, is different from a competitive engine such as Unity, which offers a C# programming language method.

The physical based rendering method of texture creation has influenced the production of in game materials, providing realistic properties comparative to an object within the real world.

Within packaged development builds, the command console can be accessed to provide data within the same testing environment that the test users receive. As frames per second (FPS) is an appropriate barometer of whether visualization is optimized to run on the test system hardware, "Stat FPS" can be used to display the FPS during run time. On the test system, the visualization produced a substantial 60 FPS, which provided a smooth experience for the user (Fig. 1).

Fig. 1. Frames Per Second data, during real time testing.

To ensure animations would initiate as intended, during simulation of the visualization, within the actor blueprint an event graph displays information to illustrate if the blueprint is entering a node correctly (Fig. 2).

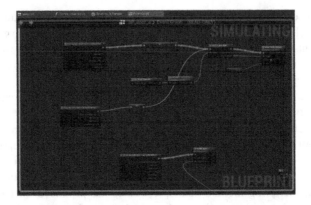

Fig. 2. Door actor blueprint, event graph

In addition to checking correct animation, revealing the collision boxes in development builds, confirmed that collision triggers were placed in correct areas to the player (Fig. 3).

Fig. 3. Rendered collision boxes, testing animation triggers

As correct lightmap resolution is critical to solving shadow irregularities within the visualization, during construction, the "Light Map Density" optimization view provided information as to whether an asset contained the "optimal" lightmap resolution (Fig. 4).

Blue coloured meshes allude to the asset perhaps needing a higher resolution, green is the ideal resolution and red is over compensating, however a balance is required as higher resolution lightmaps are more expensive in real-time. Most smaller modular sections have an exaggerated lightmap to provide sufficient shadows.

The last method to check whether "under the hood" commands execute, an output log window provides data on the specified commands, amongst other pieces of data. This window can only be accessed within the Unreal editor (Fig. 5).

Fig. 4. Lightmap Density view mode

Fig. 5. Real-time output log of executed console commands

Optimization of the solution has been extensive for the solution to work on multiple computer systems whilst still attempting to maintain standards of an industry standard visualization. Most real-time architectural visualizations require computational power that most users won't have access to, this is due to lighting calculations, scene loading and other elements all having to run in real-time when using a game engine.

However, due to the visualization running natively on a computer system rather than as a web based application, a web browser can't load detailed scenes in an efficient time

Fig. 6. A view on the presented test visualization

compared to the real-time executable application. As Liu Xiaojun et al. (2016) [13] imply within their paper, Web3D solutions can't render complex interactive scenes.

Results have been gathered by providing an executable Unreal 4 file and a video of a traditional rendered visualization which has been produced within KeyShot. These files were distributed through a Google Drive link and face-to-face. The latter testing method was conducted within a business complex on a laptop with a 970 M Nvidia Graphics Card (Fig. 6).

4   Results

To answer the question of "How can 3D Game Engines create Photo-Realistic Interactive Architectural Visualizations?", data pertaining to both technical and emotional standpoints are needed. Due to the primary target audience gathered are adults that have had experience in purchasing home and/or commercial real estate, the survey questions needed to be delivered in an understandable manner as the audience may not have the required expertise to understand how the visualization works (Fig. 7).

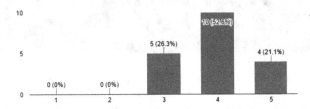

Fig. 7. Do you think the Real-time visualization's visual quality compare to that of the rendered visualization?

Results suggested that users felt that the quality was close to comparing to that of the rendered version, most responses of the survey suggested there were more objects within the rendered version which gave greater visual quality. However, many users preferred the sense of scale that can be conveyed from an interactive version as all elements are built to a 1:1 scale ratio to mimic a real-life viewing.

63.2% of users agree on interactive elements provide a benefit within the interactive solution, however some users were having issues in the control of their actions as elements such as doors could only be opened when close to the door and found that some of the collisions within the solution were frustrating (Fig. 8).

Although with these slight frustrations, interaction still provides a benefit. Almost 80% of users preferred the interactive walkthrough greatly over the video walkthrough. A frequent discussion as to why users preferred this method of delivery was largely down to being able to view everything that they wanted. Whereas the video version can only show specific portions of the visualization. Understanding of scale, floor layout among other aspects influenced their decision (Fig. 9).

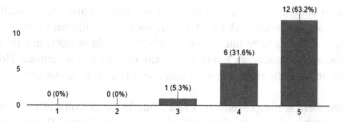

Fig. 8. Does the additional interaction (e.g. Open doors, walk through) benefit the visualization?

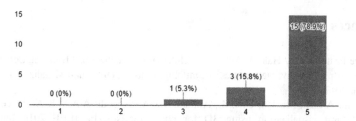

Fig. 9. Did you prefer the video presentation over the interactive walk through?

An overwhelming number of users sided with interactive visualizations having a place within the visualization industry. Although suggestions of a better methods with other technologies such as Virtual Reality and perhaps utilising mobile technologies further were given (Fig. 10).

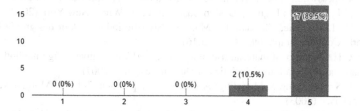

Fig. 10. Do you think interactive walk through's, have a place in the future?

On the contrary to information given from "Research and Markets" the industry suggesting that rendering software sales will rise till 2020, real-time game engine software such as Unreal 4, can provide other types of experiences that may well eclipse the use of rendering engines in the future.

5   Conclusion

A real-time game engine solution isn't distant to the rendered version in terms of visual quality, although one may conclude due to the slight limitation in achieving an exact comparison to the rendered version, would hinder the audience. Results illustrated by the outcome of both the third and fourth question asked, the audience of such real-time visualizations are interested with an interactive over the traditional solution.

For certain elements to be interactive, a sacrifice should be made in lighting quality by using moveable or stationary lights as they can be activated in runtime. However, as evident from results, the interactivity doesn't sacrifice from visual quality to a large extent.

Although, there are improvements to be made in the delivery of interactive based solutions with the inclusion of other technologies such as Virtual Reality, Augmented Reality and Mobile technologies.

References

1. Village Features 3D / Hale, J.: What is Architectural Visualization? Bluffton, South Carolina (2015). https://www.villagefeatures3d.com/blog/what-is-architectural-visualization. Accessed 10 Mar 2017
2. Rosmani, A.F.R., Mazlan, U.H.M., Ahmad, S.Z.A., Apendi, A.A.M.K.A.: Developing an architectural visualization using 3D for photo tourism. In: IEEE 2014 International Conference on Computer, Communication, and Control Technology, Langkawi, Kedah, Malaysia 2–4 September 2014. Universiti Teknologi MARA, Arau (2014). http://ieeexplore.ieee.org/stamp/stamp.jsp?arnumber=6914220. Accessed 7 Nov 2016
3. Szczepaniak, P.S.: From 3D CAD to 3D Rendering. Mach. Des. **86**(8), 54–57 (2014)
4. Research and Markets, RAM: Visualization and 3D Rendering Software Market 2016–2020 - High-End Video Games, Architectural and Product Visualization, Training Simulation, Marketing and Advertisement - Research and Markets, Dublin. (2016). http://www.businesswire.com/news/home/20160331005465/en/. Accessed 7 Nov 2016
5. Karlen, M., Benya, J.: Lighting Design Basics, 3rd edn. Wiley, New York (2017)
6. Chen, G., Li, G., Nie, Y., Xian, C., Mao, A.: Stylistic indoor colour design via Bayesian network. Comput. Graph. **60**, 34–45 (2016)
7. Faber, C.H.: Traditional material use in a digital world: a creative design methodology. In: International Association of Societies of Design Research (2007)
8. Ebert, D.S.: Texturing & Modeling: A Procedural Approach, 3rd edn. Morgan Kaufmann, San Francisco (2003)
9. McDermott, W.M.: The Comprehensive PBR Guide by Allegorithmic, vol. 1. Allegorithmic (2014)
10. McDermott, W.M.: The Comprehensive PBR Guide by Allegorithmic, vol. 2. Allegorithmic (2015)
11. Bürger, N.B.: Realtime Interactive Architectural Visualization using Unreal Engine 3.5 (2017)
12. Epic Games, EG: Quality and Innovation Take Center Stage During 'State of Unreal' at GDC 2017, Cary, North Carolina (2017). https://www.unrealengine.com/blog/quality-and-innovation-take-center-stage-during-state-of-unreal-at-gdc-2017.Accessed 10 Mar 2017
13. Liu, X., Xie, N., Tang, K., Jia, J.: Lightweighting for Web3D visualization of large-scale BIM scenes in real-time. Graph. Models **88**, 40–56 (2016)

An Efficient Human Body Contour Extraction Method for Mobile Apps

Li Wang[1], Tao Ruan Wan[2], Wen Tang[3(✉)], Yao Lin Zhu[1], and Tong Wu[1]

[1] College of Electronic and Information, Xian Polytechnic University, Xian, China
[2] Faculty of Informatics, University of Bradford, Bradford, UK
[3] Faculty of Science and Technology, Bournemouth University, Poole, Dorset, UK
wtang@bournemouth.ac.uk

Abstract. With the increasing prevalence of powerful mobile technology, many applications involve human body measurements, such as online cloth shopping. Aiming at the application of non-contact human body measurement and modeling system, this paper presents a new method for extracting human contours in complex background environment. Since the H component on the HSV color space is independent of the light changes, the hair and the lower garment can be divided. Therefore, a method of using the elliptical skin model on YCbCr color space is proposed to detect the skin color, then, automatically extract the skin samples to determine the threshold segmentation range. The combination of the two improves the skin color point recognition rate, gradually separating the body skin, clot and the hair by using these binary values of the linear fusion operation to get the final body contours. Our experiments demonstrates that this algorithm effectively reduces constraints on background environment when extracting contours.

Keywords: Contour extraction · Mobile apps · Online clothing · Gaussian mixture model · Threshold segmentation · Linear fusion

1 Introduction

The extraction of human contours is an essential part of the development of vision-based non-contact human body measurements and modeling systems. Applications of such systems are online shopping, online games, virtual reality applications. It directly affects the accuracy of subsequent body size measurements. Therefore, how to accurately extract human contours in images is a top priority [7]. Background environment directly affects the accuracy of human identification segmentation techniques.

Some research work makes a strict background requirements in order to extract accurate human body contours. Lin et al. [4,6] collected images that were pretreated by re-edge detection to extract more accurate body contours. The requirement was that the person must wear special clothing to reduce the computation workload. Deng et al. [3] have used the background difference method

© Springer International Publishing AG 2017
F. Tian et al. (Eds.): Edutainment 2017, LNCS 10345, pp. 173–181, 2017.
https://doi.org/10.1007/978-3-319-65849-0_18

to extract the body contours based on the condition that all the pixels were independent, thus, a fixed camera with a good location on the characters and scenes was needed. Camera parameters and environmental conditions error are not conducive to universal. Yang et al. [13] proposed a body contour extraction method based on the HSV color space [10], which reduced the requirements for background, clothing, and lighting. However, for backdrops and floors, the method required a solid color and the color of clothing that were distinctive from the surrounding environment to segment the skin, clothes, floor, background wall for the extraction of body contours. But the method did not establish a skin model, because the range of the skin colour difference amongst different people can be very large, so the algorithm is not highly adaptable in different situations.

The main contribution of this paper is to develop a method for body contour extraction without too many restrictions, so that it is widely applicable to various conditions for online applications such as mobile applications (mobile apps.).

2   Background

A large number of studies have shown that the main factor in the appearance of human skin color differences is due to the chromaticity. The distribution of skin colors of different people is similar to an elliptical shape in a smaller area [9]. Currently, skin detection models can be roughly categorized into threshold based method [12] and elliptical models [9]. The threshold method determines the range of the color space component in order to distinguish between the skin color and non-skin color points, albeit it is fast and efficient, it is difficult to determine the range of parameters. On the other hand, elliptical model establishes a skin color distribution by using the ellipse model to determine whether the point falls in the ellipse area, thus the pixel represents the skin colour. However, because this method is based on a large number of training samples in order to determine the overall all boundary of the skin color distribution, obtaining the training data is the core of the method. More recently, Bayesian model [1] has attached much research attentions, which requires the establishment of a skin color classifier, also a large number of training sets is needed to ensure its detection rate. The Gaussian model, including a single Gaussian model [11] and a mixed Gaussian model [8], relies on the probability density formula to determine the probability of a pixel belonging to the skin point or not. Therefore, Gaussian model can accurately detect the skin area beyond the boundary of the skin area, but the speed is slow and is affected by the color space.

From the above description, we can see that a large number of body contour extraction algorithms impose strict requirement on the visual source to be processed, such as the requirement on the scene or the background of the source materials, greatly limiting the adaptive and widespread of the use of these methods. In order to meet the real-time performance of the system, this paper combines the threshold method and the ellipse model to extract the contours of the human body to achieve efficient real-time performance. The algorithm consists of three steps: (a) Hair and shorts separation using a feature H component independent of the light changes to differentiate the hair and coat; (b) Skin division by using a CbCr color space [2,14] oval skin detection model to separate the skin, while automatically extracting human skin samples; extracting the sample HSV value as a threshold for better skin segmentation effect; (c) T-shirt division using the threshold segmentation method to extract contour, because the shirt color is single. The algorithm is robust to the background walls and floors, and gradually extracts the contours of human hair, skin and cloth to obtain the body contour. It further reduces the backdrop and the floor, the clothe of the pre-shooting requirements. Thus, the adaptability of the algorithm has also been greatly improved.

3   Improved Body Contour Extraction Method

This paper introduces a robust approach for extracting contours of human body accurately from the complex background environment. Removing a background scene to separate the human body from the scene is a difficult task due to the rapid change of the background environment. Figure 1 shows the proposed body contour extraction flow chart. The focus of this paper is on the characteristics of the human body and how to extract human body efficiently and effectively. Figure 1 outlines the extraction process, from which we can see that the main computation process for the division of clothing, hair, skin, individual differences in the body colour constitutes a very large part of this process. The use of the oval skin detection model combined with the human skin samples of HSV to maximize the effect of statistical analysis can significantly improve the skin color area recognition rate, hence, the effectiveness of the approach.

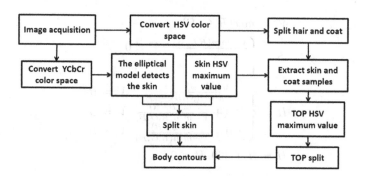

Fig. 1. Body contour extraction flow chart

RGB images taken by a smart phone were used in the experiments. Due to photo pixels, in order to improve the processing speed and reduce the amount of redundant information, the original images were compressed to 450 X 800 resolution. As shown in Fig. 2, in the experiment, a general requirement for clothing can be that participant wears a single colour vest and a dark colour shorts, and hair bundles and no shoes. The front posture of the participant

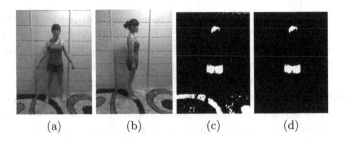

(a)   (b)   (c)   (d)

Fig. 2. RGB images (a) front image, (b)side image. (c) H binarization. (d) Processed image.

was standing with feet and arms were 45° open (Fig. 2(a)). The side pose was hands were vertical hanging straight (Fig. 2(b)). Bright lighting conditions was preferable, but the general home environment would be adequate.

3.1   HSV Colour Space and Segmenting Hair and Cloth

The HSV colour space is an oriented colour coordinate system, this colour model is close to the human colour-aware simulation model [5], where H represents the chromaticity (a measure of the composition of the color spectrum), S represents the saturation (the pure wavelength ratio in the main wavelength), indicating the degree of the same brightness of a color distance, and V represents the purity (relative to the brightness of white light). The equation for RGB transform to HSV component is Eq. 1.

$$V = max(R, G, B)$$

$$S = \begin{cases} \frac{V - min(R,G,B)}{V} & V \neq 0 \\ 0 & V = 0 \end{cases}$$

$$H = \begin{cases} \frac{60(G-B)}{V - min(R,G,B)} & V = R \\ 120 + \frac{60(B-R)}{V - min(R,G,B))} & V = G \\ 240 + \frac{60(B-R))}{V - min(R,G,B))} & V = B \end{cases} \tag{1}$$

$$H = H + 360, H < 0$$

In order to differentiate various parts of the human body, we must firstly analyze the HSV channels of the image and its histogram, as shown in Fig. 3. The color histogram is the colour features of the image, which describes proportions of different colours in the entire image. The advantages of using HSV channels are that these are that these are suitable for describing images that are difficult to automatically segment and do not need to consider objects spatial positions in the image.

In Fig. 3, histogram peak boundaries were not clear. Therefore, directly finding the threshold of the human body from the histograms can be very difficult.

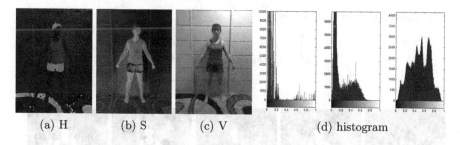

| (a) H | (b) S | (c) V | (d) histogram |

Fig. 3. HSV channel image and histogram.

Because H is almost independent to the changes in light, it can be used as colour comparison, so that images can be separated from the colorful color. Figure 3(a) shows hair and cloth colour contrast in H channel image. The three-thirds of the region below the pixel value becomes 0 and the removal of the small area can be extracted. Figure 2(d) shows the hair and shorts binary profiles.

3.2 YCbCr Colour Space and Oval Skin Detection Model

The luminance and chrominance components of the YCbCr colour space are separated, hence they are often used as colour models for detecting skin colours. In this mode Y is the brightness, Cb is the blue component of the light source, and Cr is the red component in the light source. The original RGB image conversion for YCbCr formula is as follows:

$$Y = 0.299 * R + 0.587 * G + 0.114 * B$$
$$Cr = (R - Y) * 0.713 + d$$
$$Cb = (B - Y) * 0.564 + d$$
$$R = Y + 1.403 * (Cr - d) \qquad (2)$$
$$G = Y - 0.714 * (Cr - d) - 0.344 * (Cb - d)$$
$$B = Y + 1.773 * (Cb - d)$$
$$with, d = 128, 8bit; = 32768, 16bit; = 0.5, float$$

The main factor in the appearance of the difference in colours is the skin colour variations of people represented as a skin colour distribution relative to the concentration in a smaller area, i.e. similar to the oval shape. The colour of the person can be converted to a YCbCr colour space. In the CbCr plane projection, we can get the skin colour sample set and KL transformation to establish the ellipse model. By determining whether the pixel CbCr value is in the ellipse model area, the pixel can be identified as a skin colour pixel or non-skin color pixel, separating the skin area out. The ellipse model is defined by:

$$\frac{(x - ec_x)^2}{a^2} + \frac{(y - ec_y)^2}{b^2} = 1 \qquad (3)$$

Parameter matrix is given by:

$$\begin{bmatrix} x \\ y \end{bmatrix} = \begin{bmatrix} cos\theta & sin\theta \\ -sin\theta & cos\theta \end{bmatrix} \begin{bmatrix} C'bC_x \\ C'rC_y \end{bmatrix} \tag{4}$$

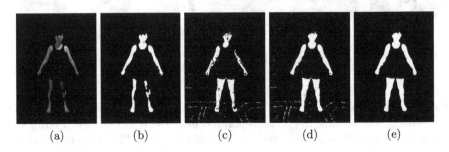

(a)   (b)   (c)   (d)   (e)

Fig. 4. Oval skin model: (a) The elliptical model for skin; (b) Ellipse models binary map. (c) Sample skin test chart; (d) Fig. 4(b) and (c) linear fusion graph; (e) Skin segmentation binary map

As shown in Fig. 4(a), the skin area is found to be defective, and the elliptical model does not fully recognize all the skin pixels, which is due to differences in the skin colour variations from person to person.

3.3   Thresholds Division of the Skin Colour

In order to solve the problem that the ellipse detection model cannot completely separate the skin, we extract the skin samples using the HSV value of the sample to determine the threshold parameters to divide the skin points. This approach helps identify the problem skin pixels and is able to mitigate the oval skin detection model deficiencies. Further, in order to define the threshold range θ_i for skin division, it is necessary to extract multiple sets of skin samples S_i of the person. Define the sample Region of Interest (ROI) which specifies the upper left corner coordinates $P_i(m_i, n_i)$ of the rectangle and the length and the width L_i, W_i of the rectangle. After a large number of experiments, it is concluded that the oval skin detection model of the leg and neck segmentations are not ideal for the distribution of human skin colour, we extracted three groups of samples from the left leg, right leg, and neck position to compensate the issues caused by the lighting.

After analyzing the sample histogram, the HSV maximum value of each sample is obtained, and it is set to separate the threshold. The pixels in the most significant range are marked as shown in Fig. 4(c), then linearly merged with Fig. 4(b) as shown in Fig. 4(d), the extraction process must have some interference points, so that removing the points and some small areas, the integration step fills the region to get more accurate results Fig. 4(e). The method of extracting the cloth area is similar to that of skin as described above. Since the cloth

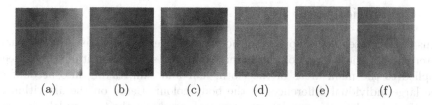

Fig. 5. Automatically extract skin ((a)–(c)) and cloth samples ((d)–(e))

colour is singular, we also extracted three areas in the middle of the image as the top cloth as shown in Fig. 5(b). Through the analysis of the top cloth sample, the maximum value was obtained and the pixels in the most valued areas were marked out, and then the three markers were linearly merged as shown in Fig. 6(a) to obtain the final cloth division as shown in Fig. 6(b).

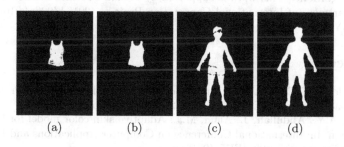

Fig. 6. (a) Linear fusion. (b) Processed image, the coat is divided. Extract the contours of the human body: (c) Integrated map; (d) Morphological operation.

The final results was shown in Fig. 6(c), which was obtained by the linear fusion of the results of Fig. 2(d), Fig. 4(e) and Fig. 6(b). Figure 6(d) was obtained by morphological closing operations applied to Fig. 6(c). Figure 7 is another example of this article, the results of the segmentation is good, but also proved the feasibility of the proposed method.

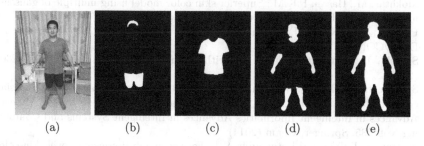

Fig. 7. Another example: (a) RGB image. (b) Hair and shorts. (c) T-shirt; (d) skin. (e) Results graph.

4   Conclusions and Future Work

This paper presents an approach of body contour extraction based on the characteristics of the surface of the human body. A set of algorithms have been applied to the main areas of the cloth, hair and skin, taking into account of the large individual differences in the body colour. Based on the algorithm of elliptical skin detection model, our approach combines the two models to automatically extract skin samples to improve the skin area Recognition rate. Finally, the results produced by the three methods were linearly merged to produce the contours via a morphological processing. Experiments show that the approach can extract the human body contours from relatively complex background scene with good results. While this work has served to propose and prototype the body extraction concept, future research will investigate algorithms to further reduce the restrictions on cloth and light and further optimization is also needed.

Acknowledgement. This work is supported by Shanxi Province Science and Technology Department of International Cooperation Projects (2016JZ026; 2016KW-043) and (2016GY-047).

References

1. Bouzerdoum, D.C.A.: A Bayesian approach to skin color classification in YCbCr color space. In: Proceedings TENCON 2000, 24–27 September 2000
2. Dawod, A.Y., Abdullah, J., Alam, M.J.: Adaptive skin color model for hand segmentation. In: International Conference on Computer Applications and Industrial Electronics, pp. 486–489. IEEE (2010)
3. Deng, W., et al.: Image extraction method of 3D human body feature based on image. J. Zhejiang University **44**(5), 837–840 (2010)
4. Jiang, L., Yao, J., Li, B., Fang, F., Zhang, Q., Meng, M.Q.-H.: Automatic body feature extraction from front and side images. J. Softw. Eng. Appl. **05**(12), 94–100 (2012)
5. Kaehler, A., Bradski, G.: Learning OpenCV 3 (2016)
6. Lin, Y.L., Wang, M.-J.J.: Constructing 3D human model from front and side images. Expert Syst. Appl. **39**(5), 5012–5018 (2012)
7. Lu, J.-M., Wang, M.-J.J.: Automated anthropometric data collection using 3D whole body scanners. Expert Syst. Appl. **35**(1–2), 407–414 (2008)
8. Mokhtar, M., Hasan, P.K.M.: Superior skin color model using multiple of gaussian mixture model. Br. J. Sci. **6**(1) (2012)
9. Peer, P., Jure Kovac, F.S.: Human skin color clustering for face detection. In: EUROCON 2003 (2003)
10. Szeliski, R.: Computer Vision: Algorithms and Applications **21**(8), 2601–2605 (2010)
11. Subban, R., Mishra, R.: Human skin segmentation in color images using gaussian color model. In: Thampi, S., Abraham, A., Pal, S., Rodriguez, J. (eds.) Recent Advances in Intelligent Informatics Advances in Intelligent Systems and Computing, vol. 235. Springer, Cham (2014)
12. Sawangsri, T., Vorapoj Patanavijit, S.J.: Face segmentation using novel skin-color map and morphological technique. In: World Academy of Science, Engineering and Technology 2 (2005)

13. Yang, M., Liu, G., Dai, H.: A study on human body contour extraction method based on HSV color space. J. Beijing Fashion Institute (Natural Science Edition) **2**, 41–46 (2015)
14. Zhang, Q.: Hand gesture segmentation based on mixed skin-color model and FCM algorithm. J. Inf. Comput. Sci. **12**(9), 3527–3536 (2015)

A Study into Autonomous Scanning for 3D Model Construction

Darryl O'Hare, William Hurst[✉], David Tully, and Abdennour El Rhalibi

Department of Computer Science, Liverpool John Moores University,
Byrom Street, Liverpool L3 3AF, UK
D.OHare@2013.ljmu.ac.uk,
{W.Hurst,D.Tully,A.Elrhalibi}@ljmu.ac.uk

Abstract. 3D scanning and printing has the potential to revolutionise the world. It offers a bridge between the virtual environment and the tangible world. The use of 3D scanners to capture and recreate defining objects is known as 3D virtualisation. It involves capturing a real-life scene using laser technology and representing its geometry using 3D modelling software or 3D printers. Despite being a relatively young technology, 3D printing has now become accessible and a part of modern industry. The printing of a 3D generated model can change the way in which an individual understands a concept, environment or communicates an idea. This has multiple benefits, for education, skills development, training and within the construction industry. However, using this technology relies on the operator having the skills and training required to generate accurate 3D models, and account for errors in the mesh after scanning. As such, this paper details the development into an automated 3D scanning system, and a cloud-based printing platform, where models are intelligently printed by multiple devices. Its development allows the readiness of 3D printing capabilities to unskilled users, who have no education or training in 3D model construction. Objects can be instantly manipulated and transferred into free-to-use open source graphic software. The access to detailed 3D model construction has never been so accessible to the untrained.

Keywords: 3D scanning · 3D modelling · Education · Real-Time

1 Introduction

3D printing has become a common tool for developing bespoke applications in construction, engineering, and computing industries. It is, however, a relatively young technology and the full applicability of 3D printing is still being investigated. One of the common prohibitive issues in 3D printing is its exclusive reliance on designers having adequate skills to create, edit and design 3D models suitable for 3D printing (Latham, *et al.,*). The creation of printable 3D models requires specialised knowledge of 3D editing software. At present, this does not favour consumers of 3D printing technology who have no 3D modelling capabilities? Therefore, model creation requires a steep

© Springer International Publishing AG 2017
F. Tian et al. (Eds.): Edutainment 2017, LNCS 10345, pp. 182–190, 2017.
https://doi.org/10.1007/978-3-319-65849-0_19

learning curve and additional expenditure in relation to 3D modelling, rendering and animation software.

Yet, architects or construction workers tend to make use of 3D construction models to plan out development and renovations. However, in practical environments, this requires the expertise of 3D modellers to construct and map out rooms or buildings inside or out in relevant 3D software. In addition, the use of off-the-shelf 3D printing technology involves techniques, which are generally slow and time-consuming.

Therefore, this project involves the development of an autonomous system for 3D room construction, object cloning and bespoke object construction. With current TOF-ready devices, it is possible to scan and image capture environments for 3D printing purposes. By autonomously converting basic measurements or images into a 3D virtual scene, an automated system would be able to 3D-clone structures or models of people etc. Additive manufacturing using a cloud-based multi-agent system can provide an approach to improve the speed of 3D printing technology (Van der Hoek *et al.*,). As such, we envision that intelligent agents can be employed to divide up 3D model structures, and distribute the segments to an arrangement of 3D printers. A selfmanaged 3D printing service, using a cloud-based model, is a relatively untried research area.

As a final objective, we will investigate how this new technology can be used by both individuals and higher education establishments to improve the way, in which, technical and complex subjects can be taught. Current 3D technologies enable a more in-depth platform for communicating information (Keskin *et al.*,). For education and teaching computer/complex theoretical concepts, adding a tangible component may change the way in which a subject is communicated (Papp *et al.*,). This paper is organised as follow. Section 2 presents a background overview on 3D model construction and 3D scanning techniques. Section 3 presents our system framework and design for an autonomous 3D scanning device. Section 3.1 presents an evaluation and discussion on the approach put forward. The future work and conclusion are presented in Sect. 4.

2 Background

When viewing a real-world tangible object, there are various aspects which require consideration. Firstly, as the reference object provides the main information for the 3D model construction, measurements need to be accurate in order to represent the realworld object as a digital output. This is a time-consuming and sometimes a costly process. Creating 3D scans using digital image capture technologies produces instant 3D rendered geometry, which is an accurate recreating of the real world object. The process is often as rudimentary as taking a series of photos or recording a video with a handheld device. Recreating an object using a camera and depth scanner has traditionally been a challenging task. However, the reality is that the post-production of a 3D scan is usually the most time consuming aspect of creating a digital representation. It is often determined by many factors, such as the GPU or CPU, which both determine the capture frame rates, and how well the hardware and the software working together actually are. The scanning process is still a task worthy enterprise and can be time consuming in its own way but this paper looks at different technologies and how this method can be improved upon making it a viable system for geometry creation. As such, in the section, related research on 3D scanning and modelling is presented.

2.1 Scanning Types

The Microsoft Kinect has a built in sensor and a high resolution RGB (Red, Green, Blue) camera capable of depth capture and 3D Mesh geometry creation (Nagori *et al.,*). Over the last 8 years Microsoft have invested significantly, both financially and through research in 3D scanning and print options; the Hololens is testament to this (Microsoft *et al.,*). They have made available free Kinect-based software to make it a viable option for users to scan an object and print out the results using a 3D printer. With the software, it is possible to create novel algorithms for motion or image capture.

In the construction industry, full-scale models can be 3D printed out from scanners attached to drones used to map out an entire cave; before any human life is put at risk venturing down (Ende *et al.,*). This now affordable technology is changing the whole perception of 3D model construction in industry. Whereas, traditionally, scanning an object, or getting a general shape, primitive techniques involved using Radar. This involves using a radio wave signal, projected out and used to shape-map an area by calculating the points where the signal would hit the object and reflect the signal back at the receiver.

More modern revolutionary techniques are found in the form of LiDAR (Tully(a), *et al.,*). Where instead of radio frequencies, a strong pulse of light is sent out and, by understanding the amount of time light takes to hit a surface and reflect back, a distance can be calculated precisely. This enables an engineer to determine the X, Y and Z coordinates of an object, which would then be used for a mapping sequence. After the first return, sequential pulses begin to create an image linking up and creating a geometry based on each coordinate created from the scanner. This would then be stored in a library of points to create a full point cloud. This is the high-end of the laser scanning spectrum, often used by geologists and meteorologists. However, LiDAR uses different laser types for various projects and conditions. Off-the-shelf scanners, like the Kinect, use a similar approach, where a scanner uses LiDAR to calculate depth.

With regards to LiDAR data, when mapping large scale environments, there are issues which may affect its accuracy. LiDAR has a high cost and, city LiDAR maps are not always up-to-date in ever changing urban environments. There is often missing data, caused by vegetation or water for which the laser used does not reflect off the object correctly. False data can also be captured from dynamic objects; vehicles, flocks of birds, swaying trees etc.

As Russel et al., state, LiDAR produces improved results of data capture in daylight hours. The issue with this is if capturing in daytime hours, multiple moving artefacts are more frequently found within the data-source. The resolution of the LiDAR maps proves troublesome in respect to processing and also data storage. Each resolution and data point count contained within each map is stated in Table 1.

Table 1. LiDAR data resolutions, dimensions, point count, and area coverage.

Resolution	Dimensions	Total points contained	Area Coverage
2 m	5002	250,000	1km$_2$
1 m	1000	1,000,000	1km$_2$
50 cm	1000^2	1,000,000	500 m^2
25 cm	2000^2	4,000,000	500 m^2

Some military organisations use LiDAR point technology in automation and rely on robots that can scan an entire building before any soldier even enters the vicinity. This helps to reduce the risk of loss of life. Figure 1 below, is an example of a LiDAR generated map.

Fig. 1. LiDAR generated map

The modern world needs to reproduce things at a rate that humans cannot keep up with. *'Time of Flight'* cameras are relatively new, in 3D scanning domain, but within photogrammetry the technique has been around for decades (Anand *et al.*,). The process works at a high frame rate and in a similar method to the LiDAR depth camera technology, where it measures the time of flight between a light signal from the camera to the object and then measures all the points it has projected onto the object. This approach is typically used in the construction industry for measuring distances between objects, measuring rooms, and also measuring the size and shape of an object.

2.2 3D and VR

Scanned 3D objects are typically deployed into virtual reality (VR) systems. VR involves user interactions between digital data in a representation of the real world (Latham, K, *et al.*,). Often, this means the user is completely immersed in an artificial environment through use of a headset, or interacts through the environment on a screen. However, creating an emulated environment is a complex procedure when modelling by hand. To develop virtualised environments, a skilled developer must create objects, as well as procedurally generated buildings, by hand or by use of algorithms (LiangKun *et al.*,). Yet, the use of 3D environments for education and learning is becoming increasingly common-place. As Zhang *et al.,* discuss, the use of a 3D virtual cloud platform can be employed for language education. As detailed in their research, the development of their system requires extensive code development and the modelling of a 3D '*game room*' for the users to interact with (Zhang *et al.*). Approaches such as this, where there is crossover between 3D modelling and games technology for real-world simulation, is becoming widespread (Tully(b) *et al.,*) as an effective way of learning and communicating. This process is known as *Game Based Learning* and its trend in recent years has been notable in pedagogic research theories (Chen *et al.,*). As such, the research presented in the paper, aims to make 3D content construction more available to the unskilled user for virtual environment creation, or 3D model construction; both for educational purposes.

3   Approach

The system put forward in this paper theorises that objects and environments can be autonomously scanned using off-the-shelf technologies and the models subsequently made accessible to the untrained. The system has a modular design, where a cloud based printing platform is employed to intelligently reconstruct accurate scale representations of the 3D scanned object. In this section, an overview of the system design is presented along with the initial experimentation. The full purpose of the system is to scan a Tangible object in real time, process the scan and output a final lower polygon mesh suitable for 3D environments as discussed above.

3.1   System Design

Figure 2 displays a high-level view of the system design. The process is completed in 4 stages which are outlined.

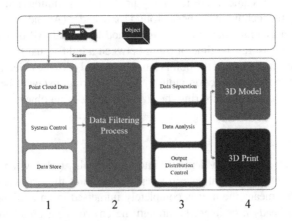

Fig. 2. System framework and process

For the scanning process, nearly all 3D scanners use a point cloud system to map and generate a shape. Each vertex created within the point cloud has its own X, Y, Z location. Combined, all these coordinates represent an entire model. Polygons can then be created from these coordinates in a 3D space. The positioning can be manipulated post process but the 3D scanner creates accurate values for each vertex and full mesh geometry can be instantly created. After the vertex locations are complete and indexed, most scanning software completes a rasterization process, turning all the newly created geometric shapes into a format capable of being seen in a renderer. At this stage textures can be applied and the model can really take shape.

To make the desired geometry of a mesh for optimizing purposes, the topology is considered. The topology is the general flow of edges, vertices and polygons of an object. Mesh optimising, creates a topology, can be crucial for frame rates and rendering, making a mesh or animation move in an environment accurately. As such, the system processes are explained as follows:

1. Object scanning is governed by the system control module, which controls the intake of point cloud data. The collected data is then placed in a temporary database.
2. The data is extracted from the temporary databased where it is filtered to check for missing values.
3. Next, in stage three, the object is divided into segments. For example, in the case of a human as the scanned object, the arms, legs, body and head would be separated and treated as different objects.
4. The model is then either sent for reconstruction in a 3D software application or printed out on a 3D cloud-based printing platform.

3.2 Case Study

To demonstrate the approach of our system, a simple scan was made of an individual participant using the Kinect v2 with minimum clothing and only scanning from the waist up. The scanning process is automated, using the system discussed in Sect. 3.1.

As the scanner employed is a Kinect v2, it meant that the polygon count was considerably high at 320,000 polygons, due to the point cloud mesh generation. This is why the third stage in the system design works to Retoplogize the new object shown in Fig. 3(b) by creating a flow of quadrilateral polygons for considerably lowering the

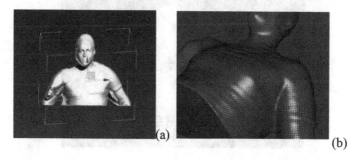

Fig. 3. 3D scanned person(a) and object after reconstruction(b)

vertices count. In Fig. 4(a), the first model is the full mesh and in (b) the texture map applies perfectly onto each triangle, as it has its own UV mapped coordinates. However once the mesh has been quadifed, the UV Map coordinates are then moved around with the new mesh geometry.

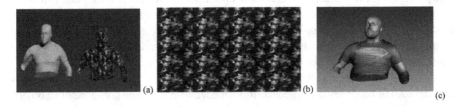

(a)   (b)   (c)

Fig. 4. Full mesh and lowered mesh(a), Texture map(b), lowered polygon model with baked textures(c)

Currently, dissecting the generated UV map at this point would be a considerable challenge for a 3D processing software. So a new texture mapping approach needs to be administered to the system.

This process, known as '*Baking*', takes the two meshes, side by side, the original mesh 1 and the new '*quadifed*' lowered mesh 2. The technique is used to transfer details from one object to another. It functions by scanning surface detail of the first object and saving the information as a texture map, using the first model's texture coordinates. The baking process takes place via the Computer Graphics software. All the texture details from mesh 1 are cast onto mesh 2. In our case study, we cast our textures onto the new lowered qualified mesh, generating a new UV Map in the process.

3.3 Output

The final output model shown in Fig. 5 demonstrates a completed modified mesh. To complete the final output for use in real time rendering applications the mesh needs to

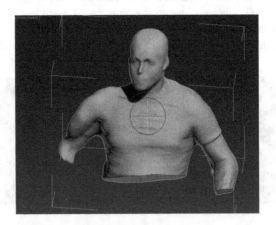

Fig. 5. Final output

be closed. An approach would be to employ a '*cap-hole modifier*', within 3D software. This would fill any holes in a mesh and remove unnecessary triangles. This however, would require training in 3D software so would not be ideal for the approach put forward. After use of a cap-hole modifier, the final output is presented in Fig. 5 and is comprised of 37,000 polygons showing a good rational of the system with 10% of the original poly count remaining with no degradation in the mesh.

4   Conclusion and Future Work

Digital scanning technology is becoming common place in education and in many industries. The use of 3D technologies can transform the way in which a concept is understood. With the increase in available off-the-shelf 3D scanning technologies such as the Kinect, 3D modelling and object reconstruction for the untrained has never before been so accessible. As such, the system presented in the paper aims to make 3D modelling more accessible to untrained users, through use of an automated scanning and modelling approach. In our future research, we will work towards the integration of artificial intelligence to understand the type of 3D object being scanned and divide the object into different parts so they can be treated as separate objects. This mean that, high detail can be captured from the correct parts and low details from the unimportant parts to ensure that file sizes are kept to a minimum.

References

Anand, C., Jainwal, K., Sarkar, M.: A high background light subtraction circuit for long range time-of-flight cameras. In: 2016 IEEE Asia Pacific Conference on Circuits and Systems (APCCAS), Jeju, pp. 487–490 (2016)

Chen, J.H., Shih, T.K., Chen, J.Y.: To develop the ubiquitous adventure RPG (role play game) game-based learning system. In: IEEE International Conference on Systems, Man, and Cybernetics (SMC), Seoul, pp. 2973–2978 (2012)

am Ende, B.A.: 3D mapping of underwater caves. IEEE Comput. Graph. Appl. **21**(2), 14–20 (2001)

Keskin, C., Balci, K., Aran, O., Sankur, B., Akarun, L.: A multimodal 3D healthcare communication system. In: 3DTV Conference, Kos Island, pp. 1–4 (2007)

Latham, K., Hurst, W., Shone, N., El Rhalibi, A., Pan, Z.: A case study on the advantages of 3D walkthroughs over photo stitching techniques. In: The International Conference on Virtual Reality and Visualization (ICVRV 2016), China (2016), submitted

Microsoft Hololens Tutorial: 2016 IEEE International Symposium on Mixed and Augmented Reality (ISMAR-Adjunct), Merida (2016)

Nagori, N.P., Malode, V.: Communication interface for deaf-mute people using microsoft kinect. In: International Conference on Automatic Control and Dynamic Optimization Techniques (ICACDOT), Pune, India, pp. 640–644, (2016)

Papp, I., Tornai, R., Zichar, M.: What 3D technologies can bring to education: the impacts of acquiring a 3D printer. In: 7th IEEE International Conference on Cognitive Infocommunications (CogInfoCom), Wroclaw, pp. 000257–000262 (2016)

Russel, S.: Artificial Intelligence: A Modern Approach, 3rd edn. Prentice Hill, New Jercy (2009)

LiangKun, S., DeTong, Z.: Polygon topology generation algorithm research based on 3D modelling. In: IEEE 2nd International Conference on Software Engineering and Service Science, Beijing, pp. 385–388 (2011)

Tully, D., El Rhalibi, I., Pan, Z., Carter, C., Sudirman, S.: Automated procedural generation of urban environments using open data for city visualisation. In: Zhang, Y.-J. (ed.) ICIG 2015. LNCS, vol. 9219, pp. 545–551. Springer, Cham (2015a). doi:10.1007/978-3-319-21969-1_49

Tully, D., El Rhalibi, A., Pan, Z., Carter, C., Sudirman, S.: Mesh Extraction from a Regular Grid Structure Using Adjacency Matrix. In: Zhang, Y.-J. (ed.) ICIG 2015. LNCS, vol. 9219, pp. 562–572. Springer, Cham (2015b). doi:10.1007/978-3-319-21969-1_51

Van der Hoek, W., Wooldridge, M.: Multi-agent systems. Found. Artif. Intell. **3**, 887–928 (2008)

Zhang, B.: Playing 3D: Digital technologies and novel 3D virtual environments to support the needs of Chinese learners in western education: Cross-cultural collaboration, gamification, well-being and social inclusion. In: 2016 22nd International Conference on Virtual System & Multimedia (VSMM), Kuala Lumpur, Malaysia, pp. 1–9 (2016)

The Analysis and Creation of Mogao Caves' Three-Dimensional Model

Yao-Lin Zhu[1(✉)], Xiao-Yu Wang[1], Tao-Ruan Wan[1],
and Yu-Qiao Yang[2]

[1] Xi'an Polytechnic University,
No.15 South Jinhua Road, Xi'an 710048, Shanxi, China
fz_zyl@126.com
[2] Chang'an University, South 2nd Loop, Xi'an 710061, Shanxi, China

Abstract. Dunhuang Mogao Grottoes is one of the most important historical and cultural sites in China. This paper proposes using three-dimensional construction method for modelling Mogao Grottoes under commercial modeling package environment to achieve realistic and accurate results in terms of dunhuang culture's preservation. Considering the complexity and fidelity of the model, the complex and irregular part of the model with limited access to the dunhuang cave details and measurement, we used image-based modeling method, and together with using geometry-based modeling method for basic environmental map configuration. In addition, this paper put forward parameterized and modular modeling method to ensure the proportion of the model not distortion and to avoid lots of repeating work, in the same time, this method will improve the modeling efficiency. At last, this paper summarizes the rules and techniques in the UV Mapping process. The results show that this method can create realistic models of Mogao Grottoes, and the model can reach the demand that the preservation of Mogao Grottoes culture and scene roaming.

Keywords: Modelling · 3D reconstruction · Maps · UV reflection

1 Introduction

Mogao Caves in Dunhuang China, as an important historical and cultural site, are suffering from considerable damage due to the combined effect of natural environment and human activities. Especially with the development of tourism, the rapid increase of tourists makes the management of this place extremely difficult, which highly accelerates the disappearance of local culture. As we all know, it is unrenewable heritage, so the digitization of cultural heritage of Mogao Grottoes conservation is imminent and significant. Hence, how to protect the Mogao Grottoes culture has become a hot research topic in recent years. Fan Jinshi, the former dean of Dunhuang Research Institution, firstly proposed the use of computer technology to preserve the Dunhuang murals and colorful art based on the idea that the digital preservation of Mogao Grottoes will be permanent.

Currently Mogao Grottoes' cultural digitization is mainly reflected in the model reconstruction of murals, painted sculptures and the like. And there are many existing

© Springer International Publishing AG 2017
F. Tian et al. (Eds.): Edutainment 2017, LNCS 10345, pp. 191–198, 2017.
https://doi.org/10.1007/978-3-319-65849-0_20

research discussing the three-dimensional (abbreviated as 3D) modeling studies: As for [1], based on Geomagic, AutoCAD and 3DMAX, 3D detailed model of the building has been constructed, which focuses on the process and method of fine ancient architecture modeling on the ground of point cloud data. Even though this modeling can meet the engineering needs, it is still wanting in terms of the removal of the point cloud noise, the reduction of point cloud splicing errors and the improvement of the automation of feature extraction and the efficiency of network modeling. As for [2], by using Bedmap2 data and ice radar data, a 3D model from Zhongshan station to Dome A section of the Gamburtsev mountain region has been created, focusing on data processing. The accuracy of this model depends on the exactness of the data and the effect of data processing. For [3], according to the relevant literature, the common methods of 3D modeling of building have been described. Besides, the process and method of 3D modeling on the basis of CityEngine have been elaborated. However, this method relies mainly on two-dimensional data obtained from total station, RTK and other specialized equipment. According to the references [4–7], multiple views modeling method based on OpenGL, VRML and spherical coordinate was introduced and modeling methods based on 3D laser scanner was proposed at the same time. From [8], an interactive and user-oriented 3D reversible modeling method was introduced. Regarding [9], the 3D modeling featured by a portable measuring device consisting of four cameras has been suggested, and it is used to obtain the data information from four directions of the object or space. About [10], image-based modeling method with the purpose of image edge detection, Hough transform processing, data acquisition model and the model creation was conducted. According to [11], a multi view 3D reconstruction method of stereo vision was proposed, and this method can be applied into the reconstruction of historical sites. The above methods can help get modeling results, but these methods either depend on the professional data collection equipment or specific modeling equipment, or even computer programming technology. Therefore, the limitations are obvious. This paper will describe a 3D modeling method based on MAYA, in order to create 3D Mogao Grottoes. Since it is a manual modeling method which does not require professional equipment and programming, modeling effects can be desirable to meet the needs of cultural scene roaming and digital preservation.

2 An Overview of Modeling Process

The nature of Maya-based modeling method is geometric modeling techniques, which requires various operations on geometric objects by a large number of multilateral surface structural 3D models. Geometric modeling technology can create fine and realistic 3D model, but for complex models, a lot of surfaces are required to reflect the details of the model, which will take enormous computing resources. This is demanding for computer performance. And the essence of the image based modeling method is to reflect the details of the model by pictures, therefore, it is not demanding for the computer hardware. Consequently, the model is far from satisfactory in roaming and vividness. The parts which are not demanding for details can be created through image-based modeling. Considering the fidelity and complexity, the mixed modeling approach involving geometric modeling and image-based modeling will be used in this work, in order to avoid weaknesses and play to their strengths.

Before model creation, it is necessary to carry out a detailed analysis of the scene to determine the model module. Good analytical work can reduce the occurrence of rework during the modeling process and improve the work efficiency. Then each module will be analyzed in detail to determine the structure of the module composition. Afterwards, different modeling methods will be selected to refine the model according to the different structural characteristics. In the following, in order to achieve realistic visual effects, it is necessary to expand the model UV, and accordingly, maps and materials balls will be made. And finally, a combination of the various parts of the model will be integrated as a whole model, aiming to complete the creation of the model. Model Create flowcharts are shown in Fig. 1.

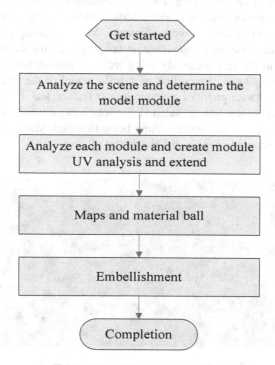

Fig. 1. Flowchart of model creation

3   The Analysis and Creation of the Model of Mogao Caves

Mogao Grottoes scenarios include nine-story (nine-story means the palace of Great Buddha), cave, cliff that cave attaches to, railings, stairs and the like. Wherein the cliff surface is the irregular planar structure, thereby, the complexity of the model will be increased if using the 3D model to reflect the undulating folds of the cliff face; meanwhile, visitors' experience will be greatly discounted if applying the 3D model into virtual roaming aspect. So the image model will be used to show the cliff surface details. The curved surfaces of tile on nine-story, though regular structures, need to be reflected by a plurality of faces; besides, given the great number of the tiles, so will be the complexity of the model. Therefore, roof will be shown in plane or cube and the details of its tiles will be reflected with pictures, for the same reason, part of the windows and doors of nine-story can also use image-based modeling method to present its hollow structure; in addition, regular and simple structures like railings and stairs will be created by geometric modeling approach; plus, caves, as the regular structure, will be presented in the geometry modeling stretched, squeezed or zoomed by a multilateral body. Because it is important to show the details the murals inside the caves, only in this way can the coming visitors get a better visual effect. Apart from that, in order to ensure the realistic effects, it is suggested to use parametric in modeling to unify and standardize the model. For the same or similar moieties, such as the promenade railings, front fence, nine-story etc., modular modeling should be adopted. Because recombination of different model modules can not only increase the reusability of modules, but also improve the work efficiency. Maya modeling provides a picture import functions for modeling convenience, in order to make the model proportions as close as possible to the real scene. By using real scenarios in the modeling process image as a modeling basis, the outline of a scale model of the real picture can be controlled. Maya software provides a picture import feature, and it is necessary to pay attention to the model view settings sided view (front view, side view or plan view), so as to maintain the ratio of the model without being distorted. Mogao Grottoes' overall external model is shown in Fig. 2, and the model of cave.

Fig. 2. Mogao Caves' overall external model

4   Model Texture

After the establishment of the 3D model, the quality of the textures plays an important role in making a difference on visual sense and realizing higher fidelity. This is what is called: modeling is 30%, while textures are 70%, because excellent textures will directly lead to excellent visual effect of a 3D model. The first crucial factor related to excellent texture is UV spin-off and display, which determines whether the textures fit with the model, otherwise, the texture will not be realized in the three-dimensional space perfectly. UV connects the model and the texture, which is the short for UV texture coordinates that identifies the positional information of each point on the texture. These points closely connect with the 3D model, and determine the position of the surface texture map, to say it inflomally, the XY coordinate on the surface of 3D model. Without UV, Maya can not make textures correspond with 3D model. NURBS model has its own UV, so the textures can be directly pasted on the model, while polygon model is more complex, so in order to make the textures correspond with the model, we need firstly to expand its UV.

UV expanding is also called UV mapping, which means the process of establishing, editing and arranging the UV and it is an important skill to get the accurate and real textures on polygon's curved surface. Maya software comes with a variety of mapping ways, including planar mapping, cylindrical mapping, spherical mapping, automatic mapping and mapping based on camera. These mapping methods use a predetermined rules to project the UV texture coordinate the model surface so that automatically create the corelation of the model surface and the texture image. Taking cavern 245 as an example, UV mapping results in using different ways of mapping. After Comparison of different mapping results of cavern 245, we can see that automatic mapping effect is the best. However, for most models, it is difficult to achieve the ideal effect only by one time UV mapping, hence, using the UV Editor (Window > UV Texture Editor) to further edit the automatic UV is also necessary. After analyzing the model structure of cavern 245, it is easy to find out that four surfaces and each side in the middle of the cave as well as the top of the cave have a large area needed to correspond with the texture. So we choose to take this part as a whole, besides, mural of niches as a whole, splitting the niche into a UV block, the rest of the porch of parts into another block; By UV editing of the model, the result of cavern 245's UV mapping is as shown in Figs. 3 and 4.

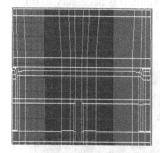

Fig. 3. Cylindrical mapping

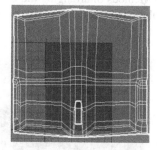

Fig. 4. Spherical mapping

Picture materials should correspond with rules of UV mapping and the model, which is usually done in image processing software of Photoshop and the model texture is shown in Fig. 5; to finish the process of making the model, we should primarily conduct the material in the material editor, and then add multi-layer to the model, the

Fig. 5. Model texture   **Fig. 6.** Cave internal rendering

results are as shown in Figs. 6 and 7. Here it is important to satisfy the following format requirements when exporting the UV:

- Format: Suggesting formats are TGA TIFF or PNG which contain channel information, and in this article, we choose the PNG format;
- Size:The size of the picture is 2n, such as 128, 256, 512 and so on. the specific size can be settled according to the requirements of the finer level of the mapping and we select 1024 * 1024 in this project;
- Memory Location:Theoretically, it is possible to customize the target position, but the truth is that it can only be exported in the default folder, which might be related to computer configuration, but it does not matter a lot;
- Name: using English name, for Maya software is in English, there will be errors when naming it in Chinese.

Methods of arranging the UV of the model are quite flexible. It is necessary to fully analyse and design properly the model structure before the UV mapping process. There

Fig. 7. Mogao Caves model

are many ways to map the UV and also will get different effects. Meanwhile, the UV editoring of polygon varies from producers who design and set different textures, but please pay attention to the following principles in the process of UV arrangement.

First, the UV mapping should be after the completion of the model; due to the UV layout directly corresponds to the model, a slight modification (such as extrusion, zoom, addition delete etc.) will lead to the change of UV, so in order to avoid duplication of useless work, modeling should be done before UV arrangement work. Second, maintain the UV undistorted; the UV spliting process is to expand a 3D model to a plane. The proportion of the map varies with the changes of the UV ratio, so if the proportion of UV do not fit the model, there might be distortion of texture's effect, so try to keep the same scaling of each surface in the same UV block. Third, avoid unnecessary overlapping of UV blocks; UV's overlapping will result in the same texture in overlapped part of the model, and also can cause incorrect display of con-cave- convex texture, so it is needed to avoid unnecessary overlapping of UV block; Conversely, if the object has any parts that the textures are the same, we can employ UV overlapping to save the texture space. Fourth, try to split edges not easy to be observed by a camera as far as possible; UV spliting is inevitable in the process of the UV mapping, but there will be an apparent juncture, if the transition on the model between both sides of the textures that were once cut is not good, so that will reduce the authentic degree of the model. Therefore, try to split more hidden positions in the process of UV production. Fifth, distribute the UV blocks reasonably; UV spliting work is for drawing the map later, so too many and cluttered UV blocks will make the following drawing work much more difficult. Hence, it is necessary to distribute the UV blocks in accordance with general visual habit of object structure which will provide convenience for following map production. UV blocks must be in distribution of 0–1 space, otherwise, UV beyond the space will be invalid. In addition, vacancies will also waste the texture space, so in the process of UV distribution, we can magnify the important parts of the UV block, so that we can get more finer details of those important parts.

5 Conclusion

The cultural sites of Mogao Caves in Dunhuang are fading fast under the mutual influence of natural environment and human activities, for this problem, this paper puts forward using Maya software to create the 3D model of the Mogao Caves to realize the idea of digital preservation of its cultural heritage. In this article, first of all, we analysed the structure of Mogao Caves and then decided to combine geometric modeling and based on image modeling methods to create the 3D model, in addition, we divided the model into two parts: external model and internal model and analysed them apart, what's more, we thoroughly introduced its creation and UV mapping processes. Then, we summarized the skill details that needed to pay attention to and the rules that should be followed in the process of UV mapping; Finally we displayed the details of the model in the article. The creation of 3D model of Mogao Caves historical and cultural relics not only can realize the digital protection of its cultural heritage, alleviating the damage caused by a large number of tourists, but also can overcome regional control at the same time, so that will greatly promote the influence of Dun-huang cultural in the worldwide. Furthermore, ideas and techniques involved in this subject also can be applied to other tourism projects or cultural heritage protection work, providing reference for cultural heritage and the new type of tourism, and will make visitors who never leave home to get a nice view of the world beautiful scenery.

Acknowledgements. This work is supported by Shaanxi Science and Technology Department of International Cooperation Projects: 2016KW-043, 2016GY-047 and 2016JZ026; 2015, Shaanxi Education Department of Special Research Program (15JK1320).

References

1. Li, Y.-Q., et al.: Study of three-dimensional geological modeling method about large antique building. J. Henan Polytech. Univ. **10**(5), 640–644 (2015)
2. Liu, C., et al.: Three-dimensional modeling of local antarctic ice sheet based on Bedmap2 and Ice Radar Data. Geodetic Geodyn. **12**(6), 957–962 (2015)
3. Qi, X.-Q., Qiao, H.: The modeling study of three-dimensional digital campus building based on city engine. Shaanxi Construct. **1**(2), 255–256 (2016)
4. Li, G.-L.: 3D modeling visualization software development based on OpenGL. China University of Geosciences, Beijing (2009)
5. Liu, W.-L.: Research of VRML-based 3D modeling in virtual reality. Wuhan University of Technology, Wuhang (2002)
6. Zhao, H.-Y., et al.: Study of multi-view 3D reconstruction based on spherical coordinates. J. Inner Mongolia Agricult. Univ. **5**(3), 146–149 (2014)
7. Wang, Y.-N., et al.: Application of three-dimensional laser scanning technology in historical building survey. Geospat. Inf. **10**(5), 116–118 (2014)
8. James, A., Hailin, J., Carlo, S.: Interactive inverse 3D modeling. Comput.-Aided Des. Appl. **6**, 881–900 (2012)
9. Peng, Q., et al.: Automated 3D scenes reconstruction using multiple stereo pairs from portable four-camera photographic measurement system. Int. J. Opt. **2015** (2015)
10. Han, L., Wang, J.: A new way to realize 3D modeling using an image. In: 6th International Conference on Measuring Technology and Mechatronics Automation (2014)
11. Xiong, J., Zhong, S.-D., Zheng, L.: An automatic 3D reconstruction method based on multi-view stereo vision for the Mogao Grottoes. In: ISPRS WG IV/7 and WG V/4 Joint Workshop on Indoor-Outdoor Seamless Modelling, Mapping and Navigation (2015)

Spherical Hybrid Curvature Images of 3D Shapes and Its Applications

Yuankui Ma[1](✉), Shusheng Zhang[2], and Xiaoliang Bai[2]

[1] School of Science, Xi'an Technological University, Xi'an 710021, China
yuankuima@126.com
[2] The Key Laboratory of Contemporary Design and Integrated Manufacturing
Technology of Ministry of Education, Northwestern Polytechnical University,
Xi'an 710072, China

Abstract. A new representation of 3D shapes is proposed using spherical hybrid curvature images. Signals like normals and curvatures are stored in spherical hybrid curvature images using spherical parameterization and partition of a sphere. The generation depends on several geometric signals, not one single geometric signal. So its colors reflect the properties of 3D shapes more clearly. With simple arrays similar to 2D image, the spherical hybrid curvature image can be post-processed easily using sophisticated image processing algorithms. Applications include segmentation, editing and model retrieval etc. Experimental results show that our method is better than other geometry image algorithms. The algorithm is simple and practical especially for models in engineering.

Keywords: Triangular mesh · Spherical hybrid curvature image · Segmentation

1 Introduction

There are already many 3D models in internet, and with the development of optical scanning, 3D modeling and 3D reconstruction [1], the number of 3D models can be shared will become more and more. How to manage and reuse these 3D models has become a hot research topic [2, 3].

Gu et al. proposed a 2D geometry image (GIM) to represent an original 3D mesh [4]. It cuts the 3D mesh open and maps it onto a unit square. The mesh is resampled onto the pixels of an image. As an added benefit, techniques such as image compression can be directly applied to the remesh. However, this extreme approach of mapping an entire mesh to a single square has limitations. Models with disconnected components require a separate geometry image per component, and complicated shapes with many extremities or topological handles have distorted parameterizations. The multichart geometry image (MCGIM) [5] presented an atlas-based parameterization to

This work is funded by Scientific Research Program Funded by Shaanxi Provincial Education Department (No. 16JK1373).

© Springer International Publishing AG 2017
F. Tian et al. (Eds.): Edutainment 2017, LNCS 10345, pp. 199–209, 2017.
https://doi.org/10.1007/978-3-319-65849-0_21

overcome the distortion problem in GIM. MCGIM consists of many irregular charts and needs a zippering algorithm to determine the pixel neighbors across charts. MCGIM solves the GIM limitation but has other problems: 1. not suitable for dynamic LOD manipulation, 2. less efficiency in packing irregular charts, 3. less efficient implementation for applications such as texture synthesis and mesh editing.

The rectangular MCGIM [6] (RMCGIM) was used to exploit rectangular patches onto tile surfaces, guaranteeing a one-to-one pixel correspondence across chart boundaries. However, it is difficult to guarantee each tiled patch with a rectangular shape. The RMCGIM still has higher distortion than MCGIM, and its packing efficiency is not too high. In contrast to multichart methods, several single chart methods such as smooth GIMs [7] and spherical parameterization [8] can reduce undersampling or distortion problem in GIMs. Although the spherical parameterization [8] only supports genus-0 meshes, this drawback is overcomed by toroidal domain tessellation [9]. Liu and Li attempted to use spherical normal image to classify genus-zero shapes [10]. In addition, AGIM [11] can achieve significant peak signal-to-noise ratio (PSNR) gain over MCGIM.

Unlike all of the above methods, the representation of triangular mesh models in engineering is proposed using spherical hybrid curvature image [12]. Signals like normals and curvatures are stored in spherical hybrid curvature images using spherical parameterization and partition of the sphere. Most models in engineering are composed by planes, spheres, cylinders and other common surfaces, which have their own features. So the generation depends on several geometric signals, not one single geometric signal. Therefore its colors reflect the properties of the triangular mesh more clearly. With simple arrays similar to 2D image, the spherical hybrid curvature image can be post-processed easily using sophisticated image processing algorithms. Applications include segmentation, editing and model retrieval etc. Segmentation is introduced in this paper in detail. Experimental results show that our method is better than other geometry image algorithms.

2 Spherical Hybrid Curvature Images

Spherical hybrid curvature image is defined as a spherical partition, which divides the sphere into multiple small areas ranged over the orderly rows. Each small area is colored after the spherical partition, and a spherical hybrid curvature image is created. The small areas can be seen as pixels of the image, whose colors can be obtained by the map of geometric signals (such as coordinates, normals, principal curvatures, curvature, etc.) from the corresponding position of the triangular mesh. So the color of the spherical hybrid curvature image reflects the properties of the triangular mesh.

The approach of transform a genus-0 triangular mesh to a spherical hybrid curvature image is: (1) parameterize the genus-0 triangular mesh by mapping to a unit ball (i.e. spherical parameterization); (2) divide the unit ball as shown in Fig. 1 (i.e. spherical partition); (3) map the geometric signals of the triangular mesh to a spherical image (i.e. coloring the spherical image). So in this section spherical parameterization, spherical partition, and coloring the spherical image are mainly described.

2.1   Spherical Parameterization

In a number of spherical parameterization methods, the progressive mesh parameterization is fast and can handle complex meshes [13], so it is used in this paper. The algorithm is as follows: (1) simplify a triangular mesh and create a progressive mesh meanwhile; (2) parameterize the simplified mesh by projection; (3) restore the original mesh and calculate the parameter of the newly inserted vertex hierarchically.

2.2   Spherical Partition

After spherical parameterization, the parameterized sphere can be divided by the following steps, as shown in Fig. 1: (1) select an inscribed hexahedral of the sphere as the initial mesh; (2) follow the topology of the cube connecting through a large arc on the sphere to divide it into six parts; (3) divide each part with a network of squares. With simple arrays similar to 2D image, the spherical hybrid curvature image can be post-processed easily using sophisticated image processing algorithms.

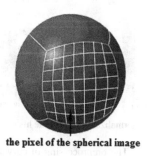

the pixel of the spherical image

Fig. 1. Spherical partition

2.3   Coloring the Spherical Hybrid Curvature Image

The colors of the pixels reflect the geometric properties of the triangular mesh model. So the process of coloring the spherical hybrid curvature image is as follows, as shown in Fig. 2: (1) calculate the geometric signals of the vertices on triangular meshes; (2) preprocess the geometric signals, such as histogram equalization; (3) get the colors of the pixels.

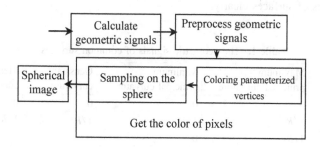

Fig. 2. Coloring the spherical image

2.3.1   Calculate the Geometric Signals

The maximum principal curvatures, minimum principal curvatures, mean curvatures and Gaussian curvatures are used in this paper. There are a lot of researches on computing the signals on meshes. The method of fitting quadratic surfaces [14, 15] is used in this paper.

2.3.2   Preprocess the Geometric Signals

After getting the geometric signals, preprocess is handled, including normalized and histogram equalization. Due to noise and large curvature (corresponding to the sharp features), the curvature of the mesh is in a large range of changes, and the curvature being interested may be only a small part of the interval. If it is mapped to color directly, most of the curvature changes can not be reflected by the colors. To solve this problem, histogram equalization is used to make that the histogram of curvature is approximately uniformly distributed [16], as shown in Fig. 3.

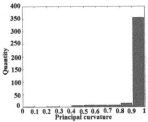 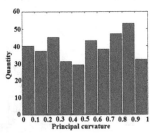

(a) The histogram of curvature after normalization   **(b)** The histogram of curvature after equalization

Fig. 3.   The preprocessing of curvature

2.3.3   Color the Pixels

Most models in engineering are composed by planes, spheres, cylinders and other common surfaces, which have their own features, as shown in Table 1. For a specific curvature, two types of surfaces may be the same, such as the common surfaces with zero Gaussian curvature are plane and cylinder. But three among them only correspond to one type of surface generally. For example, given the values of the maximum principal curvature, minimum principal curvature and Gaussian curvature, one type of surface is determined. Therefore, hybrid curvature mapping is used to distinguish different types of surfaces clearly.

Table 1.   The geometric signals of common surfaces

	Maximum principal curvature	Minimum principal curvature	Gaussian curvature	Mean curvature
Plane	0	0	0	0
Sphere	$1/R$	$1/R$	$1/R^2$	$1/R$
Cylinder	$1/R_1$	0	0	$1/(2R_1)$
Cone	$\cos\theta/\rho$	0	0	$\cos\theta/(2\rho)$

Here R, R_1, ρ, θ is the spherical radius, the cylindrical radius, the radius of the latitude circle of the cone and the half-apex angle of the cone, respectively.

The hybrid curvature mapping used in this paper is given as follows:

$$(R, G, B) = 255 \times (k_1, k_2, 1), \tag{1}$$

where k_1 and k_2 are principal curvatures after being preprocessed in Sect. 2.3.2. Different geometric signals can be selected to be mapped to different colors according to different scenes.

After coloring the parameterized vertices, the spherical hybrid curvature image can be gotten by sampling on the sphere. In order to avoid missing the details of the original mesh, dynamic sampling is used [17]. Sampling density is determined by the minimum area of the triangle in the parameter space, which ensures that the vertices with largest density can be adequately sampled.

For a sampled point on the sphere, its position must be found firstly, i.e. in which spherical triangle it is located. Then the color of the pixel is obtained by interpolating three vertices of the spherical triangle.

Denoting the colors at the three vertices P_1, P_2, P_3 of the triangle as C_1, C_2, C_3, then the color at the point P is obtained as follows,

$$C_p = \lambda_1 C_1 + \lambda_2 C_2 + \lambda_3 C_3,$$

where λ_1 is the ratio of the areas of triangle PP_2P_3 and triangle $P_1P_2P_3$, λ_2 is the ratio of the areas of triangle PP_1P_3 and triangle $P_1P_2P_3$, and λ_3 is the ratio of the areas of triangle PP_1P_2 and triangle $P_1P_2P_3$, with $\lambda_1 \geq 0$, $\lambda_2 \geq 0$, $\lambda_3 \geq 0$ and

$$\lambda_1 + \lambda_2 + \lambda_3 = 1.$$

3 Applications

Applications of the spherical hybrid curvature image include segmentation, editing and model retrieval etc., which are used in computer graphics, computer animation, reverse engineering etc. Segmentation is only introduced in this paper.

The spherical hybrid curvature image based triangular mesh segmentation is as follows: Firstly, the spherical hybrid curvature images of triangular meshes are generated, as described in Sect. 2. Secondly, the spherical hybrid curvature image is segmented based on sophisticated 2D image processing algorithms. Finally, the segmentation result of spherical hybrid curvature image is transformed into the one of triangular mesh. The algorithm is effective for non-uniform, low-resolution triangular mesh models, and need not to be post-processed. The impact of accuracy of estimated geometric properties on segmentation results is reduced, such as curvatures.

After being generated as described in Sect. 2, the spherical hybrid curvature image can be uniformly divided into six sub-blocks following the hexahedral map, and each sub-block has simple arrays similar to 2D image. So the methods of region growing and region merging for 2D image segmentation are generalized for spherical hybrid curvature image segmentation in this paper. Firstly region growing is made in each sub-block to get color types. Then the adjacent regions which are similar in color and normal are merged between the sub-blocks, so the image is represented by several colors, and color image segmentation is achieved. The algorithm is as follows:

Step1: Marking each sub-block of spherical hybrid curvature image I.

The sub-block with the same direction as the positive z-axis is denoted as P_1, and the one with the same direction as the negative z-axis is denoted as P_6; The rests are counter-clockwisely denoted as P_2, P_3, P_4, P_5, starting from the sub-block with the same direction as the positive x-axis, as shown in Fig. 4.

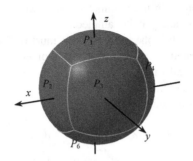

Fig. 4. Marking the sub-blocks of spherical image

Step2: Getting color groups in P_i ($i = 1, 2, ..., 6$).

The set of groups in P_i is denoted as

$$C_{in_i} = \{X_{i0}, X_{i1}, \ldots, X_{in_i-1}\},$$

with n_i the number of groups, which may be different in all sub-blocks. The number of pixels, the mean color and the mean normal of X_{ij} are denoted as n_{ij}, $\overline{c_{ij}}$, $\overline{N_{ij}}$. Two thresholds ε_1, ε_2 are selected. The first pixel is taken as the first group. Euclidean distances d_1 between $\overline{c_{ij}}$ of a known group and another pixel, and d_2 between $\overline{N_{ij}}$ are calculated. If $d_1 \leq \varepsilon_1$ and $d_2 \leq \varepsilon_2$, the group making the weighted sum of d_1 and d_2 minimum is to be searched. Then the pixel belongs to the known group. Without loss of generality, we can assume that this known group is X_{ij}. In this case, the number n_{ij} is added by one, and the values $\overline{c_{ij}}$ and $\overline{N_{ij}}$ are re-calculated. Otherwise, the pixel does not belong to all known groups. Then a new group is created, until all the color groups are convergent (i.e., the number of pixels in each group is unchanged), as shown in the following.

Input: The color c_{ik} and the normal N_{ik} of all the pixels p_{ik} in P_i, $k = 0,1,...,m-1$ (m is the number of pixels in P_i); Two thresholds ε_1, ε_2.

Output: The set of groups in P_i $C_{in_i} = \{X_{i0}, X_{i1},...,X_{in_i-1}\}$

Initializing the distances d_1, d_2;

for(k =1, k<m, k++)//starting from the second pixel
{
  n_i =1;
  for(j =0, j<n_i, j++)//The first pixel is taken as the first group
    {
      $\overline{c_{i0}} = c_{i0}$; $\overline{N_{i0}} = N_{i0}$; n_{ij}=1; Flag=TRUE;

      $d_1 = | c_{ik} - \overline{c_{ij}} |$;

      $d_2 = | N_{ik} - \overline{N_{ij}} |$;

      if($d_1 \leq \varepsilon_1$ && $d_2 \leq \varepsilon_2$)
        {
          To search the group X_{ij} making the weighted sum of d_1 and d_2 minimum, then the pixel p_{ik} belongs to the group X_{ij};
          n_{ij}++;
          The values $\overline{c_{ij}}$ and $\overline{N_{ij}}$ are re-calculated;
          Flag=FALSE;
        }
    }
  if (Flag)
    {
      The pixel p_{ik} does not belong to all known groups. Then a new group is created, of which the initial values of the mean color and the mean normal are equal to c_{ik} and N_{ik};
      n_i++;
    }
}

Step3: Merging the adjacent groups which are similar in color and normal among the sub-blocks.

The distances between the mean value of the group on the boundary of P_i and the one in the adjacent sub-block are calculated. If $d_1 \leq \varepsilon_1$ and $d_2 \leq \varepsilon_2$, the two groups are merged, not otherwise.

Step4: Getting the final color groups N.

The final color groups N is gotten as

$$N = \sum_{i=1}^{6} n_i - N_1,$$

where N_1 is the merging number in Step3.

After getting the segmentation result of spherical hybrid curvature image, with the spherical grid obtained in the partition of the sphere and the method used in paper [16], segmentation results can be mapped back to the triangular mesh model to complete the triangular mesh segmentation.

4   Experimental Results

4.1   The Spherical Hybrid Curvature Images of Triangular Meshes

Figures 5 and 6 demonstrate the spherical hybrid curvature images of triangular meshes, with (a) as the original model, (b) as the spherical parameterization and partition of the sphere, (c) as the spherical hybrid curvature image introduced in this paper, (d) as the spherical normal image introduced in paper [10], (e) as the spherical geometry image introduced in paper [4].

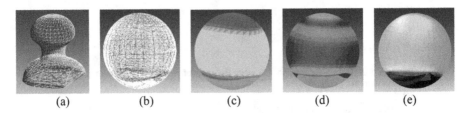

(a)   (b)   (c)   (d)   (e)

Fig. 5. Spherical images of model A: (**a**) Original model; (**b**) Spherical parameterization and partition of the sphere; (**c**) Spherical hybrid curvature image; (**d**) Spherical normal image; (**e**) Spherical geometry image.

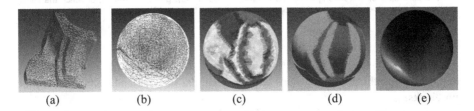

(a)   (b)   (c)   (d)   (e)

Fig. 6. Spherical images of fan-disk model: (**a**) Original model; (**b**) Spherical parameterization and partition of the sphere; (**c**) Spherical hybrid curvature image; (**d**) Spherical normal image; (**e**) Spherical geometry image.

Figures 5(c) and 6(c) show that different types of surfaces correspond to different colors. Therefore, the method in this paper can clearly distinguish the different types of surfaces, which is conducive to segmentation.

The geometry image in paper [4] (Fig. 5(e)) and the spherical normal image in paper [10] (Fig. 5(d)) can not achieve the distinction among different types of surfaces, because for different types of surface, the color of the boundary is not clear in the image. Figure 5(d) shows that the lower half of the image is clearly divided into three parts corresponding to the three connected planes of the original model from left to right (Fig. 7), which has made up the defect that the connected planes are mapped to the same color in this paper, i.e. there is no distinction in the lower half in Fig. 5(c). Therefore, the combination of spherical normal image and spherical hybrid curvature image can classify triangular mesh more clearly (Fig. 8(b)).

Fig. 7. Spherical normal image of model A

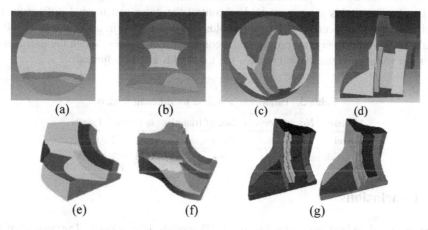

(a)   (b)   (c)   (d)

(e)   (f)   (g)

Fig. 8. Segmentation results: **(a)** Segmentation result of (c) in Fig. 5; **(b)** Segmentation result of (a) in Fig. 5; **(c)** Segmentation result of (c) in Fig. 6; **(d)** Segmentation result of (a) in Fig. 6; **(e)** Segmentation result in paper [18]; **(f)** Segmentation result in paper [19]; **(g)** The initial segmentation result and the one after merged and smoothed in paper [20].

4.2 Segmentation

Figure 8 shows the segmentation results. Figure 8(e) shows the segmentation result of fan-disk model containing 6475 vertices using the region growing method based on curvature tensor analysis and classification of curvature in paper [18]; Fig. 8(f) shows the segmentation result of non-uniform fan-disk model containing 10,921 vertices based on convex-concave signal in paper [19]; Fig. 8(g) shows the segmentation result based on random walks theory in paper [20]; Fig. 8(d) shows the one based on our method, a non-uniform fan-disk model containing 2344 vertices is used. Table 2 shows

Table 2. Time of different algorithms used for fan-disk model

Methods	No. of vertices	No. of triangles	Time/s	Per 1 K triangles/s
Our method	2344	4684	0.805	0.172
Curvature tensor [18]	6475	12946	0.624	0.048
Convex-concave signal [19]	10921	21838	1.610	0.074
Random walks [20]	11239	22474	0.764	0.034

the time of different algorithms above, on an Intel(R) Core(TM) 2 Duo 2.00 GHz CPU, together with 2 G of RAM.

It can be seen from Fig. 8 that the boundaries of the segmentation results (e), (f), (g) are not very satisfactory, especially in (g) some regions which are not the same type do not be segmented effectively, and need to be post-processed and smoothed. The segmentation results in this paper are better than the ones based on the above three methods, not needing to be post-processed. The method in this paper can segment non-uniform, low-resolution triangular mesh models effectively.

Table 3 shows the experimental parameters and time in the segmentation as shown in Fig. 8. Thresholds ε_1, ε_2 are used to control the color and normal differences in region merging, respectively. Two thresholds can be selected in a range over 0.3–0.4 and 0.1–0.2 respectively, according to the complexity of models. When the user is not satisfied with the segmentation results, the thresholds can be adjusted.

Table 3. Parameters and time for different models

Models	No. of vertices	No. of triangles	ε_1	ε_2	Time/s
Model A	1022	2040	0.4	0.2	0.31
Fan-disk	2344	4684	0.31	0.1	0.805

5   Conclusions

The spherical hybrid curvature image of 3D models is proposed. The algorithm is simple and practical. Signals like normals and curvatures are stored in spherical images using spherical parameterization and partition of the sphere. The generation depends on several geometric signals, not one single geometric signal. So its color reflects the properties of the triangular mesh surface more clearly than spherical geometry images and spherical normal images. With simple arrays similar to 2D image, spherical hybrid curvature images can be post-processed easily using sophisticated image processing algorithms. Applications include segmentation, editing and model retrieval etc. Experimental results show that our method is better than other geometry image algorithms.

References

1. Hengel, A.V.D., Dick, A., et al.: Video trace: rapid interactive scene modeling from video. ACM Trans. Graph. **26**, 861–865 (2007)
2. Johan, W., Tangelder, C., Veltkamp, R.: A survey of content based 3D shape retrieval methods. In: Proceedings of the Shape Modeling International, pp. 145–156. IEEE Computer Society Press, Washington DC (2004)
3. Sun, X.P.: The Segmentation of 3D Models and Its Applications. Institute of Computing Technology, Chinese Academy of Sciences, Beijing (2005). (in Chinese)
4. Gu, X., Gortler, S.J., Hoppe, H.: Geometry images. In: Proceedings of Computer Graphics. Annual Conference Series, pp. 355–361. ACM, New York (2002)

5. Sander, P.V., Wood, Z.J., Gortler, S.J., et al.: Multi-chart geometry images. In: Proceedings of Symposium Geometry Processing, pp. 146–155. ACM, New York (2003)

6. Carr, N.A., Hoberock, J., Crane, K., et al.: Rectangular multi-chart geometry images. In: Proceedings of Fourth Eurographics Symposium on Geometry Processing, pp. 181–190. ACM, New York (2006)

7. Losasso, F., Hoppe, H., Schaefer, S., et al.: Smooth geometry images. In: Proceedings of Eurographics/ACM SIGGRAPH Symposium on Geometry Processing, pp. 138–145. ACM, New York (2003)

8. Praun, E., Hoppe, H.: Spherical parameterization and remeshing. ACM Trans. Graphics **22**, 340–349 (2003)

9. Schreiner, J., Asirvatham, A., Praun, E., Hoppe, H.: Inter-surface mapping. In: Proceedings of ACM SIGGRAPH, vol. 204. pp. 870–877. ACM, New York (2004)

10. Liu, S.J., Li, J.: Genus-zero shape classification using spherical normal image. In: 18th International Conference on Pattern Recognition, pp. 126–129. IEEE Computer Society Press, Washington DC (2006)

11. Yao, C., Lee, T.: Adaptive geometry image. IEEE Trans. Visual. Comput. Graph. **14**, 948–960 (2008)

12. Ma, Y.K., Zhang, S.S., Bai, X.L., et al.: The spherical images of triangular mesh surfaces. In: The 12th International Conference on CAD/Graphics, pp. 119–123. IEEE Computer Society Press, Washington DC (2011)

13. Zhou, K.: Digital Geometry Processing: Theory and Applications. Zhejiang University, Hangzhou (2006). (in Chinese)

14. Zhu, X.X.: Modeling Technology of Freeform Curve and Surface. Science Press, Beijing (2000). (in Chinese)

15. Bai, X.L.: Research on Hybrid CSG/B-Rep Model Reconstruction in Reverse Engineering. Northwestern Polytechnical University, Xi'an (2005). (in Chinese)

16. Li, Q.M.: Some Applications of Wavelets in Reverse Engineering. Zhejiang University, Hangzhou (2006). (in Chinese)

17. Zhang, X.Y.: Study of 3D Modeling and Processing Based on Meshes. Zhejiang University, Hangzhou (2004). (in Chinese)

18. Lavoué, G., Dupont, F., Baskurt, A.: A new CAD mesh segmentation method based on curvature tensor analysis. Comput. Aided Des. **37**, 975–987 (2005)

19. Dong, H.W., Li, Z.H., Zhou, R.R., et al.: Mesh segmentation based on convex-concave signal. J. Comput. Aided Des. Comput. Graph. **31**, 295–304 (2009). (in Chinese)

20. Lai, Y.K., Hu, S.M., Martin, R.R., et al.: Rapid and effective segmentation of 3D models using random walks. Comput. Aided Geom. Des. **26**, 665–679 (2009)

WebPainter: Collaborative Stroke-Based Rendering Through HTML5 and WebGL

Ning Xie, Mengyuan Ren, Wu Yang, Yang Yang, and Heng Tao Shen[✉]

School of Computer Science and Engineering, Center for Future Media,
University of Electronic Science and Technology of China, Chengdu, China
hengtaoshen@hotmail.com

Abstract. Computer-aided drawing system assists users to convert the input real photos into painterly style images. Nowadays, it is widely developed as cloud brush engine service in many creative software tools and applications of artistic rendering such as Prisma [1], Photoshop [2], and Meitu [3], because the machine learning server has more powerful than the stand-alone version. In this paper, we propose a web collaborative Stroke-based Learning and Rendering (*WebSBLR*) system. Different from the existing methods that are mainly focused on the artistic filters, we concentrate on the stroke realistic rendering engine for browser on client using WebGL and HTML5. Moreover, we implement the learning-based stroke drawing path generation module on the server. By this way, we enable to achieve the computer-supported cooperative work (CSCW), especially for multi-screen synchronous interaction. The experiments demonstrated our method are efficient to web-based multi-screen painting simulation.

Keywords: CSCW · SBR · Artistic stylization · WebGL

1 Introduction

Computer-aided drawing system assists users to convert the input real photos into painterly style images. Nowadays, it is widely developed as cloud brush engine service in many creative software tools and applications of artistic rendering such as Prisma [1], Photoshop [2], and Meitu [3], because the machine learning server has more powerful than the stand-alone version.

Following the trends of mobile officing, education and creative solution, the techniques of computer-supported cooperative work (CSCW) are widely used in many aspects such as Slack [4], Microsoft Office 365, and Adobe creative cloud. The CSCW supports a group of individuals working on projects at different physical sites. It is based on the principle of group coordination and collaborative activities supported through computer systems.

In this paper, we propose a web Stroke-based Learning and Rendering (*Web-SBLR*) system for collaborative creation and education on painting for beginners. Different from the existing methods that are mainly focused on the artistic

© Springer International Publishing AG 2017
F. Tian et al. (Eds.): Edutainment 2017, LNCS 10345, pp. 210–217, 2017.
https://doi.org/10.1007/978-3-319-65849-0_22

filters, we concentrate on the stroke realistic rendering engine for browser on client using WebGL and HTML5. In detail, We apply the HTML5 artistic rendering framework called *AlloyImage* to achieve the task through CSCW across the multiple terminal such as iPad, smartphone and PC.

Moreover, the key challenge in painterly rendering is the stroke placement. A lot of significant efforts has been made to investigate how to draw a stroke with realistic brush texture in a desired shape and how to organize multiple strokes. In our web-based system, we implement a novel learning-based stroke drawing path generation module on the server.

Our paper is organized as follows. Section 2 reviews the related works. In Sect. 3, we overview our pipeline. Section 4 describes our web-based rendering module. The experimental results show from Sect. 5. Finally, we summarize the contribution of this paper in Sect. 6.

2   Related Works

Artistic stylization (AS) in non-photorealistic rendering (NPR) enables non-expert users or beginners to stylize pictures with the appearance of traditional art forms, such as pointillism painting, line sketching, or brush stroke drawing. Among these art forms, the brush stroke drawing is one of the widely used art styles across various cultures in history.

The artistic filter could be the most straightforward approach for painterly rendering with respect to art pattern design [5,6]. However, in case of online painting teaching interactively under CSCW, this artistic filter based method is not suitable. Because the artistic filter is in one-shot manner, which can not reproduce the procedure of painting stroke by stroke.

To settle these problems related to physics-based painting, the stroke-based rendering method was presented to directly simulate rendering marks (such as brush strokes, lines, or even larger primitives) on a 2D canvas. It is much practical than the series of physical brush simulation method [7,8], since the rendering power of WebGL is limit.

This stroke-based rendering [9] underpins many artistic rendering algorithms, especially on those emulating traditional brush-based artistic styles such as oil painting and watercolor [10,11]. It is extremely convenient to apply into our web-based application in drawing and creating compared with desktop softwares.

3   Overview of Our WebPainter Pipeline

In this work, we mainly aim at web-based Stroke-based Rendering (*WebSBR*) system for collaborative creation and education on painting. The pipeline is illustrated in Fig. 1. Two contributions of this work focus on proposing (1) the method on the pixel level rendering in the canvas of HTML5 and WebGL, and (2) the discreted stroke path interpolation based on Catmull-Rom Spline [12].

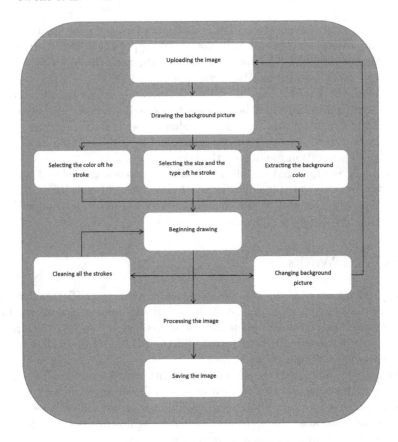

Fig. 1. The flow diagram of the proposed *WebPainter* system.

The details are shown as below:

1. Record the sampling points of user specified stroke path once user inputting.
2. Interpolate the stroke path based on Catmull-Rom Spline in Javascript on the client side.
3. Create the dataset of strokes texture with different size and transparency so as to select the specific effect of the brush texture according the speed and the strength of the users' input.
4. Map brush texture pictures according the path of users' interaction.
5. Upload the user's desired real photo for sketching as you will.
6. Set the size of the brush and the color of the pigment either from the input photo or user specified.

4   Web Stroke-Based Learning and Rendering

In this work, we build our web Stroke-based Learning and Rendering module upon AlloyImage, which is a HTML5 image processing library. AlloyImage provides the chance to process the image on web side. It can offer a variety of complicated functional operations which derive from the underlying data module encapsulation including matrix operations and fast Fourier transforms, etc. We can implement more diversified effects by fine tuning the parameters of the images within the mathematical processing modules. It has a variety of advantages including the easy-to-use practical API. Aslo, it provides several artistic filter in order to convert the color, artistic style and so on. In order to extend the ability of artistic image processing, we further implement the IRL-based stroke-based rendering (IRL-SBR) [13], and achieve a simple and practical drawing simulation web application with artistic stylization with the concept of CSCW.

4.1   Sampling Points Pre-processing

The sampling points are collected by setting the delay time and the loop call function. The key issues include how to set the delay time, serious bias in generated strokes, as well as space occupy. We modify the color and width to obtain the various effects with different sizes where the strokes could be monotonous. We can not only bring the texture result, but also use textures of different sizes or transparency according the speed and the strength of the user's input. In our algorithm, Catmull-Rom Splines is adopted to smooth the path with less computation.

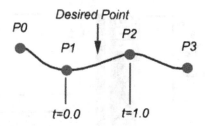

Fig. 2. Catmull-Rom Splines.

For computing the Catmull-Rom Splines, two sampling points and their adjacent points should be considered as shown in Fig. 2, where t represents the distance of the nearest two points.

$$q(t) = 0.5(1.0, t, t^2, t^3) \begin{pmatrix} 0 & 2 & 0 & 0 \\ -1 & 0 & 1 & 0 \\ 2 & -5 & 4 & -1 \\ -1 & 3 & -3 & 1 \end{pmatrix} \begin{bmatrix} p_0 \\ p_1 \\ p_2 \\ p_3 \end{bmatrix} \tag{1}$$

Transition matrix is represented as Eq. (1). The thickness of strokes tends to be different when drawing individual strokes according to the speed and strength. The distance of two sampling points also depends on the various speed of user sketching and the selected input photo. Meanwhile, the thickness and the density is also adjusted by distance computing. Moreover, the orientation of the stroke remains same to the direction of user interaction. For pigment setup, the color can be picked up from the pixel of the input picture.

4.2 Stroke Generation

The raster brush texture is applied to generate both dry and wet textures. Rendering is carried out by capturing single footprints of a brush and then stamping them along the trajectory obtained by the user sketch. We collect the reference texture of brush footprints from the scanned brush footprint images, and then sampled with different contents of ink of hollow strokes for rendering the change of the stroke texture. Then, we save them into raster textures to create our brush footprint texture libraries. Discrete series of footprint images need to be interpolated to render strokes with smooth textures. We implement this stroke generation method in AlloyImage artistic processing framework.

5 Experiment

In this section, we will give the explanation of our system and results. Within the concept of CSCW, the group participators can successfully work at the same time and even at various terminals. The overall designing style of our drawing simulation web application with artistic stylization was keep consistent with

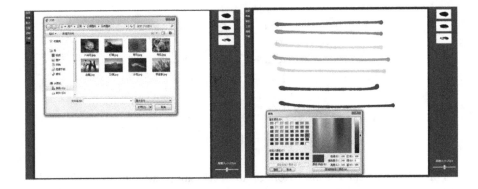

Fig. 3. The user interface of our system.

Fig. 4. The result of artistic filter in our system.

Fig. 5. Rendering results.

traditional desktop graphics softwares but more simple and practical as shown in Fig. 3. The result of the artistic filter in our system is illustrated in Fig. 4. The rendering results are illustrated in Fig. 6.

Fig. 6. Rendering results.

6 Conclusion

In this paper, we propose *WebSBLR*, which is the CSCW Stroke-based Learning and Rendering system. We implement the stroke realistic rendering engine for browser on client using WebGL and HTML5. The learning-based stroke drawing path generation module on the server. The experiments demonstrated our method are efficient to web-based multi-screen painting simulation (Fig. 5).

Acknowledgments. This work was supported in part by the National Natural Science Foundation of China under Project 61602088, Project 61572108 and Project 61632007 and the Fundamental Research Funds for the Central Universities under Project ZYGX2016J212, Project ZYGX2015J055 and Project ZYGX2014Z007. Authors are grateful to the anonymous reviewers for their careful readings and valuable feedback.

References

1. https://en.wikipedia.org/w/index.php?title=Prisma_(app)&oldid=769699619
2. https://en.wikipedia.org/w/index.php?title=Adobe_Creative_Cloud& oldid=771515328
3. https://en.wikipedia.org/w/index.php?title=Meitu&oldid=761855434
4. https://en.wikipedia.org/w/index.php?title=Slack_(software)&oldid=771140361
5. Kyprianidis, J.E., Kang, H., Dllner, J.: Helpinghand: image and video abstraction by anisotropic Kuwahara filtering. Comput. Graph. Forum **28**(7), 1955–1963 (2009)
6. Jan, E.K., Henry, K.: Image and video abstraction by coherence-enhancing filtering. Comput. Graph. Forum **30**, 593–602 (2011)
7. Chu, N., Tai, C.L.: Moxi: real-time ink dispersion in absorbent paper. ACM Trans. Graph. **24**(3), 504–511 (2005)
8. Chu, N., Baxter, B., Wei, L.Y., Govindaraju, N.K.: Detail-preserving paint modeling for 3D brushes. In: Proceedings of the 8th International Symposium on NPAR, pp. 27–34. ACM, New York (2010)

9. Hertzmann, A.: A survey of stroke-based rendering. IEEE Comput. Graph. Appl. **23**, 70–81 (2003)
10. Xie, N., Laga, H., Saito, S., Nakajima, M.: IR2s: interactive real photo to Sumi-e. In: Proceedings of the 8th International Symposium on Nonphotorealistic Animation and Rendering, NPAR 2010, pp. 63–71. ACM (2010)
11. Bousseau, A., Neyret, F., Thollot, J., Salesin, D.: ACM Trans. Graph. Video watercolorization using bidirectional texture advection **26**(3), 104 (2007)
12. Derose, T.D., Barsky, B.A.: Geometric continuity, shape parameters and geometric constructions for Catmull-Rom Splines. ACM Trans. Graph. **7**(1), 1–41 (1988)
13. Xie, N., Zhao, T., Tian, F., Zhang, X., Sugiyama, M.: Stroke-based stylization learning and rendering with inverse reinforcement learning. In: International Conference on Artificial Intelligence, pp. 2531–2537 (2015)

Digital Visualization of Design and Construction Process of Traditional Village Dwellings

Jian Zhang[✉]

Sichuan Fine Arts Institute, Chongqing 401331, China
Jianfiremax@gmail.com

Abstract. The traditional village dwellings and its construction process have been a very important part of Chinese construction culture. However, during the past decades the large scale of urbanization in China has put that tradition and culture in great danger. To protect and sustain the dwellings, in recent years the digital media technology has been applied to the implementation and development of visualizing the design and construction process of traditional village dwellings. Through the filed study on the traditional village dwellings in Sichuan and Chongqing, China, this paper explores new digital visualization concepts and approaches to exhibiting the design of dwellings, aiming to improve and enhance people's awareness and attention to the construction process and culture of traditional dwellings.

Keywords: Digital visualization · Digital media · Cultural heritage · Traditional dwellings

The countryside shall be the sources of etiquette, the foundation of traditional ethics and the cradle of Chinese farming civilization [1]. The traditional village dwellings and its construction process is an indispensable and more important part of Chinese construction culture, representing the essential wisdom and extraordinary manual ability of Chinese laboring people. The dwellings and their forming process contain massive information, in which Chinese historical civilization, as well as national historical and cultural memory is concentrated; origin of national culture form is inherited; regional material and mental culture is presented as a miniature. However, large scale of urbanization has brought modern engineering technologies and new types of buildings, which significantly compress living space of traditional village dwellings and room of its engineering development. The ancient craftsman system is collapsing, expelling traditional construction process into oblivion. Without proper maintenance with the original craftsmanship, the authentic appearance of some ancient buildings is losing gradually, which would probably disappear in the near future. Thanks to the emergence of digital media, a chance of tremendous reform on the protection of traditional village dwelling construction process has shown up. In fact, the digital visualization technology has also provided a new technical guarantee and spread thoughts for the cultural heritage and the development of traditional village dwellings construction process.

© Springer International Publishing AG 2017
F. Tian et al. (Eds.): Edutainment 2017, LNCS 10345, pp. 218–223, 2017.
https://doi.org/10.1007/978-3-319-65849-0_23

1 Background and Significance of the Digital Visualization

Since the evaluation and selection of the traditional village in 2012, there are total 2555 candidate traditional villages in China. Most of those traditional villages have been built for a long time and have accumulated abundant historical and cultural information. Meanwhile, unique buildings and building cluster with unique characteristics are also formed during the long-term changes of the rise and fall and the morphological evolution. As a historical heritage of the traditional village cluster living space, the traditional village dwellings have become such a vivid history with unique characteristics during human perennial activities; it is a unique language of space to interpret the traditional cultural customs and the specific living style of the times. For those traditional village dwellings among the historical retention, by using new media technology related to cultural heritage protection like image, audio and video in recent protection and development actions, combining with the three-dimensional data information acquisition means like the digital editing, storage and retrieval, etc., it has provided the effective means of protection to ensure sustainable development of traditional village dwellings. Thus the artistic and cultural values of those traditional village dwellings are well preserved to the largest extent.

Currently, the digital protection on material landscape heritage like the traditional village dwellings has entered into a positive cycle. However, construction technique and process that can reproduce and inherit these precious cultural landscape is as valuable as dwellings themselves. In the process of urbanization, traditional construction technique is disappearing under the impact of modern engineering expertise and new types of buildings. With the development and popularity of those digital technical means such as internet, big data, public resource platform and mobile smart device, etc., it is very critical to utilize the new methods and means to interpret the traditional village dwellings construction process and give them new significance in the era (Fig. 1).

Fig. 1. VR exhibition of traditional village dwellings

The digital visualization technology refers to realization of the digital communication and exhibition of non-material cultural heritage based on the multimedia technology, the internet of things, 4G mobile communication network, mobile intelligent application terminals, virtual reality and holographic projection, etc. [2]. Through digital exhibition technology, elimination, induction or the necessary supplementation on the information of massive traditional village dwellings construction processes can be provided. So that to record and save those content and information in a systematical and visualized way is made possible. The digital visualization of construction process of traditional village dwellings represents the characteristics of abundant diversification and extremely powerful inter-discipline property; integrating so many communication means and technical applications such as PC network platform, mobile smart apps, interactive public resource application and VR devices, etc. In addition, a sense of freshness can be maintained through those new communication forms like game, calendar, etc., guiding user's initiative for participation. The digital visualization of traditional village dwellings construction process has greatly increased user's sense of experience and intrusive sensation during the operating process. The application of mobile intelligent terminals in the digital visualization of traditional village dwellings construction process has also made it more convenient for the public to operate. The audience can also achieve more interactive experiences while sharing the cultural information. Furthermore, the improvement on the breadth and speed of communication has also enabled the construction process with even stronger communication effect, and practically achieved the purpose to exhibit and spread the traditional culture accordingly.

2   The Cultural Inheritance and Innovation of Visualization Design

A digital visualization media for intangible cultural heritage is able to exhibit the intangible cultural heritage in exact scenario visually on the digital terminals, realizing the fast and effective communication and visualization accordingly, so as to achieve the ultimate purpose for intangible cultural heritage inheritance and protection [3]. The traditional village dwellings construction process shall be the precipitation and continuation of history and culture as it has represented the evolution of Chinese traditional civilization context. Thus the cultural representation of exhibition design shall be particularly important. The cultural inheritance and innovation shall always be the focus of digital design of cultural heritage, and the dwellings shall be the effect between Chinese traditional village historical time and space and the social environment. As a result, it should both reflect the social and historical styles, and represent the certain temper of times during the digital protection or reconstruction design of traditional village dwellings construction process by focusing on the establishment of contemporary context of traditional and historical culture memory and selecting the design language for digital visualization properly.

3   The Digital Visualization of Traditional Village Dwellings Construction Process in Sichuan and Chongqing

Among those nominated national traditional villages, nearly 40% of them are located in southwest areas. Except for Guizhou province, most of traditional villages are in the areas of Sichuan province and Chongqing. Behind modern cities are those traditional villages hidden, in which, ancient dwelling and buildings such as the Stilted buildings, Blockhouse, stone towers are retained. What is more, precious construction processes in construction architecture, production processes, working methods, customs, geomantic omen, artist conception etc. are also inherited. In this paper, I focus on the study of communication and protection of traditional village dwellings and their construction process in Sichuan and Chongqing by using the digital technology, and on the basis of deep field investigation. I also integrate the theories and methods of architecture, folklore and art studies, etc. to further explore the intelligence and construction thought, ecological and craft aesthetics inside the digital visualization design of traditional village dwellings.

3.1   The Artistic Reconstruction on Building's Cultural Spirit

In his book of *Simulation and Simulacra*, the scholar Baudrillard has interpreted the transformation of modern visual paradigm from "simulated image" to "simulacra". The product of visual times - "simulated image" shall be the created object, but with the grow-up logic belonging to the independence, it was not only the "reflection" and "communication" of the world we lived in, but also created such a world [4]. In this topic, it firstly sorted and analyzed the collected information in exhibition design, made digital modeling based on the prototype object with comprehensive assumption, trying to accurately reconstruct the national cultural attributes and process procedure of the dwellings in Sichuan and Chongqing. By conducting dynamic breakdown and reconstruction of traditional engineering technique, construction process of traditional dwellings is made deductive while coding. During the design of visualization platform, by creating the memory that can be easily recognized by the user through the application of elements and symbols with the characteristics of Sichuan and Chongqing, a deep connotation on significance of traditional rural dwellings is given to the user, realizing information communication of traditional village dwellings construction process culture in Sichuan and Chongqing.

3.2   Scientific Structuring on Cultural Information

Human individuals shall have gradually increased desire on more information. However, an exhibition would usually present massive of information, giving the audience a sense of losing direction and a sense of failure to memorize such a burden of information. The audience would then choose to terminate their visits. Due to the existence of multi-ethnic settlement in the areas of Sichuan and Chongqing, there are abundant dwellings construction materials. In this case the problem faced by the research group during the long-term collection and preparation of materials is not insufficient information, but excessive information, whose content cannot be exhibited with all necessary details. Among the massive quantity of image, text, data, article and other materials, it is essential to make broad and accurate selection of these information which is to be shown on the reasonably-built platform.

In this paper, through deepened analysis on public cultural needs and proper quantitative and qualitative analysis relevant information has been classified. Repeated and similar information are filtrated, so that an information framework with logic and differences is formed dedicatedly. In addition, by utilizing the technology combining with s selective focus and artistic means, the visualized construction cultural information through the network media can be spread. The design concept for digital visualization platform of traditional village dwellings in Sichuan-Chongqing region and its construction process is promoted to the public in a professional way. All these has promoted the knowledge that originally belongs to professional fields enter into the field of public cultural communication accordingly.

3.3 Inheritance and Sustaining of Regional Culture

The multi-ethnic settlement has brought the diversified characteristics for the ethnic life in Sichuan and Chongqing region, marking the regional cultural imprinting on the dwellings in such region. The core concept for promoting p tangible and intangible cultural heritage protection through the form of digital media and extending the theoretical research with straightaway application in different contexts would simplify the profound knowledge. During digital visualization design of traditional village dwellings construction process in Sichuan and Chongqing, the designers have made efforts to find the equilibrium and harmonious point between modern technology and traditional culture, to interpret the dwellings construction process inside the traditional culture of Sichuan and Chongqing through digital visualization. The theoretical research has been extended into different contexts and is represented to the public by a straightaway means. The professional and complicated content has become quite easier to understand and to use, interpreting the construction processes of traditional village dwellings with one and another mainline stories based on historical background through various dynamic diagram interpretation to explain the materials, tools, customs, craftsman system, production processes and patterns, etc. In addition, the digital visualization has enabled the user experiencing the ethnic wisdom, culture, etiquette, life customs hidden behind the traditional village dwellings in Sichuan and Chongqing (Fig. 2).

Fig. 2. To represent traditional village dwelling construction process through 3D animation form.

4   Conclusion

By combining the disciplines of architecture, communication and the new media technologies, etc., the digital visualization has not only explored such a new path to communication and protection of traditional village dwellings construction process, but also brought a new perspective for the people to recognize traditional village dwellings construction process. By exploring the concept and new design of digital visualization, this paper concludes that the manifestation of the tradition and cultural connotation in the traditional village dwellings construction process shall be the spirit of digital visualization design, and that the interpretation on regional characteristics and cultural connotation should be fully respected, restoring and completing artistic expression to the design accordingly.

Acknowledgements. This work is a periodical finding of the two projects: (1) Humanities and social science research project of Chongqing Municipal Education Commission in 2017 [17SKG131]; *(2)* The institution reform project of Sichuan Fine Arts Institute - *The Crossover and melange - the study on "information and interaction" curriculum system and teaching mode under the trans-disciplinary context* in 2016 [2016JG31].

References

1. Zhang, F.: The new countryside construction, de-urbanization and rural renaissance. Acad. J. Guizhou Normal Univ. (social science edition) (06), 14–19 (2013)
2. Wang, J., Wang, S., Chen, S.: The study on the protection measures of intangible cultural heritage based on digital technology. Softw. Guide (08), 49–51 (2011)
3. Zhang, X.: The study on digital exhibition media of intangible cultural heritage. Packag. Eng. (05), 20–23 (2015)
4. Ding, L.: The visual art innovation under digital media context. Nanjing Arts Institute, Nanjing (2013)

GPGPU-Based Painterly Rendering for Mobile Environment

Seulbeom Kim[1], Dongwann Kang[2], and Kyunghyun Yoon[1(✉)]

[1] Chung-Ang University, Seoul 06974, Korea
khyoon@cau.ac.kr
[2] Bournemouth University, Fern Barrow, Poole BH12 5BB, UK

Abstract. This paper presents a method for the real-time implementation of brush stroke-based painterly rendering in a mobile environment using the General-Purpose computing on Graphics Processing Units (GPGPU). We parallelize brush search and comparison, and accelerate them using GPGPU to improve the computation time. Through this approach, a 35 times higher computational speedup was achieved for high-resolution images compared to the previous Central Processing Unit (CPU)-based painterly rendering algorithms.

Keywords: Non-photorealistic rendering · Painterly rendering · Mobile environment

1 Introduction

Painterly rendering refers to the technique of stylizing an image based on painters' drawing style. Painterly rendering can be classified into two categories. One is the style transfer method which considers a painting image itself as a reference and transfer its style into the original input image. The other method is to algorithmically imitate the way in which painters draw paintings. This method takes the drawing elements, such as the images of real brush strokes, as a database, and attempts to draw a painting similar to the input image by locating strokes on empty canvas [1, 2]. Compared to style transfer methods, painterly rendering methods based on a brush strokes database are more predictable and can produce more natural images. However, they have the disadvantages in aspect of computation speed because many brush strokes should be painted to mimic real painting. Moreover, due to insufficient computational resources, previous research on painting rendering in mobile environments [3] were based on processing on CPU.

To obtain high-quality painterly rendered results for high-resolution images in a mobile environment, we propose a brush-stroke-based painterly rendering method employing parallelized computation which can be accelerated by using GPGPU. By parallelizing the processes of dividing the image into grids of a certain size, searching for the appropriate brush for each grid, and applying the brush, as used in previous systems, we significantly enhance the speed of searching for the optimal brush for each grid.

© Springer International Publishing AG 2017
F. Tian et al. (Eds.): Edutainment 2017, LNCS 10345, pp. 224–227, 2017.
https://doi.org/10.1007/978-3-319-65849-0_24

2   Brush-Based Painterly Rendering Method

Figure 1 shows an overview of a typical brush stroke-based painterly rendering method. After generating a multi-layered canvas of the same size as the resulting image, each layer of canvas is divided into brush grids with a pre-defined size. Normally, the grid size of upper layer is smaller than those of lower layer. Then, the processes of finding the best brush stroke which is similar to the original image from the database and applying the brush stroke on the canvas are performed repeatedly for each grid of a layer. The best brush stroke is found by searching the brush stroke ($I_{brush}(id)$) in the database whose color difference from original input image (I_o) is minimum. At this time, brush strokes are rotated by using an interval with certain degree to find best matching angle, consequently the best brush stroke is defined as the ID (id) and rotated angle (θ) as shown in Eq. (1). During this process, when a grid of a layer is chosen to find its best brush stroke, if the part of canvas (I_c) corresponding to the grid was previously drawn on lower layers, the best brush stroke which is selected to be drawn on the grid on current layer is drawn only in case of that the color distance between newly drawn part (I_r) and original input image is lesser previous one (Eq. 2). This avoids not only the decline of painting quality but also excessive over painting. At this time, error tolerance e is used to allow slight artistic error.

$$\text{argmin}_{id,\theta} Dist\left(I_o, I_{brush}(id, \theta)\right) \tag{1}$$

$$Dist\left(I_o, I_c\right) - Dist\left(I_o, I_r\right) > e \tag{2}$$

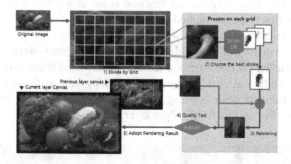

Fig. 1. An overview of a typical brush stroke-based painterly rendering method.

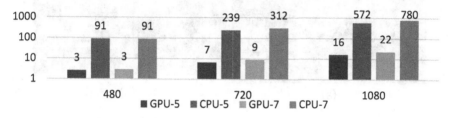

Fig. 2. Comparison of computation time results between CPU and GPGPU versions (sec).

At each step of moving to the next layer, the grid size is reduced to represent a more detailed expression. However, if the grid size is too small, or if too many layers are specified, the number of computing operations increases geometrically and the result is more photorealistic rather than artistic.

Among these stages, the stage that causes main bottleneck effect in the overall computational process is the search for best brush stroke at each grid. A large amount of time is spent on calculating the color distance between each pixel to compare between a brush stroke and a grid (original image or canvas) for similarity. This paper aims to improve the speed by processing this stage in parallel.

3   Parallel Processing and Hardware

Two aspects have been accelerated through parallel processing in this paper. One is a searching process for the best brush stroke for each grid, and the other is a pixel-wise parallel processing during image comparison.

The reason for parallelizing in this manner is to optimize the process for GPGPU. In GPGPU libraries, such as CUDA or OpenCL, a group of threads is organized as a block, and a group of blocks is organized as a grid. This configuration optimizes the cache memory usage between the neighboring cores of a GPU, as the threads that form a single block can share the local memory, allowing memory optimization.

We aim to optimize the cache memory usage by fetching the brush stroke and image data to local memory inside the image comparison function (used for finding best brush stroke for each grid and comparing between, before and after applying the brush stroke). In other words, the image comparison function is set as a single thread block, and a multiple of these functions are applied on each brush grid, to search for the best brush stroke for multiple grids simultaneously.

To enhance the quality of the resulting image, multiple grids were overlapped on a single layer. While the previous method searches for a single brush stroke and places it on a single position for each grid, our method overlaps these grids, so that more brush strokes can be identified while drawing a single layer. The resulting images in Fig. 3 were obtained by overlapping 64 grids per layer.

(a)   (b)

Fig. 3. Original input image (a) and result of this paper (b).

4   Experimental Result

For the experiment, SONY Xperia Z1 was used, and the actual computation time was measured after closing all the applications except the basic ones and that used for the experiment. To measure the results, three different images containing people, scenery, and objects were used, and the resolutions were adjusted close to 480p, 720p, and 1080p, respectively. Moreover, with a fixed number of layers, the same number of grids was used for computation in both the CPU and GPGPU versions. The overall computation time was evaluated using the average of the three images.

Figure 2 shows a comparison graph between the computation times of each different versions of the application. From the experimental results, it can be observed that the resolution has a greater impact than the number of layers, and this is attributed to the fact that the number of grids increases in proportion with the square of the resolution. The CPU version takes around 5 min for 720p, which is considered inappropriate for the smartphone application environment. However, the GPGPU-based version exhibits a maximum computation time of 22 s even with a 1080p resolution, which indicates that the present method is capable of converting high-resolution images that were difficult to process with the previous algorithm.

5   Conclusion

This paper proposed a system that can produce high-resolution painterly images in a mobile environment by parallelizing the existing brush database-based painterly rendering system and accelerating it using GPGPU. The experimental result indicates a 35-fold performance improvement with high-resolution images compared to the previous system based on CPU only. Based on this performance improvement, painterly images with better quality could be obtained using a greater number of grids per layer.

Future works may consider the technique of drawing a clear straight line similar to that drawn with an oil painting knife. Further, there is a technique for accentuating the colors in the original image. Both the techniques are expected to enhance the quality of the painterly images.

Acknowledgement. This work was supported by the National Research Foundation of Korea (NRF) grant funded by the Korea government (MSIP) (No. NRF-2017R1A2B4007481).

References

1. Lim, H.T., Shim, H.O., Yoon, K.H.: A painterly rendering system in mobile environment. In: HCI Korea Conference, pp. 115–117 (2014)
2. Seo, S., Park, J., Yoon, K.: A painterly rendering based on stroke profile and database. In: Proceeding of Fifth Eurographics Conference on Computational Aesthetics in Graphics, Visualization and Imaging, pp. 9–16 (2009)
3. Song, H.W., Seo, S.H., Ryu, S.T.: Development of an iPhone-based real-time painterly rendering system. J. Korean Soc. Comput. Game **23**, 175–182 (2010)

Generating Stained Glass Animation

Dongwann Kang[1], Doan Quang Vu[2], and Kyunghyun Yoon[2(✉)]

[1] Bournemouth University, Fern Barrow, Poole BH12 5BB, UK
[2] Chung-Ang University, Seoul 06974, Korea
khyoon@cau.ac.kr

Abstract. Generating stained glass animation from a given video is a challenging issue in computer graphics. It requires to maintain the temporally coherent stained glass pieces between all frames in video. To cope up with this problem, we propose a method for generating stained glass animation with panoramic image. In this method, we first extract temporally coherent segments from a given video. We then divide each big segment into sub-segments by dividing the panoramic image. As a result, we obtain temporally coherent segments as glass pieces. Then, we generate stained glass pieces by employing image-based stained glass rendering method to each sub-divided region.

Keywords: NPR · Panoramic image · Temporal coherency

1 Introduction

Stained glass, which means colored glasses, has been produced since ancient times. Initially, stained glass was crafted for the need of building, especially for windows of the Gothic church. In the stained glass, small pieces of glass are arranged to form patterns or pictures, and are held together by lead came, because a stained glass which consists of large sized glass pieces is architecturally unstable.

In Non-photorealistic rendering field, several studies focused on imitating stained glass effect. Mould [1] firstly proposed a method for generating a stained glass image utilizing morphological operations, color palette, and displacement-mapping to manipulate and render segmented regions. Brooks [2] also proposed image-based stained glass method for transferring the color of real stained glass example into input image. In spite of these studies, rendering stained glass animation methods for video input are not proposed yet. So, in this study, we aim to generate an animation with stained glass style from video input.

2 Proposed Method

2.1 Video Segmentation

To obtain overall form of glass pieces from input video, we segment each video frame by using mean-shift video segmentation [3]. Mean-shift is a technique to seek local maxima of density in the feature space and widely used in image and video segmentation.

© Springer International Publishing AG 2017
F. Tian et al. (Eds.): Edutainment 2017, LNCS 10345, pp. 228–232, 2017.
https://doi.org/10.1007/978-3-319-65849-0_25

However, especially for video, it produces too many segments even if parameters are appropriately adjusted. To avoid over-segmentation, we extract the low frequency layer from input video by using image decomposition technique [4], and apply mean-shift segmentation to the layer of video frames. Figure 1 shows the results.

Fig. 1. Input video frames (top) and segmented results (bottom)

Although the segmented regions we obtain are not over-segmented, some regions are too large to be used as glass pieces. However, glass pieces should be proper-sized to be architecturally stable. A recent study for rendering stained glass [5] proposed a method for resegmenting such regions to obtain regular regions. Similarly, we also sub-divide large segments. To create coherent glass pieces between video frames, this sub-division should consider temporal coherency. To achieve this, we first obtain a panoramic image which is synthesized by merging each segmented region between frames, we then sub-divide it into several small regions. To generate panoramic image, we extract the feature points between each region (I_i) in frames by using the ASIFT algorithm [6] which is a fully affine invariant feature detector. F_{ij} a set of features on I_i which are matching points between I_i and I_j is as follow.

$$F_{ij} = \left\{ f_{ij}^k | i, j \in N, k \in K_{ij} \right\} \tag{1}$$

Here, N is the number of source images, K_{ij} is feature points between I_i and I_j. We calculate F_{ij} between a region I_i and a region I_j in adjacent frame by using ASIFT. We then deform each region by moving features F_{ij} to synthesize panoramic image. For this, we employ image deformation methods using moving least squares [7]. Figure 2 shows regions in frames and synthesized panoramic image.

Fig. 2. Segmented regions (a–c) and synthesized panoramic image (d).

We then sub-divide the panoramic regions of which the size is larger than pre-defined threshold value. To achieve this, we employ Voronoi diagram. We first generate random seed points within the panoramic image, then apply Voronoi diagram to them. At this time, we assign random weights to the sites, and apply weighted Voronoi diagram to obtain arbitrary shape and size. Figure 3 shows the sub-divided results.

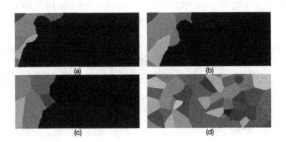

Fig. 3. Sub-divided region in frames (a–c) and weighted Voronoi diagram on panoramic image.

2.2 Stained Glass Rendering

Brooks [2] proposed an image-based stained glass method which generates stained glass image by transforming each segment of image to match real segments of stained glass from an example stained glass database. We employ his approach, and render each stained glass piece by using real stained glass example image. In this process, we only use the low-frequency layer which is extracted in Sect. 2.1 to avoid excessive detail. By using Brooks' method, we compute the color distance and texture distance between each sub-divided region in video volume and real stained glass piece in the database (Fig. 4 (a)), and find the piece of which distance is minimum as the best matching piece. We then transfer the color of the best matching piece to corresponding sub-divided region by using Reinhard's method [8] (Fig. 4 (b)). In addition, to express many small facets on the surface of glass pieces, we add Perlin noise to transferred regions (Fig. 4 (c)).

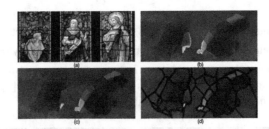

Fig. 4. Stained glass rendering process: real stained glass example (a), color-transferred result using the example (b), the result with glass facet effect (c), and the result with lead came (d)

In real stained glass, there are lead came which holds glass pieces together. In this study, we mimic lead came by simply drawing black curves with pre-defined width along to the boundary of glass pieces (Fig. 4 (d)).

Figure 5 shows the results of stained glass animation generated by proposed method. As shown in the figure, stained glass effects are coherently maintained in frames.

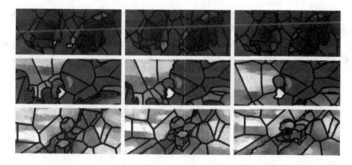

Fig. 5. Stained glass animation results: stained glass effect is coherently maintained in frames.

3 Conclusion

This paper presents a method for generating stained glass animation from a given video. To achieve this, we segment video frames into coherent regions by using mean-shift segmentation. We then sub-divide large regions into smaller sub-regions. To obtain temporally coherent regions, we merge each region in frames to a panoramic image, and sub-divide it by using weighted Voronoi diagram. To render these sub-divided regions into stained glass pieces, we find the best matching glass piece from example stained glass piece database, and transfer its color to the region. Finally, we draw lead came on the boundary of regions, consequently obtain temporally coherent stained glass animation of input video.

In this study, we utilize the low-frequency layer of input video to omit the detail which disrupts video segmentation and color transfer. However, this also causes the lack of important detail in results. In traditional stained glass, detail was usually painted on the glass directly. In future work, we will enhance the detail by adding detail part through painterly rendering techniques.

Acknowledgement. This work was supported by the National Research Foundation of Korea(NRF) grant funded by the Korea government(MSIP) (No. NRF-2017R1A2B4007481).

References

1. Mould, D.: A stained glass image filter. In: Proceedings of EGSR, pp. 20–25 (2003)
2. Brooks, S.: Image-based stained glass. IEEE TVCG **12**(6), 1547–1558 (2006)
3. Wang, J., Thiesson, B., Xu, Y., Cohen, M.: Image and video segmentation by anisotropic kernel mean shift. In: Pajdla, T., Matas, J. (eds.) ECCV 2004. LNCS, vol. 3022, pp. 238–249. Springer, Heidelberg (2004). doi:10.1007/978-3-540-24671-8_19
4. Subr, K., Soler, C., Durand, F.: Edge-preserving multiscale image decomposition based on local extrema. ACM Trans. Graph. **28**(5), 1–9 (2009). Article No. 147
5. Doyle, L., Mould, D.: Painted stained glass. In: Expresive 2016, pp. 1–10 (2016)
6. Morel, J.M., Yu, G.: Asift: a new framework for fully affine invariant image comparison. SIAM J. Imaging Sci. **2**(2), 438–469 (2009)

7. Schaefer, S., McPhail, T., Warren, J.: Image deformation using moving least squares. ACM Trans. Graph. **25**(3), 533–540 (2006)
8. Reinhard, E., Ashikhmin, M., Gooch, B., Shirley, P.: Color transfer between images. IEEE Comput. Graph. Appl. **21**(5), 34–41 (2001)

E-Learning and Game

Web3d Learning Platform of Furniture Layout Based on Case-Based Reasoning and Distance Field

Peihua Song[1], Youyi Zheng[2], and Jinyuan Jia[1(✉)]

[1] School of Software Engineering, Tongji University, Shanghai 201804, China
sph2000@126.com, jyjia@tongji.edu.cn
[2] School of Information Science and Technology, ShanghaiTech University, Shanghai 200120, China

Abstract. For non-professional designers, it is a difficult task to arrange furniture to the right position without the interior designer's guidance. We have developed a web3d learning platform of furniture layout, which can automatically generate a reasonable layout to help people learn knowledge of interior design and improve efficiency. First the non-rectangular room shape normalization algorithms are proposed. Next, four layout modes, namely, coupled mode, enclosed mode, matrix mode and circular mode are introduced; the coupled mode and enclosed mode are solved using the case-based reasoning and distance field, respectively. Finally the furniture layout algorithm of non-rectangular bedroom and that of non-rectangular living room are given. The experimental results show that layout results of the algorithms are similar to the real designs of non-rectangular room, and the running time of the algorithms can meet the needs of the online furniture layout.

Keywords: Furniture layout · Case-based reasoning · Distance field · Learning platform

1 Introduction

The scene layout problem can be widely found in many domains such as city planning, architectural design, interior design, and three-dimensional scene modeling. It is the research focuses in computer graphics, ergonomics and optimization design. Furniture layout is one of the most important research subjects in the scene layout, which are traditionally performed manually. With the development of the internet technology and web 3D technology, there are many online three-dimensional interior design platforms, such as Home-style online platform developed by Autodesk Company. An ordinary user who has no professional interior designer knowledge can now arrange furniture using these online platforms semi-automatically, and don't need to install the off-line interior design software. However, since the furniture layout contains a lot of ergonomic knowledge which requires professional skills, it is not an easy task for ordinary user to arrange furniture in appropriate location without the guide of the designer teachers.

© Springer International Publishing AG 2017
F. Tian et al. (Eds.): Edutainment 2017, LNCS 10345, pp. 235–250, 2017.
https://doi.org/10.1007/978-3-319-65849-0_26

To solve the problem, many scholars have proposed automatic furniture layout algorithms to guide users to arrange furniture, which also can help ordinary users to learn knowledge of interior design while reducing workload and improving efficiency for interior designer. In particular, at the international SIGGRAPH conference in 2011, two scholars have discussed this issue further [1, 2]. However, those algorithms mainly use a single case study technology or intelligent algorithm, and some of those algorithms are of long running time, and off-line. Few studies have focused on online automatic furniture layout. The requirements of online furniture automatic layout algorithms are the effectiveness, robustness, and real-time response. There remains a need for furniture layout algorithms.

In this paper, we first present the room shape standardization algorithm to extract the rectangular layout region from the non-rectangular rooms. Next we introduce four layout modes: coupled mode, enclosed mode, matrix mode and circular mode, and propose corresponding algorithms to the individual modes based reasoning and the distance field. Finally the bedroom layout algorithms and living room layout algorithms are given. Experimental computations suggest that the algorithms are extremely efficient.

2 Related Work

There exist many algorithms to the furniture automatic layout problem. Those algorithms can be divided into two categories: the algorithms based on optimization model and the algorithms based on case study.

2.1 Algorithms Based on Optimization Model

Those algorithms first give an evaluation function according to furniture layout rules defining the distance between the furniture and the angle and so on. Then, the layout result was calculated by using the evaluation function and intelligent algorithms [1–5]. Yu et al. [1] presented an algorithms based on the simulated annealing algorithm. The evaluation function of the algorithm mainly considers accessibility, visibility, pathway constraints and so on. Merrell et al. [2] presented an interactive furniture layout system based on interior design guidelines. The algorithm incorporates the layout guidelines as terms in a density function, and then generates layout suggestions. Chen et al. [3] presented a hierarchical optimization strategy and used particle swarm optimization to solve the furniture layout problem. Akase et al. [4] introduced a way of construction of gene expression and evolution process for interactive evolutionary computation. Liu et al. [5] proposed the composite model for home furnishing generation based on furniture configuration process.

The result of those algorithms depends on the rule values setting at the beginning of the layout. If the information of the furniture and that of room are changed, the rule values need to be reset and the parameters of the intelligent algorithm need to be artificially adopted.

2.2   Algorithms Based on Based on Case Study

Akazawa et al. [6] used the distances between furniture to denote the constraint relationships stored in the database. The query furniture is arranged by retrieving the database. Germer et al. [7] also presented an algorithm based on case study. But the two algorithms do not consider the relationships between the furniture layout and position of door and window. Kjølaas [8] used a set of default templates provided for most common room and furniture types to solve the furniture layout problem. Fisher et al. [9] presented a method for synthesizing 3D object arrangements from examples. The method synthesizes a diverse set of plausible new scenes by learning from a database. In the authors' previous work [10], an algorithm for rectangular room has been introduced, but the algorithm cannot solve the problem of non-rectangular room furniture layout. In this paper, we adopt the room shape standardization algorithms, improved case - based reasoning algorithms and distance field to deal with the problem of non-rectangular room furniture layout.

3   Learning Platform Overview

Figure 1 gives an overview of interaction with our platform. First the users create the room and select the furniture in a library using the online three-dimensional platform. Next, a rectangular layout region is extracted by room shape standardization algorithms. Then individual algorithms for the coupled mode and enclosed mode are introduced based on case-based reasoning and distance field. We omit the algorithms for the matrix and circular mode as they are simple and can be similarly solved. Finally the platform generates layout result to the users. The layout result and the layout case library can assist the users to learn arrange furniture knowledge, to reduce the labor intensity and to improve the labor efficiency. The uses can obtain the desired layout form the platform.

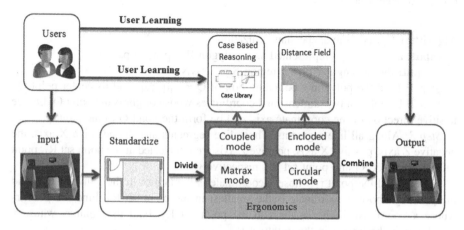

Fig. 1. Platform overview.

4 Room Shape Standardization Algorithm

The aim of room shape standardization algorithm is to extract the rectangular layout region from the non- rectangular room. Next we propose the bedroom shape standardization algorithm and the living room shape standardization algorithm.

4.1 Bedroom Shape Standardization Algorithm

A room shape is represented as a polygon $P = p_1p_2 \cdots p_n$ (see Fig. 2(a)). The polygon P contains two sets: a set of vertex $P = \{p_1, p_2 \cdots p_n\}$ and a set of line segments $L = \{p_1p_2, p_2p_3 \cdots p_{n-1}p_n, p_np_1\}$. A line segment p_ip_{i+1} represent a wall in the room with $1 \leq i \leq n$. The point p_{door} and point p_{window} represent the door position and window position, respectively. Our aim is to extract a rectangular layout region form the polygon P. The bedroom shape standardization algorithm works as follows. First, we find the bounding box of the polygon P, namely rectangle $Q = q_1q_2q_3q_4$, and its center point O (see Fig. 2(b)). Next, we obtain four midpoints of edges of layout rectangular region, namely point r_1, point r_2, point r_3 and point r_4, by those walls (see Fig. 2(c)). Finally, as is shown in Fig. 2(d), we obtain the rectangular layout region $S = s_1s_2s_3s_4$ according those midpoints. The algorithm is given below.

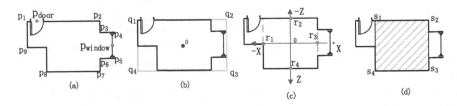

Fig. 2. An example of bedroom shape standardization algorithm. (a) The shape of a bedroom. (b) The bounding box of the room. (c) The midpoints of edges of the rectangular layout region. (d) The rectangular layout region.

Algorithm 1. Bedroom shape standardization

Input: a room shape represented as a polygon $P = p_1p_2 \cdots p_n$.

Output: the rectangular layout region $S = s_1s_2s_3s_4$.

Step 1: Find the polygon's bounding box of $Q = q_1q_2q_3q_4$ and its center point O.

Step 2: Establish a two-dimensional coordinates whose origin is the point O. Let the positive direction of the coordinate axis x to be form the point O to the point p_{window}.

Step 3: Along all line segments. Those line segments and the negative X axis, the negative Z axis, positive X axis, positive Z axis are intersected at the point set R_1, point set R_2, point set R_3 and point set R_4, respectively.

Step 4: Find the point r_1 whose x coordinate is the largest in the point set R_1. Find the point r_2 whose y coordinate is the smallest in the point set R_2. Find the point r_3 whose x coordinate is the smallest in the point set R_3. Find the point r_4 whose y coordinate is the largest in the point set R_4.

Step 5: Construct the rectangular layout region $s_1s_2s_3s_4$ by the point r_1, point r_2, point r_3, point r_4 and point O, and then return the region $s_1s_2s_3s_4$.

4.2   Living Room Shape Standardization Algorithm

As is shown in Fig. 3(a), the polygon $P = p_1p_2 \cdots p_n$ represent a living room shape. The rectangle $s_1s_2s_3s_4$ is the sofa and TV layout region which is extracted using living room shape standardization algorithm. The algorithm is given below.

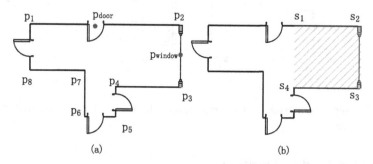

(a)   (b)

Fig. 3. An example of living room shape standardization algorithm. (a) The shape of a living room. (b) The rectangular layout region.

Algorithm 2. Living room shape standardization
   Input: a living room shape represented as a polygon $P = p_1p_2 \cdots p_n$.
   Output: the sofa and TV layout rectangular region $S = s_1s_2s_3s_4$.
   Step 1: Find the three walls p_1p_2, p_2p_3, p_3p_4 which are adjacent to the window.
   Step 2: Find all the door position set D on the walls p_1p_2, p_3p_4, and then calculate the distance between the point p_{window} with the point p_1, point p_4 and the points in set D. Find the point p_{min} to be of minimum distance. As is shown in Fig. 3(b), the point p_{min} is p_4.
   Step 3: Construct the rectangular layout region $s_1s_2s_3s_4$ using the point p_2, point p_3 and point p_{min}, and then return the region $s_1s_2s_3s_4$.

5   Furniture Layout Mode

A furniture layout mode refers to the layout relationship between the furniture and room. We define four layout modes. (1) Coupled mode is to require the furniture and room to maintain a certain distance and angle to each anther, such as the bed and bedside cabinet (see Fig. 4(a)). It can be divided into two categories: furniture and furniture coupled mode, furniture and room coupled mode. (2) Enclosed mode is to require the furniture first to be placed at the corner, and then to be placed along the wall, and finally to be placed in the middle of the room, such as the desk in the study (see Fig. 4(b)). (3) Matrix mode is to require the furniture to be placed in a rectangular region, such as the desks in the classroom (see Fig. 4(c)). (4) Circular mode is a layout mode to require the furniture to be placed around the circular furniture, such as the circular dining table and chairs (see Fig. 3(d)). The combination of the four modes is called combination mode, such as the bedroom layout. The distance and angle between furniture in those layout models need to meet the ergonomic. The matrix mode and circular mode solution to be relatively easy, the distance and angle between the furniture are obtained according simply calculating. In the following section, we give the algorithms of coupled mode and enclosed mode.

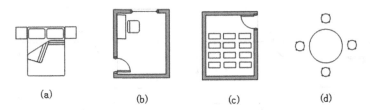

(a)   (b)   (c)   (d)

Fig. 4. Furniture layout mode. (a) Coupled mode. (b) Enclosed mode. (c) Matrix mode. (d) Circular mode.

6 Coupled Mode Algorithm

6.1 Mathematical Model

The mathematical model represents the layout relationship between the furniture in the coupled mode. Coupled mode consists of one chief furniture and n pieces of attached furniture. We use k to denote the number of the furniture, k = 1, 2... n. All the attached furniture is the same. The chief furniture contains n layout points, and each pieces of attached furniture has one layout point. As shown in Fig. 5, the chief furniture is the desk, and the attached furniture is the stool. We use the axis-aligned bounding box to represent a piece of furniture. Let l, w and h denote the length, width and height of the furniture, respectively. $S = (l/2, h/2, w/2)^T$ is the length matrix, S_0 is the chief furniture length matrix, and S_k is the attached furniture k length matrix. $P = (x, y, z)^T$ is the furniture position, P_0 is the chief furniture position, and P_k is the attached furniture k position. a is the furniture rotation angle in the Y-axis direction, $a = \{0, 90, 180, 270\}$, a_0 is the chief furniture rotation angle, and a_k is the attached furniture k rotation angle. The main idea of coupled mode algorithm is to find the chief furniture and attached furniture layout points, and then to obtain the layout results through those layout points and matrix transformation. The position relationship between the attached furniture k and chief furniture can be expressed by the mathematical model as follows:

$$
\begin{aligned}
P_k &= G_k + T_\mathbf{k} + D_k, \\
G_k &= M_k S_k, \\
T_k &= P_0 + R_k S_0.
\end{aligned}
\tag{1}
$$

Where, $G = (g_{ij})_{3\times1}$, G_k is the attached furniture k layout point; $T = (t_{ij})_{3\times1}$; T_k is the chief furniture layout point relative to the attached furniture k; $D = (d_{ij})_{3\times1}$, D_k is

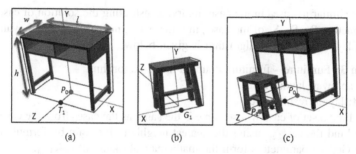

(a)   (b)   (c)

Fig. 5. An example of coupled mode. (a) The information of chief furniture. (b) The information of attached furniture. (c) The information of coupled mode.

the attached furniture k distance matrix; $M = (m_{ij})_{3\times3}$, M_k is the attached furniture k transformation matrix; $R = (r_{ij})_{3\times3}$, R_k is the chief furniture transformation matrix relative to the attached furniture k; P_0, S_0 and S_k are known. a_k, M_k, R_k and D_k are set according to ergonomics and the layout [11].

As is shown in Fig. 5, the parameters of the mathematical model of the desk and stool are as follow:

$$a_0 = 0,\ a_1 = 0.$$

$$\mathbf{M}_{01} = \begin{bmatrix} 0 & 0 & 0 \\ 0 & 0 & 0 \\ 0 & 0 & 1 \end{bmatrix}, \mathbf{M}_1 = \begin{bmatrix} 0 & 0 & 0 \\ 0 & 0 & 0 \\ 0 & 0 & 1 \end{bmatrix}, \mathbf{D}_1 = \begin{bmatrix} 0 \\ 0 \\ 20 \end{bmatrix}$$

6.2 Furniture-Furniture Coupled Mode Algorithm

Case-based reasoning has been widely used to solve various problems [12]. Now we use it to solve the coupled mode. The layout case consists of two parts: the layout problem description and the layout solution description. The layout problem is described by the vector $\mathbf{q} = (l_0, w_0, h_0, l_1, w_1, l_1)^\mathrm{T}$, where $l_0, w_0, h_0, l_1, w_1,$ and l_1 denote the length, width, and height of the chief furniture, the length, width, and height of the attached furniture, respectively. The layout solution is the model parameters. The layout case name is composed of the chief furniture name, the attached furniture name and the total amount of attached furniture. Case similarity is defined as the Euclidean distance between the two layout cases. We use the nearest neighbor algorithm (K-Nearest Neighbor algorithm, K = 1) to retrieve cases.

$$\min_i \{\mathrm{Dis}(\mathrm{case}_0, \mathrm{case}_i) = (\sum_{j=1}^{6} (\mathbf{q}_{0,j} - \mathbf{q}_{i,j})^2)^{1/2}\} \tag{2}$$

Where, case_0 is an await layout case, and case_i is a layout case whose name is the same as the case_0, i = {1, 2, ..., m}. $\mathbf{q}_0$ is the problem description of case_0, and $\mathbf{q}_i$ is the problem description of case_i. The minimization returns the best case $\mathrm{case}_{\mathrm{best}}$ which is the most similar to $case_0$ in the case library. Substituting the solution of $case_{best}$ and three parameters P_0, S_0, S_k of the $case_0$ into the mathematical model and evaluate, we obtain the layout result. The algorithm is given below.

Algorithm 3. Furniture - furniture coupled mode Algorithm
 Input: an await layout $case_0$.
 Output: layout results of $case_0$.
 Step 1: Find a set of case whose name is the same as the $case_0$ from the case library.
 Step 2: Find the $case_{best}$ using the nearest neighbor algorithm by formula (2).
 Step 3: Get the parameters form the mathematical model of $case_{best}$.
 Step 4: Assign the parameters to the mathematical model of $case_0$ and calculate using formula (1).
 Step 5: Obtain and return the layout result of $case_0$.

6.3   Furniture-Room Coupled Mode Algorithm

When there is a coupled layout mode between furniture and a room, we can take the room as a piece of furniture, which is converted into the furniture - furniture coupled mode. If the room shape is non-rectangular, we first need to extract its rectangular region using room shape standardization algorithm in Sect. 3, then define the coupled mode between the rectangular region and furniture. We summarize the common furniture layout rule of furniture - room coupled as follows. (1) The tables are placed in the middle of the conference room (see Fig. 6(a)). (2) The sofas should be placed along the windows of the living room (see Fig. 6(b)). (3) The bed is placed along the windows of the bedroom (see Fig. 6(c)), the distance D is decided by the room size.

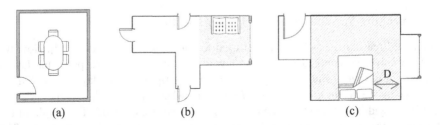

(a)   (b)   (c)

Fig. 6. Furniture - room coupled mode. (a) Meeting room. (b) Non-rectangular living room. (3) Non-rectangular bedroom.

7   Enclosed Mode Algorithms

7.1   Distance Field

In order to solve the enclosed mode layout problem, we use the distance field to fit the bedroom and living room furniture layout rules. Before constructing the distance field, we should make room's floor discretization. We use 1 unit to represent 1 cm in real world. For example, the length of a room is 4 m and width is 3 m, then the size of the

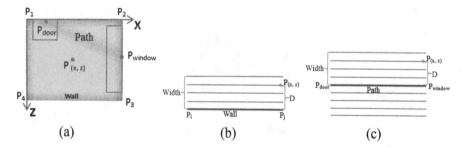

Fig. 7. (a) The distance field of a bedroom. (2) The distance field of a wall. (3) The distance field of a path.

room's floor is expressed as 400 * 300 after discrete processing. The room distance field consists of two parts: walls distance field and paths distance field. The line segment p_{window} p_{door} is called a path. For example, a bedroom distance field is shown in Fig. 7(a).

A wall distance field is an attractive energy to the furniture. We define the wall maximum energy intensity of t (t > 0). If the shortest distance from the point P (x, z) to the wall p_ip_j is D, the point P (x, y) energy value generated by the wall p_ip_j is calculated as follows.

$$V\left(P(x,z), Wall\left(p_ip_j\right)\right) = \begin{cases} \left(\frac{D}{Width}\right) * t, & P(x,z) \text{ inside the room and } D < Width \\ 0, & P(x,z) \text{ outside the room or } D > Width \end{cases}$$

(3)

A path distance field is a repulsive energy to the furniture. We define the path maximum energy intensity of s (s < 0). If the shortest distance from the point P (x, z) to the path $p_{door}p_{window}$ is D, the point P (x, z) energy value generated by the path $p_{door}p_{window}$ is calculated as follows.

$$V(P(x,z), Path(i)) = \begin{cases} \left(\frac{D}{Width}\right) * s, & P(x,z) \text{ inside the room and } D < Width \\ 0, & P(x,z) \text{ outside the room or } D > Width \end{cases}$$

(4)

When the room shape, the doors and the windows position are determined, using the formulas 3 and 4, we can calculate any point energy value in the room as follows.

$$V(P(x,z)) = \sum_{i=1}^{n} V(P(x,z), Wall_i) + \sum_{j=1}^{m} V\left(P(x,z), Path_j\right)$$

(5)

Where, n and m is the number of walls and paths, respectively.

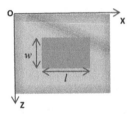

Fig. 8. Furniture energy

7.2 Furniture Energy and Furniture Energy Maximization

The furniture energy value is the sum of the energy values of the points occupied by the furniture. As is shown in Fig. 8, the rectangle is the bottom of the furniture bounding box, and the furniture energy is calculated as follows.

$$E(P(x,z), S(l,w)) = \sum_{i=x-l/2}^{x+l/2} \sum_{j=z-w/2}^{z+w/2} V(P(x,z)) \tag{6}$$

Where, point p(x, z) is the furniture position, l and w denote the length and width of the furniture, respectively.

In the formula (6), when the following two cases occur, the furniture energy value is zero: (1) There is a collision between the furniture with the placed furniture or the door rectangular box (see Fig. 7(a)). (2) There is a collision between the furniture with the window rectangular box and the height of the furniture is greater than the height of the window (see Fig. 7(a)).

Furniture energy maximization is to search the position in the room where the furniture energy value is the largest, which is represented as follows.

$$\max_{x,z} E(P(x,z), S(l,w)) \tag{7}$$

Where $E(P(x,z), S(l,w))$ is the energy value of the furniture in position point(x, z), and the furniture can be rotated 90°. To improve the computational efficiency, the energy value of the furniture in current position can be deduced according the energy value of the furniture in previous position [10]. Compared with the formula of distance field in [10] to be suitable for the rectangular room, this paper's formula of distance

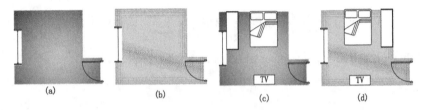

Fig. 9. (a) The energy distribution using the formula of distance field in [10]. (b) The energy distribution using the formula (5). (c) The layout result using the layout method in [10]. (d) The layout result using our layout method.

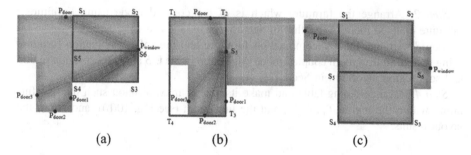

(a)   (b)   (c)

Fig. 10. (a) The energy distribution of finding the layout region of sofa and TV in a living room. (b) The energy distribution of finding the layout position of the dining-table in a living room. (c) The energy distribution of a bedroom.

field is more consistent with non-rectangular room. For example, Fig. 9(a) show the distance field of a bedroom using the formula of distance field in [10], and Fig. 9(b) show the distance field of the same bedroom using formula 5. Figure 9(c) show the layout result using the layout method in [10], and Fig. 9(d) show the layout result using our layout method. Our improved distance field places the furniture better.

8   Living Room and Bedroom Furniture Layout Algorithm

We now give detailed algorithmic descriptions to real cases using our furniture models and the corresponding reasoning methods. As the length requirement of the paper, we propose three cases, the living room layout, the bedroom layout, and the classroom.

8.1   Living Room Furniture Layout Algorithm

In a living room, we need arrange furniture include sofa, television, dining-table, and so on. The region of arranging television and sofa is called the television region and the sofa region, respectively. When the sofa and TV layout rectangular region is found using the living room shape standardization algorithm, we also need to extract the television region and sofa region from it, which is called television region and sofa region algorithm. First, we divide the rectangle $s_1s_2s_3s_4$ into two small rectangles: $s_1s_2s_5s_6$ and $s_3s_4s_5s_6$. Then, we calculate the energy values of the two small rectangles using formula 4 (see Fig. 10(a)). Finally, the small rectangle of the more energy value, that is $s_1s_2s_6s_5$, is placed the sofa, and the other small rectangle $s_3s_4s_5s_6$ is placed the television. The algorithm is summarized below.

Algorithm 4. Living room furniture layout Algorithm
   Input: the living room shape and await furniture.
   Output: layout results of furniture in the living room.
   Step 1: Extract the sofa and TV layout rectangular region using the living room shape standardization algorithm in Sect. 3 and calculate the distance field of the living room using formula 3 and formula 4.

Step 2: Arrange the furniture which is of the coupled mode using Furniture - furniture coupled mode Algorithm in Sect. 5.

Step 3: Arrange the TV combination furniture and the sofa combination furniture using the Furniture - room coupled mode Algorithm in Sect. 5 and the television region and sofa region algorithm in Sect. 7.

Step 4: Arrange dining-table and make its energy maximization such that the furniture within the region $T_1T_2T_3T_4$ and the ling room (see Fig. 10(b)), and return the layout results.

8.2   Bedroom Furniture Layout Algorithm

In a bedroom room, we need to arrange furniture include bed, television, wardrobe, and so on. When the rectangular layout region is found using the bed room shape standardization algorithm, we also need to extract the television region and bed region. The extract method of the television region and bed region in the bedroom is similar with the extract method in living room (see Fig. 10(c)). Bed room furniture layout Algorithm is summarized below.

Algorithm 5. Bed room furniture layout Algorithm

   Input: bed room shape and await furniture.

   Output: layout results of furniture in the bed room.

Step 1: Extract the bed and TV layout rectangular region using the bed room shape standardization algorithm in Sect. 3 and calculate the distance field of the living room using formula 3 and formula 4.

Step 2: Arrange the furniture which is of the coupled mode using Furniture - furniture coupled mode Algorithm in Sect. 5.

Step 3: Arrange the bed combination furniture and the television combination furniture using the Furniture - room coupled mode Algorithm in Sect. 5 and the television region and bed region algorithm in Sect. 7.

Step 4: Sort the others furniture of awaiting layout by height and area.

Step 5: Arrange the others furniture one by one and make its energy maximization within the region $s_1s_2s_3s_4$ (see Fig. 10(c)), and return the layout results.

8.3   Classroom Furniture Layout Algorithm

In a classroom, we need to arrange furniture include a teacher's desk and the student's desks and stools. The classroom furniture layout algorithm is summarized below.

Algorithm 6. Classroom furniture layout Algorithm

   Input: a rectangular classroom, a teacher's desk and student's desks and stools.

   Output: layout results of furniture in the classroom.

Step 1: Arrange the student's desks and stools using Furniture - furniture coupled mode Algorithm in Sect. 5.

Step 2: Arrange the student's desks and stools according the matrix mode.

Step 3: Arrange the teacher's desk and the combination furniture of the student's desk and stool using the Furniture - room coupled mode Algorithm in Sect. 5.

Step 4: Return the layout results.

9   Experimental Results

We developed an online furniture layout platform using WebGL and C sharp language in Visual Studio 2015. We designed 16 common cases of furniture layout to store in database of SQL Server 2012. The computation was performed on a computer with a processor of Dual-core 2.6 GHz, main memory 4G, operation system Microsoft Windows 8 64bit and Chrome browser.

9.1   Comparisons with Prior Art

To further evaluate our method, we compare with two most recent methods, [2, 5] respectively. As there are no detailed parameters on the scene of living room and furniture sizes in [5], we manually extracted these information from their paper and used our method on their scenes and compare the running time with their method. Figure 11 and Table 1 shows the visual results and the detailed running time. In both case, our method generates comparative results to theirs while the running time is significantly faster (a factor of 30x).

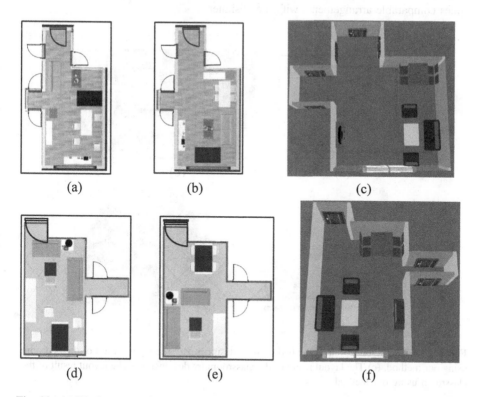

Fig. 11. (a) The layout result using the method in [2]. (b) The layout result using the method in [5]. (c) The layout result using our method. (d) The layout result using the method in [2]. (e) The layout result using the method in [5]. (f) The layout result using our method.

Table 1. Statistics of running time comparisons with [2, 5]

Method	Computer configuration	Programming tools	Average running time (s)
Method in [2]	RAM 4 GB, and 3.4 GHz CPU Intel Core i7-2600	Matlab and VS2008	217
Method in [5]	RAM 4 GB, and 3.4 GHz CPU Intel Core i7-2600	Matlab and VS2008	50.3
Our method	RAM 4 GB, and 2.6 GHz CPU Intel Core i5-3230	WebGL and VS2015	1.5

9.2   Comparison with Real Designs

We also invite an interior designer to manually design some furniture arrangements using our online system but without any algorithmic inference. The designer is allowed to manually drag an object and move it along the floor plane to place it properly given a room layout. It took almost an hour for him to finish the classroom and bedroom design whereas our system took 2.3 s. Figure 12 shows the visual results. Our method generates comparable arrangements with the designer.

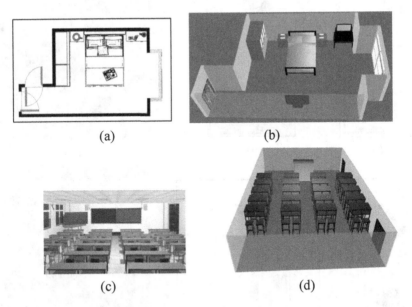

Fig. 12. (a) The layout result of the bedroom by designer. (b) The layout result of the bedroom using our method. (c) The layout result of the classroom by designer. (d) The layout result of the classroom using our method.

10 Conclusion and Future Work

In this paper, a learning platform of furniture layout has been developed using the furniture layout algorithms based on case-based reasoning and distance field. It can automatically generate a layout to help the users to learn knowledge of furniture layout and obtain the desire layout. Compared with the traditional layout algorithms using a single method to all the different scenes, our algorithms use different layout mode to solve the different scenes layout problem. First the non-rectangular room shape normalization algorithms are presented according the room shape features. Then, four layout modes, namely coupled mode, enclosed mode, matrix mode and circular mode, are introduced by analyzing the distribution in a room. Next, we propose the algorithm of coupled mode based on the mathematical model and case-based reasoning. We also present the algorithm of enclosed mode based on the distance field. Finally we give the furniture layout algorithm of non-rectangular bedroom and that of non-rectangular living room. The experimental results show that the layout results of our method are similar to the real designs and the running time can meet real-time response requirements of online layout. In future, we plan to explore automatic furniture layout for large scale and mixed scenes. How to automatically generate the layout for mixed places such as the office and shopping malls scenes using our layout modes is worth further exploration.

Acknowledgments. The authors appreciate the comments and suggestions of all anonymous reviewers, whose comments significantly improved this paper. This work is supported by The Key Research Projects of Central University of Basic Scientific Research Funds for Cross Cooperation (201510-02), Research Fund for the Doctoral Program of Higher Education of China (No. 2013007211-0035) and Key project in scientific and technological of Jilin Province in China (No. 20140204088GX).

References

1. Yu, L.F., Yeung, S.K., Tang, C.K., et al.: Make it home: automatic optimization of furniture arrangement. ACM Trans. Graph. **30**(4) (2011). Article No. 86
2. Merrell, P., Schkufza, E., Li, Z.Y., et al.: Interactive furniture layout using interior design guidelines. ACM Trans. Graph. **30**(4) (2011). Article No. 87
3. Chen, G., Li, G., Liu, P., et al.: Hierarchical constraints with particle swarm optimization for furniture arrangement. J. Comput. Aided Des. Comput. Graph. **26**(10), 1603–1612 (2014)
4. Akase, R., Okada, Y.: Automatic 3D furniture layout based on interactive evolutionary computation. In: Proceedings of the 2013 Seventh International Conference on Complex, Intelligent, and Sofaware Intensive Systems, pp. 726–731. IEEE Computer Society, USA (2013)
5. Liu, M.-L., Jiang, H., Mao, T.-L., Wang, Z.-Q.: Composite model for home furnishing generation. Chin. J. Comput. **39**(2) (2016)
6. Akazawa, Y., Okada, Y., Niijima, K.: Automatic 3D scene generation based on contact constraints. In: Eighth International Conference on Computer Graphics and Artificial Intelligence, pp. 593–598 (2002)

7. Germer, T., Schwarz, M.: Procedural arrangement of furniture for real-time walkthroughs. Comput. Graph. Forum **28**(8), 2068–2078 (2009)
8. Kjølaas, K.A.H.: Automatic furniture population of large architectural models. Massachusetts Institute of Technology, Cambridge (2000)
9. Fisher, M., Ritchie, D., Savva, M., et al.: Example-based synthesis of 3D object arrangements. ACM Trans. Graph. **31**(6), 439–445 (2012)
10. Song, P.-H., Jia, J.-Y.: Online furniture layout method based on case-based reasoning and distance fields. J. Syst. Simul. (10), 2438–2447 (2016)
11. Zhang, Q.-M., Zheng, S.-Y.: Interior Design Data Set. China Construction Industry Press, Beijing (1991)
12. Kolodner, J.L.: An introduction to case-based reasoning. Artif. Intell. Rev. **6**(1), 3–34 (1992)

What's Wrong with the Feedback?

Alain Simons[✉], Karsten Pedersen, Jose Fonseca,
and Simant Prakoonwit

Bournemouth University, Poole House, Talbot Campus, Poole BH12 5BB, UK
{asimons,kpedersen,jfonseca,
sprakoonwit}@bournemouth.ac.uk

Abstract. It has already been for a while that educational institutions and researchers tried to find an answer to the recurrent critics of learners on how feedback is delivered. Many emerging technologies have been used with a limited success, therefore there must be some other factors. What we learned from observing different feedback was that written feedback is not very attractive. Most of the feedback was not enjoyable to consult or difficult to access. This research proposes an answer to how to make feedback more appealing, especially when artefacts are submitted, and formulate some recommendations to develop an effective feedback tool. This research is not aiming for feedback on written reports where tools such as Turnitin are sufficient.

Keywords: Higher education · Feedback · Marking · Video feedback · Recorded feedback · Visualization

1 Introduction

Usually marking and feedback are released to learners at the same moment. The feedback summarizes the pros, cons and advice to improve the delivered work. Substantively most given feedback meets the justification criteria as the feedback is provided by professionals in their field. Interested learners will go through a process where they first identify the score and secondly try to figure out what justify that score. Non-interested learners will ignore the feedback.

Early research in 2004 at the University of Wolverhampton [1] indicates that students even don't collect their assessed work. Other research done by Wojtas in 1998 [2] as well shows that the students have little interest in their feedback. They only consult the feedback if the mark is not confirming their expectations. Being still confronted in 2017 with the same problems discussed in 2004 (despite many attempts were undertaken over the years to improve the situation) indicates that the problems persist. Within our own department tutors were even confronted in a harder way due the large amount of creative assessments (artefacts).

Therefore, the main aim of our research is to meet demands of tutors and students on feedback for artefacts. Tutors mentioned they spent a lot of time to provide the feedback (a lot of recurring work) and students didn't feel to be attracted to consult the feedback.

© Springer International Publishing AG 2017
F. Tian et al. (Eds.): Edutainment 2017, LNCS 10345, pp. 251–261, 2017.
https://doi.org/10.1007/978-3-319-65849-0_27

Summarized this research is going to create and discuss different prototypes to develop a feedback and marking tool which meets the following requirements:

Reduce the workload for the feedback providers

- Time saving.
- Excellent usability.
- Freedom.
- Availability of creative tools.
- Integration in existing VLRs.

Visualize feedback in a more attractive way for learners

- Attractive presentation.
- Perception of easy processing.
- Clear correlation.
- Structured.
- Neat.

This research won't consider the actual content of the feedback but how it is presented to the learner. Four prototypes have been setup, discussed and tested to formulate recommendations to use in the development of a common marking and feedback tool. Note that as output for the feedback and marking will be an output on a screen (digital). So, new technologies (video, audio, interactivity) can be also implemented later.

2 Previous Research

Various research was conducted on feedback and marking in higher education. Many of them were focused on the improvement of the actual content of the feedback. Less seems to be interested in how the feedback could be presented in a more attractive way to the learner.

In 2016 The Higher Education Academy presented a Framework for transforming Assessment in Higher Education [3]. This research is focused on a better integration of feedback in the assessment process, which is absolute a necessity, but again not covering how feedback can be presented in a more visual, attractive way to learners. Concept mapping, mind mapping and argument mapping are techniques now used for education-related purposes [4]. In fact, this is a visualization of an analysis of different part of an assignment setup so the use of visualization is not a novelty in Higher Education.

Feedback is very important as a learning tool that guides students' progress and the need for improvement on their performance. It has a scaffolding function, as it may enable students to further develop their performance level. As said before, research on assessment feedback has been essentially focused on ways to improve the quality of written based documents, whether for summative or formative assessment, and independently of being driven by a more developmental dimension, an encouraging or fairness one. Seven principles of good feedback practice were identified by Nicol and

Macfarlane-Dick [5], aiming to facilitate the students' self-regulation of their own performance, in terms of their thinking, motivation and behaviour during the learning process. The 3rd principle, about delivering high quality information to students about their learning, has been more and more reflected on the UK NSS surveys. Curiously, this principle focuses on the quality of the content and has no mention to the quality of the way feedback is delivered or presented to students. However, for the feedback to be useful to students, they must understand the feedback first, as pointed out by Lizzio and Wilson [6], alluding to a potential discrepancy between the meaning of academic's feedback and its interpretation by students. This difficulty, commonly felt by students, in understanding written comments, which are usually vague and in an imposing style, was also referred by Duncan [7], who highlighted that a "clear advice on how to improve the quality in subsequent work" was often neglected in feedback sheets. Understanding how students make sense of feedback and how they use it to support their learning process, has also been object of research (Higgins et al. [8]; Hepplestone and Chikawa 2014 [9]; Pitt and Norton [10]).

Per Nicol [11] "the quality of the students' interaction" with the feedback comments is as important as (or maybe even more important than) the quality of the comments they receive. Surprisingly enough, being this interactive characteristic considered so important, no examples were found of the use of interactive capabilities, offered by new technologies and devices, applied to the assessment feedback process.

The use of audio to provide feedback have been widely discussed and became an available option, usually, as discussed by Savin-Baden [12], who suggests the use of podcasting to deliver feedback, within a dialogic learning framework, because students seem to like it, although it does not necessarily improve grades, and despite staff tending to show some resistance, considering it more time-consuming. Lunt and Currant [13] also discuss the introduction of audio feedback, delivered to students via a VLE or email, with very positive results, showing that students are at least 10 times more likely to open audio files compared to collecting written feedback. Hussey and Smith [14] refer to an innovative solution that provides audio feedback which can be accessed by students with a simple digital audio player.

3   Research Methodology

The initial plan was to set up several test cases covering one or both proposed requirements. To create the prototypes two techniques were used:

- Rapid Application Development (RAD)
- Template

As RAD the FileMaker platform was used which is a standout leader for Rapid Application Development [15]. Despite it is a great software it still has some restrictions in the creative areas. But nevertheless, it's good to have some insight in this kind of software to figure out if it can be used to develop the final tool. To have completely free hand in creativity Adobe Illustrator was chosen to create the templates. Using templates had the disadvantage that there was no database connection resulting in the template based prototypes totals of the marks were done manually which must be taken in account that this won't be the case in the final tool.

When our brains perceive information, they catalogue how easy it is to process the available data. This can make the difference that a learner will be focused on the feedback or not. Young learners have a lot of distractions those days and want to catch information in a snap. Figure 1 shows us what the two main issues are, gaining interest and keeping that interest.

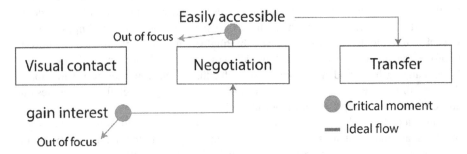

Fig. 1. Visualization of the fragile perception

This research is focused on delivering feedback for Artefacts. In our department, this could be used by units teaching creative assets and programming. The covered topics by the different prototypes were:

- Software programming.
- Texturing and lighting for games.
- Animation for games.
- Programming for Graphics and Games.

The first prototype was created to formulate an answer to the growing concern about the workload feedback providers had. A programming unit, Software Programming, was used as a test case. To develop the prototype a RAD (Rapid Application Development) tool was used. Whilst this offered quick iteration times during development which were crucial in receiving initial test results, it quickly proved to be inflexible once requirements evolved from these initial results. In the past, there were complaints from learners that the provided feedback was a copy/paste work. This is not the way to gain confidence from the learners and it will reduce the value of the proposed feedback. The developed prototype allowed to adjust predefined sentences when they were used as feedback. Beyond, there was a nice overview of the learning outcomes combined with their appropriate values and scores. Figure 2 shows the setup of the prototype.

A second prototype was used for feedback on a texturing assignment which is a good example of an artefact submission. Knowledge from graphic design and the advertisement world [16] was implemented. At the same moment, it looks very structured and polished. Basic idea behind the setup was that creative students are not keen to read textual feedback and have a more visual focus. This is template based solution.

MARKING SOFTWARE PROGRAMMING 2015 - 2016

Student Name █████	Student Group █████	Student ID █████	**55.30**
Analysis - 20%			**100**

		Remarks
Analysis Problem	60	- The analysis is well done.
Analysis IPO	40	- Using separate modules use a function for each module is well done.
Analysis Diagram	35	- You could use also diagrams for the analysis.
Analysis CPO	55	- An IPO overview should be convienent.
Total Analysis	**47.50**	**/100**

Design - 30%

		Remarks
Module design	60	- You have a lot of diagrams some are not visible but most important once are there.
Design techniques	55	- There are 3 functions now, You could have split up everything in more different functions.
Module IPO	45	- Structs are used for card and hand which is good.
Detailed diagram	65	
Total Design	**56.25**	**/100**

Implementation - 50%

		Remarks
Modularity	60	- The actual game play is all right but there is problem executing the loops in the right way.
Programming style	60	- Invalid value at bet (character instead of number) will end in a infinite loop.
Strategy results	65	- UI of play is very basic, could be more user friendly, clear.
Discussion - Concl.	50	- You have to enter each time to move on in the game but it is not mentioned anywhere.
System requirem.	50	- Ace High or low, here is a fall back but also not mentioned at the beginning which key has to be used.
Underst. principles	60	- There is a running Execute which is good.
Underst. techn. iss.	60	- Try to use other references, for example C++ books, decent learning video tutorials.
Total Implement.	**57.86**	**/100**

Fig. 2. Structured feedback for each of the learning outcomes. Remarks are predefined but can be adjusted.

Colours played also an essential role in the prototype. From our daily lives, we know green is **GO**, orange is **TAKE ATTENTION** and red is **DANGER**. The combination of those colours was used to indicate the level of quality of the delivered work. Colour was applied on text and arrows. Figure 3 is showing a first implementation. Notice the use of arrows as a visual guidance, the large numbers of screenshots from the students work and the application of some rules used in the advertisement world. Figure 5 shows the areas of importance to place our data. For our prototype, title, marks, learning outcomes and a part of the visualization are situated in the high interest area part. There's also a brand identity included in this example by using the logo of Bournemouth University in quite a large size. Notice also that all prototypes have a landscape orientation and an aspect ratio of 16:9 and are perfect viewable on HD screens. All prototypes were exported in the same way. A high-quality pdf was generated which could easily been shown full screen (Fig. 4).

The third prototype was created to give feedback on an animation unit and the goal was to combine the positive elements from both previous prototypes. Feedback on animation is more complex compared to texturing. The assignment covered the use of curves and their influence on the behaviour of the animation. Once again a RAD solution was used. Notice that the characteristics of advertising rules were still more or less implemented but in a less efficient way. The marking and the demands related to the learning outcomes plays a larger part here. There was no spontaneously approval.

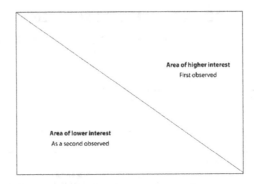

Fig. 3. Visual representation of the lower and higher interest areas.

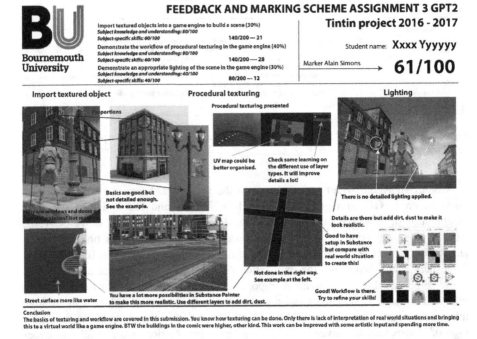

Fig. 4. Knowledge from graphic design and the advertisement world was implemented in prototype 2.

Prototype 3 showed the feedback providers that it's not always easy to define what is a 6 or 7 as a mark. There is a grey area which can cause discussions with students "why a 6 and not a 7". To avoid that kind of discussions prototype 4 had been adjusted to a more verbal judgment for the marking but strong related to the learning outcomes. The conclusion area changed position to a more important area.

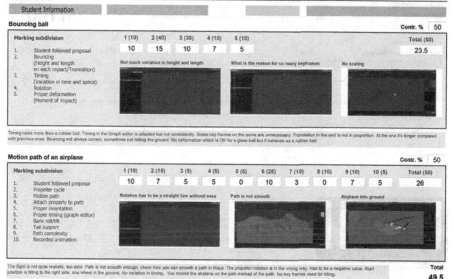

Fig. 5. Prototype 3 is a solution for an animation assignment. The small images were not a great success.

4 Results

4.1 Results from the Learner Perspective

It may be no doubt that the RAD solutions were faster to generate feedback. Features as drop-down lists to select predefined feedback and the ability to do calculations made it more user friendly compared to the template based solutions. The predefined feedback was also adaptable which made that the given feedback could be easy personalized. On the other hand, it restricted the creation of a more "creative" feedback.

4.2 Results from the Leaner Perspective

Take in account that during the testing phase of the prototypes learners were not informed that a research was going on. Instead of using surveys we waited for a response from the learner side. We didn't trigger anything, the appreciation had to come by itself, for us the only way to be certain they could appreciate the used method. Perhaps a weird approach to get a feedback from the learners but if it was appreciated it should come up during the student forums spontaneously (Fig. 6).

After the release of the feedback and marks it was waiting for a response from the learners through the student forums. After the release of the texturing assignment the feedback came without any demand of our part. Spontaneous the learners indicated that

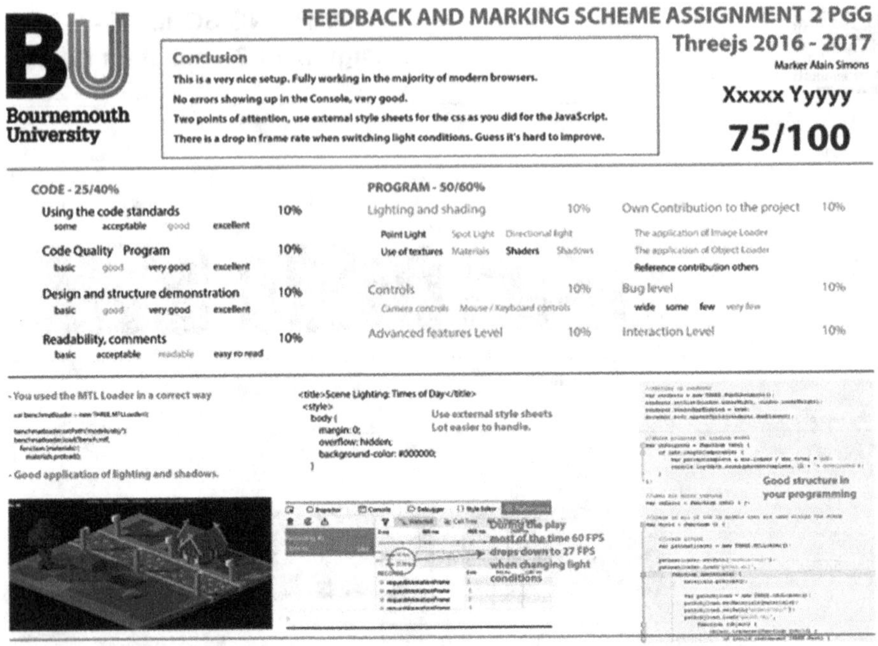

Fig. 6. Prototype 4, the learning outcomes and related marks are prominent present.

they liked the way the feedback was provided. Something similar happened after the release of the PGG marks. The visual approach was successful for both the creative and programming assignments. Prototype 1 and 3 didn't deliver a spontaneous feedback from the learners. There was space for improvements in some areas of the content but it seems to be overshadowed by the visual presentation of the feedback. In a way, it delivers the proof that the package is more important than the actual content. From an academic view that can be argued but it's a fact that decent visualization gets more learners involved in the feedback and marking, especially learners who otherwise wouldn't have consult their feedback. Prototype 2 and 3 succeeded in gaining the attention of the learner (Table 1).

Table 1. From the feedback provider perspective.

	Time saving	Excellent usability	Freedom	Creative	Integration	Used feedback for
Prototype 1	X	X				Programming software
Prototype 2			X	X		Texturing
Prototype 3	X	X				Animation
Prototype 4			X	X		Programming graphics

It was clear that the biggest impact was on the artefact and programming assignments. The software and animation feedback was great in presenting the link between the ILOs and the marks but still looks to dull to make students enthusiastic. A wrong approach to visualize the graphs (difficult to read, too small) on the–animation feedback taught us that the visualization of the feedback must be done in a perfect way if it wants to have some impact (Table 2).

Table 2. From the learner perspective.

	Attractive	Ease	Correlation	Structure	Neat	Used feedback for
Prototype 1			X	X	X	Programming software
Prototype 2	X	X	X	X	X	Texturing
Prototype 3		X	X	X		Animation
Prototype 4	X	X	X	X	X	Programming graphics

5   Future Developments

To provide software which will allow the system to store the data needed to generate the correct output whilst at the same remaining as non-invasive as possible to the user, some further developments are planned.

The first aim is to tightly integrate the software with the operating system itself so that it can become part of the work review process that the marker goes through. For example, if at any point the marker decides to make a comment, they can press a known hot-key and rather than any software loading and distracting from their original train of thought, simply the task they want to perform will appear, such as highlighting a piece of work and adding a comment box. This should mean that no windows will pop up, breaking the flow of marking. As part of this aim, it is important that the examiner builds up a feedback sheet in a similar way to the final output that a student will receive. This WSYWYG (What you see if what you get) design flow will help ensure that the feedback response will be more personal and relevant than anything that could potentially be generated from data or even WYSWYM (What you see is what you mean).

The second aim is to provide the user with an easy and obvious way to upload the final marked items to a server. Opening web browsers and navigating web interfaces often causes large breaks in workflow when the marked work is all ready and waiting on the user's machine. For this we will be looking in to potential ways that the marked work can be selected and committed in a similar way to existing GUI version control software such as Tortoise SVN. This also means that plugins could be written to connect the software to a variety of Virtual Learning Environments (VLEs) in a common and uniform manner requiring little training when joining a new institution. Supporting a variety of media is important for the proposed system to work. For example, examiners may well want to embed audio clips and videos onto the feedback "sheets" where the students can then click to enable them as needed. A storage and recovery facility that allows for this will need to be slightly more flexible than simply storing i.e., PDF files.

A final aim is to ensure the software is fast and easy to set up and portable to a variety of platforms that instructors must use such as not only Windows but also Mac OS X, Linux and FreeBSD. This ensures that work can be marked on the systems it was intended for such as MAX MSP on Mac OS X, Maya on Linux etc. For this reason, we intend to write the software using the C++ language and a portable GUI toolkit such as wxWidgets.

6 Conclusion

Our research proved that a good visualization of feedback will help students to get more interested, more engaged in the marking and feedback of their assessed work. Previous research already proved that feedback is a very important part of the learning process and that it deserves all appropriate attention. This research was an attempt to focus as learning specialists not only on the content of the feedback but more specific on how it is presented to learners. The prototypes can be presented on a wide range of screens such as for mobile phones, tablets and computers. Prototypes 2 and 4 were the most effective. Based on these two a final prototype will be developed which can be used as a blueprint to create a feedback and marking tool. Video and audio must be integrated in this setup so that they are not a standalone solution anymore to provide feedback. To be affective it's much better they are integrated in a feedback solution. As mentioned in future developments chapter the lay-out of the feedback provider will be the same as the one shown to the learner, a kind of scrapbook were the feedback provider can stick his comments. Research on RAD solutions (prototype 1 and 3) showed us that it's hard to use such a solution to meet all mentioned requirements to satisfy learners and feedback providers. Usability (feedback provider) and attractive (learner) will be the keywords when developing a blueprint for a feedback and marking tool.

References

1. Winter, C., Dye, V.L.: An investigation into the reasons why students do not collect marked assignments and the accompanying feedback. Learn. Teach. Proj. 2003/2004 **9**, 133–141 (2004)
2. Wojtas, O.: Feedback? Just give us the answers. Times High. Educ. Supplement September 25 (1998)
3. Elkington, S.: Introducing a framework for transforming assessment in higher education. Transforming assessment webinar (2016). https://wwwheacademy.ac.uk/system/files/trans forming_assessment_webinar.pdf. Accessed 23 Mar 2017
4. Davies, M.: Concept mapping, mind mapping and argument mapping: what are the differences and do they matter? High Educ. **62**(279–301), 23 (2010)
5. Nicol, D., Macfarlane-Dick, D.: Formative assessment and self-regulated learning: a model and seven principles of good feedback practice. Stud. High. Educ. **31**(2), 199–218 (2006)
6. Lizzio, A., Wilson, K.: Feedback on assessment: students' perceptions of quality and effectiveness. Assess. Eval. High. Educ. **33**(3), 263–275 (2008)

7. Duncan, N.: 'Feedforward': Improving students' use of tutors' comments. Assess. Eval. High. Educ. **32**(3), 271–283 (2007)
8. Higgins, R., Hartley, P., Skelton, A.: Getting the message across: the problem of communicating assessment feedback. Teach. High. Educ. **6**(2), 269–274 (2001)
9. Hepplestone, S., Chikawa, G.: Understanding how students process and use feedback to support their learning. Pract. Res. High. Educ. **8**(1), 41–53 (2014)
10. Pitt, E., Norton, L.: Now that's the feedback I want! 'Students' reactions to feedback on graded work and what they do with it. Assess. Eval. High. Educ. **42**(4), 499–516 (2017)
11. Nicol, D.: From monologue to dialogue: improving written feedback processes in mass higher education. Assess. Eval. High. Educ. **35**(5), 501–517 (2010)
12. Savin-Baden, M.: The sound of feedback in higher education. Learn. Media Technol. **35**(1), 53–64 (2010)
13. Lunt, T., Curran, J.: Are you listening please? The advantages of electronic audio feedback compared to written feedback. Assess. Eval. High. Educ. **35**(7), 759–769 (2010)
14. Hussey, T., Smith, P.: The Trouble with Higher Education: A Critical Examination of our Universities. Routledge, Abingdon, Oxon (2010)
15. FileMaker.com. Rapid application development software (2016). http://info2.filemaker.com/rapid-application-development.html. Accessed 23 Mar 2017
16. Gomez Palacio, B., Vit, A.: Cover Image for Graphic Design, Referenced: A Visual Guide to the Language, Applications, and History of Graphic Design Graphic Design, Referenced: A Visual Guide to the Language, Applications, and History of Graphic Design, 1st edn. Rockport Publishers, Beverly (2009)

A Measure of Student Engagement for Serious Games and IoT

John Henry$^{(\boxtimes)}$, Stephen Tang, Martin Hannenghan, and Chris Carter

Department of Computer Science, Faculty of Technology and Environment,
Liverpool John Moores University,
James Parsons Building, Byrom Street, Liverpool L3 3AF, UK
j.melthis@2015.ljmu.ac.uk,
{s.o.tang,m.b.hanneghan,c.j.carter}@ljmu.ac.uk
http://www.ljmu.ac.uk

Abstract. *Student Engagement* has been a strong topic of research for the avoidance of student drop out and the increase in grading. *Serious games* have highlighted benefits in engaging students, primarily through *edutainment*, educating via games. This article suggests a *Computer Algorithm*, purposed at measuring and encouraging student engagement. In addition, the algorithm accounts for sensor networks accessed both directly and through the Internet, extending its application to the *Internet of Things* (IoT).

1 Introduction

Student Engagement is a multifaceted theory that constitutes of three factors; behavioural, emotional and cognitive engagement, as described in the research review conducted by J. Fredricks et al. [1]. Student engagement is usually measured through surveys based on self and/or academic self-reflection [2–6]. This paper proposes a computer algorithm that measures student engagement based on class attendance and punctuality in addition to self-perception. The calculated sum serves as data points that can be utilised in games, gamification, serious games and smart serious games.

Serious games are computer games built for non-entertainment domains, and have a presence in industries including health, advertisement, training, education, science, research, and others [7]. By harnessing the power of entertainment that gaming provides, serious games and gamification have provided a number of research and industrial solutions [8–11]. Serious Games have displayed an increase of student engagement in previous literature [12–14].

Furthermore, this paper introduces the Internet of Things (IoT) as a utility of measuring real world environmental effects on student engagement. IoT was firstly introduced by Kevin Aston [15] in 1999, aiming to identify unique objects and their virtual representations in an internet-like structure. IoT enables the connectivity of anything from any time to any place. Nowadays, researchers have expanded IoT with more technologies including sensors, network, data analysis, and various applications. Its applications include diverse and wide fields such

© Springer International Publishing AG 2017
F. Tian et al. (Eds.): Edutainment 2017, LNCS 10345, pp. 262–270, 2017.
https://doi.org/10.1007/978-3-319-65849-0_28

as industries [16], environments [17], cities [18], transportation [19] and health-care [20]. IoT consists of interconnected devices or Things that operate in Smart Environments and communicate data with virtual identification and/or person-alities [21]. In addition, IoT accounts for an ecosystem, which is comprised of middle-ware [22], users and interconnected devices.

This paper outlines as follows; Sect. 2 details current research on Serious Games and the Internet of Things, in respect to the future of this research. Section 3 discusses the new terminology of Smart Serious Game, a genre of seri-ous games that directly relates to this project. Section 4 explains the process of quantifying student engagement based on their actions in the physical world, and proposes a computer algorithm that measures, and potentially improves engage-ment through a game. Section 4 also presents the methodology for uncovering the proposed algorithm. Section 5 states the continuation of this research by val-idating the algorithm on students. Finally, the paper concludes and considers this research's limitations.

2   Student Engagement and Serious Games

Engagement is understood to be the involvement of people in an activity rather than the intensity of interaction [2]. Engaged students select tasks and learn-ing objectives at the border of their comprehension and adopt a positive and optimistic approach to learning [5]. E. Skinner and M. Belmont outlined a psy-chological model, which drew a correlation between the competencies of students and their levels of engagement [5].

The student engagement theory is utilised for analysing dropouts in schools [2,23]. Research by J. Appleton et al. outlines four subtypes of engagement: Academic, behavioural, cognitive and psychological [2]. Behaviour manipula-tion can be intrinsically or extrinsically triggered [1,24]. Intrinsic engagement stems from the engagement of following an instruction for the activity itself whereas extrinsic engagement relates to the desire to achieve goals and objec-tives related to an activity. A review conducted by J Fredricks et al. categorised student engagement into three elements: behavioural, emotional and cognitive [1]. Behavioural engagement relates to positive in-class conduct, involvement in learning relating (effort, concentration, contribution to class) and participation in activities (competitions, membership). Emotional engagement describes the feelings of students such as interest, anxiety, boredom and others. Finally, cog-nitive engagement focuses on the desire to complete extra curriculum activities and tasks, and the demonstration of strategic and methodical approaches to learning.

M. Handlesman et al. created a questionnaire in an attempt to measure course engagement based on a four-factor dimension. The four factors com-prised of skills, emotion, participation and interest, and performance. After performing validation tests against student grades they discovered correlations between engagement factors and grades, however due to the sample size acquired, their research could only provide an indication towards the questionnaire's effectiveness [4].

All included research into student engagement provide the psychological measures needed to monitor and evaluate engagement. All research recognises the existence of behavioural, emotional and cognitive engagement. Therefore, the algorithm and game will include these aspects of student engagement their measurements. Scientific research has proven games are engaging and immersive. In detail, research by R. Garris et al. focuses on the instructional games and their engagement to learners to accomplish better learning outcomes [12]. Their suggested Input-Process-Output Game Model details an iterative Game Cycle that comprises of User Judgement, User Behaviour and System Feedback and encourages interacting with a game. This game cycle remains true in Smart Serious Games for student engagement.

The key difference lies in the mechanisms used to implement such an iterative cycle. User Behaviour and Judgement can now be monitored and inputted into the game through the use of network distributed sensors rather than direct input. Additionally, predictive algorithms and machine learning add another layer of information that can aid in understanding engagement from external factors, like never before.

Research into the gamification of learning experiences by A. Domnguez et al. presented a solution focused on cognitive, social and emotional engagement, in an attempt to improve learning outcomes [13]. Their research provided an indication of emotional and social engagement on students; however, they noted no significant improvement on learning outcome.

Research by V. Guilln-Nieto et al. acknowledged that serious games can generate engagement and stimulation in educational environments, but focused on the effectiveness of serious games for learning [14]. Their empirical findings indicated that serious games are effective as learning tools providing that the developed solution include classroom procedures and clearly outlined learning objectives as well as game cycle and game dimensions. The structure of the serious game V. Guilln-Nieto et al. developed provides a useful insight into game elements that must be included in effective serious games for educational settings.

The core difference between the aforementioned research and this project lies in the methods of data collection and data analysis. The Student Engagement Instrument [2], and others, obtain data through questionnaires, either during classroom time, or at random intervals. This project embeds attendance as a measure, achieved through a hybrid sensor network [25], and utilises IoT to predict and inform.

The combination of IoT and Serious Games has recently been termed as Smart Serious Games (SSGs) [26]. SSGs are the merger of smart technologies, including devices and services, and the principles of Serious Games [26]. Sharma et al. detail the combination of the advantages of both technologies and its future utilisations including analytics for corporations, a tool for solving serious problems and others.

IoT serves a pivotal role in developing predictive and reactive algorithms that measure engagement through games. The combination of a sensor network with real world data will allow correlations to be drawn. These data association allow for personalised prompting based on behaviour pattern. In detail, if a student tends to be absent on a rainy day, a personalised prompt can be created for the next time it rains to highlight that fact to the student. Prompting aside, the manipulation of data points and bonus scores can transverse the immersion of gaming into student engagement.

3   Quantifying Student Engagement

In the previous section, we highlighted research relating to serious games and student engagement, and identified they commonly measure engagement through qualitative feedback acquired from questionnaires. By introducing IoT, it is possible to quantify elements of student engagement, particularly behavioural. By monitoring class attendance and punctuality we receive quantitative data related to each student's engagement. Monitoring attendance and punctuality is not a new measure for student engagement, however obtaining the data through a wireless sensor network generates accurate data that has been captured in a less invasive manner. Traditional attendance monitoring systems involve pen and paper, which is susceptible to student forgery. Recent systems include Radio-Frequency Identification (RFID) cards and receivers, however this is still more invasive than IoT solutions, and can disrupt class flow.

Figure 1 presents the engagement model we utilise for monitoring student engagement. Student attendance and punctuality is tracked through a wireless sensor network. Based on the time of their presence, game points are allocated for attendance and punctuality. A breakdown of the point allocation can be seen in Appendix A. Game points are also allocated through a questionnaire that is embedded into the game. The scoring system for the questionnaire follows the principles set by aforementioned research projects that utilise the same means for obtaining a measure of student engagement. In detail, a rating of $1 - 4$ is given to questions that monitor distribution, effort, contribution, concentration, interest, boredom, anxiety, happiness, desire, and strategy.

The game points accumulated from sensor networks and questionnaires will allow for an aggregate scoring to be produced that can indicate a student's level of engagement. Further detail on this is provided in Sect. 4.

4   Measuring Student Engagement

This section presents the equation for calculating student engagement and the methodology behind it. The measure of student engagement will be visualised in game as a score, where a high value equates to high engagement levels.

We calculate the value by accounting for class attendance, punctuality, and the views of academics and students, gathered by game embedded questionnaires. Physical activities (attendance and punctuality), provide a static score each time they are completed. Students that complete a streak of game objectives will receive further rewards. For example, a student that attends all classes in a week will receive a bonus reward that directly increases the engagement score.

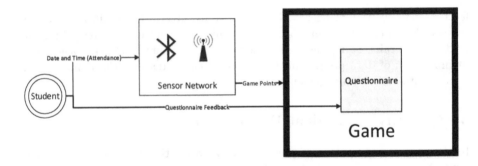

Fig. 1. An illustration of the model used for quantifying student engagement

In detail, a set game objective requires players to attend a class, this awards five points. Attending all classes in a week is a separate game objective that rewards an additional ten points if met. This method of scoring provides a points balance between those who are engaged and those who are disengaged. It is pivotal that the encouragement received in gameplay does not outscore an engaged student's score, as it can hinder the purpose of the game. Section 4.1 provides further detail on data points and the methodology used.

$$En = \left[\frac{1}{2}(Ca + Cp + \frac{Wt}{d})\right] \tag{1}$$

The equation above calculates En, which represents the total engagement score achieved and forms the core measurement of achievement in game. Ca and Cp are the weekly total of game points amounted by class attendance and punctuality, respectively. Wt symbolises the questionnaire weekly scores, calculated using Eq. 2. In detail student engagement En is formed by averaging the sum of data points achieved and the weekly total Wt score divided by the number of timetabled days for students. We divide by 2 as Ca and Cp require student presence for positive scoring, and is therefore considered as one factor of student engagement.

$$Wt = \left[\frac{Cs}{2} + \frac{Cs}{2}..\right] \tag{2}$$

Wt is calculated by averaging the total class score (Cs) from student and academic, and summing up the value of average class scores obtained through a timetabled week. Using attendance as a quantifiable measure of engagement is supported by J. Frederick et al. as they deem behavioural engagement to be a crucial factor in preventing student drop-out and achieving positive academic results [1]. Referring to Fig. 1, the algorithm ensures all three elements of student engagement are accounted for. Behavioural engagement will be quantified through presence and punctuality. A non-intrusive attendance system obtains these measurements [25]. Emotional and cognitive engagement measure through qualitative responses. Quantifying these elements would require intrusive technology, such as head scanners.

It is possible that IoT can provide an indicator of cognitive engagement. If a student chooses to attend class with severe weather conditions, high traffic congestion, or out of scheduled time, their cognitive engagement is assumed. We will conduct further research to investigate any possible correlation.

4.1 Engagement Simulation

We undertook a form of data simulation to identify the range of scores between engagement levels, and to determine the best equation for aggregating the total of data points. All data simulation was performed utilising spreadsheet software. To begin with, data obtained from the Web regarding traffic, weather and sunlight duration was exported into the spreadsheet. A timetable copy for a live module at Liverpool John Moores University was utilised, providing the amount of classes in a week and their respective details. At this stage three personae were developed.

Each persona represented a point in the spectrum of student engagement, therefore producing disengaged, engaged and neutral personae. We performed simulations over two hypothetical weeks. The first week utilised assumptions based on each persona. Disengaged achieves around 20% of weekly maximum $Ca+Cp$ and scores low on Wt, neutral obtains 88% of $Ca+Cp$ with medium Wt score, whereas engaged is allocated with top scores.

These assumptions tested resiliently the scoring system and the equation for a balance in scores. By manipulating the points of reward through multiple iterations of calculation with the equation, a fairer score was produced and data anomalies were solved, ultimately changing the equation itself. Utilising spreadsheet software for the production of data algorithms therefore proved extremely useful as simulated data ensures a strong data algorithm is used before an application is built, reducing development time.

Simulating based on persona assumptions provided the foundation to game fairer rewards, however when taking this equation and points system to real students, further anomalies could occur. In an attempt to test this, prior to development of the game, we randomised all scores for the second week utilising embedded functionality provided by the spreadsheet software. For the second randomised week, the engaged and disengaged personae produced disengaged scores whereas neutral remained within a neutral range of score. This occurred as the attendance allocated to them by picking a random number (between 0 and 10) directly affected their respective engagement scores. An illustration of the results is located in Appendix A, where an engaged factor is symbolised with white, neutral with grey and disengaged with black.

As aforementioned, we are utilising attendance to quantify engagement, therefore the results produced indicated no preliminary issues. By utilising spreadsheet software and mathematical equations it is therefore possible to detect data anomalies before the development cycle begins, aiding in reducing it.

5   Research Challenges and Future Works

At this stage, the algorithm has been validated using data simulations of occurring and random nature. This can categorise the study as preliminary. It is important to note the focus of this paper, to propose a new algorithm for quantifying student engagement, and to document the methodology of validating a computer algorithm through data simulations, performed in spreadsheet software.

Developing the serious game and embedding the suggested algorithm ensues, allowing us to validate it with real students. We will also attempt to draw meaningful correlations between real world data and student engagement through IoT. This will provide a unique perspective on student engagement and may alter the equation's format in future, pending results from experimentation.

Post experimentation, findings will be disseminated to update on the progress of this research project. A possible fall back with our future works, students may choose to disengage with the game completely, skewering results. In this instance, participants will be questioned regarding their reasons for withdrawing.

6   Conclusion

Concluding, this paper introduces a computer algorithm for quantifying measuring student engagement based on an aggregate of their attendance, punctuality and subjective feedback. This data algorithm caters for Serious Games, gamification and edutainment as it utilises game points to portray results. By including IoT we acquire behavioural engagement data that we correlate against real world events. The results of this correlation aim to encourage and alert students to facts regarding their engagement. We also presented the use of data simulation for validating the data algorithm, using personae, and spreadsheet software. As aforementioned, the study is preliminary, with data from experimentation with real students needed, to validate the algorithm's effectiveness. This will be carried out as part of this research project and the findings will be disseminated accordingly.

A   Spreadsheet

Game Objectives (Weekly Scores)			
Attendance (Behavioural Engagement)			
Punctuality	Score	Classes	Score
Over 10 minutes late	2	Attended a class	5
Between 5 and 10 minutes late	3	Attended all classes in a week	10
Less than 5 minutes late	5	Attended all classes in a month	20
Less than 5 minutes late in a week	10	Attended all classes in a semester	40
Less than 5 minutes late in a month	20		
Less than 5 minutes late in a semester	40		

		WEEK 1	
		Weekly Scores (Re-occuring)	
Personas	Attendance	Questionnaire	Factor
Engaged	120	80	100
Neutral	105	60	83
Disengaged	24	10	17

		WEEK 2	
		Weekly Scores (Randomised)	
Personas	Attendance	Questionnaire	Factor
Engaged	38	40	39
Neutral	73	54	64
Disengaged	50	20	35

References

1. Fredricks, J.A., Blumenfeld, P.C., Paris, A.H.: School engagement: potential of the concept, state of the evidence. Rev. Educ. Res. **74**, 59–109 (2004)
2. Appleton, J.J., Christenson, S.L., Kim, D., Reschly, A.L.: Measuring cognitive and psychological engagement: validation of the student engagement instrument. J. Sch. Psychol. **44**, 427–445 (2006)
3. Coller, B.D., Shernoff, D.J.: Video game-based education in mechanical engineering: a look at student engagement. Int. J. Eng. Educ. **25**, 308–317 (2009)
4. Handlesman, M.M., Briggs, W., Sullivan, N., Towler, A.: A measure of college student course engagement. J. Educ. Res. **98**, 184–192 (2005)
5. Skinner, E.A., Belmont, M.J.: Motivation in the classroom: reciprocal effects of teacher behavior and student engagement across the school year. J. Educ. Psychol. **85**, 571–581 (1993)

6. Brockmyer, J.H., Fox, C.M., Curtiss, K.A., McBroom, E., Burkhart, K.M.: The development of the game engagement questionnaire: a measure of engagement in video game-playing. J. Exp. Soc. Psychol. **45**, 624–634 (2009)
7. Tang, S., Hanneghan, M., Carter, C.: A platform independent game technology model for model driven serious games development. Electron. J. e-Learn. **11**, 61–79 (2013)
8. Blohm, I., Leimeister, J.M.: Gamification: design of IT-based enhancing services for motivational support and behavioral change. Bus. Inf. Syst. Eng. **5**, 275–278 (2013)
9. Burke, J.W., McNeill, M.D.J., Charles, D.K., Morrow, P.J., Crosbie, J.H., McDonough, S.M.: Optimising engagement for stroke rehabilitation using serious games. Vis. Comput. **25**, 1085–1099 (2009)
10. Girard, C., Ecalle, J., Magnan, A.: Serious games as new educational tools: how effective are they? a meta-analysis of recent studies. J. Comput. Assist. Learn. **29**, 207–219 (2013)
11. Aldrich, C.: The Complete Guide to Simulations and Serious Games : How the Most Valuable Content will be Created in the Age Beyond Gutenberg to Google, Pfeiffer Essential Resources for Training and HR Professionals, p. 533. Pfeiffer Publishing, San Francisco (2009)
12. Garris, R., Ahlers, R., Driskell, J.E.: Games, motivation, and learning: a research and practice model. Simul. Gaming **33**, 441–467 (2002)
13. Domnguez, A., Saenz-De-Navarrete, J., De-Marcos, L., Fernndez-Sanz, L., Pags, C., Martnez-Herriz, J.J.: Gamifying learning experiences: practical implications and outcomes. Comput. Educ. **63**, 380–392 (2013)
14. Guilln-Nieto, V., Aleson-Carbonell, M.: Serious games and learning effectiveness: the case of its a deal!. Comput. Educ. **58**, 435–448 (2012)
15. Ashton, K.: That 'Internet of Things' Thing, RFID J. **22** (2009)
16. Jia, X., Feng, Q., Fan, T., Lei, Q.: RFID technology and its applications in internet of things (IoT). In: 2nd International Conference on Consumer Electronics, Communications and Networks, vol. 21, pp. 1282–1285 (2012)
17. Sun, C.: Application of RFID technology for logistics on internet of things. AASRI Procedia **1**, 106–111 (2012)
18. Zanella, A., Bui, N., Castellani, A., Vangelista, L., Zorzi, M.: Internet of things for smart cities. Internet Things J. **1**, 22–32 (2014)
19. Guerrero Ibanez, J., Zeadally, S., Contreras-Castillo, J.: Integration challenges of intelligent transportation systems with connected vehicle, cloud computing, and internet of things technologies. IEEE Wirel. Commun. **22**, 122–128 (2015)
20. Yang, P., Hanneghan, M., Qi, J., Deng, Z., Fan, D., Dong, F.: Improving the Validity of Lifelogging Physical Activity Measures in an Internet of Things Environment. In: (CIT/UCC/DASC/PICOM) (2015)
21. Atzori, L., Iera, A., Morabito, G.: The internet of things: a survey. Comput. Netw. **54**, 2787–2805 (2010)
22. Khalid, Z., Fisal, N., Rozaini, M.: A survey of middleware for sensor and network virtualization. Sensors **14**, 24046–24097 (2014)
23. Finn, J.D.: Withdrawing from School. Rev. Educ. Res. **59**, 117–142 (1989)
24. Eccles, J.S., Wigfield, A.: Motivational beliefs, values, and goals. Annu. Rev. Psychol. **53**, 109–132 (2002)
25. Melthis, J., Tang, S., Yang, P., et al.: Topologies for combining the internet of things and serious games. J. Intell. Fuzzy Syst. **31**, 2685–2696 (2016)
26. Sharma, D., Lakhmi, J.C., Favorskaya, M., Howlett, R.J.: Fusion of Smart, Multimedia and Computer Gaming Technologies. Springer International Publishing, Heidelberg (2015)

Implementation of the Unity Engine for Developing 2D Mobile Games in Consideration of Start-Up/Student Developers

Jack Brett and Alain Simons[✉]

Bournemouth University, Fern Barrow, Bournemouth BH12 5BB, UK
{i7668967, asimons}@bournemouth.ac.uk

Abstract. The Unity 3D engine is used by a large majority of developers to create games. It owns a forty five percent market share and is considered one of the biggest development tools today; this is due to its simple and fast development process which allows for rapid production of game prototypes. However, with over a hundred different options available to develop games, one must ask whether using an engine such as Unity to generate simple 2D mobile games is necessary. This paper aims to discover whether the use of the Unity engine is appropriate for beginner developers who are looking to create 2D mobile games whilst also providing insight into how influential Unity is within education and whether learning more programming orientated applications is beneficial in regards to universal application and longevity. We will define the criteria for selecting a development methodology and create a 2D mobile game within the Unity engine and replicate this game using Corona SDK. The development process for both implementations will be reviewed and compared then the game will be tested using a benchmark application on various devices to help demonstrate which method was the most optimised and therefore appropriate for mobile development.

Keywords: 2D game · Unity · SDK · Generic software · Mobile game · Education

1 Introduction

Today, mobile games consume a vast market share within the games industry, it is expected that in 2018 mobile gaming will account for 43 percent of the gaming market revenue and currently there are over a third of Americans playing mobile games daily [1]. In regards to genre; the most popular games are brain puzzle games (with over 37 million users per month playing one), closely followed by matching puzzle games e.g. *Candy Crush* [2]. According to the UKIE's games industry map, there are nearly a thousand games companies in London. Out of these, roughly seven hundred are working on the mobile platform and over two hundred were formed in the last five years. Not all of these companies will be run by younger developers but it is safe to assume that at least a small portion of them are. Considering that nearly two billion

© Springer International Publishing AG 2017
F. Tian et al. (Eds.): Edutainment 2017, LNCS 10345, pp. 271–278, 2017.
https://doi.org/10.1007/978-3-319-65849-0_29

Fig. 1. Dominant marketplace position of Unity.

mobile devices are running a Unity-made game, it is probable that quite a large majority of these new companies will be using Unity to develop mobile games (Figs. 1, 2, 3, 4, 5 and 6).

It has been established that mobile games are becoming increasingly popular and that most users will play a puzzle or match game – a basic, more than likely, 2D game. The problem which arises is that new developers who want to create popular mobile games will assume that Unity is the correct tool for implementation. However, alternatives may offer simpler solutions but younger developers will be discouraged due to the ideology that using an SDK or graphical API is too complicated which may have been reinforced by using Unity through education.

The core objective of this paper is to determine whether Unity is the correct choice for younger developers creating mobile games. In order to achieve this objective a mobile game will be created using both Unity and Corona SDK. The development process will be documented and compared against specific criteria then both games will be tested to compare performance and set a benchmark across a multitude of devices.

2   Previous Research

2.1   Software Comparison

It is important to note that game development software is mostly specific to certain platforms so when comparing engines with one another the components which focus on creating mobile games are compared and nothing else as this is a false representation. For example, real time particle effects, a 3D graphics algorithm, cannot be used in mobile games but the engine may use it for a higher level platform.

Game engine selection methodology has been defined by [3]. In order to make a comparison, criteria must be defined; they defined this criteria as audio-visual fidelity, functional fidelity, composability, accessibility, networking and heterogeneity. Then they break these criteria down into smaller sections – not all criteria will be used in this research as their criteria applies to all game development rather than just mobile. A key criteria which falls under the 'accessibility' heading is the 'learning curve', this is an important factor in consideration for amateur developers as some methods will appear to be much easier but occasionally a steeper learning curve can be more beneficial.

A similar paper compared game engines which derived some of the criteria from Petridis' work [4]. Although the research focuses on building to multiple platforms, the conclusions drawn upon take into account how suitable each engine is depending on what platform is used. There is a focus on ease of learning too, this an important factor to consider with amateur developers who require guidance with complex issues. Also taken into account is what programming language is used for each software which has universal application within the gaming industry. The conclusion describes which engine was best in regards to specific criteria and genre; there was no one main winner but it appears choosing software for development relied on two main things: experience of the developer and the type of game one wishes to create.

2.2 Software Testing

Creating a fair testing environment for mobile games is quite different to other games, in this example testing refers to the performance of the mobile application rather than the user experience. Mobile application testing guidelines have been created by [5] who states that not only do mobile applications have to work anywhere and at any time, they also should work across platforms, different operating systems, display sizes and not drain battery life. They later split testing into separate goals; quality of service testing, reliability and scalability, interoperability testing – these are the relatable testing methods which will help achieve a fair conclusion. Finally, they outline different approaches for testing a mobile application. Device-based testing requires multiple devices and time but for this scale seems the most appropriate for it can "…verify device-based functions, behaviours, and QoS parameters that other approaches cannot" [5].

Another decision must be made regarding mobile game testing and that is the choice to manually test or to automatically test. In [6] research on mobile application testing he found that manual testing may be more time consuming but doesn't require the programming skill to initially set up the automation for automatic testing, moreover, for testing performance and playability using real people gives more accurate results. Finally, [7] mentions that "that all code can be subject to change…" in order to test for performance or errors one must expect extreme values.

3 Our Research

3.1 Previous Comparison

Interviews with independent game developers were conducted by the author to help understand the reasoning behind why they chose certain software to develop their games. The overall consensus left Unity in a positive light, most developers claimed that they had used it in the past and the experience was quick and relatively easy. However, those who had more experience in this field and had developed more games had slightly differing opinions, stating that it is a useful and powerful tool but lacks freedom of control, universal application and the fact that one can build to a large array of platforms meant that the overall quality of the build was poor i.e. quantity over quality wasn't a balanced exchange. An extra anecdote; those who could not find many issues with using Unity (or similar engine) were also those who had little experience in other methodologies of development and those of whom did have experience in other software claimed that the learning curve may be steeper for programming orientated implementations but also has a larger scope of application.

This solution aims to eliminate the issue that beginner developers face when deciding on which software to use when developing mobile games. In this paper, we compare and analyse the two different implementations of a 2D mobile game, using Unity as the engine and Corona SDK.

Criteria to compare the two development:

- Audio visual fidelity which consists of mainly 2D sprite animation
- Functional fidelity which is scripting and language efficiency,
- Composability – import/export limitations and available content
- Accessibility: learning curve, documentation and support, licensing and cost
- Heterogeneity (multiplatform support)

The game which will be created must feature the basics of a 2D mobile puzzle type game so it is applicable to the general consensus. Therefore, the game must contain specific elements:

- UI system; a menu in which users can navigate through the game
- Layered background elements which feature parallax scrolling (basic animation)
- Basic enemy AI and a scoring system
- Collision with enemies and a life system
- Touch controls and basic player movement linked to touch controls

Fig. 2. Example of the game.

3.2   Unity Implementation

Creating the basics of a game within the Unity engine is an easy task; dragging the required assets from a folder and dropping them into the editor was simple and fast. Once assets had been imported, initial backgrounds were placed – here we used multiple images and layered them in front of one another. Parallax scrolling was implemented by transforming the sprite images into textures, placing them onto a 3D quad then attaching a script which offset the textures by a rate which is changeable. It is important to note that this process requires mathematics but due to the rich documentation, understanding said mathematics was not necessary as someone has already calculated these variables. Additionally, the default shader applied to this object was not changed – it was default and changing it meant learning a new library regarding shaders.

Creating the animating ships was carried out using sprite animation. The animator window within the Unity editor is simple and easy to follow; the main issue was once again, ignorance of what was happening. Dragging a sprite sheet with multiple images into the editor meant that Unity could create the animation and when the game played the animation begun – this may appear as a good thing but with over two years of using Unity in education one should understand how sprite animation works in detail. Creating 'enemies' for the player to avoid involved creating a script which moved an enemy left to right with a sine wave for some random movement. Spawning these enemies was carried out by instantiating them within one function and using a Unity function which allows a specific function to be looped with a given time and rate. Collision was a matter of attaching a collider (something which can detect a hit) to the player and the enemies, then a script would tell the game what to do if an enemy collided with the player.

Scripting within the Unity editor can be a tedious task if only small changes need to be made. Using mostly Monodevelop (which is included with Unity) to edit code, making a small change then switching back to the editor to test the change took much longer than needed. Due to the sheer size of the engine and the speed of compilation within Monodevelop, there was a lot left to be desired when making a small mobile game which requires a lot of small details to be changed.

3.3   Corona SDK Implementation

Learning Corona SDK and Lua (a scripting language) from scratch may appear to be a somewhat daunting task but once the basics have been laid out the rest seems to flow. Using Microsoft Visual Code to edit the code meant that the project loaded instantly and changes could be made at rapid speeds. The initial set up of loading images and creating a layered background was the same as the Unity implementation only carried out using code rather than re sizing an image with a visual editor. Unlike Unity, Corona SDK only uses 2D libraries so parallax scrolling could not be carried out using texture offset of a 3D quad. In any case, a simpler solution was used. By placing an image on the screen and a copy just behind, a function could be set up which moved the first image then the second when it had reached the end of the screen – a process which relied on logic over demonstration.

Creating sprite animation was rather straight forward due to the documentation on the Corona website. The idea behind sprite animation is to tell the engine the size of each individual image, for example, a square image of 128 pixels with four images would mean that each image is 32 pixels in size. Implementing touch mechanics in order to move the ship was carried out by using code found online but the basics of it are that the engine will recognize where a touch was started and a runtime event will 'listen' for where it was let go.

In terms of difficulty; there is certainly a steeper learning curve in comparison to using Unity but the experience and knowledge gained surpasses Unity. There is no room for ignorance and therefore true logic and programming knowledge must be used. For example, spawning enemies could not be carried out by using a function which can repeat certain actions as there is no such function. This action must be carried out using a slightly more complex programming convention. Creating a table (or array) then adding the enemy to this table meant that multiple instances of the same object could be generated. Using a public variable, one can state how many enemies can spawn and a runtime event will call the function depending on how many values were in the table. This is a core concept of programming and game development yet the first time it has been used correctly, as educational institutions only use Unity there has never been a reason to understand this logic. Finally, making small changes such as spawn numbers etc. were compiled almost instantly and as a result made the development process much more streamline.

4 Results

To test performance of a mobile game it must be tested across different devices with varying scenarios. Due to the nature of video games being unpredictable two levels were created; one which plays as a normal game where the player must avoid hazards and another which tests extreme variables – this level features 70 enemies spawning at once and serves the purpose of performance testing not playability. Five devices were used for testing; from low end mobile phones to high end tablets, for this scenario the lowest end mobile, the mid-range mobile and the high end tablet will be used to demonstrate performance.

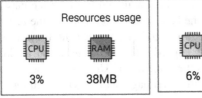 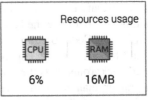

Fig. 3. Corona SDK version performance results. Corona SDK version tested on *Samsung Galaxy SIII* (Low end device). Left shows normal level and right shows extreme values.

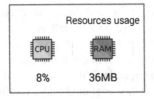 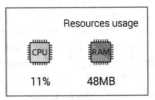

Fig. 4. Unity version tested on *Samsung Galaxy SIII*. Left shows normal level and right shows extreme level.

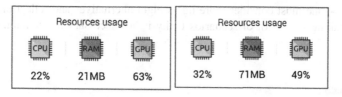

Fig. 5. *Sony Experia L* Test. Both are on extreme value level, left shows Corona version and right shows Unity version.

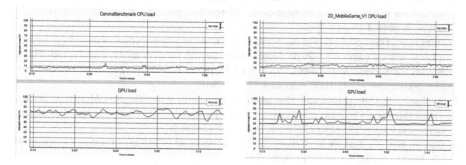

Fig. 6. Performance graphs for both versions. Right shows Corona and left shows Unity. Testing on Samsung *Galaxy Tab A*. Both tests are performed on the extreme values level.

5 Conclusions

Results show that Unity may not be the most practical solution for inexperienced developers to create 2D mobile games. Although one may presume it is used by a lot of developers and games can be made with in short time frames with relative ease, this does not mean it is the ideal game engine. Testing shows that for small mobile games Unity does not perform as well as other software; it consumes much more RAM and CPU usage which in turn will drain battery life faster than other applications and will drop in performance quicker than other games.

In addition, if one were to learn Unity throughout education and only Unity they would be limited in regards to actual knowledge of game development. For example, learning C++ with a graphical API will give a student understanding about the key fundamentals of how to draw an image to a screen, basic mathematics such as dot product etc. This knowledge is invaluable as it can be applied to any game development system whereas using Unity and allowing someone with more expertise to carry out complex tasks will only build ignorance towards more complex systems and as a result will restrict what they can do quickly.

To summarise, Unity or similar engines are great for producing prototypes at a rapid rate, however they can also limit understanding and as a result will produce very similar games. The choice of which software to use is somewhat subjective; it depends on which game one wishes to create and how much expertise is possessed. Using Unity is suitable for generating mobile games but amateur developers should not take it as the best option – one must consider more lightweight alternatives and reflect on the game they are making – in a lot of scenarios Unity is not necessary for creation of mobile games.

References

1. Augmented Reality Statista: Statistics and facts on Mobile Gaming (2017). https://www. statista.com/topics/1906/mobile-gaming/. Accessed 10 Apr 2017
2. CH Verto Analytics: The most popular mobile game genres: Who plays what, when? (2016). http://www.vertoanalytics.com/the-most-popular-mobile-game-genres-who-plays-what-when/. Accessed 10 Apr 2017
3. Petridis, P.; Dunwell, I.; de Freitas, S., Panzoli, D.: An engine selection methodology for high fidelity serious games. In: 2010 Second International Conference on Games and Virtual Worlds for Serious Applications (VS-GAMES), pp. 27–34. IEEE (2010). http://ieeexplore. ieee.org/document/5460160/. Accessed 12 Apr 2010
4. Akekarat, P.: Comparison and evaluation of 3D mobile game engines. Master of Science Thesis (Masters). Chalmers University of Technology (2014). http://publications.lib.chalmers. se/records/fulltext/193979/193979.pdf. Accessed 12 Apr 2014
5. Gao, J., Bai, X., Tsai, W.T., Uehara, T.: Mobile application testing: a tutorial. Computer **47** (2), 46–55 (2014). Accessed 13 Apr
6. Amen, B.M., Mahmood, S.M., Lu, J.: Mobile Application Testing Matrix and Challenges. http://airccj.org/CSCP/vol5/csit53503.pdf. Accessed 13 Apr
7. Manouchehri, P.: In-depth: Unit testing in Unity. GamaSutra (2012). http://www.gamasutra. com/view/news/164363/Indepth_Unit_testing_in_Unity.php. Accessed 12 Apr

Game-Enhanced and Process-Based e-Learning Framework

Rawad Hammad[✉]

Software Engineering Research Group (SERG),
Department of Computer Science and Creative Technology, Faculty of Environment and
Technology, University of the West of England, Bristol, UK
Rawad.Hammad@uwe.ac.uk

Abstract. Despite the importance of game-enhanced e-learning approaches/
artefacts, their processes, design choices, gamification mechanisms still need
further development to increase their flexibility, agility and effectiveness. This
paper critically reviews the current game-enhanced e-learning models to identify
the research gap and proposes a new e-learning framework. This framework
combines the following technologies: (i) *business process* to model and enact
game-enhanced e-learning processes, (ii) *ontology* to contextualise the e-learning
process, (iii) *service-oriented architecture* to dynamically map e-learning
processes and their elements/activities to a set of software services. Such framework allows to abstract from technical details and to keep the game-enhanced e-
learning process agile and more responsive to e-learner requirements. Further
work is needed to develop this framework and test it in real case scenarios.

Keywords: Game-enhanced e-learning · Process-based e-learning ·
Technology-enhanced learning · e-learning · Service-oriented e-learning ·
Semantic e-learning

1 Introduction

Learning is one of the very oldest human activities that have been practiced since the
dawn of humankind. Throughout the course of history, learning has been approached in
different ways according to its surrounding environments, goals, available technologies
and other contextual inputs. Learning took different forms, such as: traditional schools/
classrooms, learning discovery, e-learning, and blended learning. A variety of terms
with different definitions have been used in relation to utilising technology in learning
such as e-Learning and Technology-Enhanced Learning (TEL). Similarly, tools used
for this utilisation vary in their goals, scope, adopted strategies, etc. Examples of such
tools include: Learning Management System (LMS), Adaptive e-Learning Systems, and
Game-enhanced e-Learning Systems.

Generally, utilising technology in a certain domain (e-learning, e-business, etc.) aims
at increasing the effectiveness and the efficiency of the current processes (e.g., learning
processes, business processes). Such improvements include: better approaches to
achieve the overall goal and better design for e-learning artefacts (e.g., flexible design,

© Springer International Publishing AG 2017
F. Tian et al. (Eds.): Edutainment 2017, LNCS 10345, pp. 279–284, 2017.
https://doi.org/10.1007/978-3-319-65849-0_30

agile development processes, and coherence e-learning experience delivery [1]. However, the effective application of gamification techniques in a complex cognitive domain (i.e., e-learning) is more challenging due to e-learning particularities such as the social nature of learning [2] and the implicit mechanism of learning [3]. This work will investigate the state of the art in the game-enhanced learning domain and propose a new flexible design based on a combination of various technologies. The rest of this paper is structured as follows: Sect. 2 reviews the related literature, Sect. 3 proposes a new Game-enhanced and Process-based e-Learning Framework, and Sect. 4 briefly discusses and concludes the paper.

2   Literature Survey

Recently, the use of games in education and other domains gains momentum. This is described in literature in different terms, such as: Gamification and Serious Games. *Gamification* refers to the use of game design elements in non-games contexts [4] or, in a border sense, refers to the use of game-based mechanics, aesthetics and game thinking to engage people, motivate action, promote learning and solve problems [5]. Nonetheless, *Serious Games* refer to games designed for specific pre-defined purposes [6]. Serious games repurpose games in order to offer activities that go beyond entertainment, but gamification use game design to enhance stakeholder's willingness to participate to originally non-playful experiences [7]. Therefore, this research uses the term "Game-Enhanced Learning (GEL)" as an umbrella to cover the above-mentioned definitions/ models. Game creates a flow (e.g., goals, rules and feedback) that is necessary for learning. Psychologically during such flow learners experience gratification and their immersion in the experience are at peak creativity and performance which is an ideal situation for learning [8, 9].

Motivating e-learners and engaging them are the two key derivers behind GEL development. Games ability to reframe learners' failure as a part of learning experience is an example on motivation [10]. The continuous feedback and joyful experience to develop positive learners' qualities, such as: persistence and discovery is another example [11]. Key GEL advantages are classified as: (i) cognitive, where games provide adaptive routes to success based on complex rules through active experimentation and discovery [12], (ii) emotional, as they induce frustration, curiosity, etc. and can transform from one emotional state to another and (iii) social, because e-learners continuously try to find new identities suitable for them [10]. Literature evidences [13] reveal how GEL can positively impact e-learner's experience, while empirical evidences [14] reveal GEL positive impact on behavioural and psychological outcomes. This explains why GEL techniques have been embedded in different e-learning models, such as: ITSs [15, 16] and LMSs [6].

However, gamifying e-learning is challenging and not straightforward due to the following reasons. *First*, it requires heavy involvement by instructor and other team members in complex gamification stages, such as understanding audience/context and structuring the e-learning experience [17]. *Second*, it might absorb instructor resources and teach learners to learn based extrinsic rewards [10]. *Third*, evidences from literature reveal mistakes in applying gamification concepts (e.g., instructors try to gamify outcomes instead of behaviour [17]), which requires close monitoring during the development (i.e., time consuming process). *Fourth*, it requires long-time of fine-tuning of course contents, teaching scenarios, learning processes, assessment strategies and feedback. *Fifth*, the currently adopted design approach is not user-centred, and consequently instructors are neglected from the design which leads to poor adoption rate [18]. *Sixth*, the gamification approaches are cemented into the design of the e-learning scenarios and processes. Consequently, it is challenging to reuse the existing game-enhanced e-learning scenarios. In other words, it is difficult to compose a new game-based scenario from the existing game-enhanced e-learning artefacts. Therefore, the agility of such systems and the flexibility (i.e., giving the e-learners more control on their e-learning processes) need to be improved.

3   The Proposed Framework

To respond to the above-mentioned research gap, a new architectural Game-enhanced and Process-based e-Learning Framework will be proposed to improve the flexibility of game-enhanced e-learning artefacts. This framework depends on the following key technologies/pillars as follows. *First*, modelling and specifying a generic game-enhanced e-learning process using an industrial standard Business Process Modelling Notation, such as BPMN. This generic e-learning process model will describes a generic game-enhanced e-learning scenario, its activities and interactions between the e-learner(s) and the system. This process model allows to abstract from the technical details and separate the domain-oriented considerations/assumptions from their operational counterparts. *Second*, since e-learning processes are context-dependent, effective contextualisation mechanisms are required. However, the current process modelling notations, including BPMN, cannot effectively capture the context, which will negatively impact the ability of the proposed framework to specialise the generic e-learning scenario for a certain e-learner based on her preferences and goals. Therefore, an e-learning ontology will be designed to capture related information about the e-learners, their preferences, achievements, goals, interactions with their peers, etc. This ontology will provide the proposed e-learning framework with the proper information about the e-learner so that the generic e-learning process can be customised according to the e-learner goals and achievements.

Third, the modelled e-learning processes, and its correspondent Business Process Execution Language (BPEL) script needs to be enacted using business process execution engine in a service-oriented architecture/environment (SOA), where various web services can be identified, discovered and mapped into the e-learning process activities. This structure will allow more control for e-learning on their e-learning processes. For instance, they will be able to choose how to tailor their e-learning process, therefore, there is a need to ensure the pedagogical usefulness of any customised e-learning process. So, a selected set of validated e-learning scenarios/approaches (e.g., behavioural e-learning approaches or social-based e-learning processes) [19] must be represented in the *fourth* pillar in a certain format that is compatible with other technologies (i.e., e-learning processes, ontology and SOA). This framework is presented in Fig. 1.

As explained in the figure, the first layer is dedicated for interface-oriented functionalities/capabilities, while the second layer represents the game-enhanced e-learning process model, its roles, activities, gateway and conditions, potential data artefacts, etc. This process is modelled using BPMN 2.0 standard, which is sufficient to model e-learning activities but needs further contextualisation. This contextualisation is solved by the e-learning ontology component, while the e-learning services component enables the execution of the semantically-enriched e-learning processes through a set of software services. Finally, the Learning Scenarios/Approaches component must model a selected set of potential e-learning approaches that could be useful in the context of the game-enhanced learning environment.

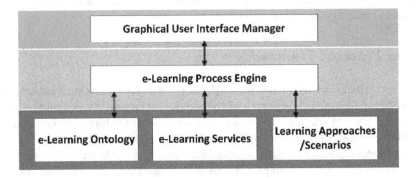

Fig. 1. The game-enhanced and process-based e-learning architectural framework

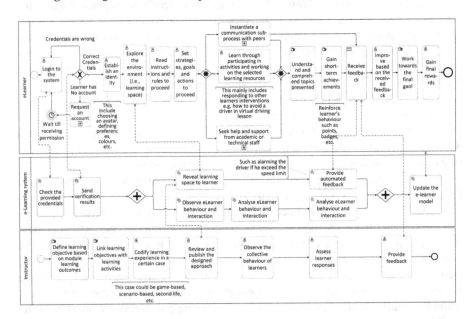

Fig. 2. Game-enhanced e-learning process model

The e-learning process engine is the core part of the proposed e-learning framework. This component is backed by a BPMN model for a game-enhanced e-learning process as explained in Fig. 2.

The process is self-explanatory, but generally, e-learners will log in to the e-learning framework, establish their identity (e.g., choose an avatar, setup a certain machine to play with and so on), explore the learning environment, participate in learning, receive feedback, and improve and work towards the final goal achievement. Such process needs certain contextual information about the e-learner so that the preferred avatar or character can be recommended automatically. Similarly, the preferred type of feedback can be presented to the e-learner based on her preferences.

4 Discussion and Conclusion

To increase the flexibility, agility and effectiveness of game-enhanced e-learning arte-facts, a new architectural e-learning framework is introduced. The proposed framework combines the following three technologies: (i) business process modelling notation to model and enact e-learning processes, (ii) ontology to contextualise the process with related information, (e.g., e-learner preferences, goals, etc.), (iii) service-oriented architecture so that e-learning business processes can be enacted using a set of software services. A rigorous instantiation process needs to be developed in order to instantiate this conceptual framework and tackle its potential challenges. Such challenges include the coherence of the designed e-learning scenarios. Giving further control to the e-learners on their learning processes might lead to weak e-learning processes. Therefore, this control should be limited based on well-identified constraints. For example, the e-learner cannot choose any avatar/ identity model for all games, the chosen identity must be related to the context of games. Additional service-oriented concerns should be solved, such as service identifications and discovery from e-learning business process models.

References

1. Hammad, R., Odeh, M., Khan, Z.: eLearner experience model. In: The International Arab Conference on Information Technology (ACIT), Morocco, pp. 43–51 (2016)
2. Wenger, E.: Learning in landscapes of practice: recent developments in social learning theory (2013)
3. Graf, S., Kinshuk, : Adaptive technologies. In: Spector, J., Merrill, M., Elen, J., Bishop, M. (eds.) Handbook of Research on Educational Communications and Technology. Springer, New York (2014)
4. Deterding, S., et al.: From game design elements to gamefulness: Defining gamification. In: Proceedings of the 15th International Academic MindTrek Conference: Envisioning Future Media Environments, pp. 9–15 (2011)
5. Kapp, K.M.: The Gamification of Learning and Instruction: Game-Based Methods and Strategies for Training and Education. Wiley, San Francisco (2012)
6. Kiryakova, G., Angelova, N., Yordanova, L.: Gamification in education. In: Proceedings of 9th International Balkan Education and Science Conference, Edirne, pp. 679–683 (2014)

7. Boughzala, I., Michel, H., Freitas, S.D.: Introduction to the serious games, gamification, and innovation minitrack. In: 48th Hawaii International Conference on System Sciences (HICSS), pp. 625–625 (2015)

8. Miller, C.: The gamification of education. Develop. Bus. Simul. Exp. Learn. **40**, 196–200 (2013)

9. Csikszentmihalyi, M.: Flow: The Psychology of Optimal Experience. Harper & Row, New York (1990)

10. Lee, J.J., Hammer, J.: Gamification in education: What, how, why bother? Acad. Exch. Q. **15**(2), 146 (2011)

11. McGonigal, J.: Reality is Broken: Why Games make Us Better and How They Can Change the World. The Penguin Press, New York (2011)

12. Domínguez, A., et al.: Gamifying learning experiences: practical implications and outcomes. Comput. Educ. **63**, 380–392 (2013)

13. Giang, V.: Gamification techniques increase your employees' ability to learn by 40%. Business Insider, 18 Sept 2013

14. Hamari, J., Koivisto, J., Sarsa, H.: Does gamification work?–a literature review of empirical studies on gamification. In: 2014 47th Hawaii International Conference On System Sciences (HICSS), pp. 3025–3034 (2014)

15. McNamara, D.S., Jackson, G.T., Graesser, A.: Intelligent Tutoring and Games (ITaG), pp. 44–65. IGI Global Hershey, Hershey (2010)

16. Jackson, G.T., McNamara, D.S.: Motivation and performance in a game-based intelligent tutoring system. J. Educ. Psychol. **105**, 1036 (2013)

17. Huang, W.H., Soman, D.: A Practitioner's Guide to Gamification of Education. Rotman School of Management, University of Toronto, Toronto (2013)

18. Kiili, K., Arnab, S.: Integrating games into the classroom: Towards new teachership. In: de Freitas, S., et al. (eds.) New Pedagogical Approaches in Game Enhanced Learning: Curriculum Integration, pp. 114–135. IGI Global, Hershey, PA (2013)

19. Hammad, R., Odeh, M., Khan, Z.: Towards a generalised e-learning business process model. In: The 7th International Conference on Business Intelligence and Technology (BUSTECH), Athens, Greece, pp. 20–28 (2017)

Mobility and Edutainment in ESL Learning via Podcasting

Galina G. Artyushina$^{(\boxtimes)}$, Olga A. Sheypak, and Roman S. Golov

MAI – National Research University, Moscow, Russia
gartyushina@gmail.com, oasheypak@gmail.com,
roman_golov@rambler.ru

Abstract. As listening is considered one of the most difficult communication competence in English language learning this paper analyses the difficulties and shows how to overcome them, using such new modern technologies as mobile learning (m-learning) and Edutainment. The article analyses integration of m-learning and Edutainment via podcasts during the English second learning. Students of the XXI century are digital natives. Educators should embrace all the opportunities the digital era presents. Teachers have been trying to keep up with the fast-changing world of information technology while shaping their mind. Digital formats allow interactive, entertaining, and motivating activities. The five-year experience of using mobile phones for listening has shown that it is interesting, easy and comparatively a new approach as it allows learning the English language outside the classrooms. Next step – the gradual transition from the state of a passive listener to a creator of the own podcasts using mobile phones has shown that a combination: podcast – mobile phone gives a birth to a new mobile technology in learning foreign languages.

Keywords: ESL learning · Communication competence · Mobile learning · Edutainment · Podcasts

1 Introduction

The value of the competence approach in English language learning is being discussed with interest among experts of education. Listening is considered to be one of the difficult competence in comparison with reading, writing, and speaking. There was an opinion if a teacher focuses only on speaking and provides to master this skill a student will be able to understand a foreign speech spontaneously without special purposeful teaching. Now, this view is disapproved both by the theoretical and practical arguments. It is stated that even people speaking a foreign language fluently have difficulties when they listen to English native speakers. For example, there is a study that 93.5% fifth-year linguistic students have difficulties when they perceive a fluent foreign speech [1]. From the other side, psychologists give convincing evidence that perception and comprehension of the foreign speech are rather difficult mental activity. It is undoubted that the main difficulty in listening is the impossibility to control the activity. Listening is the only type of speech activity where nothing depends on the person who does listening. Listening requires extremely intensive mental activity,

© Springer International Publishing AG 2017
F. Tian et al. (Eds.): Edutainment 2017, LNCS 10345, pp. 285–289, 2017.
https://doi.org/10.1007/978-3-319-65849-0_31

and that is why it causes fast tiredness and prevents from concentrating. It is obvious that effective listening requires such technique that takes into consideration these difficulties and ensures getting over them.

2 Difficulties in Listening

Difficulties in listening can be connected with the following four peculiarities of the audio material: vocabulary, contents, listening conditions, and sources [1]. Let's touch upon these difficulties in more detail.

1. The unknown vocabulary and new grammar in the listening material are easy to overcome when there are exercises teaching to understand words, word combinations and phrases with the help of conjectures. Also, it is important to use short (5–6, at least 8–9 words) rather than long sentences. Next, it should be mentioned that simple sentences are much easier to keep in the mind than compound and complex sentences.
2. The role of the contents of the listening material cannot be overestimated. It is a well-known fact that it is impossible to make a person listen to attentively if the information in the audio material is not interesting. Studies have shown that students understand and memorise better difficult and interesting texts rather than easy and primitive.
3. Speaking about conditions we mean how many times you listen to the audio material and what is the rate of the speech. The researchers show the replay listening is widely practised, but experts think it is not effective for improving listening skills [7]. While when we use the audio material to teach speaking, replay listening is essential: it helps to remember the vocabulary and grammar. It is known that a high speech rate normally causes difficulties. That is because there are differences between speech and hearing rate in languages (see Table 1).

Table 1. Differences between speed and hearing rate in languages.

Rates	Russian language (wpm)	English language (wpm)
Low speech	60–80	100–110
Normal speech	90–100	140–150
Everyday life speech	120–140	160–200
Hearing rate	130–170	180–240

So, to overcome this disproportion is possible when speech and hearing rates are equal. It is possible when we listen to low speech rate. For example, low speech rate or learning rate is a usual technique in podcasts recorded by the educational site www.eslpod.com [6].

4. Audio materials are the most complicated sources of information as they do not have visual support and also because they use unknown for listeners voices. Experts assume that personal peculiarities such as voice timber and voice pitch influence listening in the following way: the lower male voice and the softer its timber,

the easier this speech will be perceived. Also, precise and expressive speech facilitates perception rather than flabby and rambling speech.

We have analysed the four difficulties above to find effective sources of the audio materials to teach first-year students listening. Firstly, we have chosen podcasting as it is a mobile technology which has acknowledged possibilities in developing both listening and speaking skills [2]. Teaching English as a second language embraces the podcast for various reasons: to provide students with extra practice, develop critical thinking, provide background knowledge and a broad context, which students tend to lose, while "googling" for information, in pursuit of getting answers to very targeted questions.

3 Podcasts in English Language Learning

Podcasting is the latest technological innovation to reinforce language teaching and learning. Podcasts have great educational potential in developing students' listening and speaking skills while learning from authentic materials about the burning issues of today and current events, they could be easily loaded onto any mobile device and listen to when convenient [4]. Still one of the major features of podcasts is their mobility which is an important characteristic of modern education. According to Yamaguchi, "A computer is better than a mobile phone or handling various types of information such as visual, sound, and textual information, but the mobile phone is superior to a computer in portability. Further, some students do not have their own computers" [3]. Moreover, podcasting as a mobile learning technology has a rapid pace of development from a teacher – learner text – based approach to a forthcoming multimedia supporting technology. In addition, podcasts make the online interaction between teachers and students possible in a convenient way without any time and space limitations. This mobile technology gets learning away from classroom environment with little or no access to the teacher. That is why podcasts appear to be creative and entertaining on the one hand, and very motivating educational tool on the other as they are quickly and regularly updated, often free, especially for students, and may be available at any time through mobile devices. Nowadays podcasts revive rebirth due to the high-speed Internet. It has become possible to listen to a podcast by means of mobile phones and tablets based on iOS, Android, and Windows.

3.1 ESL Podcasts in Russia

Academic podcasts to study English as a second language started in Russia in 2008 and as an unusual technology was used to develop listening and speaking skills. As academic podcasts introduce diversity in the process of learning English, they arouse real interest among students and introduce elements of entertainment into the educational process that was proved by some researchers [5]. Among many educational sites we have chosen www.eslpod.com as it satisfies the following requirements: flexibility, user control, mobility and allows for time-shifting and multitasking. One more advantage of the podcasts was their strict structure with different rates of speech or words per minute

Table 2. The structure of the podcast [6].

The part of the podcast	Duration (min)	Rate of speech	wpm
Introduction	1–1,5	Learning	100
Training text or a dialogue	2	Learning	100
Vocabulary explanation from the training text	12–14	Learning	100
Replay of the training text	1.3	Normal	150
Conclusion	0.5	Very high	235

(see Table 2). Different record speech rates allow students to adjust to the English language phonation and improve their skills to percept audio materials of the podcasts and sequentially move on to percept English speech in everyday life.

3.2   The First Experience

We began working with podcasts in 2010. As the podcasts have been chosen as the basis for student self-studies outside the classrooms to increase effectiveness we worked out an educational supply for students "Guide to Listening" including a workbook with comprehension tasks, instructions, and a student's guide list [2]. By 2015 we have accumulated some interesting experience [5]. The four-year experience of introducing podcasts into our English teaching program and the results of the final English exam of the first-year students indicate the improvement of their listening skills and increase in motivation to go on with their studies of English [2]. Answering the question, "Would you like to use podcasts further?" about 63% of the students said "yes". The most frequent explanations why the student liked learning English using podcasts were that they enjoyed listening to native speakers through mobile phones, as well as the topics under review, students learned a lot about the everyday life of the English-speaking world. The majority of them underlined that it was their first experience of using phones to develop their listening skills out of the classrooms and that it was just entertaining.

3.3   Podcasts in Practice

The motto of the ESLpod site "Download - Listen and Learn – Start Speak English!" and students' achievements encouraged us to move on to the next stage. In 2016 our Masters began to create their own podcasts in English. It was those Masters who have been working with podcasts at our Department of Foreign Languages since 2012. The fact that to master spoken patterns in Business English is given too little time in the curricular urged us to include this task into Masters' podcasts. So, using a strict structure of the pattern podcast (see Table 2) and reproducing authentic materials [6] allowed our students to realize their skills in successful communication recording their own podcasts on the following topics: "Introducing a Speaker", "How to Give a Successful Presentation", "Holding Structured and Unstructured Meetings" and others from the Business English Language course. We have found out one more advantage of this work. Many of our students had difficulties during public speaking. Now they have a chance to speak alone recording their audio files in MP3 format and just send them to the tutor using a mobile phone. In return, the tutor sends a Master his comments to correct mistakes. Such approach allows monitoring the progress in speaking and getting a sound-recording portfolio for each Master.

4 Conclusion

In this paper we have looked at the introduction mobile phones through podcasts into English language teaching, especially listening and speaking Bachelors and Masters at the technical university. Podcasts provide "stepping stones" by means of their structure, which students follow and do not "get lost" in the Internet space when working on the tasks. Podcasts provide students with authentic and comprehensive Internet and digital resources, which motivate students to study English and compensate the lack of knowledge and life experience. In addition, modern digital technologies such as mobile phones allow students to learn languages even on go, demonstrating educational mobility. Regardless of the limitation, this study provided evidence that, even though some difficulties and inconvenience might occur in podcasting, language learners still hold positive attitudes toward the use of podcasts in language listening, and this type of podcasts are possibly beneficial to learners' improvement in listening, speaking and vocabulary knowledge. The results of this study thus encourage further exploration into how and to what degree such podcasts can assist learners in enhancing the identified language aspects. Also, podcasts appear to become efficient in organising self-studies. They allow educators to organise and monitor the learning process on-line. With the recent design and features of mobile devices, future studies on improving listening and speaking skills are recommended.

References

1. Eluhina, N.V.: Education of listening to foreign speech. IYSH **5**, 20–22 (1996)
2. Artyushina, G., Baguzina, E., Plekhova, O., Sheypak, O.: Developing communicative competence through Internet and digital technologies. In: Kryachkov, D.A., Yastrebova, E.B., Kravtsova, O.A. (eds.) The Magic of Innovation. New Techniques and Technologies in Teaching Foreign Languages, pp. 43–67. Cambridge Scholars Publishing, Newcastle upon Tyne (2015)
3. Yamaguchi, T.: Vocabulary learning with a mobile phone. In: Program of the 10th Anniversary Conference of Pan-Pacific Association of Applied Linguistics, Edinburgh, UK (2005)
4. Darmi, R., Albion, P.: A review of integrating mobile phones for language learning. In: 10th International Conference on Mobile Learning, pp. 93–100. International Association for Development of the Information Society (2014)
5. Artyushina, G.G., Sheypak, O.A., Golov, R.S.: Podcasting as a good way to learn second language in e-Learning. In: IC4E 2017, pp. 51–55 (2017) doi:http://dx.doi.org/10.1145/3026480.3029590
6. English as a Second Language Homepage. http://www.eslpod.com. Last accessed 20 Mar 2017
7. Voice as a psychologist and master of style. http://www.constudio.ru. Last accessed 10 Apr 2017

Young Peoples' Views of Online Historical Archives

Holly Crossen-White[✉] and Angela Turner-Wilson

Bournemouth University, Bournemouth, UK
{hcrossen,aturnerwilson}@bournemouth.ac.uk

Abstract. Digitized collections are 'a rich source of instructional material for history teachers' [1, p. 314] but it has been noted these 'remained largely underused'. There is 'a growing interest in both improving the user experience and in justifying the creation of digital collections to multiple stakeholders' [2, p. 339]. Within the UK an estimated £130m has been invested in digitisation projects [3]. Recent changes to the UK National Curriculum for history have placed greater emphasis upon the importance of understanding methods of historical enquiry and the use of evidence. Therefore, the digitized collections created by this investment should be a vital classroom tool. This study set out to investigate within the UK the level of awareness of these resources and their value to young learners aged 8–16 years. There were two stages to this qualitative study. Stage one was the delivery of a workshop which introduced young learners to a range of digital archives. After this the young people were given a period of time to use the online archives and explore the different forms of historical evidence. Stage two involved focus groups with a sample of the young people during which participants were asked to discuss their end-user experience. Key findings included enhanced personal learning experience, development of a personal connection to the past, and identification of issues related to usability and practical application in a classroom learning context.

Keywords: Digital heritage · Learning technology · Self-directed learning · UK research · Young learners

1 Introduction

Digital technology has transformed the ways in which the past can be explored [4, 5]. Within this social shift historical evidence has become much more accessible [6] and has offered the opportunity to make links with this type of material in ways that previously could never have been attempted. One example from the UK would be the London Lives digital project which resulted in a greater understanding of the lives of individuals living in the capital between 1690 and 1800 [7]. However it is also recognised that with this ability to link different sources of historical evidence comes ethical issues for researchers as it is now much easier to 'discover' the personal stories of long forgotten individuals [8]. It is this potential of online archives to bring the past back to life that makes them a powerful learning resource.

To discover, anecdotally, that some teachers were unaware of these resources and young learners were potentially not accessing them was an interesting insight. This was

© Springer International Publishing AG 2017
F. Tian et al. (Eds.): Edutainment 2017, LNCS 10345, pp. 290–293, 2017.
https://doi.org/10.1007/978-3-319-65849-0_32

particularly relevant given that between the late 1990 s and 2005 an estimated £130 million had been spent within the UK on creating these types of resources [3]. It would appear that this investment was being underutilised by the education sector.

A search of the literature indicated that studies largely focused upon who were using specific collections with the purpose of capturing data that would lead to technical refinements [2]. Other studies indicated that there was high usage by academics within higher education [9]. However little research had been undertaken into the personal experience of other end-user groups, or indeed who they were, their purpose of accessing and satisfaction with results.

2 Study Design

A two stage study was undertaken that involved the delivery of a workshop session to young learners in stage one. This was followed by a period when the young people could access and use the online archives by themselves. The participants were asked to keep a record of the online archives they visited, what they searched within this, what content they found and note how helpful or informative the search had been. These personal records were then used to construct a sample of young people who were invited to take part in the focus groups which were stage two of the study. The focus groups were audio recorded and transcribed and thematic analysis undertaken. A key limitation of the study was the small sample size which made the findings not generalizable, however the intension of the study was to scope out topics for further research, and it should be noted that the findings offer some valuable insights.

3 Sample

Participants for the study were aged between 8 and 16 years and drawn from two sources, one a youth group and the other a primary school. Some of the participants were not fully engaged with mainstream education and some among the sample reported no interest in history prior to joining the study. In total 42 young people participated in stage one and 20 in stage two. Ten of the young people from the youth group who were aged between 12 and 16 years took part in a focus group, and 10 from the primary school. These participants were all aged between 8 and 9 years. The sample was randomly selected based upon their recorded usage of the online archives with three being drawn from each of three groups: high, medium or low usage. A tenth was selected at random from the remaining personal usage records.

4 Findings

- None of the young people were aware of digital archives so the workshop session was their first introduction to this type of learning resource.
- Although a number of the participants self-reported that history held no real interest all of the participates used the archives after their workshop session and several talked

of how using the online archives had captured their interest which led them to search for particular historical content.

- The young people enjoyed the opportunities that the online archive offered for self-directed learning.
- The young people were able to recall in detail the content of the historical evidence that they viewed, even though a period of time had elapsed between access and the focus group.
- The participants valued the online archives and wanted to use them further in their learning but recognised how it might be difficult to regularly use during lesson time due to practical issues such as access to computers. However, all age groups identified ways these resources could be incorporated into their learning experience.
- The participants discussed usability issues and indicated what features were of value.
- There appeared to be a raised self-esteem among the learners. Many discussed how pleased they were that access to the online archives had given them the opportunity to find historical evidence to use in their topic of study that others in their group did not know.

5   Conclusion

Online historical archives are a valuable resource to young learners. The content on offer has the potential to nurture students' enthusiasm and to engage them in self-direct learning. In addition it can raise their self-esteem by enabling them to discover and share their new knowledge with their peers and others. Given the positive feedback from young learners about these resources future research is required to identify how teachers can be made more aware of and practically use these resources within the classroom environment.

References

1. Pattuelli, M.C.: Modeling a domain ontology for cultural heritage resources: a user-centred approach. J. Am. Soc. Inf. Sci. Technol. **62**(2), 314–342 (2011)
2. Kelly, E.J.: Assessment of digitized library and archives materials: a literature review. J. Web Librariansh. **8**(4), 384–403 (2014)
3. JISC Digitisation in the UK: The Case for a UK Framework. JISC (2005)
4. Floud, R., Shoemaker, R., Spaeth, D.: From computers and history to digital history: a retrospective (2013). http://www.history.ac.uk/podcasts/digital-history/computers-and-history-digital-history-retrospective
5. Allen, R.B., Sieczkiewicz, R.: How historians use historical newspapers. In: Proceedings of the American Society for Information Science and Technology, Pittsburgh, USA, vol. 47, pp. 1–4. Wiley (2010)
6. Tanner, S.: The value and impact of digitized resources for learning, teaching, research and enjoyment. In: Hughes, L.M. (ed.) Evaluating and Measuring the Value, Use and Impact of Digital Collections, pp. 103–120. Facet, London (2012)
7. Hitchcock, T., Shoemaker, R., Howard, S., McLaughlin, J., et al.: London Lives, 1690–1800 (2012). www.londonlives.org

8. Crossen-White, H.: Using digital archives in historical research: what are the ethical concerns for a 'forgotten' individual? Res. Ethics **11**(2), 108–119 (2015)
9. Alcencer-Brayner, A.: British Library Digital Scholarship survey: how are users engaging with our digital content? http://blogs.bl.uk/digital-scholarship/2014/11/bl-digital-scholarship-survey-how-are-users-engaging-with-our-digital-content.html. Accessed 21 Mar 2017

Research on Multidisciplinary Integration in Game Art Higher Education

Chenyang Cui[✉]

School of Media & Animation, China Academy of Art, Hangzhou 310024, China
cuicy@caa.edu.cn

Abstract. The Game art is a comprehensive discipline, which contains literature, art, music, film, psychology, communication, sociology, computer science and other disciplines. How to construct the subject system of game art education reasonably and effectively is the problem that colleges and universities need to face in view of the characteristics of game discipline. This paper analyzes the situation of the current game art higher education and gives the suggestions of talents training of multidisciplinary integration from the perspectives of discipline construction, teacher training, the establishment of incentive mechanism and the combination of industry and academia.

Keywords: Game art · Multidisciplinary integration · Higher education

1 A Summary of Game Art Education

The global game industry was born in the seventies of last century, the vigorous development of the game industry, gave birth to a large number of needs of the game industry talent, and further promoted the construction of game education [1]. In 1994, DigiPen Polytechnic Institute which was the first educational organization of game art in the world, and Nintendo created a game education base to train computer game technology and design-related professionals [2]. Then the game has gradually become an independent discipline, the major colleges and universities in Europe and the United States, Asia and other regions have carried out game education from undergraduate to doctor at different levels of education talents. There are probably the following types of school engaged in game art education: (1) Art institute. Academy of Art University in the United States focuses on the visual performance of the game and provides undergraduate and masters degree education in game art design [3]. (2) Comprehensive colleges: Cornell University focuses on training technical personnel in the field of game art design, a game design creative laboratory was established in 2003, which was based on its computer Institute and Intelligent Information Systems [4]. The game design professional in the University of Southern California pays more attention to the culture factors in the game, School of Game and Entertainment Media in Santa Cruz, University of California trains undergraduate students in the game development technology and postgraduate in game culture research [5]. (3) Vocational training schools: Vancouver Film Academy in Canada trains the practical talents needed in the game industry [2].

© Springer International Publishing AG 2017
F. Tian et al. (Eds.): Edutainment 2017, LNCS 10345, pp. 294–298, 2017.
https://doi.org/10.1007/978-3-319-65849-0_33

All above institutes partially meet the needs of the talents for game market. The Game is a comprehensive art discipline, how to construct the subject system of game education reasonably and effectively is the problem that colleges and universities need to face in view of the characteristics of game discipline [6].

2   Game and Education

After a long study of human games, Holland famous historian Huizinga [7] found that all existing cultural forms in human society, such as law, war, poetry, philosophy, art and so on, should have come from the "game". For example, the ancient sacrifice ritual originated from the game. With the passage of time, the initial game became sacred and solemn and the rules of the game were further clear, then, the sacrifice became an independent activity. In this view, Huizinga not only regarded the game as a human instinctive activity, but also discussed the importance of the game in human civilization from the perspective of cultural anthropology.

In the 21st century, due to the ever-changing technology, the form and content of the game art has increasingly become rich. The game has a huge impact on the human politics, economy, culture, media, daily life and so on, eventually, the game industry was developed. Simultaneously, colleges and universities constructed game art discipline to meet the needs of talents for game market. Professor Rune Klevier of the Media Institute at the University of Bergen, Norway, believed that the ability of digital games to express the world is growing rapidly with the development of digital technology, the game art education should be paid the same attention as the other disciplines. Just as the game "journey" made by Chinese American Chen Xinghan showed, many people began to pursue a deeper level of thinking in the game. So the game art education should cultivate innovation and compound talents for the game field, and not only meet the needs of the talents for the current game market. Game art education should return the game to its original place in history that has an impact on human culture.

3   An Analysis of the Present Game Art Education

In the media age, to distinguish the different types of art is becoming more and more difficult. The game as a comprehensive art is getting the attention of society and integrates many disciplines such as literature, painting, sculpture, dance, music, film, sociology, communication, psychology, computer science and so on. For example, in the World of Warcraft Created by the Blizzard, involving the religion, history, art, music, computer science, sociology, etc., there are regular guild organizations and social structures, this game can not be simply regarded as a pure game for entertainment.

But the current game education focused on a variety of skills training for the game industry, which leads to a big problem in multidisciplinary integration talents training. Just as the game art integrates the different arts, the early education of mankind is not divided into the different disciplines. Leonardo da Vinci naturally combined the aesthetic manifestations of the world and the rational exploration of the world in his "comparative theory". For Leonardo da Vinci, all knowledge is unified. After modern times, discipline classification happens. The separation of natural and human sciences, the separation of art and science, the separation of truth and seeking beauty is the cost of being a modern man. By the end of the twentieth century and in the twenty-first century, people realized that it is wrong to separate science and art, so, people tried to reunite art and science. Game art just provides an opportunity to integrate science and art, and to integrate different disciplines into ones. So, how to construct the subject system of game education reasonably and effectively is the problem that colleges and universities need to face.

4 Suggestions on Multidisciplinary Integration Talent Training in Game Art Education

Education is to stimulate people's inner potential and interest, rather than professional skills training. The game is a kind of human instinctive purposeless activity and has a huge influence on the formation of the culture in the historical process of human development. The construction of game art subject system should be based on the nature of education and the nature of game. On this basis, further education and vocational education will be combined. Here, the following are the suggestions on multidisciplinary talent training in game art education:

(1) Constructing a big discipline including different known disciplines.

The previous game education pays more attention to the skills training and ignores the comprehensive training. The suggested game art education can be divided into three stages including primary stage, intermediate stage, advanced stage. In the primary stage, some basic training in art, literature, science, music, psychology and so on will be given to every student, then the students can learn more about the different disciplines of the game, better understand the game design, and collaborate better with each other in game design in the future. In the intermediate stage, the students will spend more time on their favorite subjects that are found through learning in the primary stage, while the knowledge of other disciplines learned at the initial stage will also help them to better study their favorite subjects. In the advanced stage, a complete game project can be done by oneself or the team. Multidisciplinary integration will be helpful to enhance the quality of the game art disciplines.

(2) Establishing an incentive mechanic for multidisciplinary integration.

The game market has a serious impact on the construction of game art subject system. The vocational skill training can rapidly meet the needs of game market, but it is harmful to the long-term development of the game art discipline. So, a reasonable incentive mechanic is needed to avoid completely following the game market. The school manager can draft a set of rules to encourage the teachers to lead the students to carry out the experimental exploration of the nature of the game design and the future forms of the game.

(3) Cultivating high quality teachers for game art education.

Now, most of the teachers in the game art have single discipline training. As we know, the success of the construction of the game art subject system strongly depends on the quality of the teachers. So, it is very important to cultivate high quality teachers who should be trained based on the multidisciplinary integration. For example, a teacher with a computer science background needs to accept a certain degree of art such as music, art, literature training or nurturing, likewise, a teacher with an art or painting background maybe need to receive mathematics and computer science training. If a student is always able to get what he wants to know from his teacher, or is always able to discuss some topics in time that he is interested in with his teacher, he will keep his curiosity to the greatest extent. That will have a huge influence on his future development.

(4) Combination of industry and academia

Because the game is a special form of art and different from the traditional art such as oil painting, sculpture and so on, it not only shows the ideas of the game designer, but also needs to accept the market test. The game higher education can enrich the game design theory and encourage the students to explore creative game from the contents to the forms. The industrial projects can help enrich the practical experience of game production. So, combination of industry and academia will benefit to the students and teachers in game art education. The creative game items and the industrial game projects should be simultaneously encouraged in the game art education.

5 Conclusions

Game as an integrated art form including literature, music, painting, film and television, computer science, psychology, communication and other disciplines, is getting more and more concerned by the society. The combination of film and games has gained a very prosperous market, so, the game art education has be paid more and more attention.

In the future, the game art education will focus on the multidisciplinary integration training, and emphasize the academic high point of game research, which makes the game art education become a new way to cultivate the correct outlook on life and values.

References

1. Chen, Y.B.: Industrialization of professional education structure in animation. J. Zhejiang Inst. Commun. (2006)
2. Zhu, B., Song, J.W.: Research on game discipline construction and talent training system in western higher education. J. Cult. Mon. **4** (2012)
3. Di, Y.L.: An analysis of the present situation of game discipline. J. China Electr. Power Educ. **13** (2010)

4. Zhang, F., Pan, R.F., Ye, F.J.: Discussion on the construction of digital game design specialty. J. Press (2011)
5. Li, Y., Bian, Y.B.: A survey of computer and game applied research in Europe and America. J. Res. Electr. Educ. (2008)
6. Fu, Z.Y.: The orientation of digital entertainment design and the cultivation of compound talents. J. Decoration (2007)
7. HuiZinga, J.: Homo Ludens. China Academy of Art Publishing House, Hangzhou (1996)

Exploring the Shape of Digital Textbook for the Classroom in the Mobile Age

Jeong Yong Ahn$^{(\boxtimes)}$ and Kyung Soo Han

Department of Statistics (Institute of Applied Statistics),
Chonbuk National University, 567 Baekje-Daero, Deokjin, Jeonju 54896, Korea
{jyahn,kshan}@jbnu.ac.kr

Abstract. Digital textbooks come in many different forms such as read-on-demand computer-based textbooks, print-on-demand e-textbook, and curriculum-based electronic textbooks. This article is to explore the dimension and shape for the future of digital textbooks. We suggest some design strategies to develop digital textbooks for instructor-led classroom in the online and mobile age. The strategies are based on the principles of learning.

Keywords: Digital textbook · Functionalities of digital textbook · Instructor-led classroom · Learning activities · Learning effectiveness

1 Introduction

Digital textbooks, originally known as electronic books (e-books), are defined as the digitalized forms of printed textbooks, which can be read, seen and listened through wired or wireless networks. Since 2007, however, they have been called digital textbooks to emphasize their teaching and learning functions and roles in classroom [1]. There are three types in which digital textbooks exist as follows: The first type may be defined as the simply scanned pictures of the print version of the book. Secondly, the digital textbook may be considered as a digital book with some kind of additional functionality like interactivity, term searching, and links to more information and related web sites. The last type may be a digital offering from a publisher that may not reassemble a book at all [2].

The main focus of the current development of digital textbooks is to completely transfer the contents of all printed textbooks to computer-based books. This effort is worthwhile to give birth to new forms of future education materials [3]. However, the question is what educational effect we can expect from the type of digital textbook. More specifically how should digital textbooks evolve as they get used in educational institutions? This paper has been designed to answer this question. We believe that digital textbooks should focus on the implementation of various instructional methods to provide more diverse learning activities and improve student learning achievement with greater efficiency and effectiveness. In this article, we design a digital textbook for the classroom based on the principles of learning introduced by Thorndike [4]. We firstly

© Springer International Publishing AG 2017
F. Tian et al. (Eds.): Edutainment 2017, LNCS 10345, pp. 299–302, 2017.
https://doi.org/10.1007/978-3-319-65849-0_34

suggest some design strategies to develop digital textbooks, and present the prototype learning objects of the digital textbook.

2   Design Principles

A key element of the revolution in education is the emphasis on interactive, exploratory, and collaborative learning activities. Many of these activities will be implemented using tablet devices that are connected, through the cloud, to the systems and devices used by other students, teachers, parents, content publishers, and educational institutions [5]. Digital textbooks can support richer learning content with a combination of various learning materials, including not only textbooks, reference books, workbooks, dictionaries, and hyperlinks, but also multimedia content, such as audio, 3D graphics, animations, video, and virtual and augmented reality [3].

The main functions of digital textbooks include the basic features of printed textbooks and the supplementary features of information technology and digital media. These additional features can include display functions, input functions, moving to a particular page, and search functions, in addition to the multimedia features and learning support functions such as hyperlinks, interactions, file transmissions, assessments, creating learning content [6]. Arenas and Barr [2] listed some new functionalities that digital textbooks should have. The model of digital textbooks is defined by the learning needs and demands of the future students and the teachers and institutions that help them learn. In this section, we suggest some design strategies to develop new generation digital textbooks.

- Questions and responses: Questions and responses are the most fundamental and important activities in education, and a great way to grasp the understanding level of each student on specific learning contents. Digital textbooks, therefore, should have the facility to support them, in particular instructor's questions and students' reaction, in themselves, and to collect and manage the data relative to questions and answers on further steps.
- Monitoring students based on learning data: To grasp students' understanding and to provide feedback, instructors should monitor student learning activity data. Learning data is a highly meaningful resource to observe document learning behaviors. A lot of research has shown that using data for instructional decisions can lead to improved student performance [7].
- Assessment: Another factor of digital textbooks is the facility to support assessment. There are many alternatives to traditional assessment types that can be used to broaden the scope of the teacher's classroom assessment activities [8]. The typical techniques of the alternatives are self, portfolio, and peer assessment. The next generation digital textbooks should support to alternatives as well as traditional types of assessment.
- Experimental learning and learning by doing: Involving students with in-class activities is a pedagogical method intended to promote active learning. Digital textbooks should support to create various activity-based objects for experimental learning or learning by doing. This is the facility that paperback books can never provide. Digital

books should incorporate a variety of learning activities and cloud-based resources such as immersive simulation environments for practice, collaborative/individual homework, and adaptive testing and assessments.

- Including some functionalities of learning management system (LMS) and course management system (CrMS): The next generation digital textbooks will not be restricted to duplication of the printed page on a digital device, and be able to provide more types of learning contents and digital tools. To do that, they should include many functionalities of LMS and CrMS.

3   Learning Objects for Digital Textbooks

Educational psychologists and pedagogues have established some principles of learning, also referred to as laws of learning. These principles provide additional insight into what makes people learn most effectively. This section presents some learning objects designed for teaching in the classroom based on the learning laws.

Firstly digital textbooks should include student/classroom response systems such as clicker system [9]. It'd be more efficient that the systems are run integrally with other learning objects. Figure 1 presents an example of questions and responses including a digital textbook developed in this study. Instructors can generate questions where they want. The responses of students are immediately collected, provided to instructor as well as students, and used for further data analysis. Figure 2 shows an example of activity-based object for experimental learning and/or learning by doing. Activity-based object can lead to improved degree of concentration and satisfying feeling.

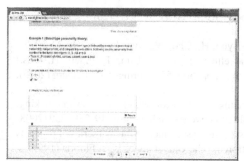   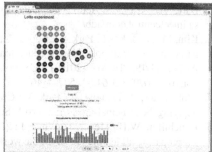

Fig. 1. Question and response   **Fig. 2.** Activity-based object

4   Discussion and Conclusion

There have been ongoing some discussion on the future of digital textbooks. Young [10] argued that the publishers may soon control not just the textbook material but the course content as well. In their push to increase the interactivity and usefulness of digital textbooks, publishers have included interactive content such as dynamic quizzes that feed results back into LCMS (learning and course management systems) grade books. Junco and Clem [11] described that the merger of textbook companies with LCMS, adaptive learning, and learning analytics products hints at the future of digital textbooks. Valjataga et al. [12] emphasized the roles of teachers and students as creators and authors of content. With these concepts, we think an important factor of digital textbooks is that they should be designed to support the learning principles.

In this article, we explored the design principles of digital textbooks for the classroom based on the laws of learning, and presented some prototype learning objects available in digital textbooks. As mentioned in Arenas and Barr [2], there are many forces re-shaping higher education, and whatever future faculties teach it is likely that much of that teaching will be done differently. We expect digital textbooks will evolve in completely different from now to help teachers teach and students learn.

Acknowledgments. This work was supported by the National Research Foundation of Korea (NRF) grant funded by the Korea government (MSIP) (NRF-2016R1A2B1010253).

References

1. Jung, E.: Status and future direction of digital textbook, vol. 1347, pp. 14–22. Institute for Information Technology Advancement, Weekly Technology Trends (2008)
2. Arenas, E., Barr, A.: The digital book in higher education: Beyond the horseless carriage. Proceedings of the ASCILITE Conference, pp. 63–67 (2013)
3. Park, C.S., Kim, M., Yoo, K.H.: Design and implementation of a problem-based digital textbook. Int. J. Softw. Eng. Appl. **6**, 213–222 (2012)
4. Thorndike, E.L.: Educational Psychology: Briefer Course. Columbia University Press, NY (1914)
5. Barr, A.: IEEE - Actionable Data Book. IEEE ADB project (2014). https://ieee-sa.imeetcentral.com/adb/
6. Kim, M., Yoo, K.-H., Park, C., Yoo, J.-S., Byun, H., Cho, W., Ryu, J., Kim, N.: An XML-based digital textbook and its educational effectiveness. In: Kim, T., Adeli, H. (eds.) ACN/AST/ISA/UCMA -2010. LNCS, vol. 6059, pp. 509–523. Springer, Heidelberg (2010). doi:10.1007/978-3-642-13577-4_46
7. Wohlstetter, P., Datnow, A., Park, V.: Creating a system for data-driven decision-making: applying the principal-agent framework. Sch. Effectiveness Sch. Improv. **19**, 239–259 (2008)
8. Bouchillon, W.H., Meyer, T., White, J.: 21st century assessment (One in a series of products for preparing all learners PAL for the workforce). The University of West Florida (1999)
9. Bruff, D: Clickers: A classroom innovation, vol. 25, pp. 5–8. National Education Association Advocate (2007)
10. Young, J.: The object formerly known as the textbook. The Chronicle of Higher Education (2013). http://chronicle.com/article/Dont-Call-Them-Textbooks/136835/
11. Junco, R., Clem, C.: Predicting course outcomes with digital textbook usage data. Internet High. Educ. **27**, 54–63 (2015)
12. Väljataga, T., Fiedler, S.H., Laanpere, M.: Re-thinking digital textbooks: students as Co-authors. In: Li, F., Klamma, R., Laanpere, M., Zhang, J., Manjón, B., Lau, R. (eds.) ICWL 2015. LNCS, vol. 9412, pp. 143–151. Springer, Cham (2015). doi:10.1007/978-3-319-25515-6_13

An Investigation into Usability and First Time User Experiences Within a Mobile Gaming Context

Lawrence Barnett[✉], Christos Gatzidis, and Carlo Harvey

Faculty of Science and Technology, Bournemouth University, Poole, UK
{i7244586,cgatzidis,charvey}@bournemouth.ac.uk

Abstract. With scientific research regarding usability and guidance plus First-Time User Experiences (FTUEs) in video games currently sparse, it is imperative to assist existing and future developers in the field build usable games and effective guidance systems. For the work presented in this publication, research was conducted to investigate the effects of guidance on mobile game usability using two independent groups; featuring two commercial games with and without the presence of a First-Time User Experience. The results show, with significance, that guidance via a FTUE increases one element of usability, 'information quality'. However, overall usability is not increased by the presence of a FTUE.

Keywords: Usability · FirstTtime User Experience (FTUE) · Game design

1 Introduction and Background

Usability, as defined by ISO 9241-11 (Guidance on usability) is termed as "The extent to which a product can be used by specified users to achieve specified goals with effectiveness, efficiency, and satisfaction in a specified context of use" [1]. Unlike software and other tools whereby usability techniques are employed to aid production or productivity, games are played for the sole reason and purpose of enjoyment/satisfaction. The key distinction arguably changes the weighting of the three areas identified above by ISO 9241-11, from an equal weighting to a hierarchy. Satisfaction needs to be prioritised, with efficiency and effectiveness following. In the following passage, we contextualise the three areas defined by ISO 9241-11 (effectiveness, efficiency and satisfaction) for our interest in games [1].

Satisfaction: Enjoyment and fun can be seen as the primary and sole motivation for an individual to engage in a computer/video game. Myers' study of Game Player Aesthetics [3], identified "challenge" as "the most preferred characteristic", highlighting balance as an important variable to tune regarding Satisfaction. Myers' finding supports and provides strong reasoning for the use of the widely accepted heuristic of creating an interface and control method that can be learned, used and mastered with as little resistance as possible, preparing and enabling the player to enjoy and utilise all available mechanics and, ultimately, strategies [3]. Optimising the complexity and interactions of an interface can aid escapism and support immersion [4]. Effectiveness: In the context of games, this can be attributed to how accurately and effectively the players can express

F. Tian et al. (Eds.): Edutainment 2017, LNCS 10345, pp. 303–306, 2017.
https://doi.org/10.1007/978-3-319-65849-0_35

themselves via the available interface and interactions to achieve specific goals, achievements or desires. Efficiency: Similarly, efficiency in computer games usability represents the relationship between the inputs and interactions, plus the success on specific goals, achievements or desires. The inputs may require considerable dexterity in order to enable the player to achieve success, or they may be achievable with comparatively little skill.

With usability contextualised to our interest in games, we can begin to discuss the effects of usability in games. As represented in Adams' Story Engine Diagram, the interface is the source of both input and output [5]. Furthermore, in the Mechanics, Dynamics and Aesthetics (MDA) framework, it can be noted that the aesthetics of a game are the first and foremost of its elements to be experienced by the player [6]. Usability affects the player's immediate and most intimate mechanism, allowing all of the game's elements to function and ultimately be enjoyed. Schell [4] describes and illustrates the importance of designing and building effective interactive systems in games. Schell's recommendations are also echoed in Google's User Experience Principles [8].

The design heuristics mentioned above aim to create and establish a fundamental/ native usable system, aiding the visceral and primitive nature of the user's experience. However, beyond the fundamental design of an application, usability can be aided through effective guidance and teaching, often referred to as 'onboarding' [8]. We will be exploring the First Time User Experience and specifically the use of FTUEs embedded in games on mobile devices. This is towards discovering how, and indeed if, these are effective at increasing usability.

2   Method – Games and Protocol

Two games were selected to review the effect of guidance upon usability; 'Super Mario Run' and 'Linia'. The experiment was conducted on an iPhoneSE, with 20 participants of mixed gender, selected from various courses at Bournemouth University. The games were selected based on their similar yet contrasting interaction complexity, since they can both be controlled with one finger. However, the combinations and precision of interactions, along with other gameplay manipulations such as pace, challenge the player's inputs past the seemingly 'simple' one-touch interaction. With two groups, control and treatment, the participants were introduced to the questionnaire with a brief overview of the protocol and events to come. Once the participants had confirmed they were unfamiliar with the games, they were placed in either the control or treatment group (based on a sequential placement). Random counterbalancing was used to determine the first game. Depending on whether the participant was administered guidance and information (Treatment) or not (Control), they would either receive 90 s (Treatment) or 60 s (Control) to play the game. This time differential exists due to the additional dialogs, cutscenes and other learning and guidance material found present in the Treatment group's experience. The participants were instructed to try their best at completing whatever goal or objective they believed they should be attempting to achieve. The termination clauses were either time limit (as outlined above) or the completion of the level/section. Once the session terminated, the participants were asked to complete an adapted IBM PSSUQ, scoring the usability over 11 questions on a 7-point Likert scale [7]. Upon completing the questionnaire, the participants would then be asked to play the remaining game and complete the relevant second questionnaire. The questions were as follows; 1. Overall, I am satisfied with how easy it is to play this game, 2. It was simple to play this game, 3. I could effectively complete the objectives and challenges, 4. I was able to complete objectives and challenges quickly, 5. I was able to efficiently complete objectives and challenges, 6. I felt comfortable using this system, 7. It was easy to learn to play this game, 8. Whenever I make a mistake in the game, I recover easily and quickly, 9. The organisation of information on the game screens is clear, 10. The interface of this game is pleasant and, finally, 11. I like using the interface of this game.

3 Results and Discussion

The results seen in Fig. 1 display correlations between guidance (existence of FTUE) and usability scores, collected and measured using an adapted (i.e. with the language contextualised to games) version of the IBM PSSUQ. Combining the groups among Mario and Linia allows for the comparison of control versus treatment across both games, providing insight into cross-genre correlations regarding the presence of guidance. Using the non-parametric Mann-Whitney U test [2], the two groups differed significantly in regards to Information Quality (Questions 8 and 9 Av.), reporting $U = 125.5$, $Z = -2.035$ and $p = .043$, displaying a positive correlation between the games' usability, specifically the information quality and guidance. The authors' belief is that with guidance comes understanding, allowing the player to utilise all available information, from UI elements to in-game mechanics, thus improving usability. In contrast to this, Overall Usability (Q1 to Q11) returns $U = 170.5$, $Z = -799$ and $p = .429$, which conveys that there is no significant result for the correlation of overall usability between the Control and Treatment groups. We believe that the design of the intuitive design and interaction model is crucial to usability, with guidance only aiding

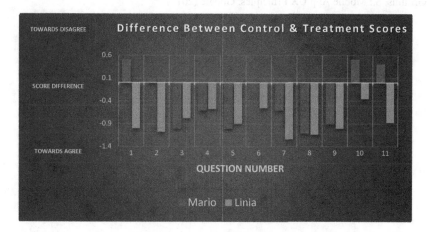

Fig. 1. Difference between control & treatment scores

a game's usability. An interesting result is observed for the Mario game (Control and Treatment), whereby Q1 scored a lower mean score in the Control group (Mean = 1.9), whereas in the Treatment group it has a Mean = 2.40. Although it is not significant ($U = 26.5, Z = -1.867, p = .075$), it does approximate a significant result and we believe it deserves noting.

The above highlights the possibility of a negative correlation between "Overall satisfaction of ease of play" and guidance via a FTUE. It is our belief that the increase in overall satisfaction can be attributed to the player's self-discovery of the controls and interface (Control Group), where they are free to learn with full agency/autonomy. This is the kind of autonomy and agency that is unavailable to the players presented with a FTUE, because of forced scenarios and intrusive dialogs (Treatment Group).

In the work in this paper it is shown that FTUEs have the power to affect user perception in elements of usability. From a game design perspective, this is impactful. A macro view of this is useful, however, it is yet unclear on the micro scale what influences control this effect. Future work will consider trying to elicit several heuristics to guide game designers in the generation of FTUEs.

References

1. ISO 9241-11: Ergonomic requirements for office work with visual display terminals (VDTs) - Part 11: Guidance on usability. ISO (1998)
2. Field, A.: Discovering Statistics Using IBM SPSS Statistics, 4th edn. Sage Publications, Thousand Oaks (2013)
3. Myers, D.: A Q-study of game player aesthetics. Simul. Gaming 21(4), 375–396 (1990)
4. Schell, J.: The Art of Game Design: A Book of Lenses, 2nd edn. CRC Press, Boca Raton (2014)
5. Adams, E.: Fundamentals of Game Design, 3rd edn. New Riders, Thousand Oaks (2013)
6. Hunicke, R., LeBlance, M., Zubek, R.: MDA: a formal approach to game design and game research. In: Challenges in Games AI Workshop (2004)
7. Lewis, R.J.: IBM Computer Usability Satisfaction Questionnaires: Psychometric Evaluation and Instructions for Use. IBM Human Factors Group,Boca Raton (1995)
8. Griffiths, S.: Mobile App UX Principles. Google (2015)

Author Index

Printed in the United States
By Bookmasters